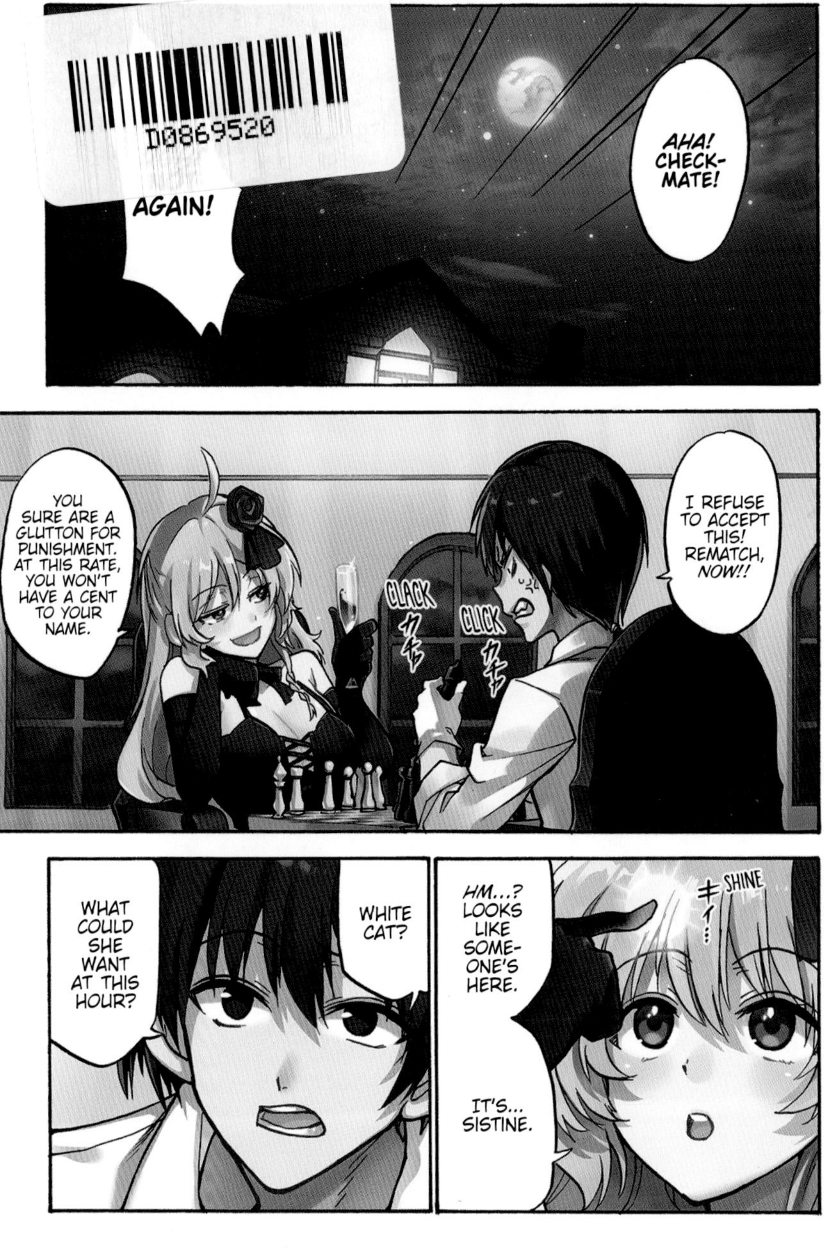
AHA! CHECK-MATE!
AGAIN!
I REFUSE TO ACCEPT THIS! REMATCH, NOW!!
CLICK
CLACK
YOU SURE ARE A GLUTTON FOR PUNISHMENT. AT THIS RATE, YOU WON'T HAVE A CENT TO YOUR NAME.
SHINE
HM...? LOOKS LIKE SOME-ONE'S HERE.
IT'S... SISTINE.
WHITE CAT?
WHAT COULD SHE WANT AT THIS HOUR?

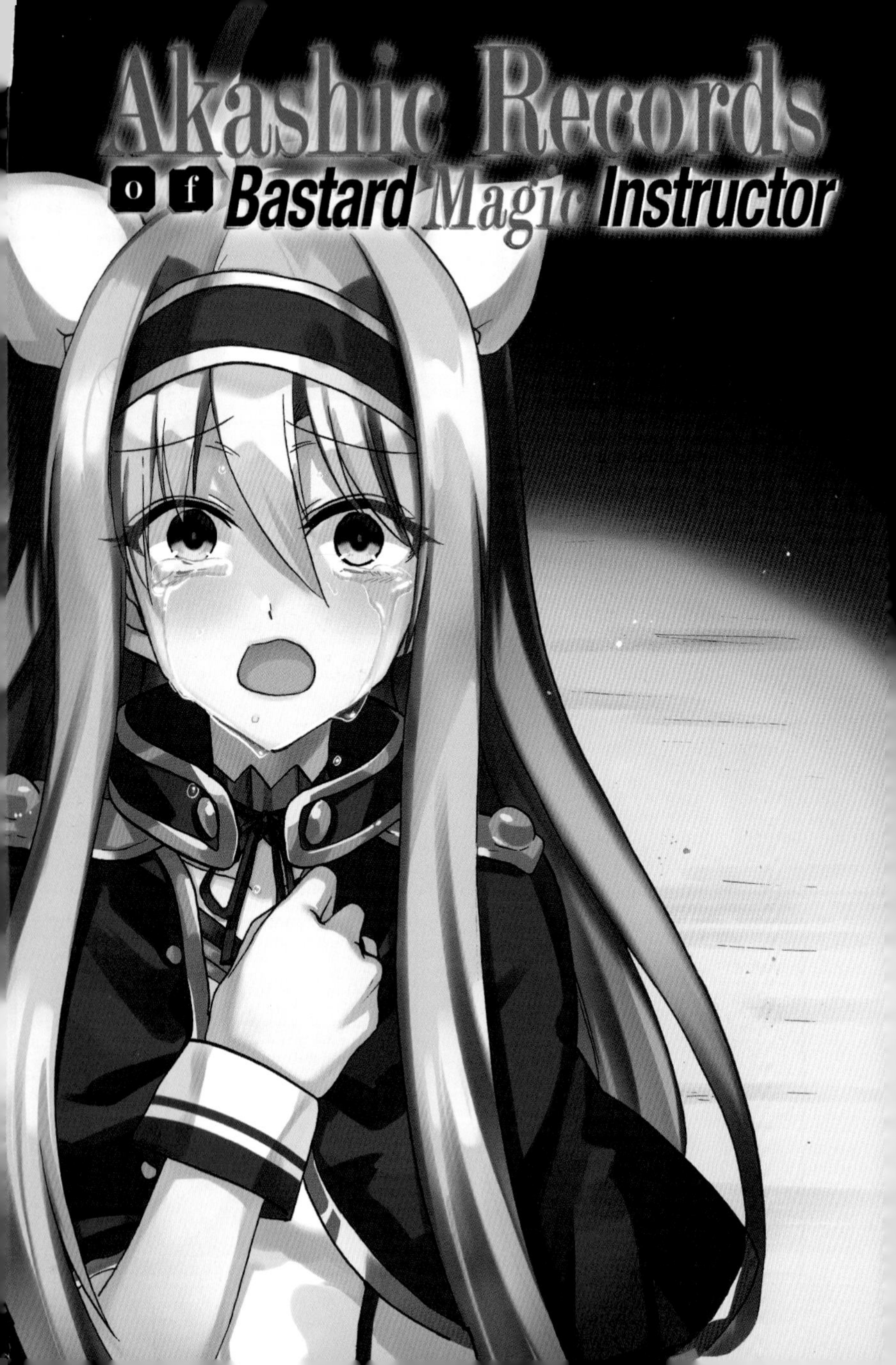
Akashic Records
of Bastard Magic Instructor

Lecture LIII

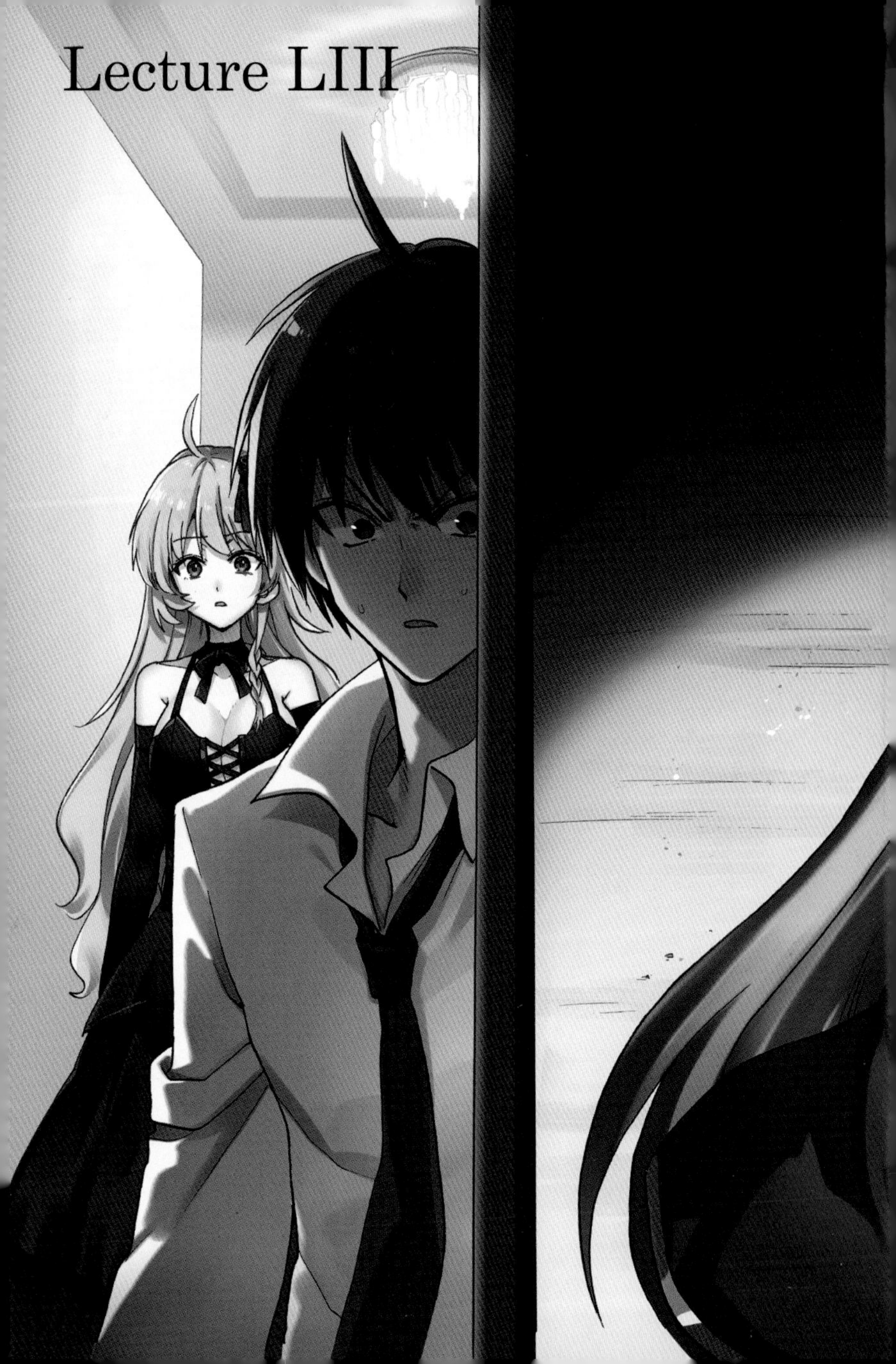

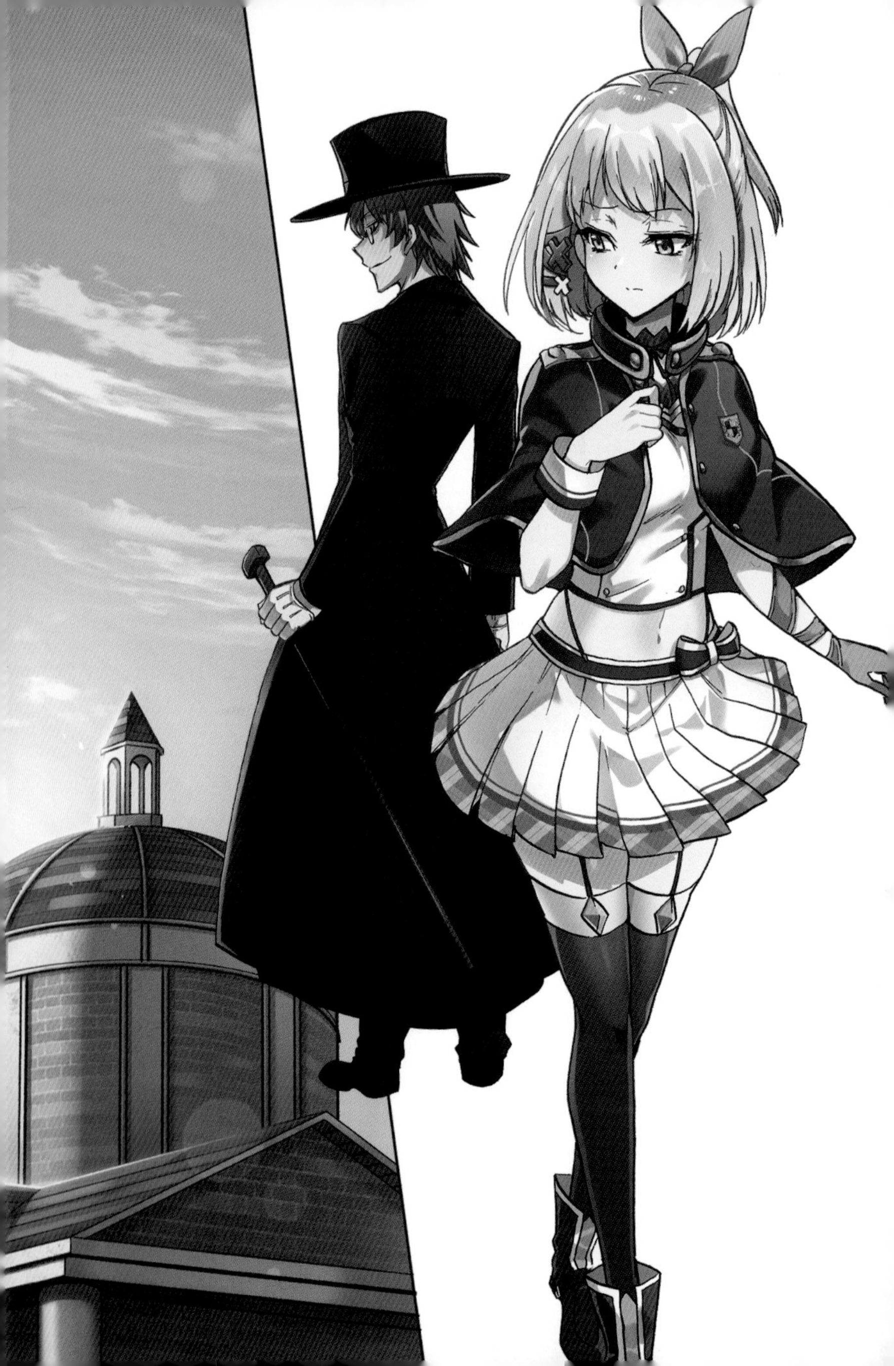

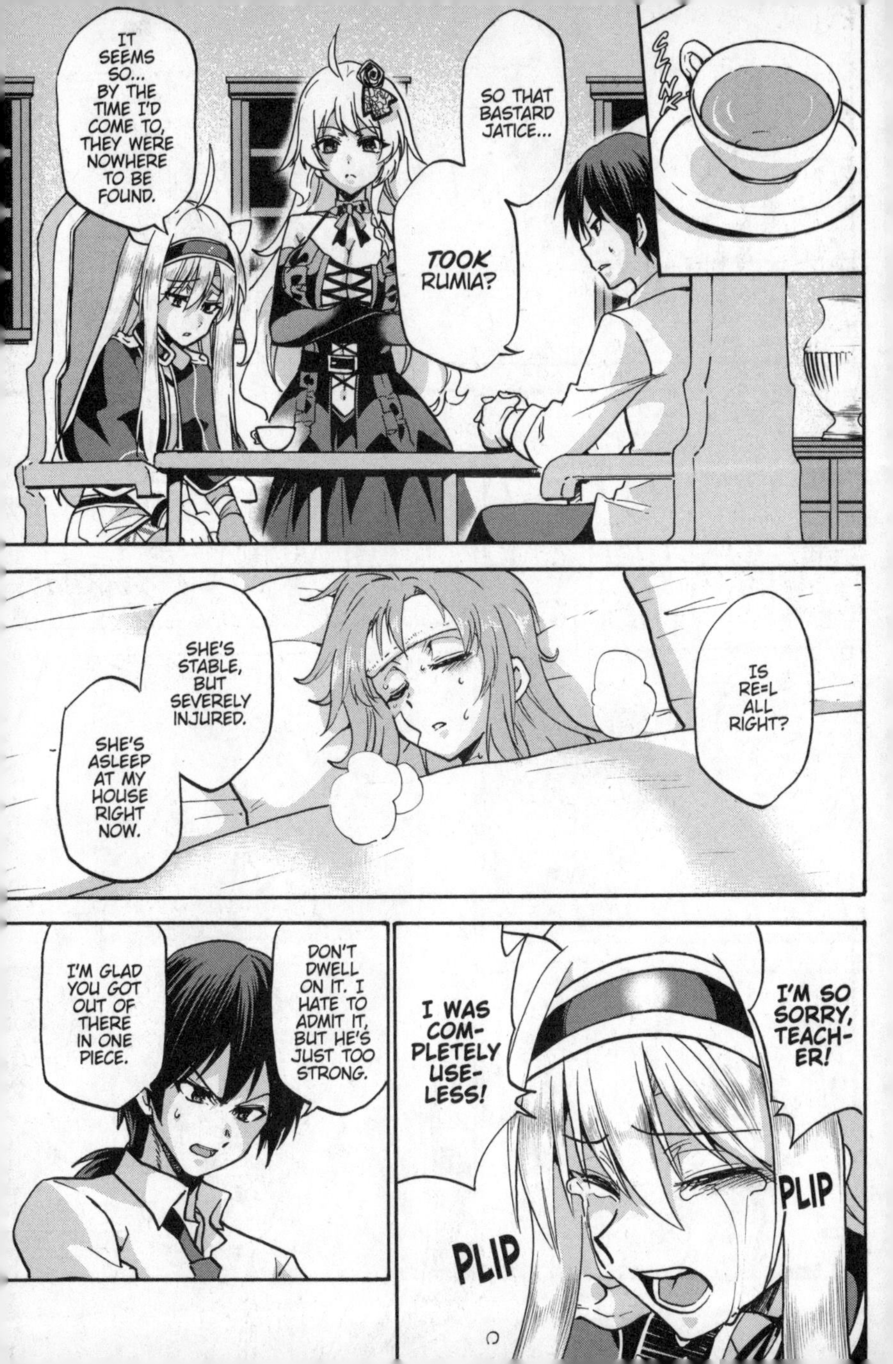
CLINK
SO THAT BASTARD JATICE...
TOOK RUMIA?
IT SEEMS SO... BY THE TIME I'D COME TO, THEY WERE NOWHERE TO BE FOUND.
IS RE=L ALL RIGHT?
SHE'S STABLE, BUT SEVERELY INJURED.
SHE'S ASLEEP AT MY HOUSE RIGHT NOW.
I'M SO SORRY, TEACHER!
I WAS COMPLETELY USELESS!
PLIP
PLIP
DON'T DWELL ON IT. I HATE TO ADMIT IT, BUT HE'S JUST TOO STRONG.
I'M GLAD YOU GOT OUT OF THERE IN ONE PIECE.

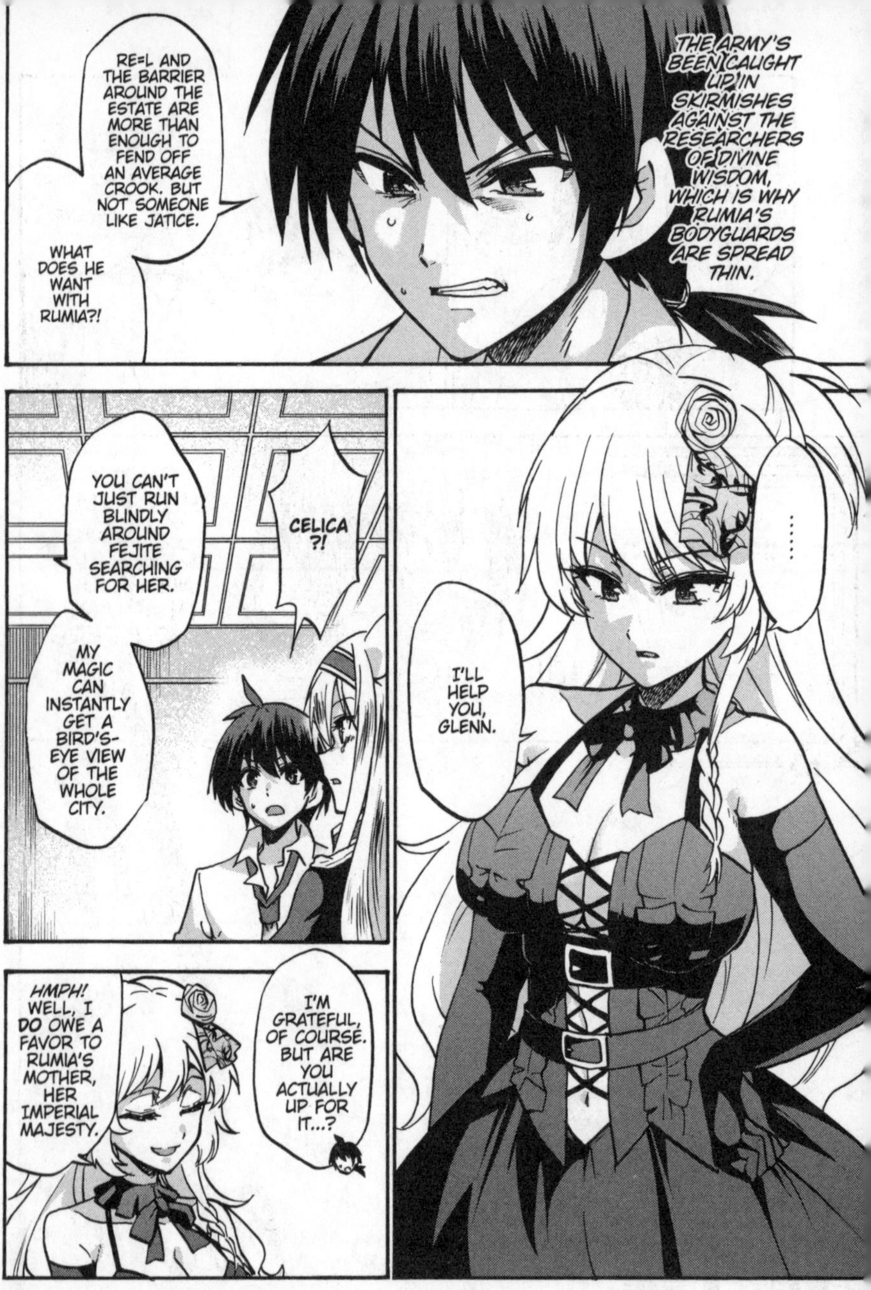
THE ARMY'S BEEN CAUGHT UP IN SKIRMISHES AGAINST THE RESEARCHERS OF DIVINE WISDOM, WHICH IS WHY RUMIA'S BODYGUARDS ARE SPREAD THIN.
RE=L AND THE BARRIER AROUND THE ESTATE ARE MORE THAN ENOUGH TO FEND OFF AN AVERAGE CROOK. BUT NOT SOMEONE LIKE JATICE.
WHAT DOES HE WANT WITH RUMIA?!
......
I'LL HELP YOU, GLENN.
CELICA?!
YOU CAN'T JUST RUN BLINDLY AROUND FEJITE SEARCHING FOR HER.
MY MAGIC CAN INSTANTLY GET A BIRD'S-EYE VIEW OF THE WHOLE CITY.
I'M GRATEFUL, OF COURSE. BUT ARE YOU ACTUALLY UP FOR IT...?
HMPH! WELL, I DO OWE A FAVOR TO RUMIA'S MOTHER, HER IMPERIAL MAJESTY.

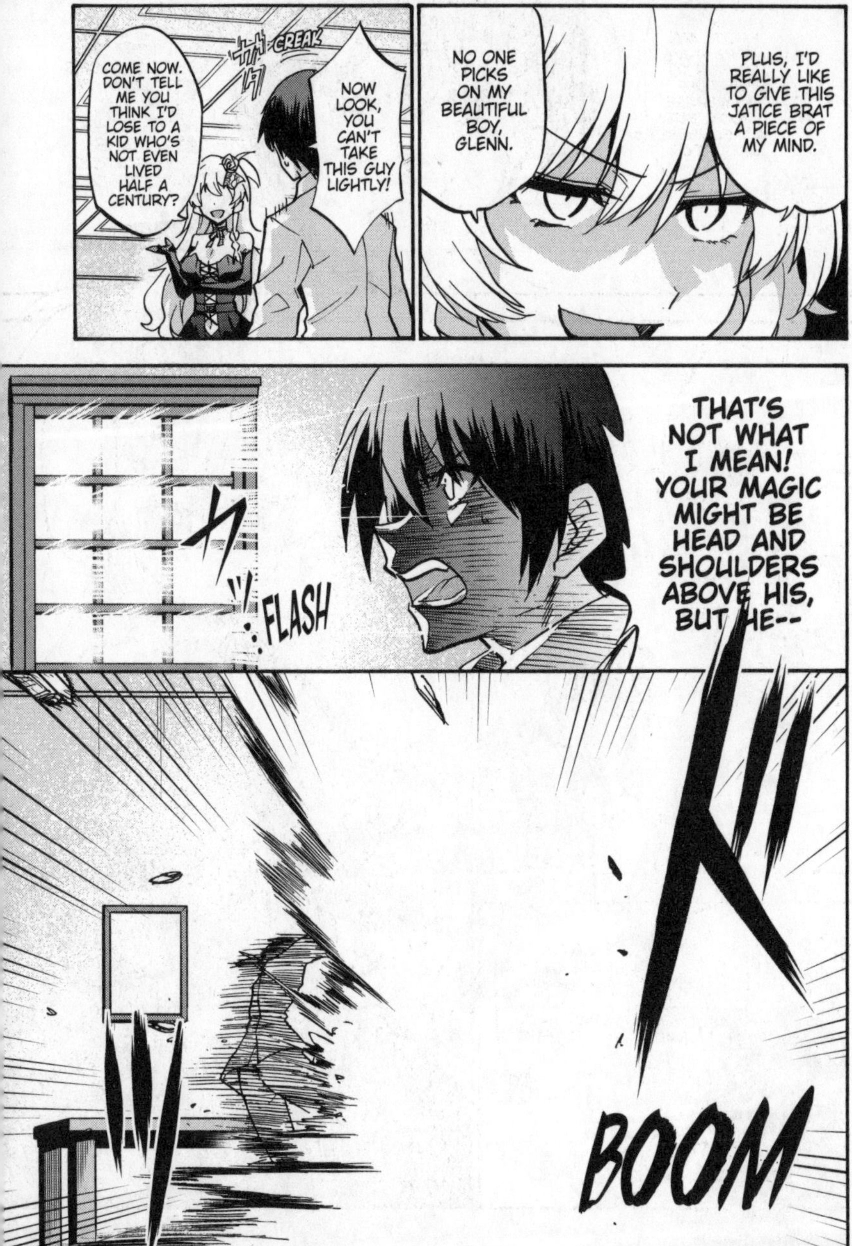

CREAK
NOW LOOK, YOU CAN'T TAKE THIS GUY LIGHTLY!
COME NOW. DON'T TELL ME YOU THINK I'D LOSE TO A KID WHO'S NOT EVEN LIVED HALF A CENTURY?
PLUS, I'D REALLY LIKE TO GIVE THIS JATICE BRAT A PIECE OF MY MIND.
NO ONE PICKS ON MY BEAUTIFUL BOY, GLENN.
THAT'S NOT WHAT I MEAN! YOUR MAGIC MIGHT BE HEAD AND SHOULDERS ABOVE HIS, BUT HE--
FLASH
BOOM

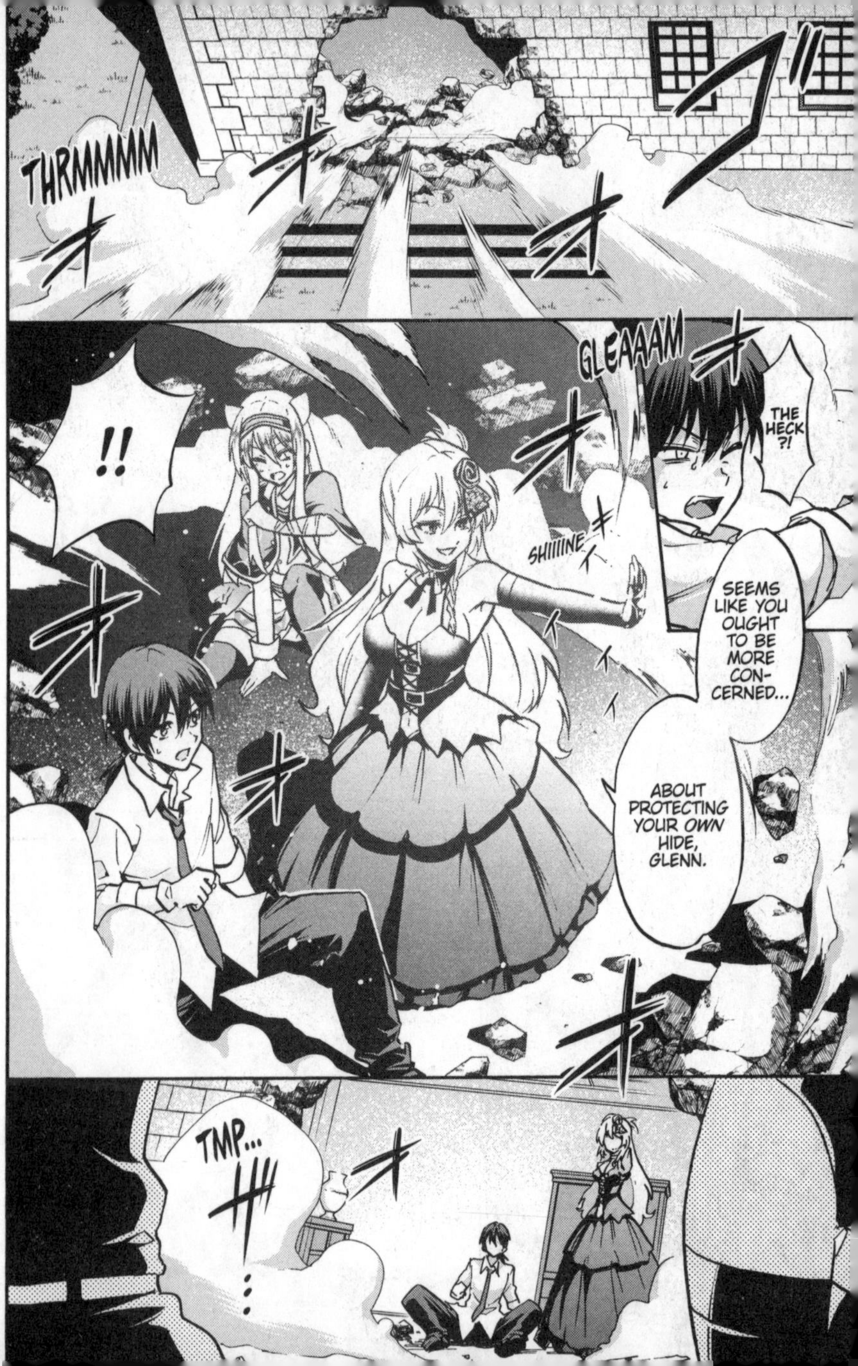
THRMMMM
GLEAAAM
THE HECK?!
!!
SHIIIINE
SEEMS LIKE YOU OUGHT TO BE MORE CON-CERNED...
ABOUT PROTECTING YOUR OWN HIDE, GLENN.
TMP...
...

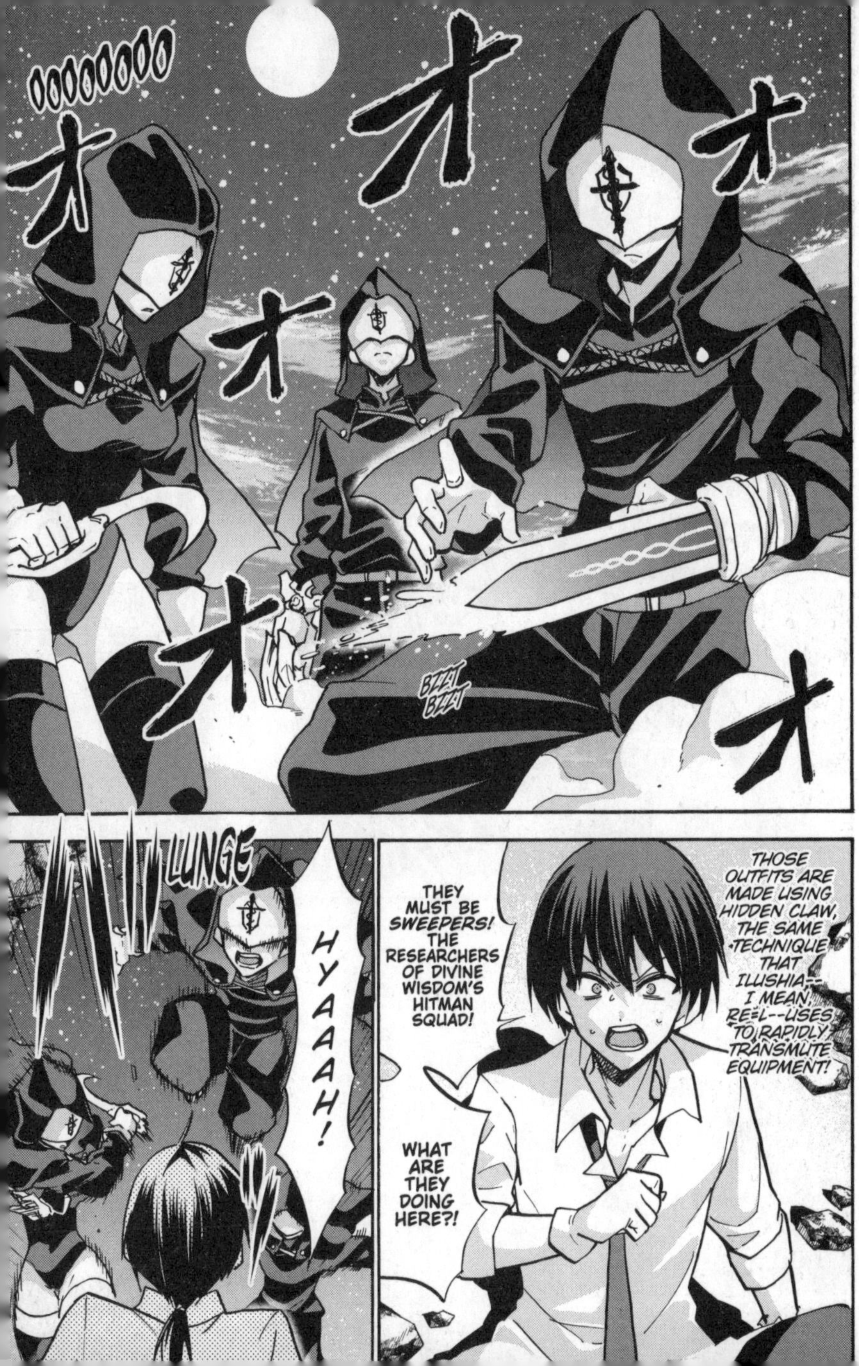
OOOOOOO
BZZT BZZT
THOSE OUTFITS ARE MADE USING HIDDEN CLAW, THE SAME TECHNIQUE THAT ILUSHIA-- I MEAN, RE=L--USES TO RAPIDLY TRANSMUTE EQUIPMENT!
THEY MUST BE SWEEPERS! THE RESEARCHERS OF DIVINE WISDOM'S HITMAN SQUAD!
WHAT ARE THEY DOING HERE?!
LUNGE
HYAAAAH!

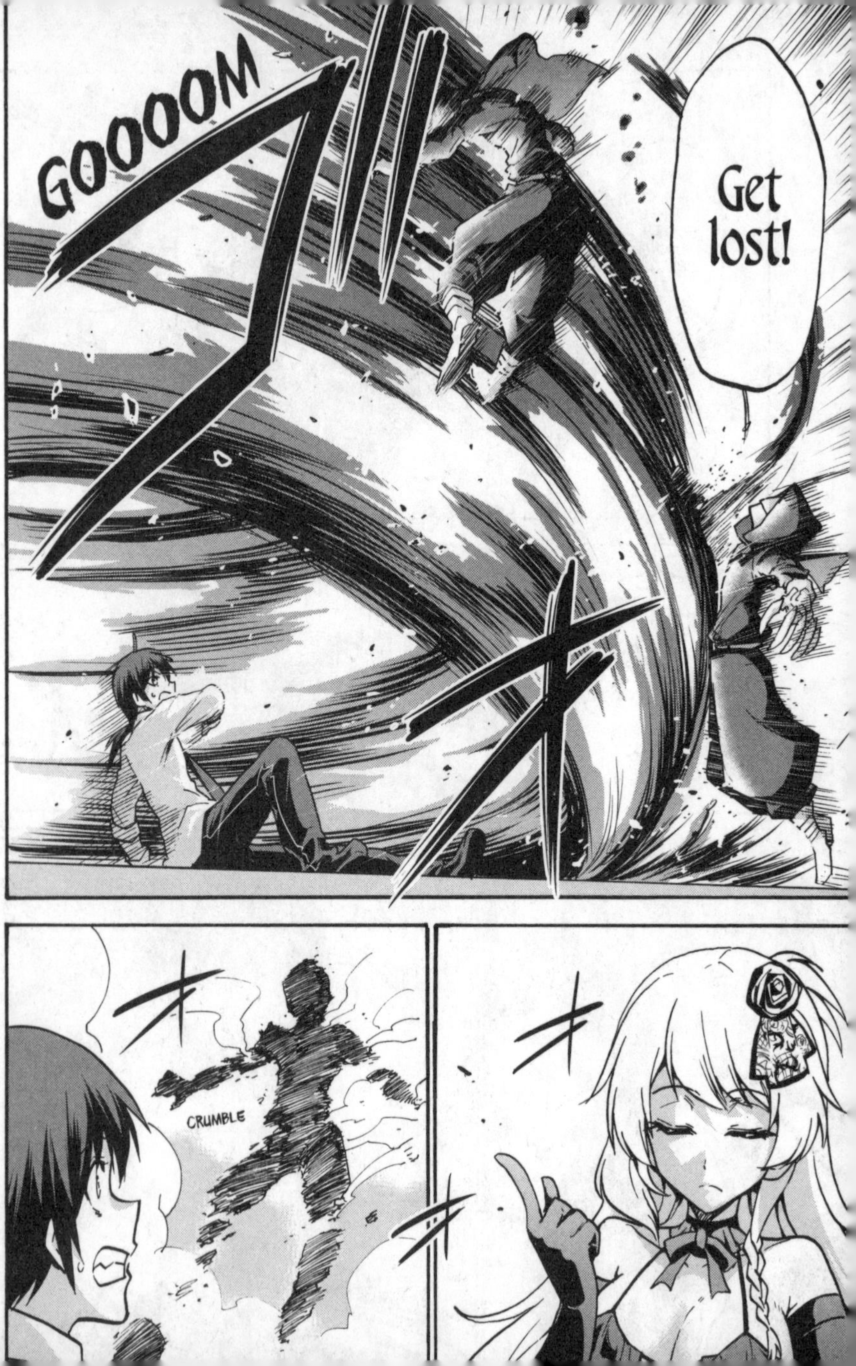
Get lost!
GOOOOM
CRUMBLE

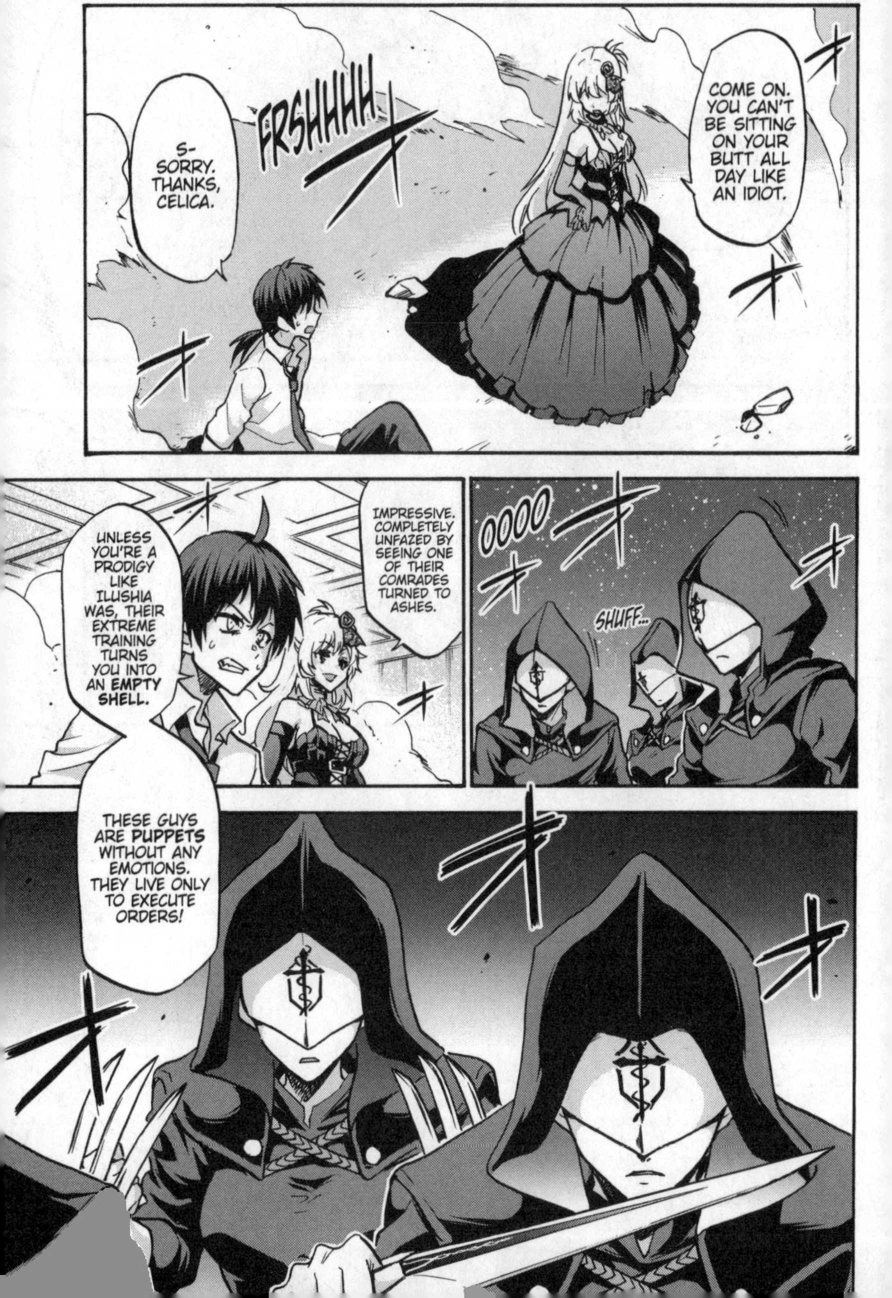
COME ON. YOU CAN'T BE SITTING ON YOUR BUTT ALL DAY LIKE AN IDIOT.
FRSHHHH
S-SORRY. THANKS, CELICA.
OOOO
SHUFF...
IMPRESSIVE. COMPLETELY UNFAZED BY SEEING ONE OF THEIR COMRADES TURNED TO ASHES.
UNLESS YOU'RE A PRODIGY LIKE ILUSHIA WAS, THEIR EXTREME TRAINING TURNS YOU INTO AN EMPTY SHELL.
THESE GUYS ARE PUPPETS WITHOUT ANY EMOTIONS. THEY LIVE ONLY TO EXECUTE ORDERS!

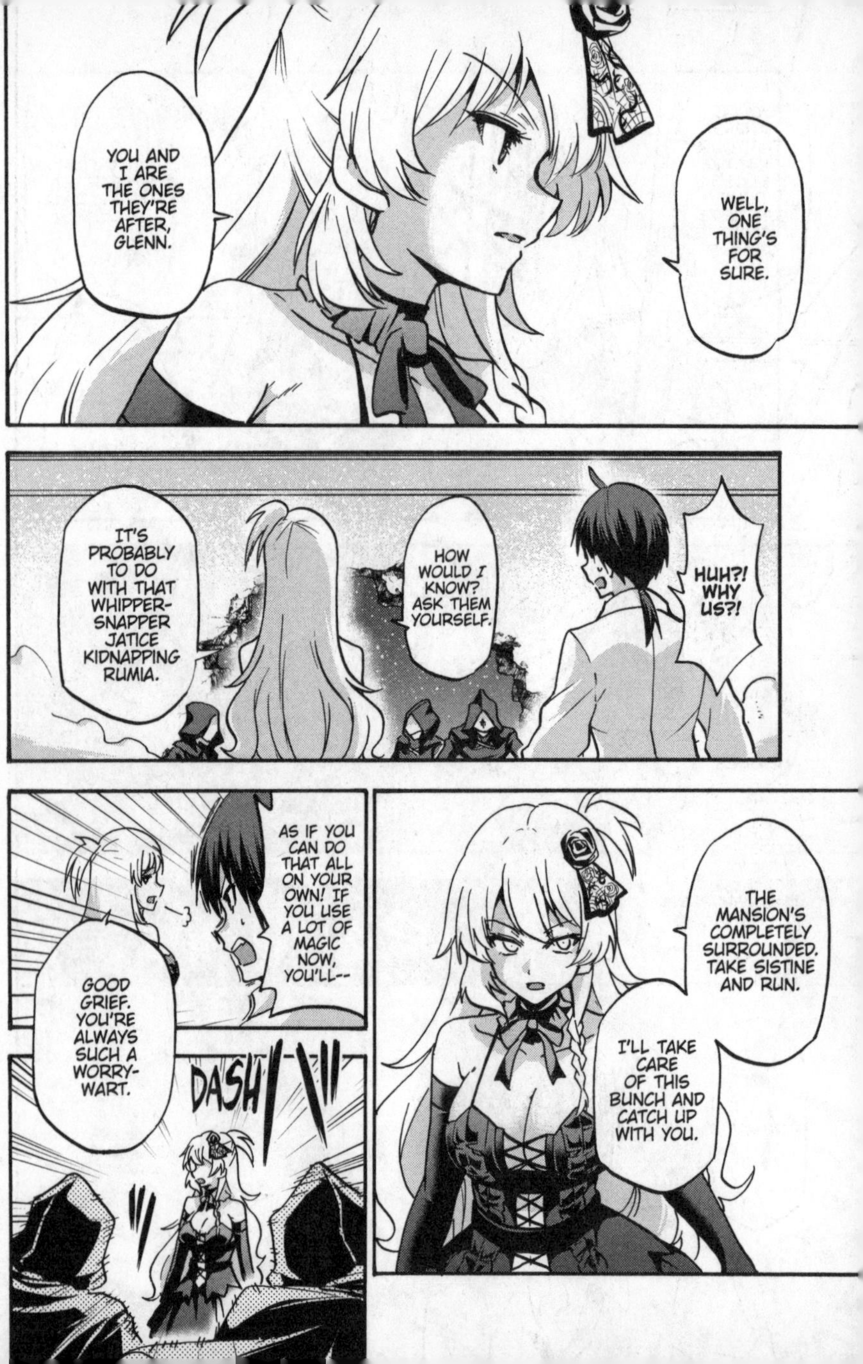
WELL, ONE THING'S FOR SURE.
YOU AND I ARE THE ONES THEY'RE AFTER, GLENN.
HUH?! WHY US?!
HOW WOULD I KNOW? ASK THEM YOURSELF.
IT'S PROBABLY TO DO WITH THAT WHIPPER-SNAPPER JATICE KIDNAPPING RUMIA.
THE MANSION'S COMPLETELY SURROUNDED. TAKE SISTINE AND RUN.
I'LL TAKE CARE OF THIS BUNCH AND CATCH UP WITH YOU.
AS IF YOU CAN DO THAT ALL ON YOUR OWN! IF YOU USE A LOT OF MAGIC NOW, YOU'LL--
GOOD GRIEF. YOU'RE ALWAYS SUCH A WORRY-WART.
DASH

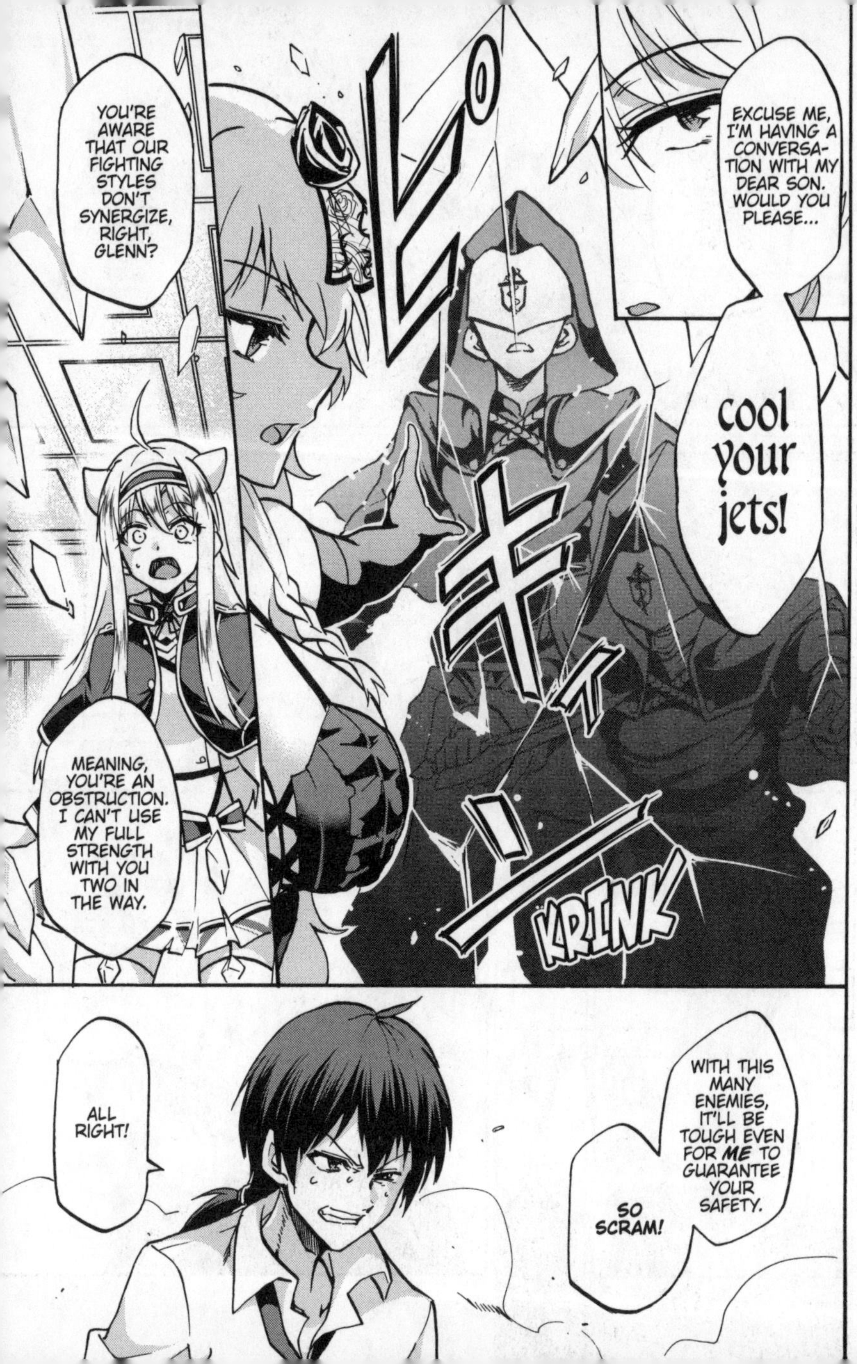
EXCUSE ME, I'M HAVING A CONVERSATION WITH MY DEAR SON. WOULD YOU PLEASE...
cool your jets!
YOU'RE AWARE THAT OUR FIGHTING STYLES DON'T SYNERGIZE, RIGHT, GLENN?
MEANING, YOU'RE AN OBSTRUCTION. I CAN'T USE MY FULL STRENGTH WITH YOU TWO IN THE WAY.
KRINK
WITH THIS MANY ENEMIES, IT'LL BE TOUGH EVEN FOR ***ME*** TO GUARANTEE YOUR SAFETY.
SO SCRAM!
ALL RIGHT!

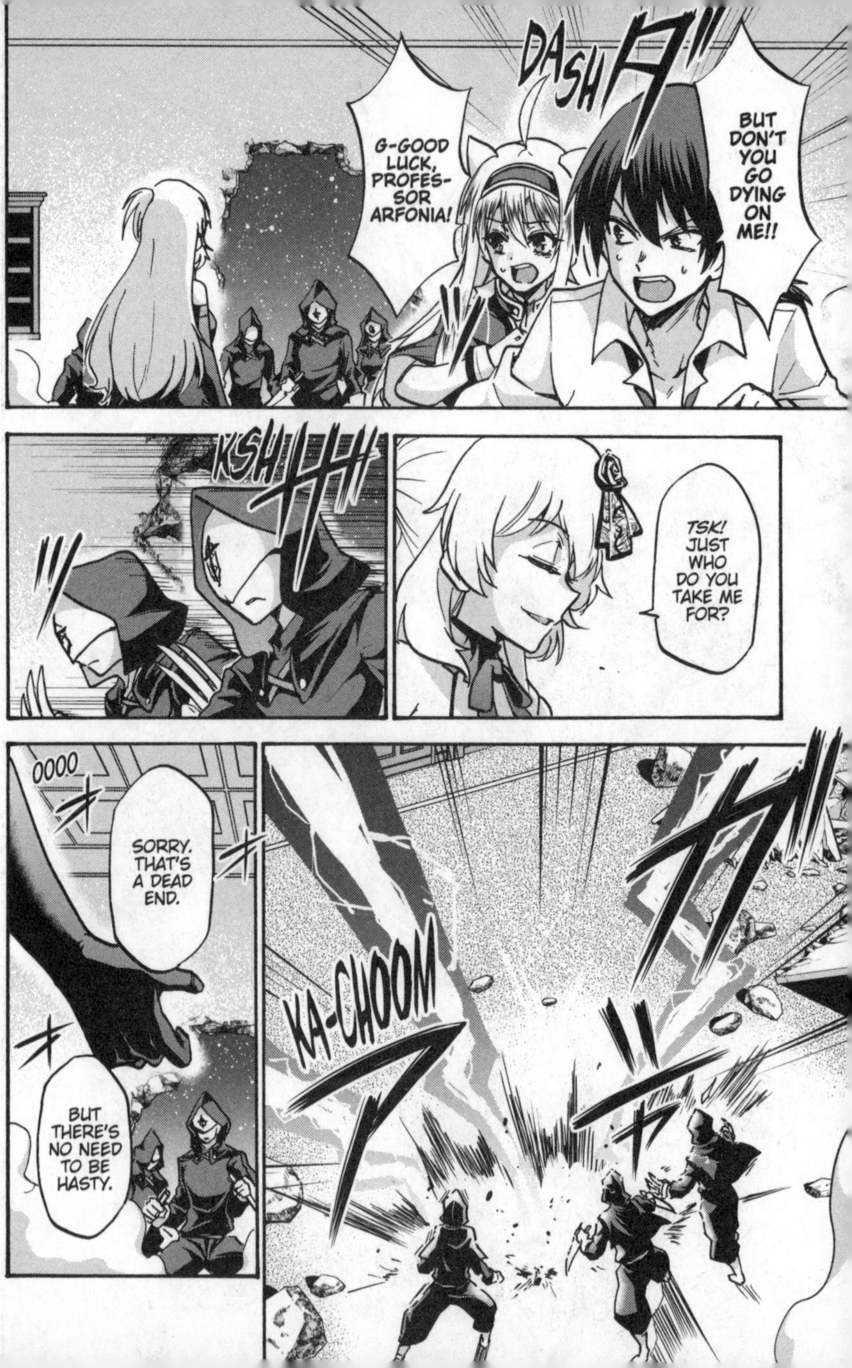
DASH
BUT DON'T YOU GO DYING ON ME!!
G-GOOD LUCK, PROFES-SOR ARFONIA!
TSK! JUST WHO DO YOU TAKE ME FOR?
KSH
KA-CHOOM
OOOO
SORRY. THAT'S A DEAD END.
BUT THERE'S NO NEED TO BE HASTY.

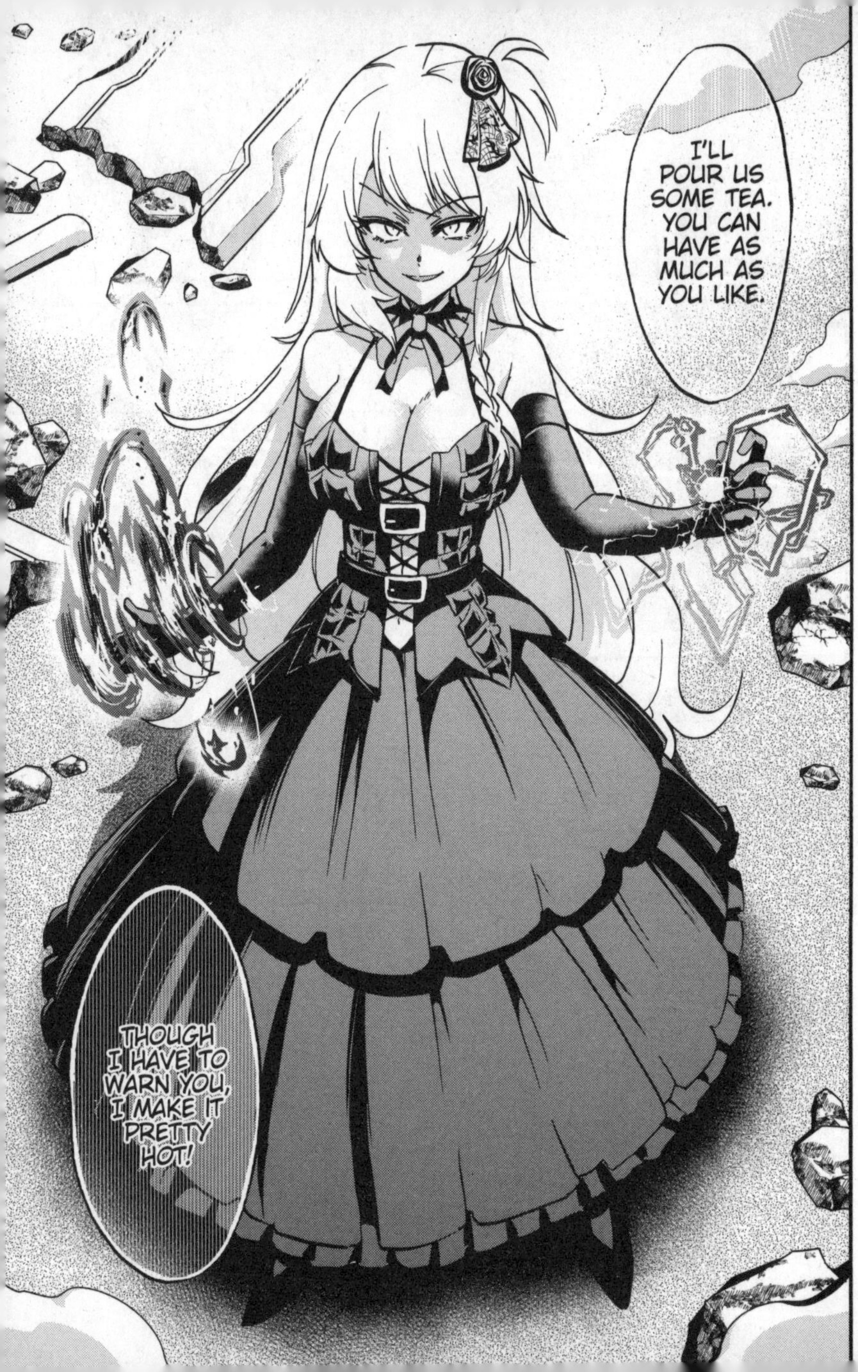
I'LL POUR US SOME TEA. YOU CAN HAVE AS MUCH AS YOU LIKE.
THOUGH I HAVE TO WARN YOU, I MAKE IT PRETTY HOT!

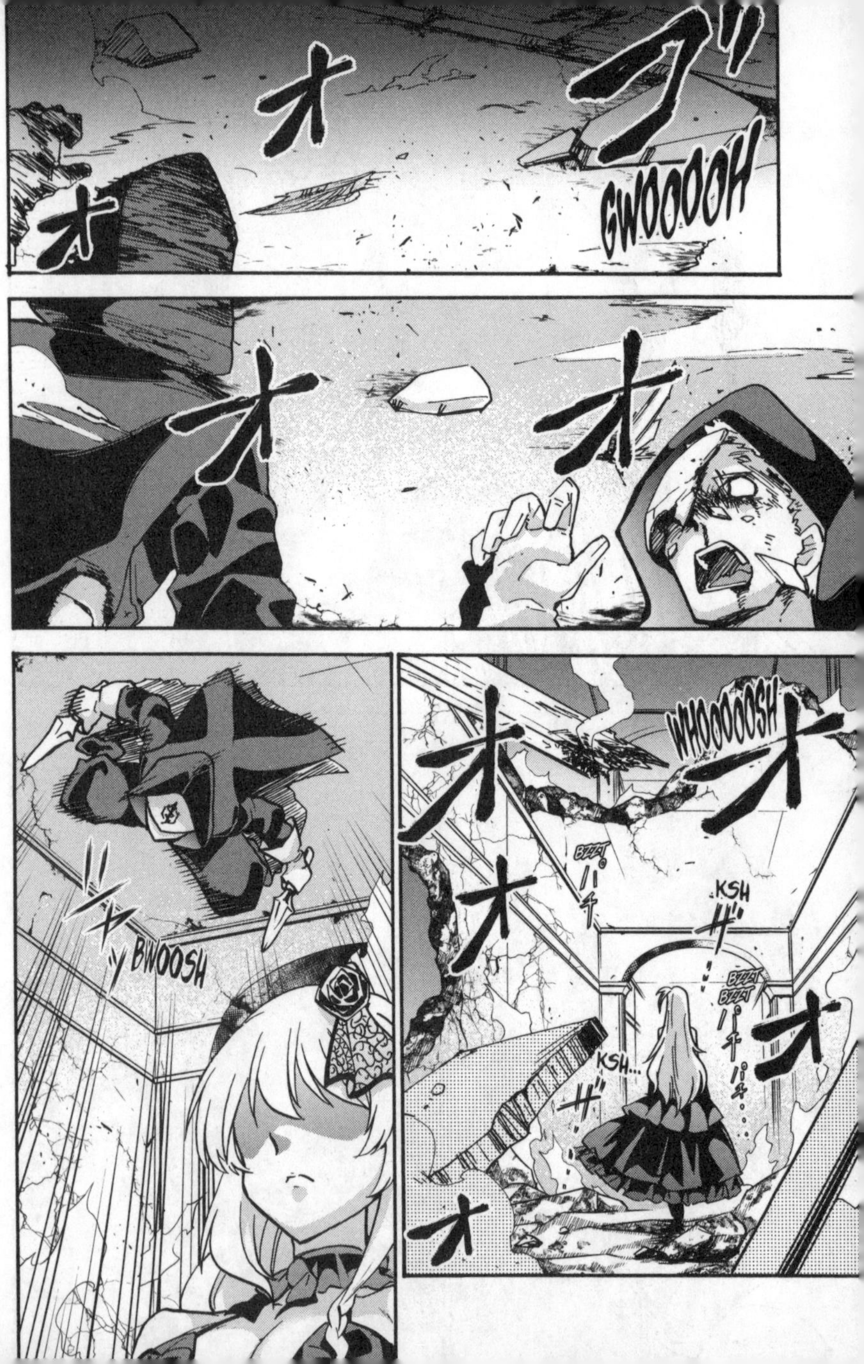

ゴ
オ
オ
GWOOOOH
オ
オ
WHOOOOSH
オ
オ
オ
BZZT!
パチ
KSH
ザ…
BZZT BZZT
パチパチ…
KSH…
ザ
オ
オ
バッ
BWOOSH

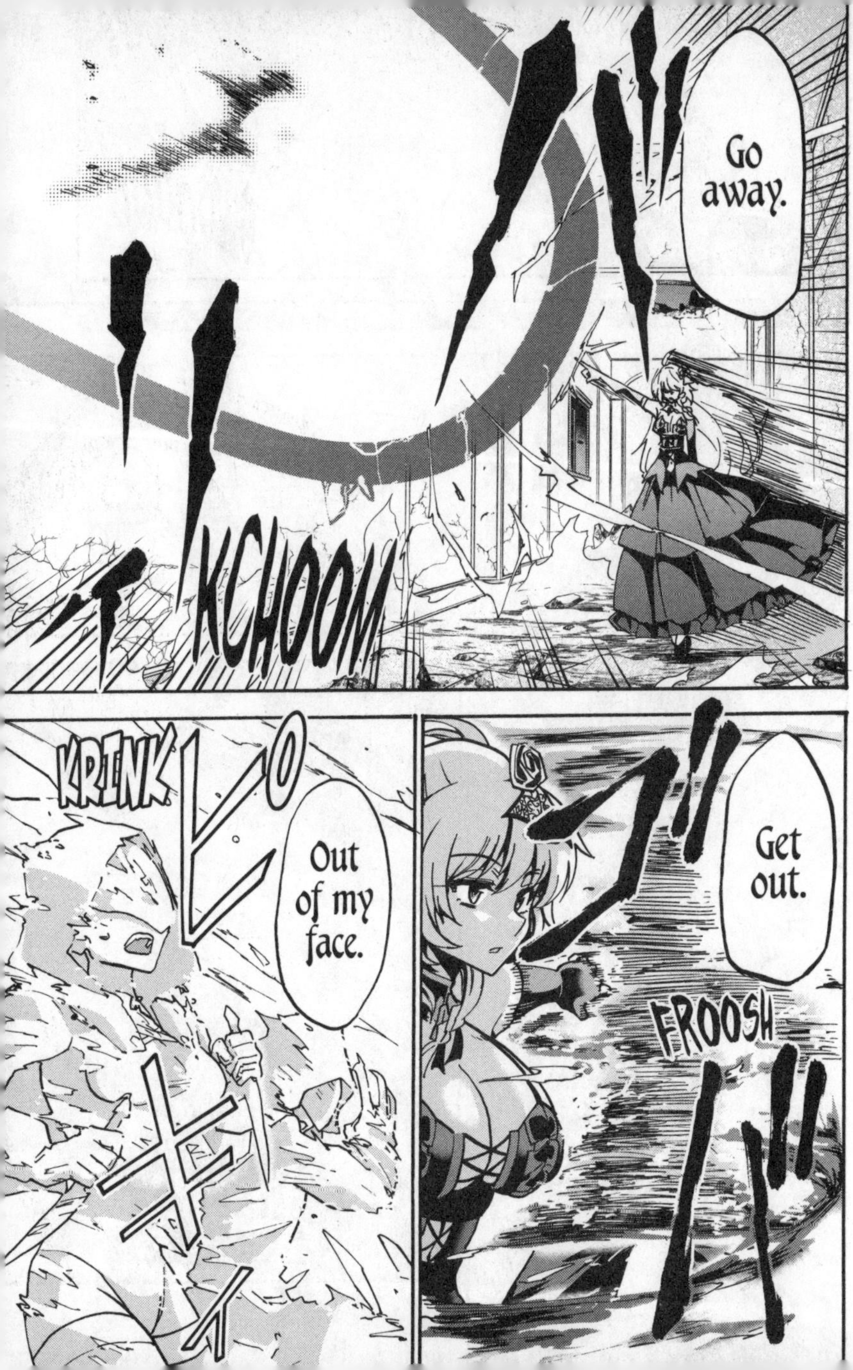
Go away.
KCHOOM
Get out.
FROOSH
Out of my face.
KRINK

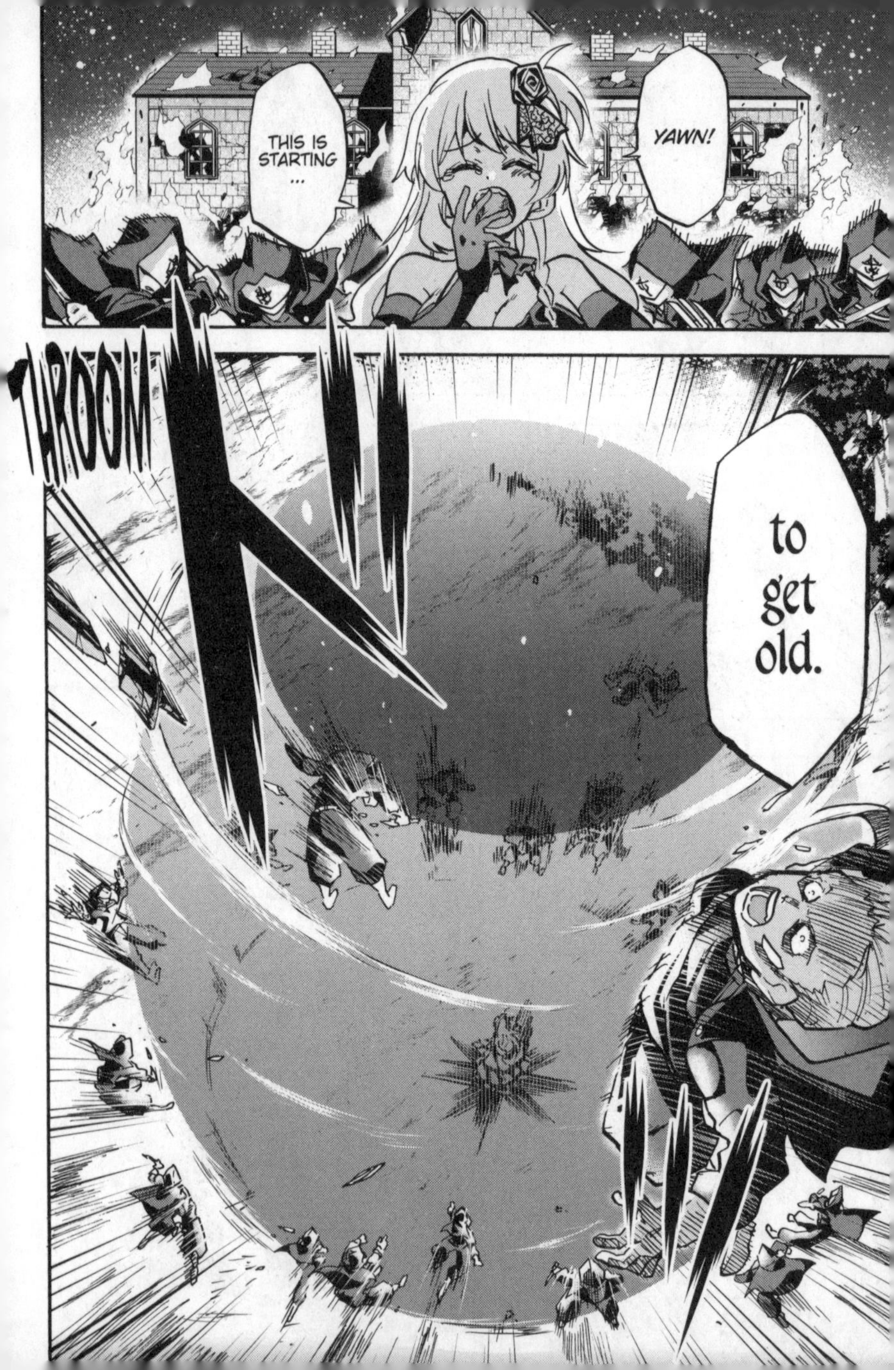
YAWN!
THIS IS STARTING ...
THROOM
to get old.

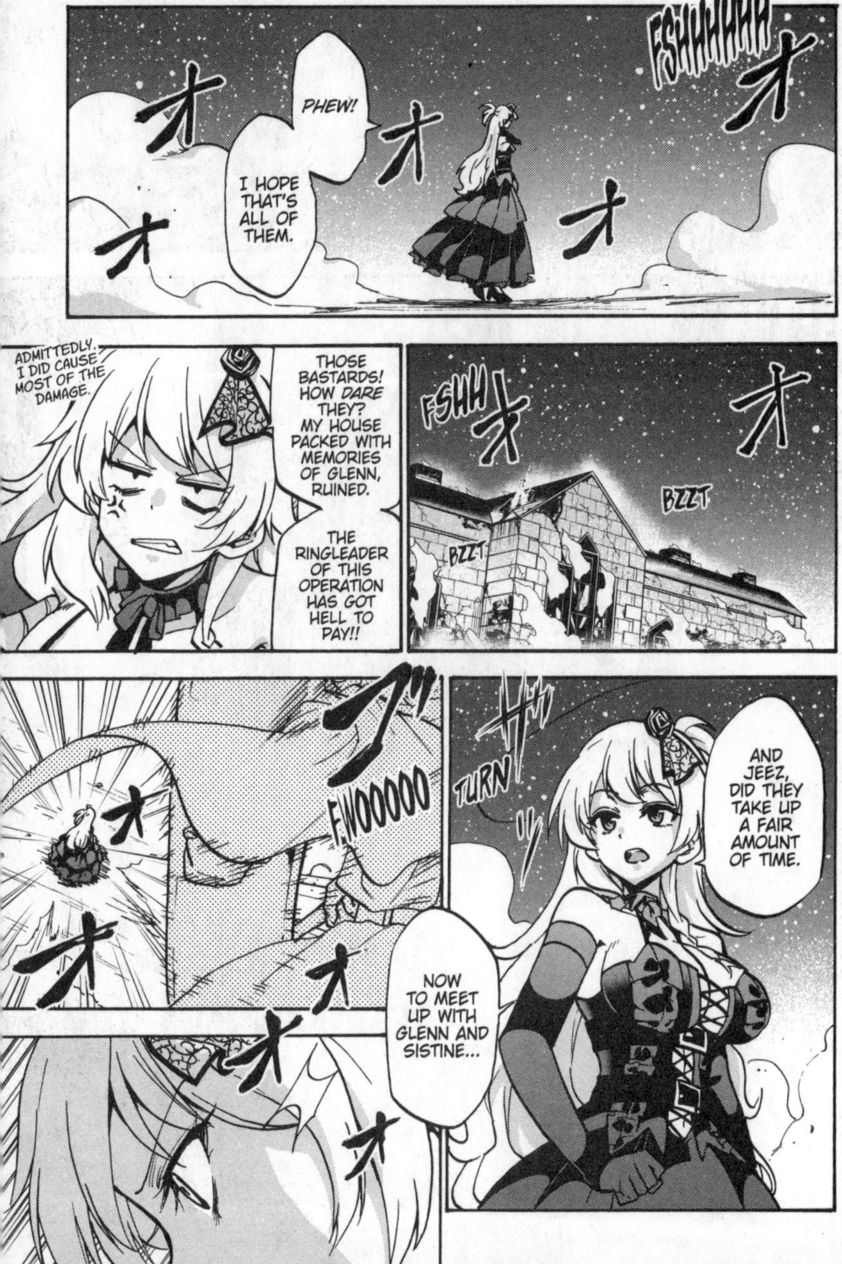
FSHHHHHH
PHEW!
I HOPE THAT'S ALL OF THEM.
FSHH
BZZT
BZZT
THOSE BASTARDS! HOW *DARE* THEY? MY HOUSE PACKED WITH MEMORIES OF GLENN, RUINED.
THE RINGLEADER OF THIS OPERATION HAS GOT HELL TO PAY!!
ADMITTEDLY, I DID CAUSE MOST OF THE DAMAGE.
TURN
AND JEEZ, DID THEY TAKE UP A FAIR AMOUNT OF TIME.
NOW TO MEET UP WITH GLENN AND SISTINE...
FWOOOOO

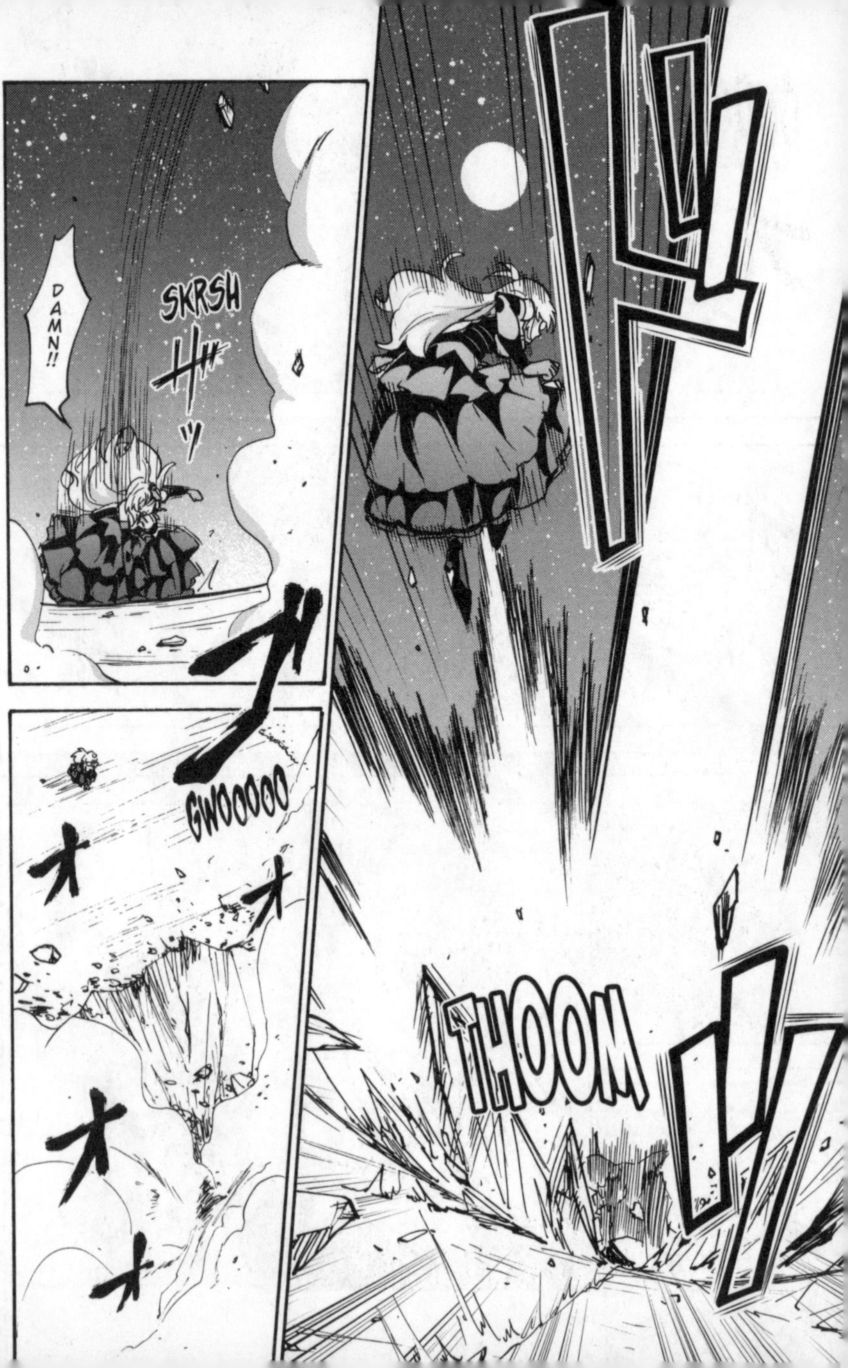
THOOM
DAMN!!
SKRSH
GWOOOOO

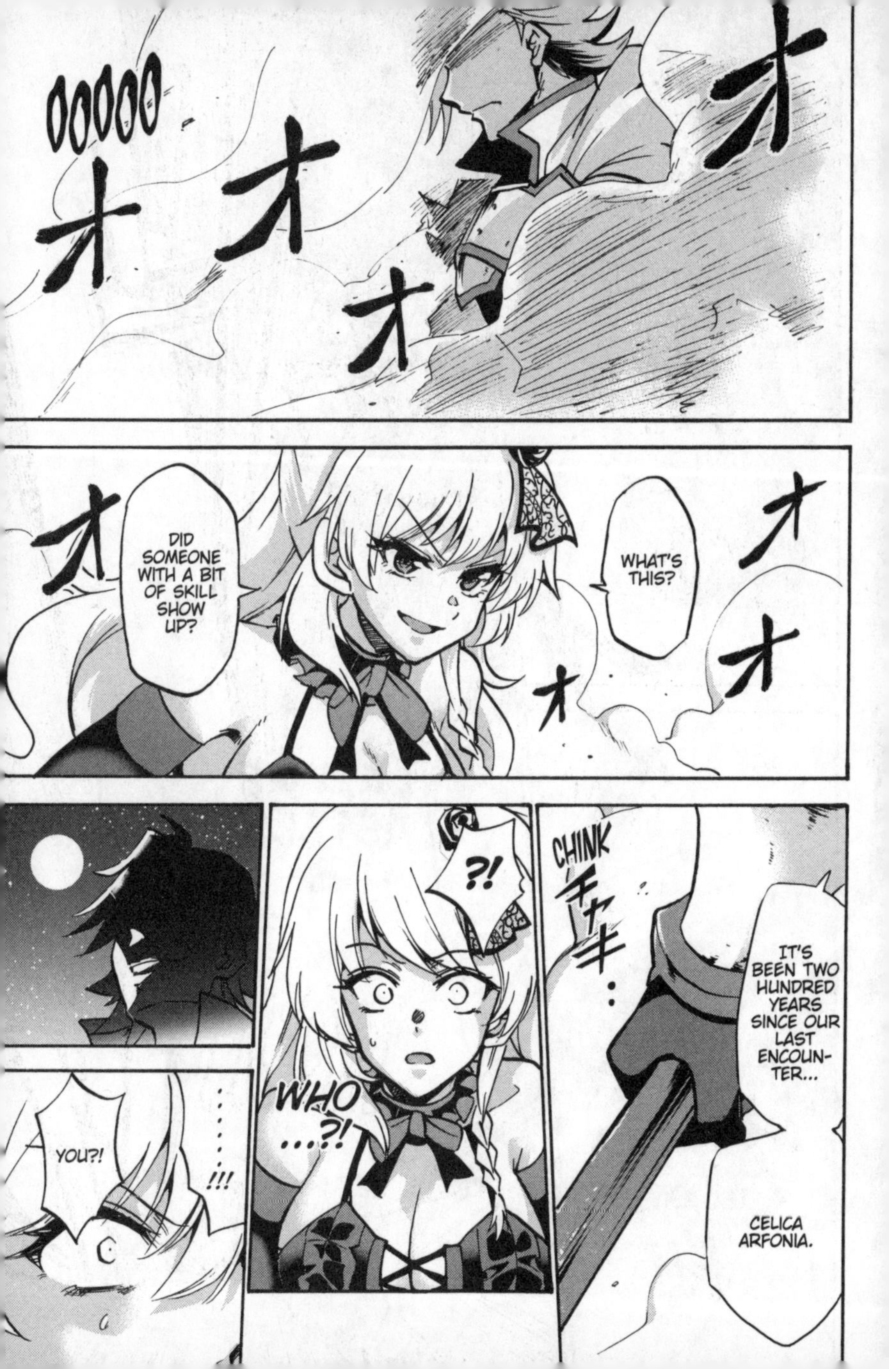
OOOOO
オオオオ
WHAT'S THIS?
DID SOMEONE WITH A BIT OF SKILL SHOW UP?
オオオオ
CHINK
チャキ
IT'S BEEN TWO HUNDRED YEARS SINCE OUR LAST ENCOUNTER...
CELICA ARFONIA.
?!
WHO...?!
...!!!
YOU?!

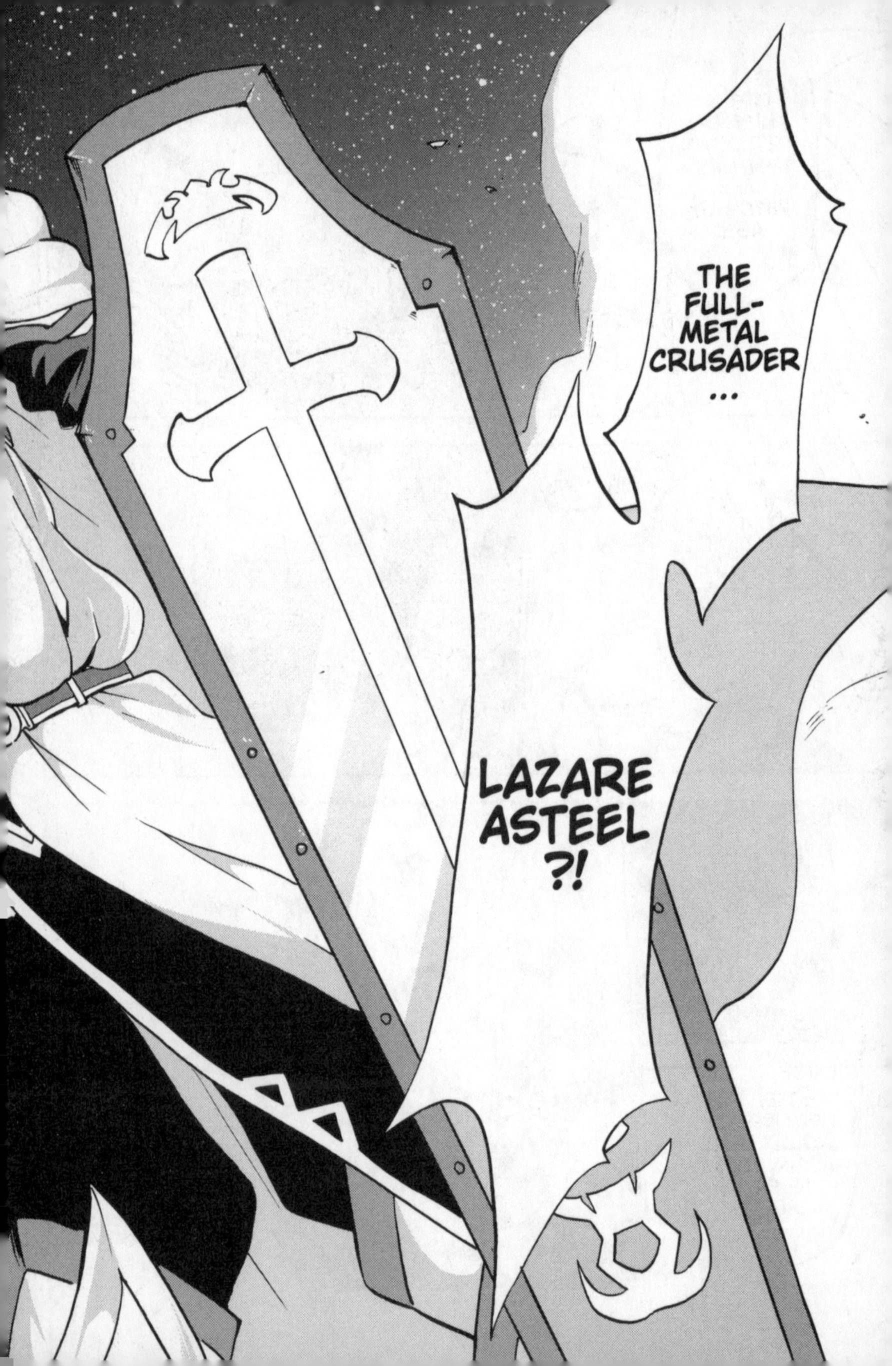
THE FULL-METAL CRUSADER...
LAZARE ASTEEL?!

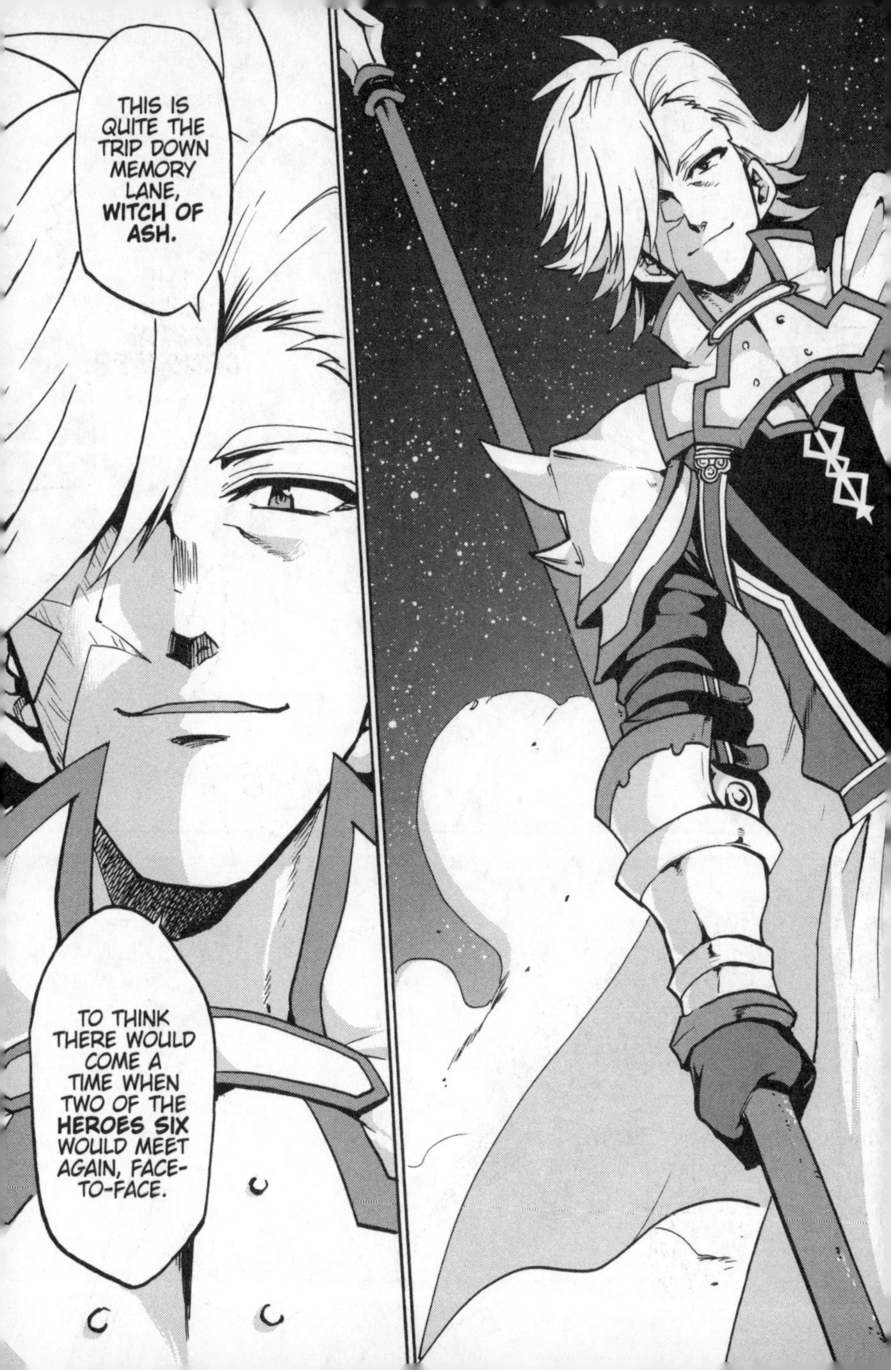
THIS IS QUITE THE TRIP DOWN MEMORY LANE, WITCH OF ASH.
TO THINK THERE WOULD COME A TIME WHEN TWO OF THE HEROES SIX WOULD MEET AGAIN, FACE-TO-FACE.

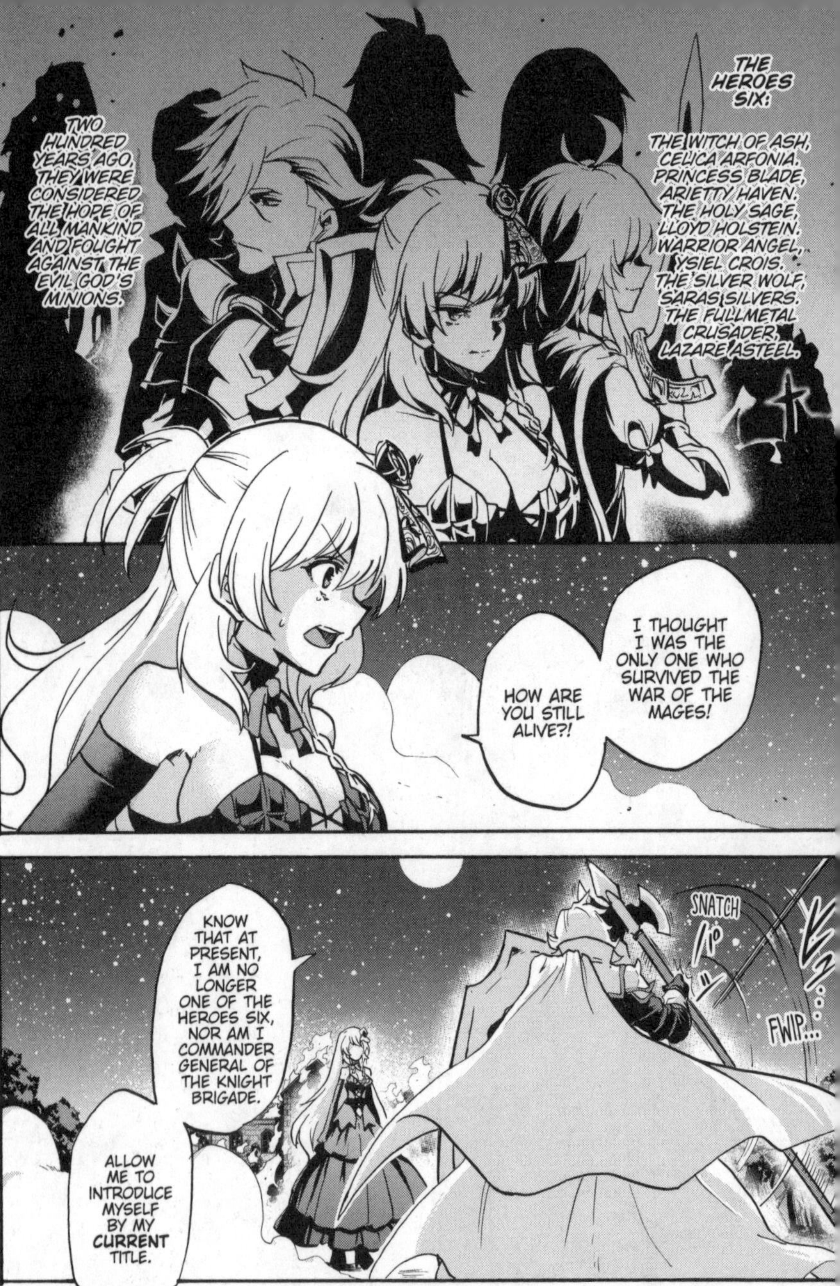
THE HEROES SIX:
THE WITCH OF ASH, CELICA ARFONIA. PRINCESS BLADE, ARIETTY HAVEN. THE HOLY SAGE, LLOYD HOLSTEIN. WARRIOR ANGEL, YSIEL CROIS. THE SILVER WOLF, SARAS SILVERS. THE FULLMETAL CRUSADER, LAZARE ASTEEL.
TWO HUNDRED YEARS AGO, THEY WERE CONSIDERED THE HOPE OF ALL MANKIND AND FOUGHT AGAINST THE EVIL GOD'S MINIONS.
I THOUGHT I WAS THE ONLY ONE WHO SURVIVED THE WAR OF THE MAGES!
HOW ARE YOU STILL ALIVE?!
SNATCH
FWIP...
KNOW THAT AT PRESENT, I AM NO LONGER ONE OF THE HEROES SIX, NOR AM I COMMANDER GENERAL OF THE KNIGHT BRIGADE.
ALLOW ME TO INTRODUCE MYSELF BY MY CURRENT TITLE.

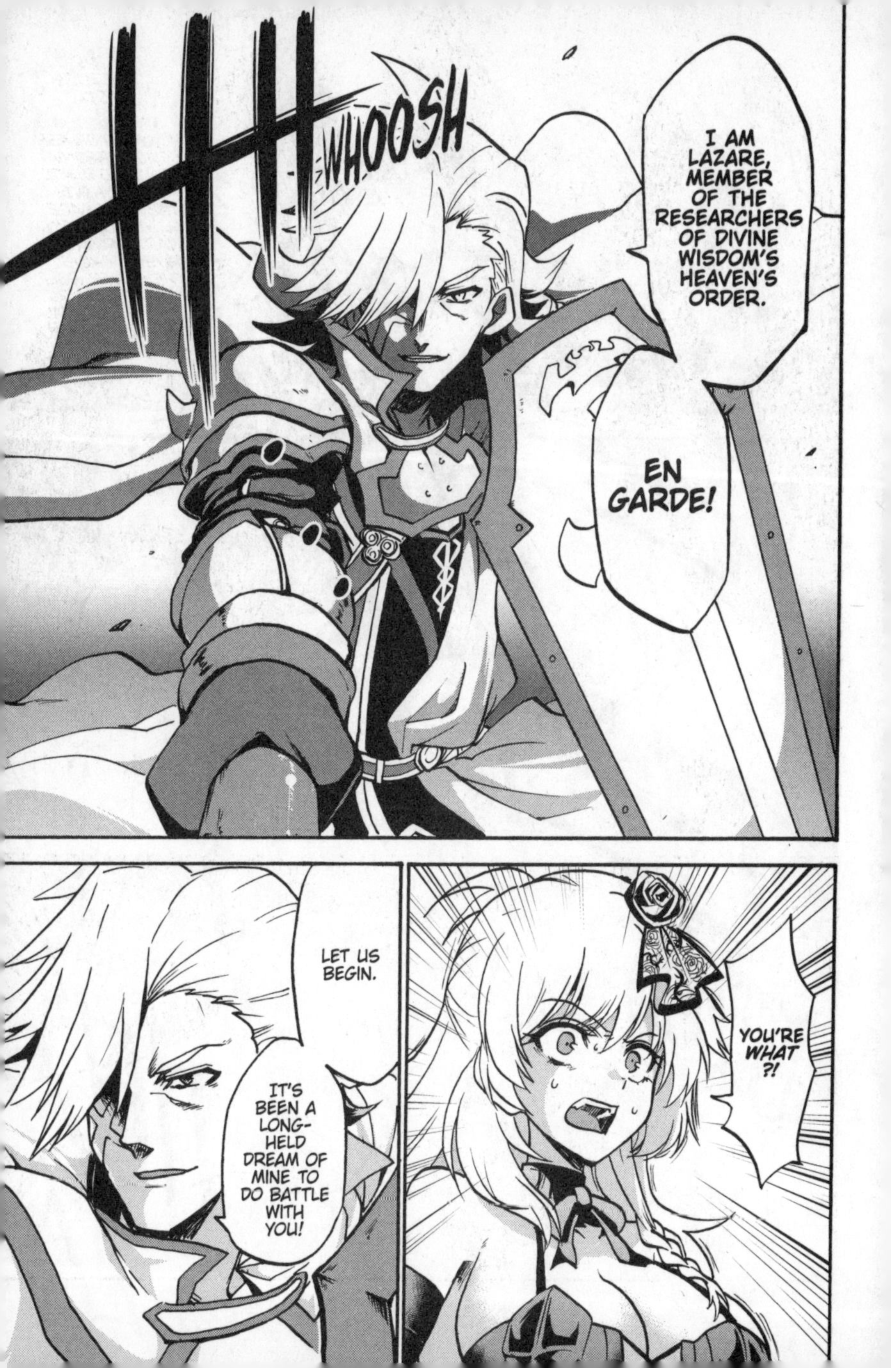
WHOOSH
I AM LAZARE, MEMBER OF THE RESEARCHERS OF DIVINE WISDOM'S HEAVEN'S ORDER.
EN GARDE!
YOU'RE WHAT ?!
LET US BEGIN.
IT'S BEEN A LONG-HELD DREAM OF MINE TO DO BATTLE WITH YOU!

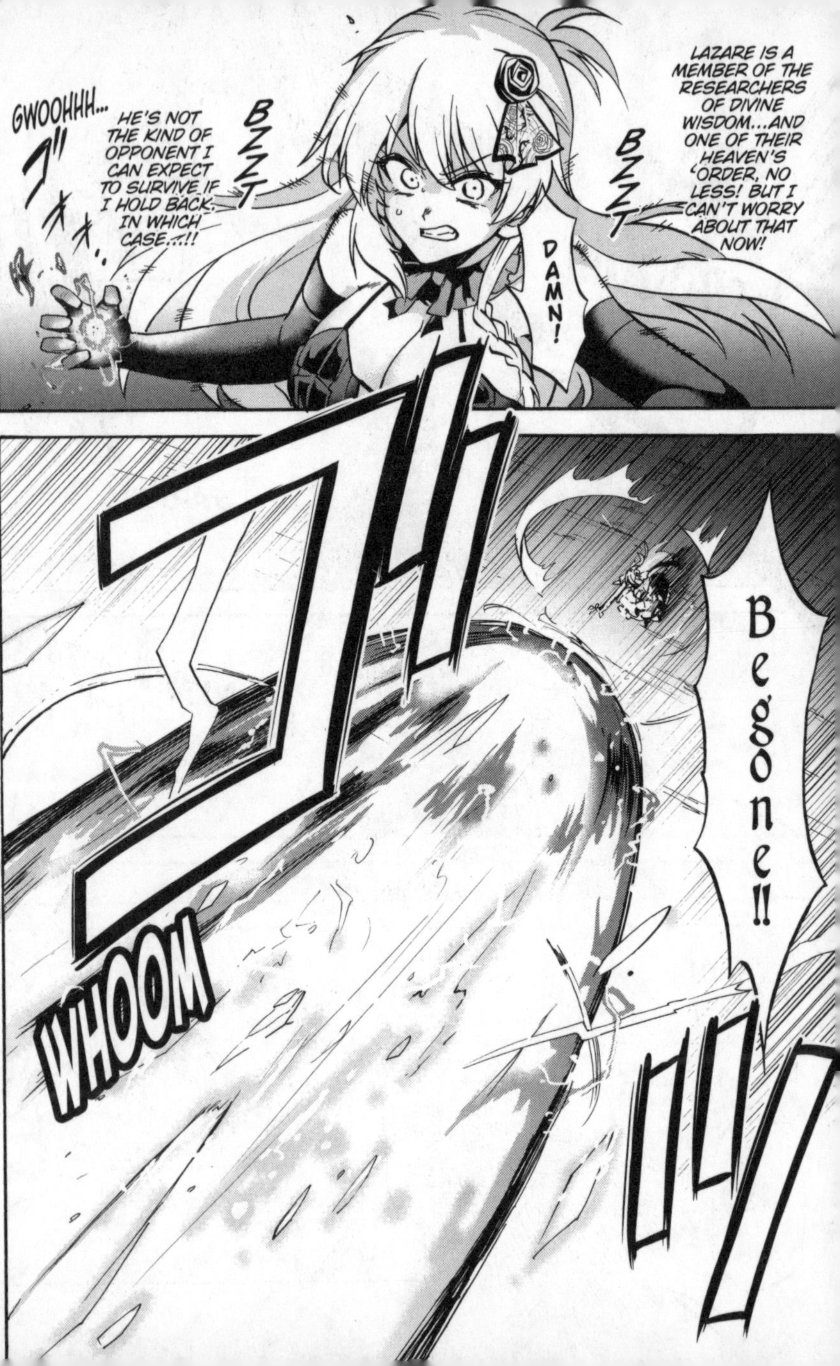

LAZARE IS A MEMBER OF THE RESEARCHERS OF DIVINE WISDOM...AND ONE OF THEIR HEAVEN'S ORDER, NO LESS! BUT I CAN'T WORRY ABOUT THAT NOW!
BZZZT
DAMN!
BZZZT
HE'S NOT THE KIND OF OPPONENT I CAN EXPECT TO SURVIVE IF I HOLD BACK. IN WHICH CASE...!!
GWOOHHH...
ゴォォ...
Begone!!
WHOOM

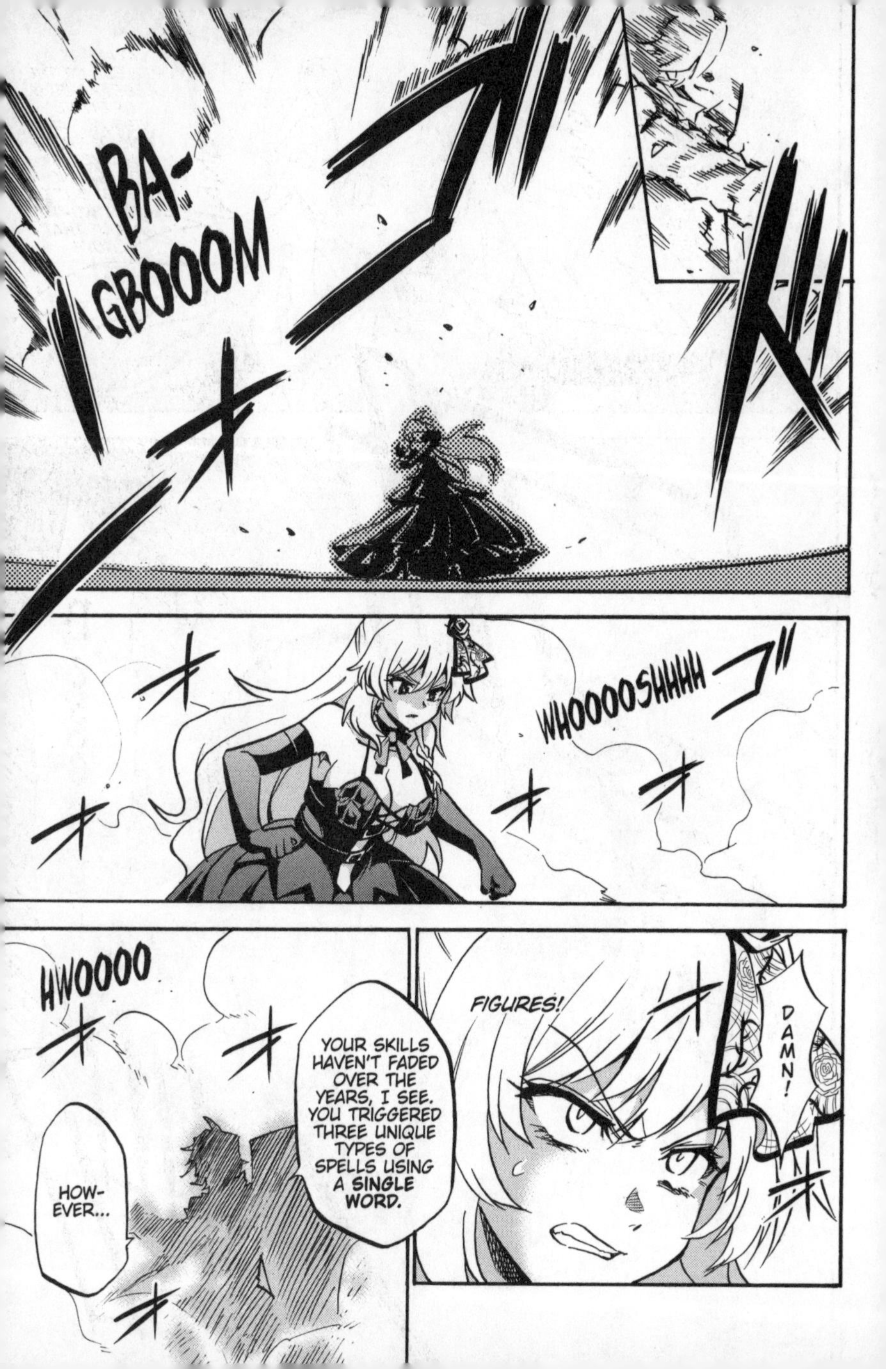
BA-
GBOOOM
WHOOOOSHHHH
HWOOOO
DAMN!
FIGURES!
YOUR SKILLS HAVEN'T FADED OVER THE YEARS, I SEE. YOU TRIGGERED THREE UNIQUE TYPES OF SPELLS USING A SINGLE WORD.
HOW-EVER...

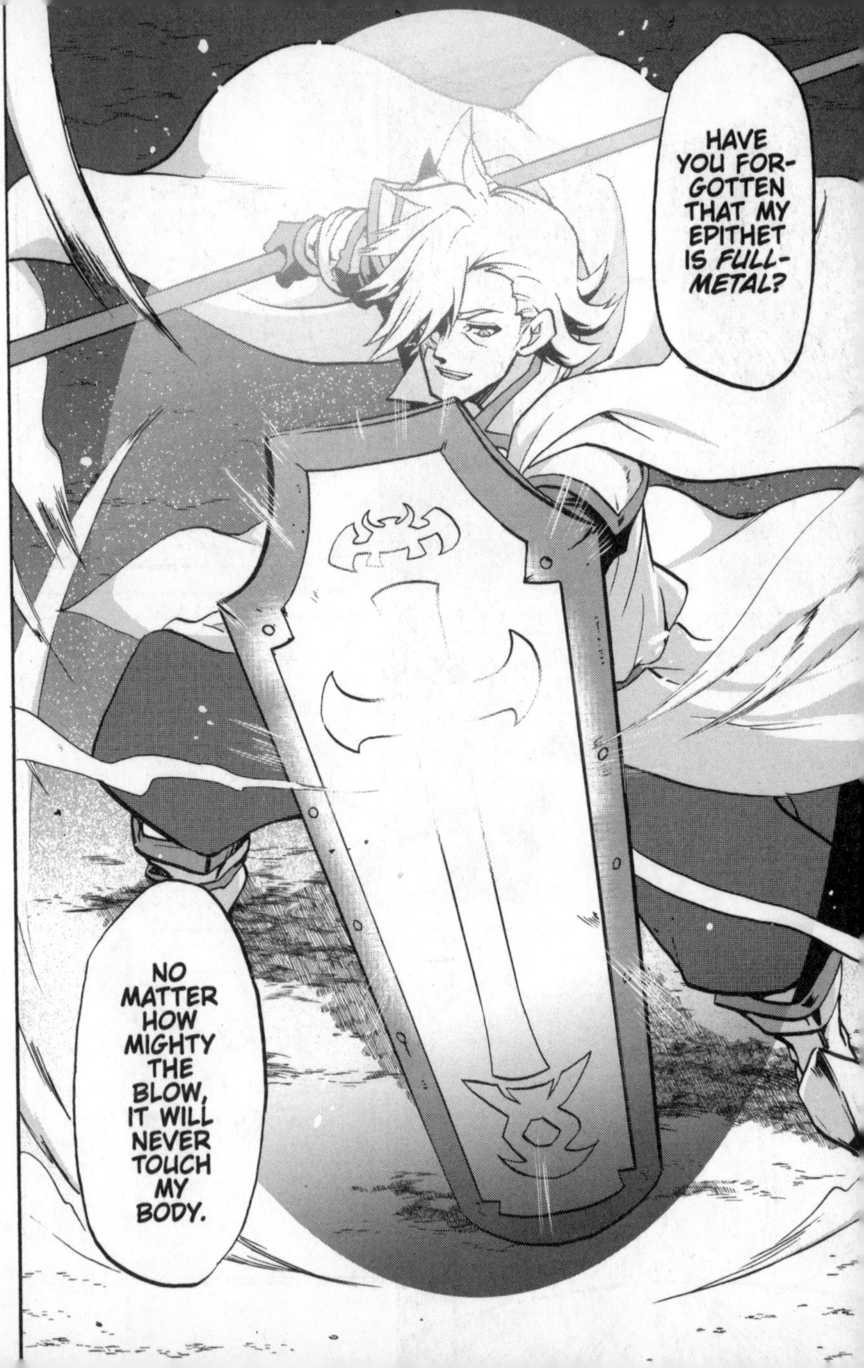
HAVE YOU FOR-GOTTEN THAT MY EPITHET IS *FULL-METAL*?
NO MATTER HOW MIGHTY THE BLOW, IT WILL NEVER TOUCH MY BODY.

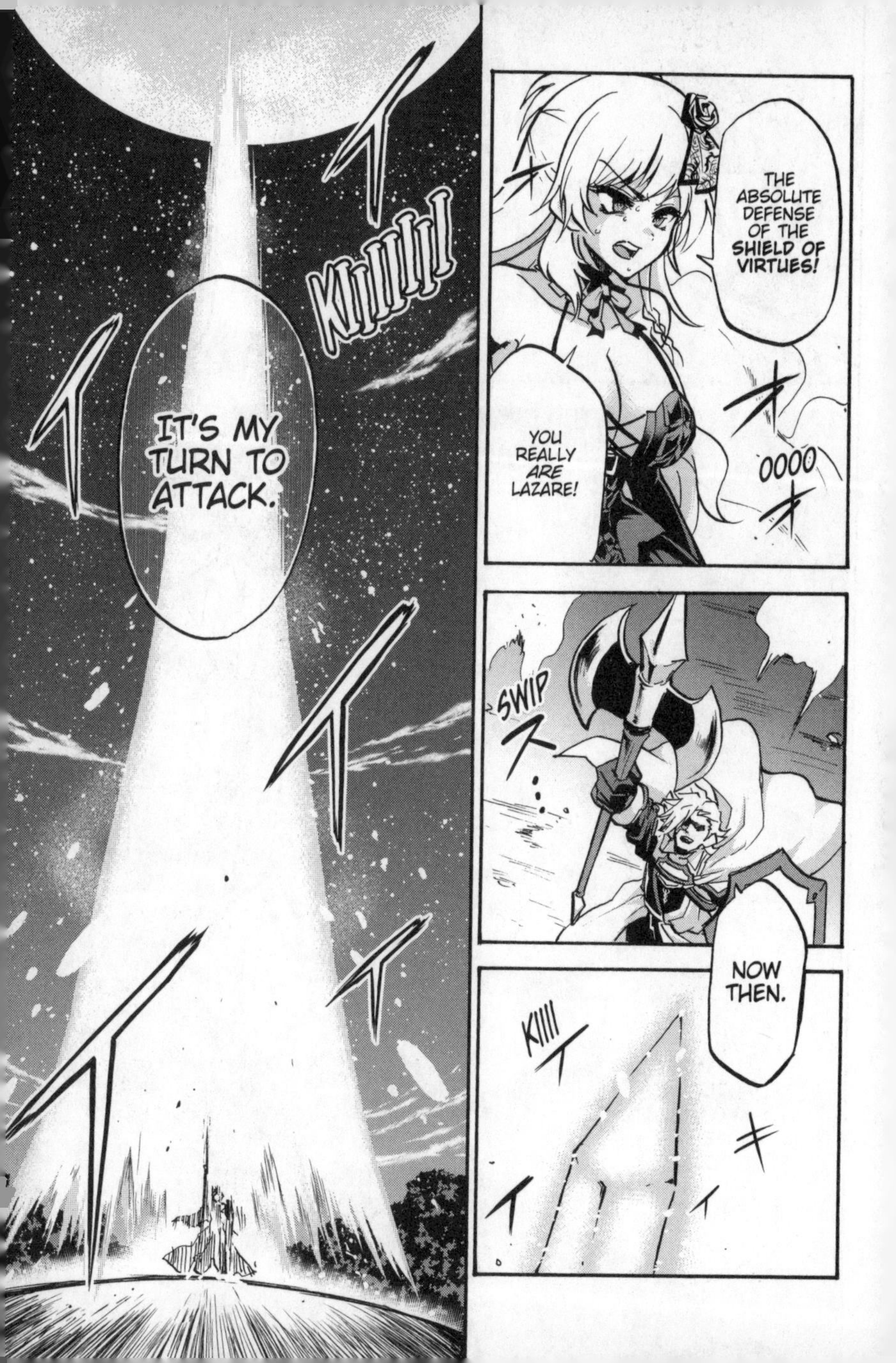
THE ABSOLUTE DEFENSE OF THE SHIELD OF VIRTUES!
YOU REALLY ARE LAZARE!
OOOO
SWIP
NOW THEN.
KIIII
IT'S MY TURN TO ATTACK.
KIIIIIII

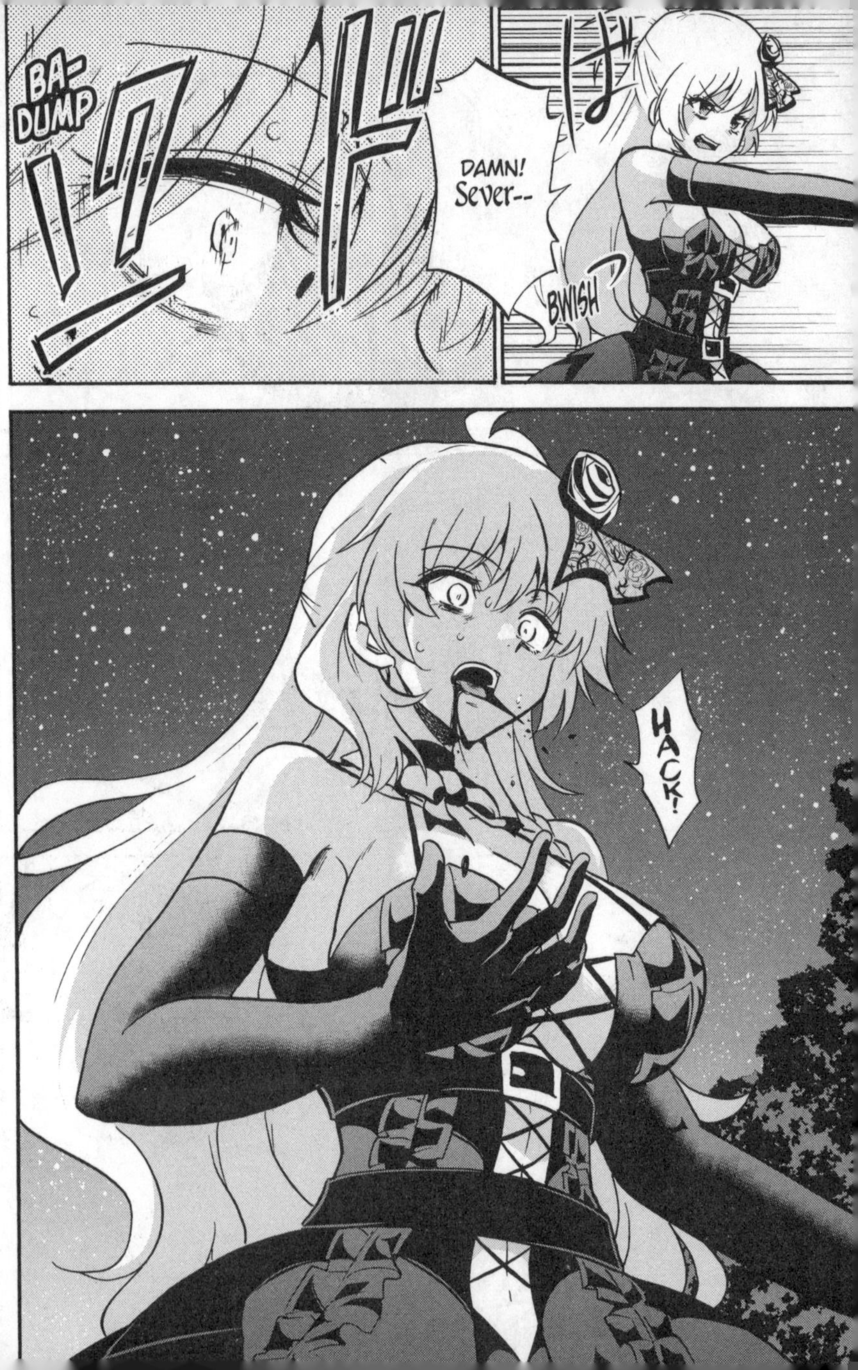
BA-DUMP
DAMN! Sever--
BWISH
HACK!

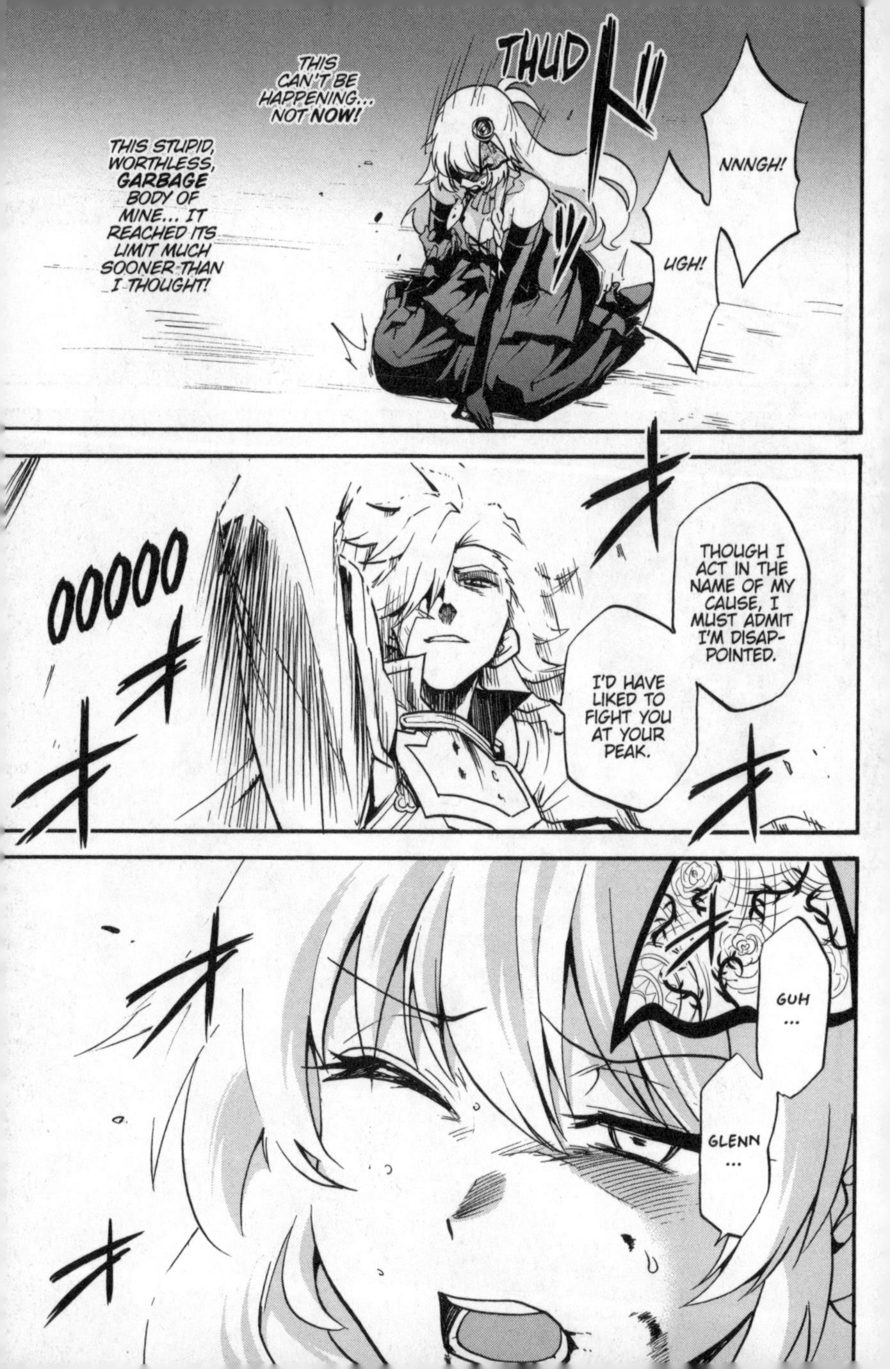
THUD
NNNGH!
UGH!
THIS CAN'T BE HAPPENING... NOT NOW!
THIS STUPID, WORTHLESS, GARBAGE BODY OF MINE... IT REACHED ITS LIMIT MUCH SOONER THAN I THOUGHT!
THOUGH I ACT IN THE NAME OF MY CAUSE, I MUST ADMIT I'M DISAPPOINTED.
I'D HAVE LIKED TO FIGHT YOU AT YOUR PEAK.
OOOOO
GUH...
GLENN...

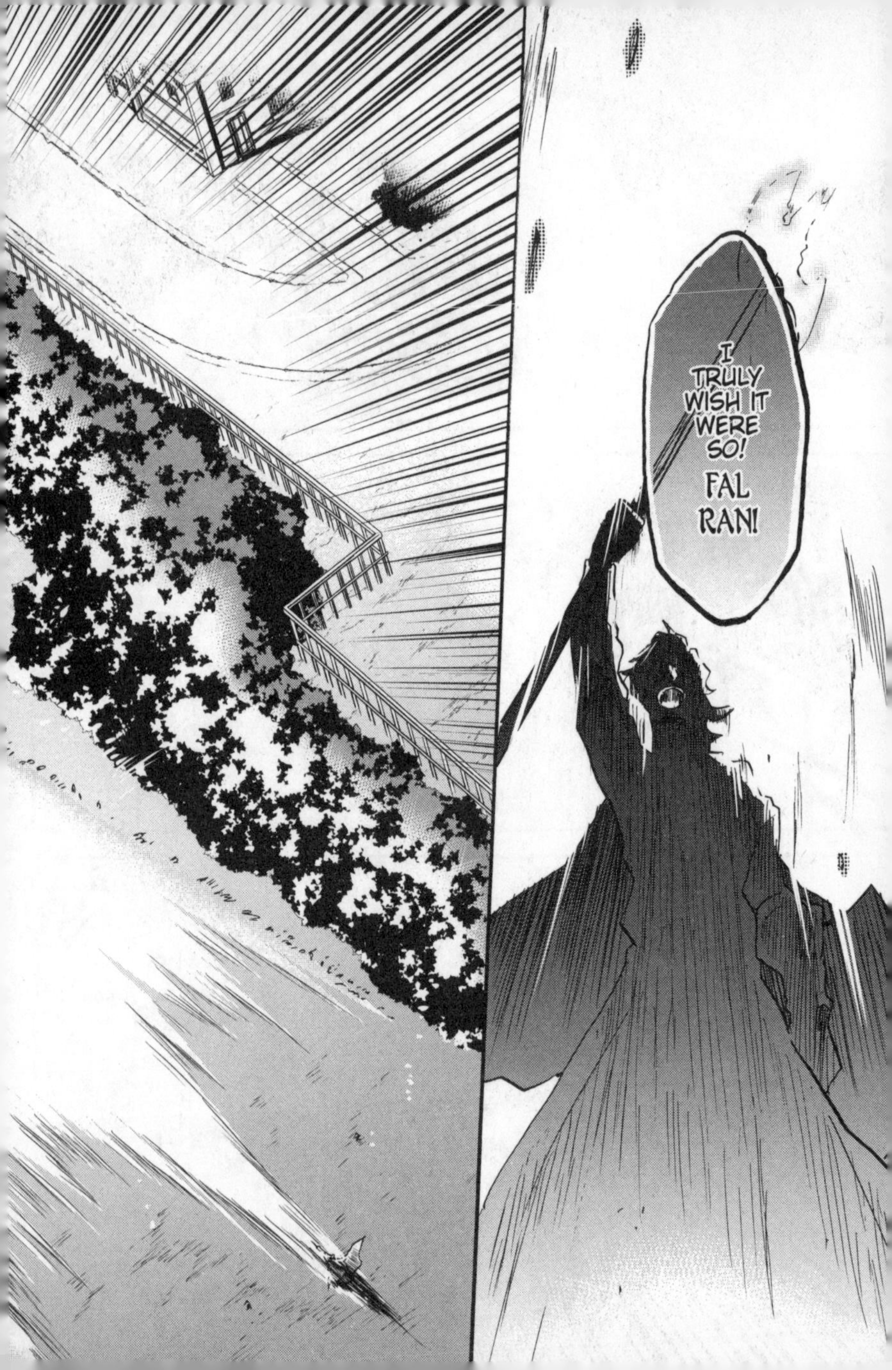
I TRULY WISH IT WERE SO! FAL RAN!

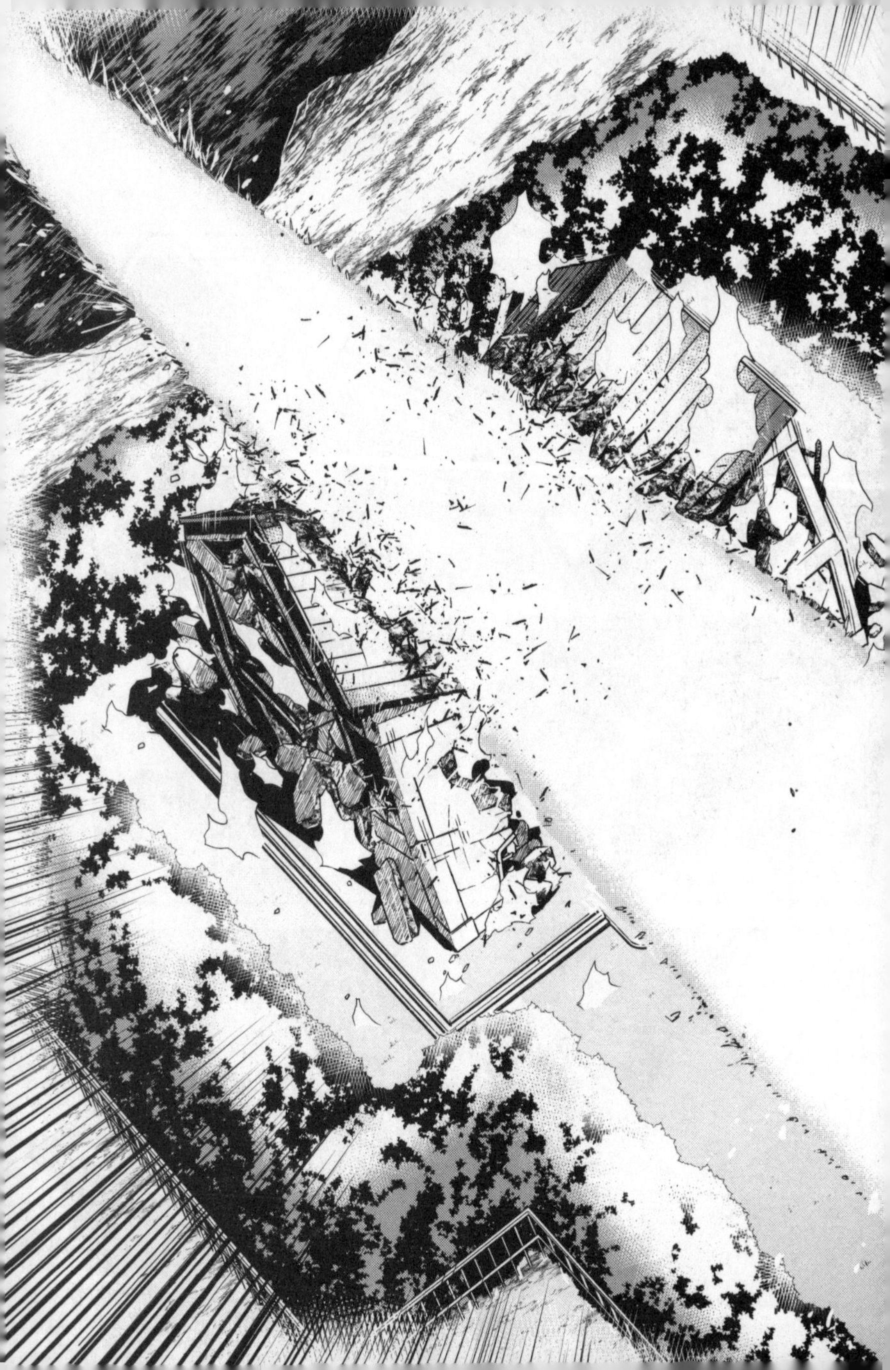

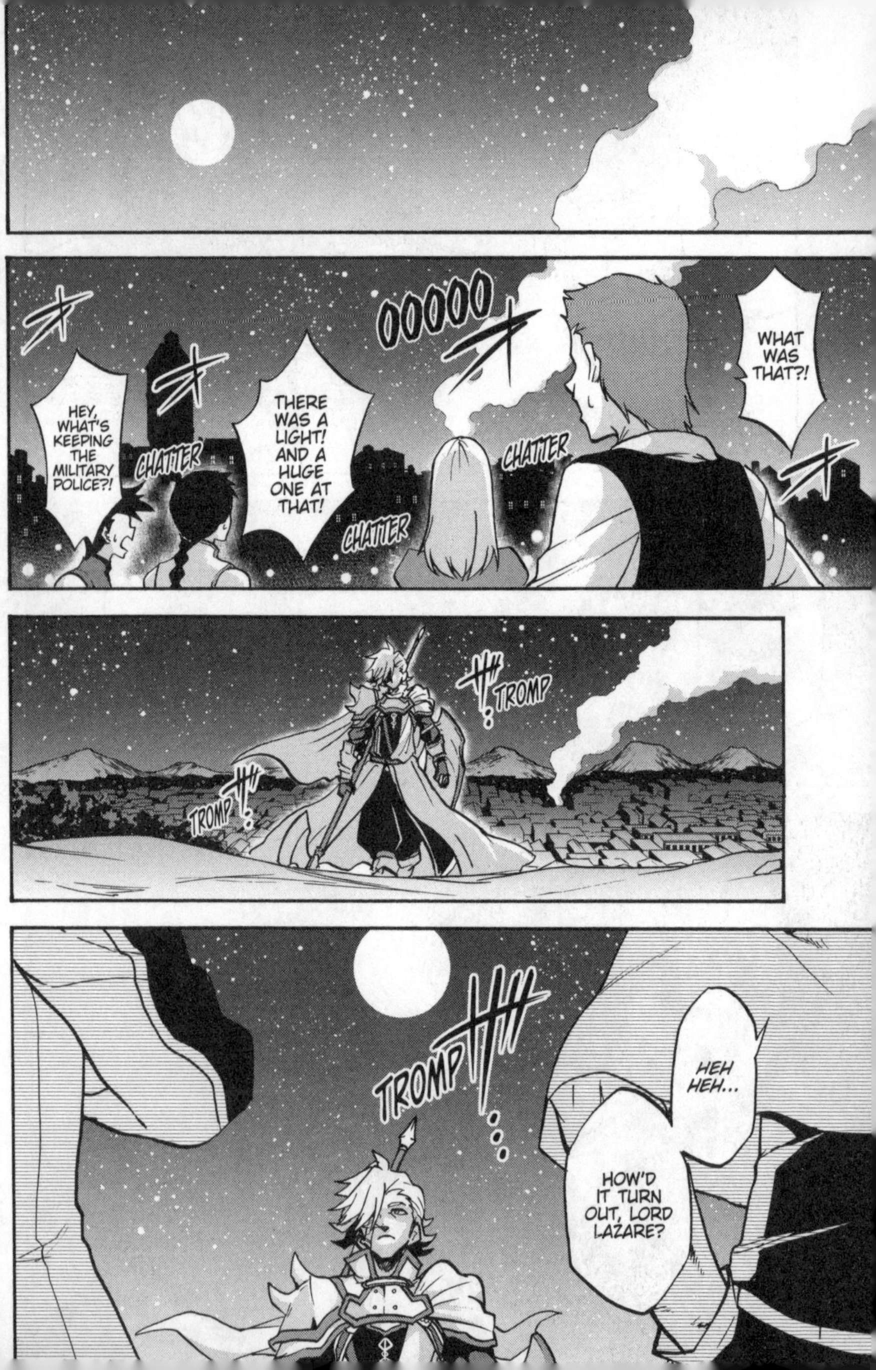
WHAT WAS THAT?!
OOOOO
CHATTER
THERE WAS A LIGHT! AND A HUGE ONE AT THAT!
CHATTER
HEY, WHAT'S KEEPING THE MILITARY POLICE?!
CHATTER
TROMP
TROMP
TROMP
HEH HEH...
HOW'D IT TURN OUT, LORD LAZARE?

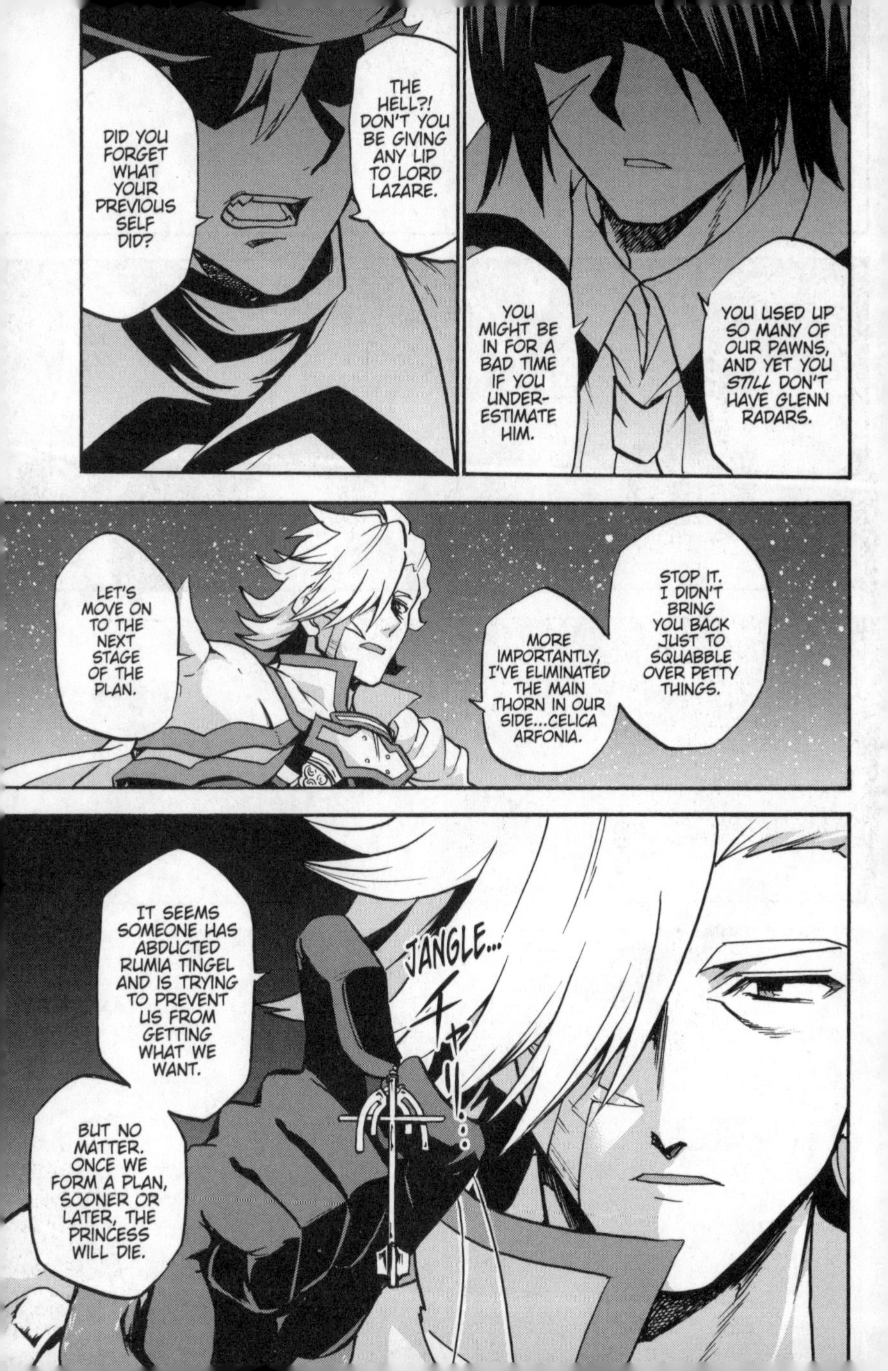
YOU USED UP SO MANY OF OUR PAWNS, AND YET YOU *STILL* DON'T HAVE GLENN RADARS.
YOU MIGHT BE IN FOR A BAD TIME IF YOU UNDER-ESTIMATE HIM.
THE HELL?! DON'T YOU BE GIVING ANY LIP TO LORD LAZARE.
DID YOU FORGET WHAT YOUR PREVIOUS SELF DID?
STOP IT. I DIDN'T BRING YOU BACK JUST TO SQUABBLE OVER PETTY THINGS.
MORE IMPORTANTLY, I'VE ELIMINATED THE MAIN THORN IN OUR SIDE...CELICA ARFONIA.
LET'S MOVE ON TO THE NEXT STAGE OF THE PLAN.
IT SEEMS SOMEONE HAS ABDUCTED RUMIA TINGEL AND IS TRYING TO PREVENT US FROM GETTING WHAT WE WANT.
JANGLE...
BUT NO MATTER. ONCE WE FORM A PLAN, SOONER OR LATER, THE PRINCESS WILL DIE.

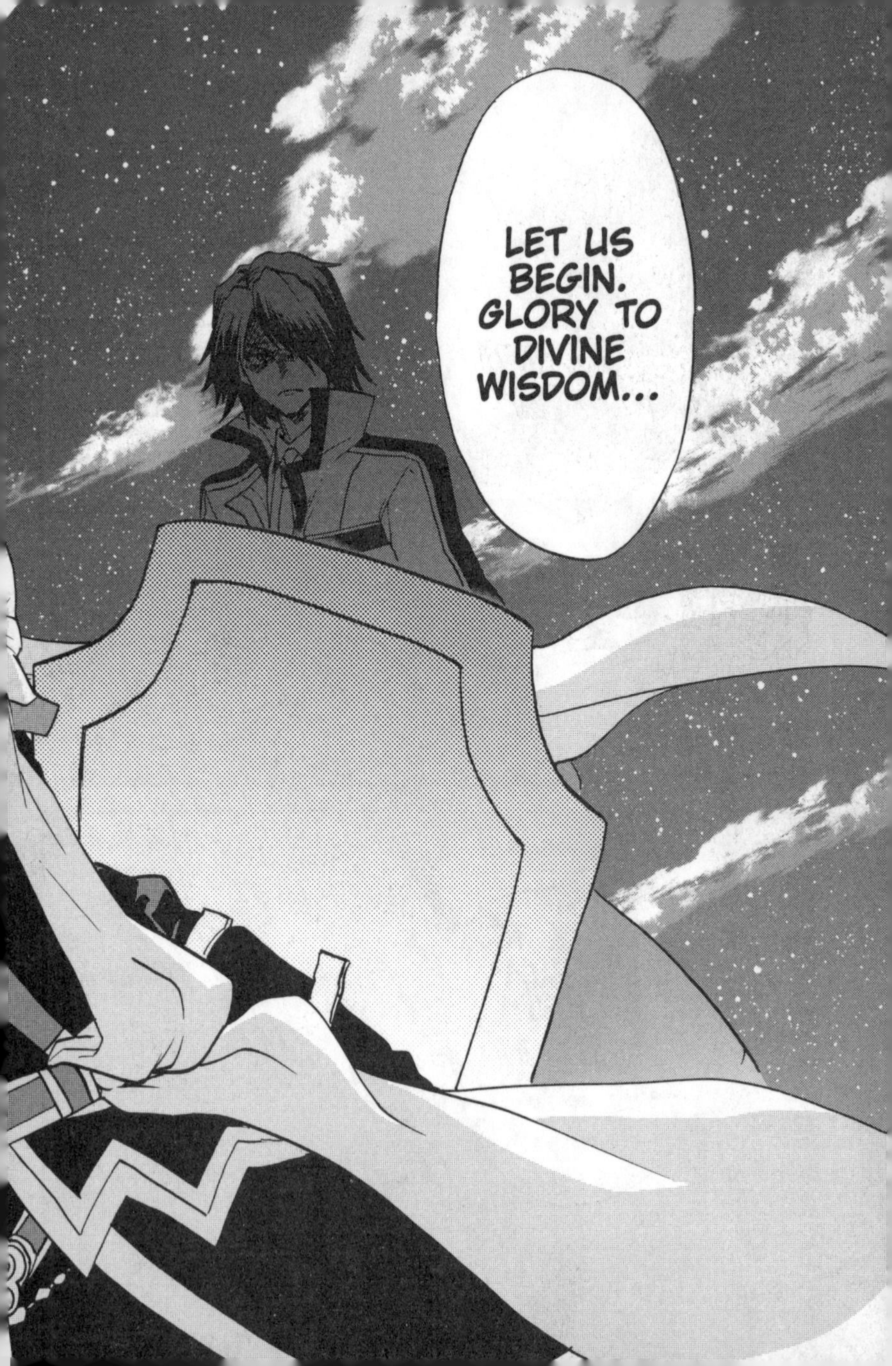
LET US BEGIN. GLORY TO DIVINE WISDOM...

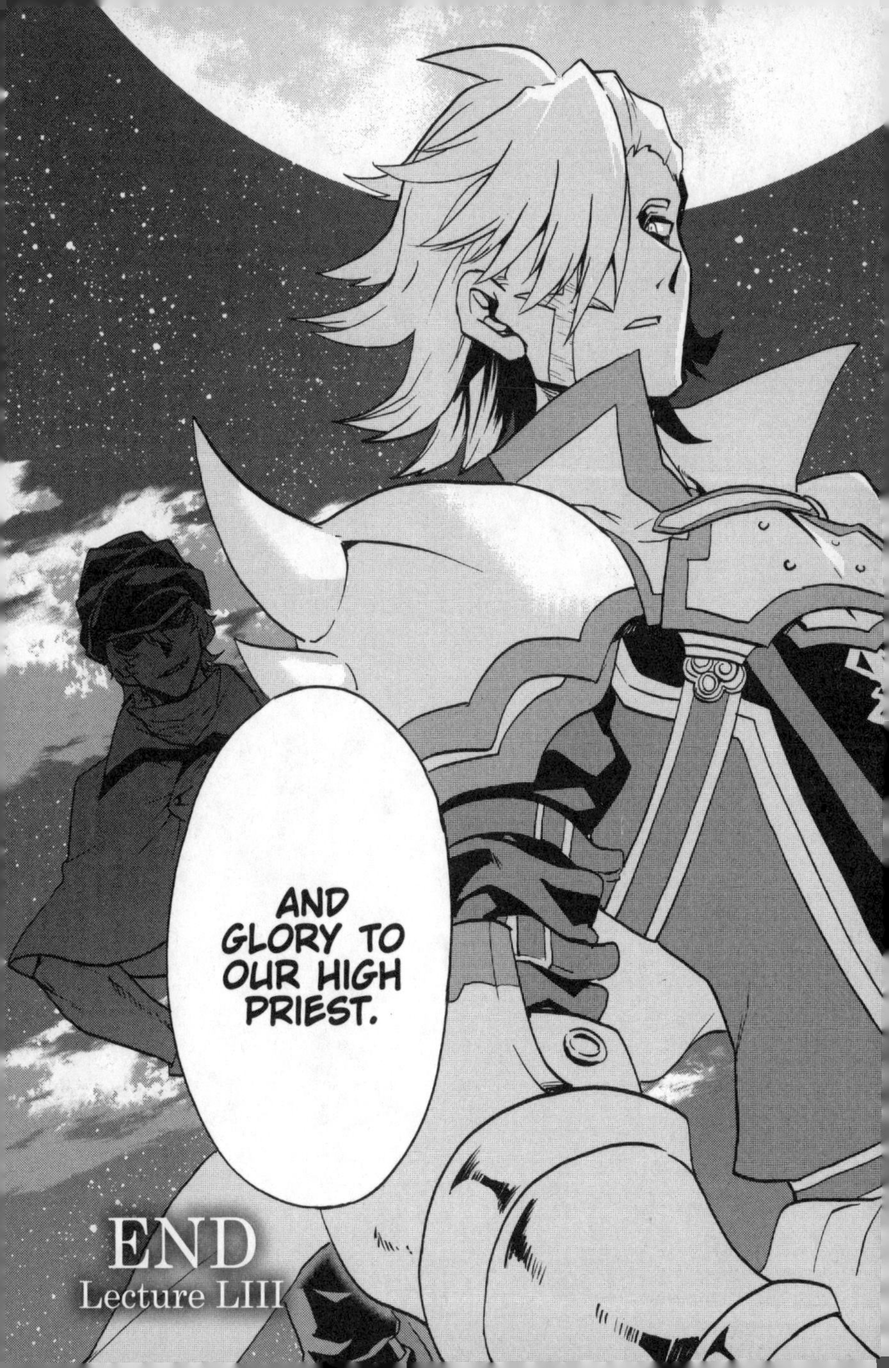
AND GLORY TO OUR HIGH PRIEST.
END
Lecture LIII

Akashic Records

of ***Bastard*** Magic ***Instructor***

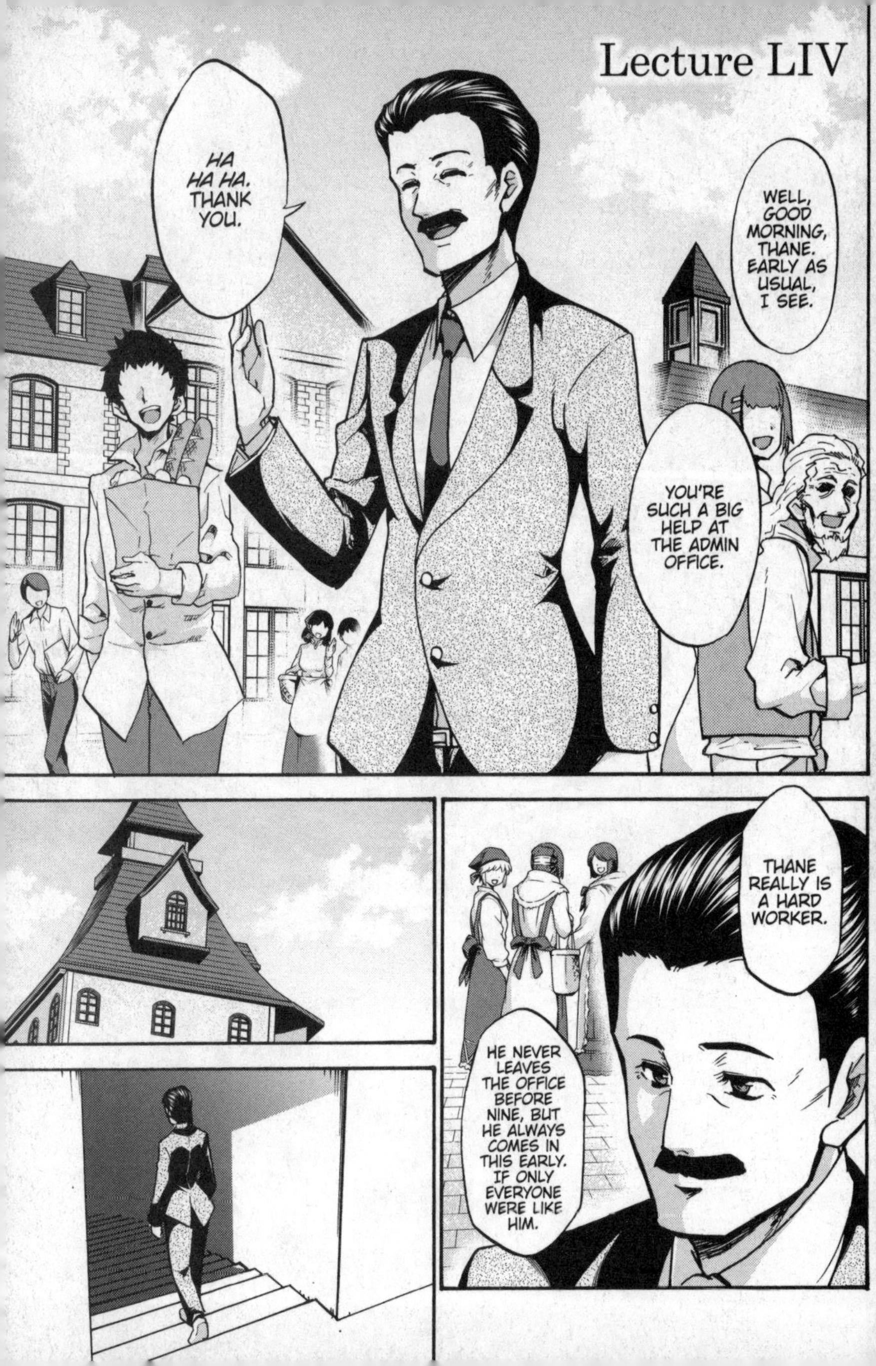
Lecture LIV
WELL, GOOD MORNING, THANE. EARLY AS USUAL, I SEE.
YOU'RE SUCH A BIG HELP AT THE ADMIN OFFICE.
HA HA HA. THANK YOU.
THANE REALLY IS A HARD WORKER.
HE NEVER LEAVES THE OFFICE BEFORE NINE, BUT HE ALWAYS COMES IN THIS EARLY. IF ONLY EVERYONE WERE LIKE HIM.

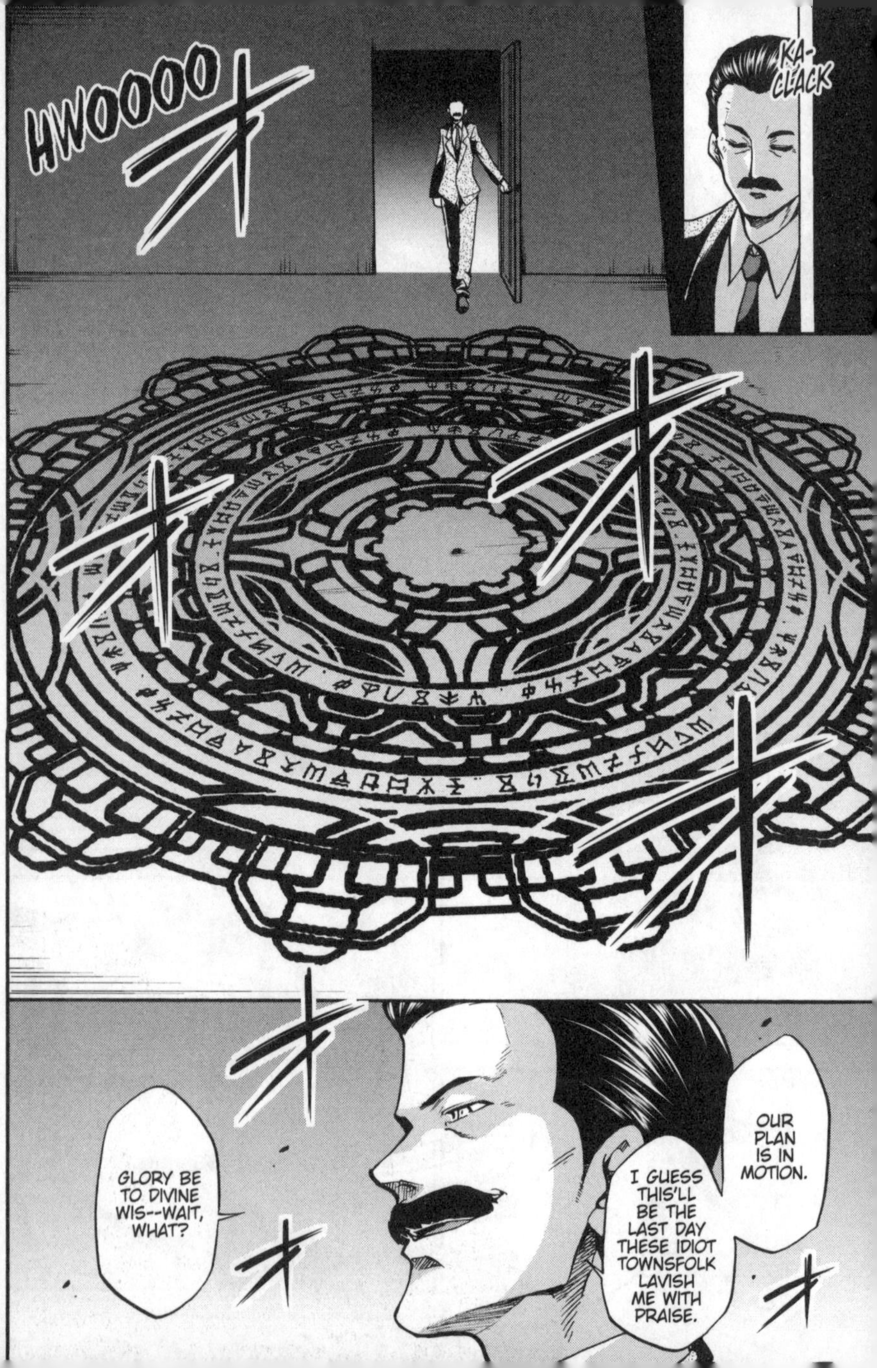
HWOOOO
KA-CLACK
OUR PLAN IS IN MOTION.
I GUESS THIS'LL BE THE LAST DAY THESE IDIOT TOWNSFOLK LAVISH ME WITH PRAISE.
GLORY BE TO DIVINE WIS--WAIT, WHAT?

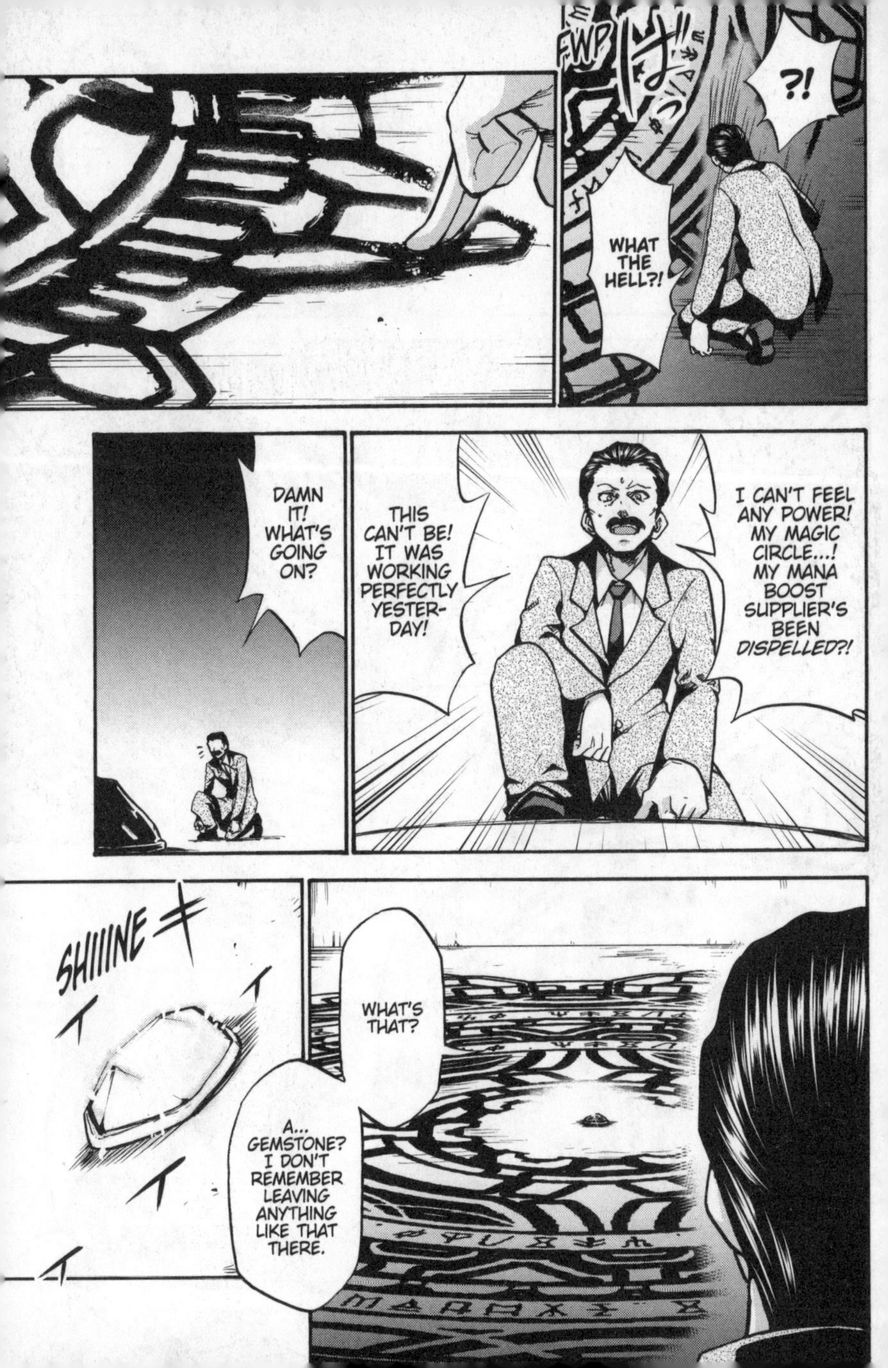
FWP
?!
WHAT THE HELL?!
I CAN'T FEEL ANY POWER! MY MAGIC CIRCLE...! MY MANA BOOST SUPPLIER'S BEEN DISPELLED?!
THIS CAN'T BE! IT WAS WORKING PERFECTLY YESTER-DAY!
DAMN IT! WHAT'S GOING ON?
WHAT'S THAT?
A... GEMSTONE? I DON'T REMEMBER LEAVING ANYTHING LIKE THAT THERE.
SHIIINE

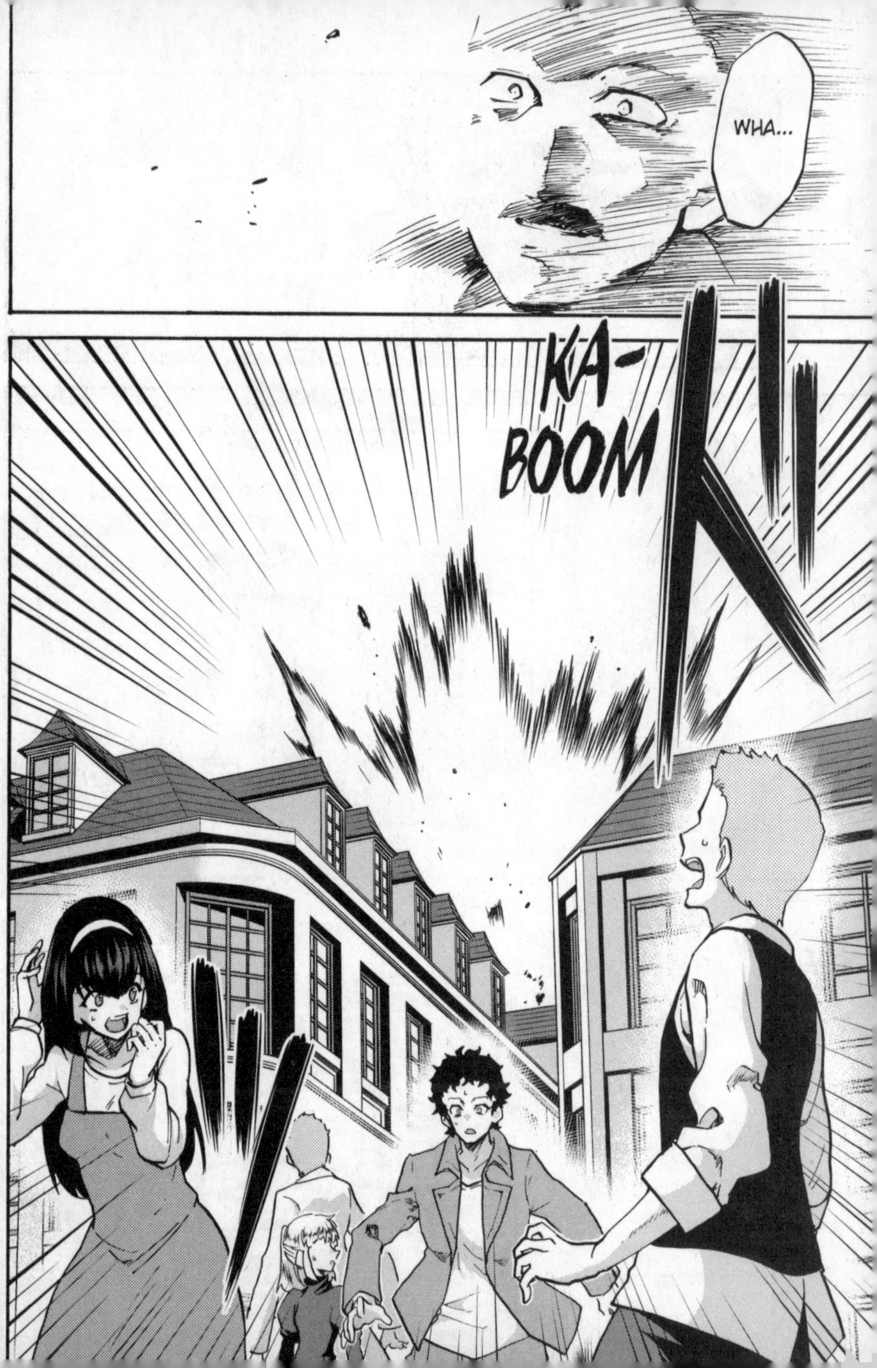
WHA...
KA-BOOM

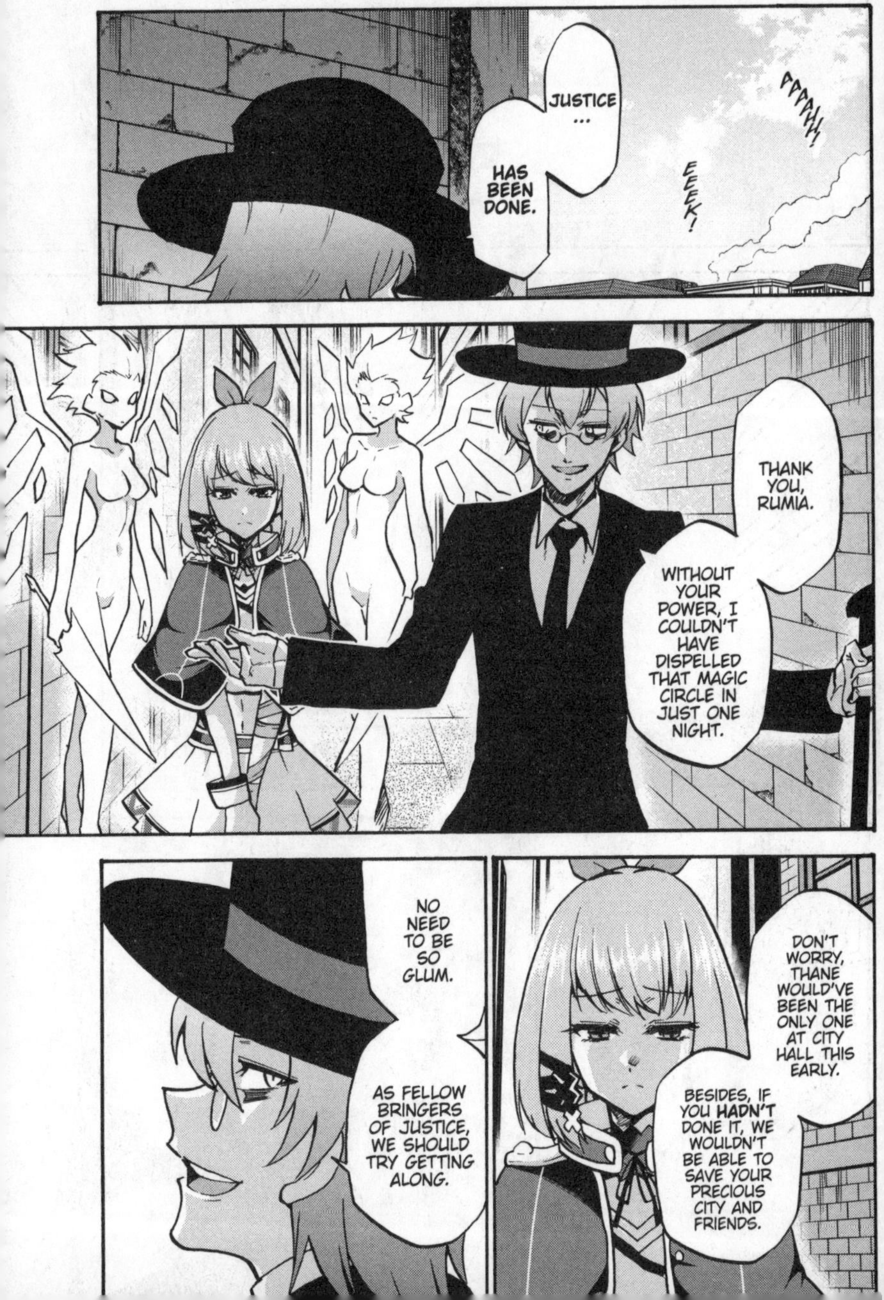
JUSTICE ... HAS BEEN DONE.
AAAAHH!
EEEEK!
THANK YOU, RUMIA.
WITHOUT YOUR POWER, I COULDN'T HAVE DISPELLED THAT MAGIC CIRCLE IN JUST ONE NIGHT.
NO NEED TO BE SO GLUM.
AS FELLOW BRINGERS OF JUSTICE, WE SHOULD TRY GETTING ALONG.
DON'T WORRY, THANE WOULD'VE BEEN THE ONLY ONE AT CITY HALL THIS EARLY.
BESIDES, IF YOU **HADN'T** DONE IT, WE WOULDN'T BE ABLE TO SAVE YOUR PRECIOUS CITY AND FRIENDS.

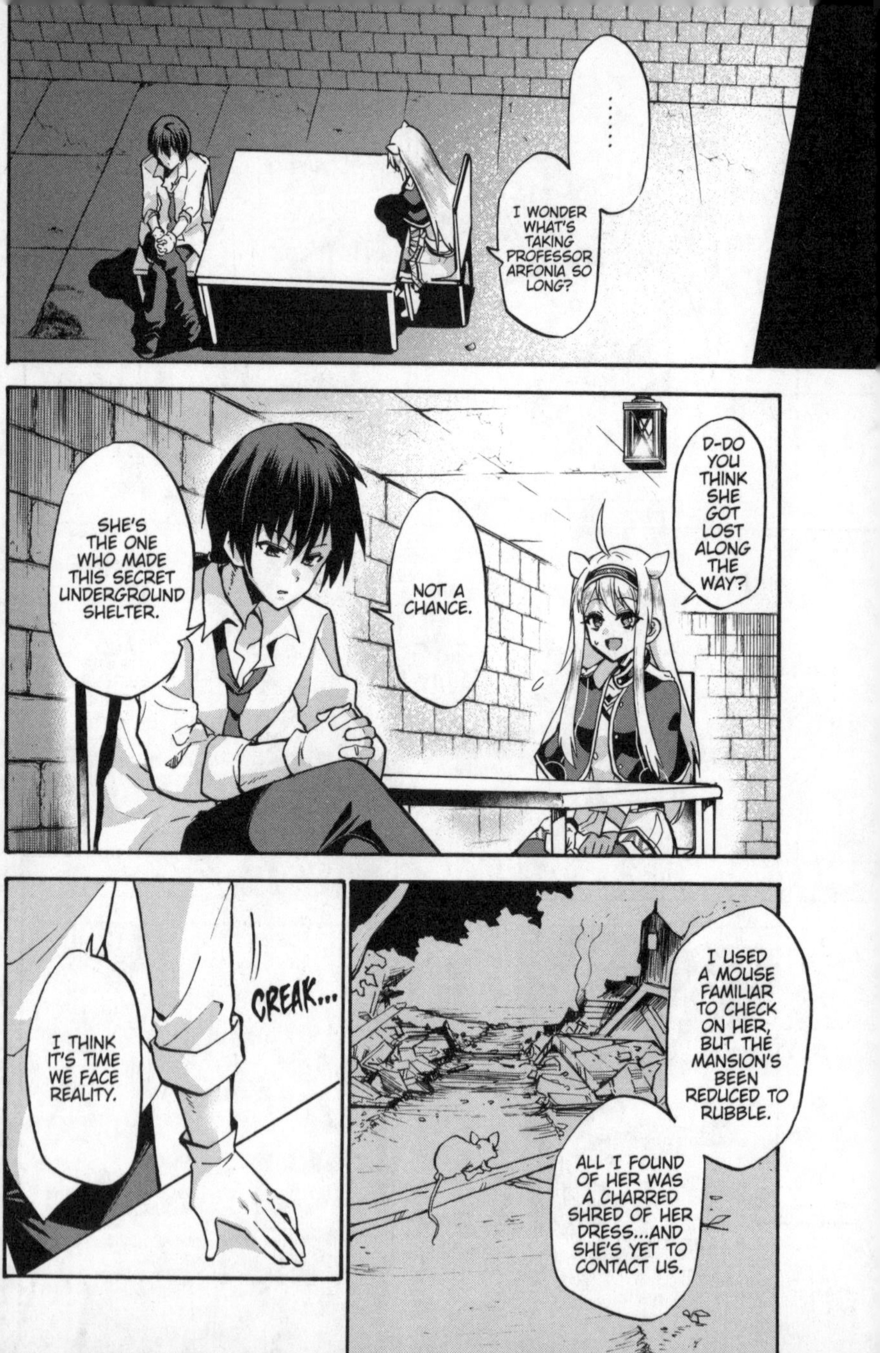
......
I WONDER WHAT'S TAKING PROFESSOR ARFONIA SO LONG?
D-DO YOU THINK SHE GOT LOST ALONG THE WAY?
NOT A CHANCE.
SHE'S THE ONE WHO MADE THIS SECRET UNDERGROUND SHELTER.
I USED A MOUSE FAMILIAR TO CHECK ON HER, BUT THE MANSION'S BEEN REDUCED TO RUBBLE.
ALL I FOUND OF HER WAS A CHARRED SHRED OF HER DRESS...AND SHE'S YET TO CONTACT US.
CREAK...
I THINK IT'S TIME WE FACE REALITY.

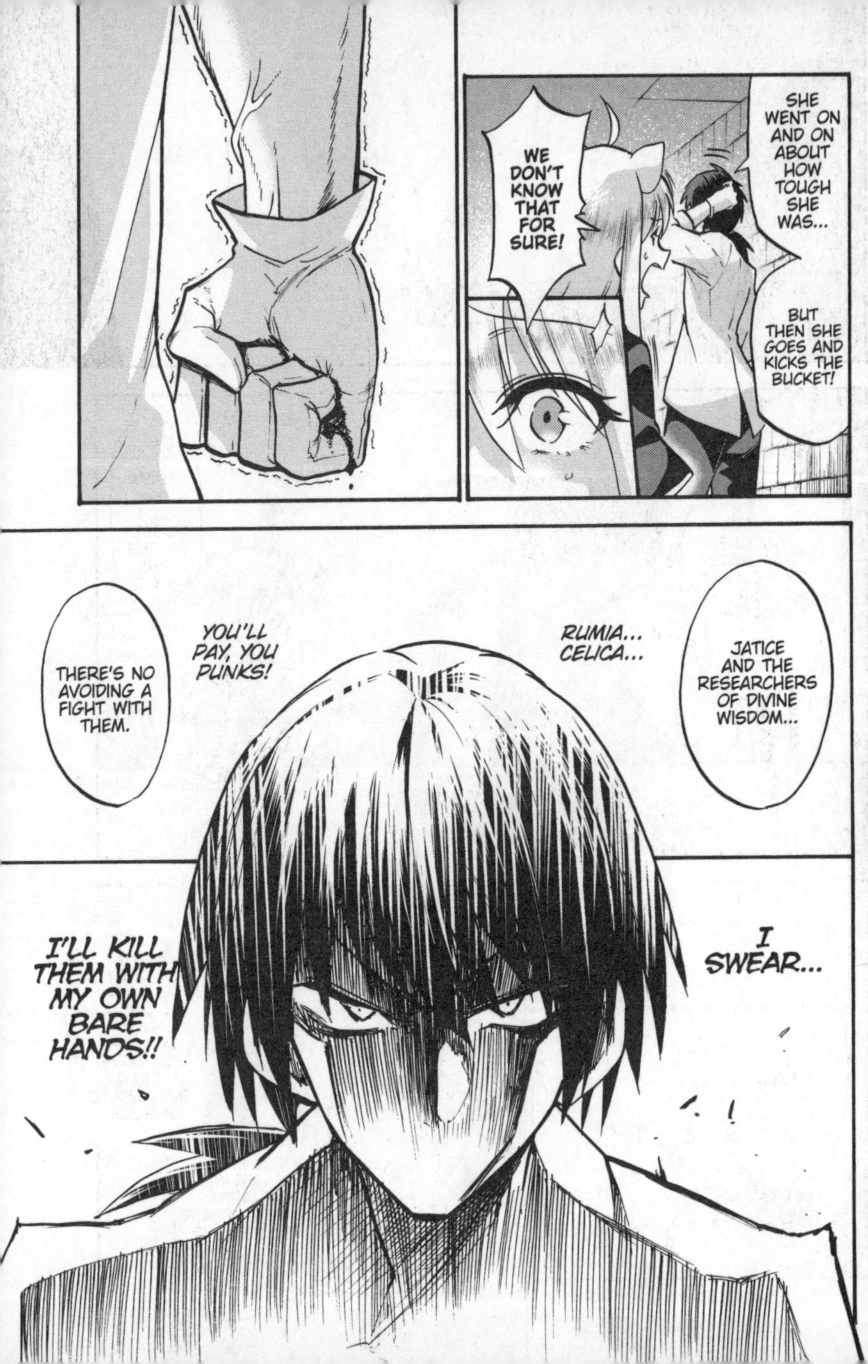
SHE WENT ON AND ON ABOUT HOW TOUGH SHE WAS...
BUT THEN SHE GOES AND KICKS THE BUCKET!
WE DON'T KNOW THAT FOR SURE!
JATICE AND THE RESEARCHERS OF DIVINE WISDOM...
RUMIA... CELICA...
YOU'LL PAY, YOU PUNKS!
THERE'S NO AVOIDING A FIGHT WITH THEM.
I SWEAR...
I'LL KILL THEM WITH MY OWN BARE HANDS!!

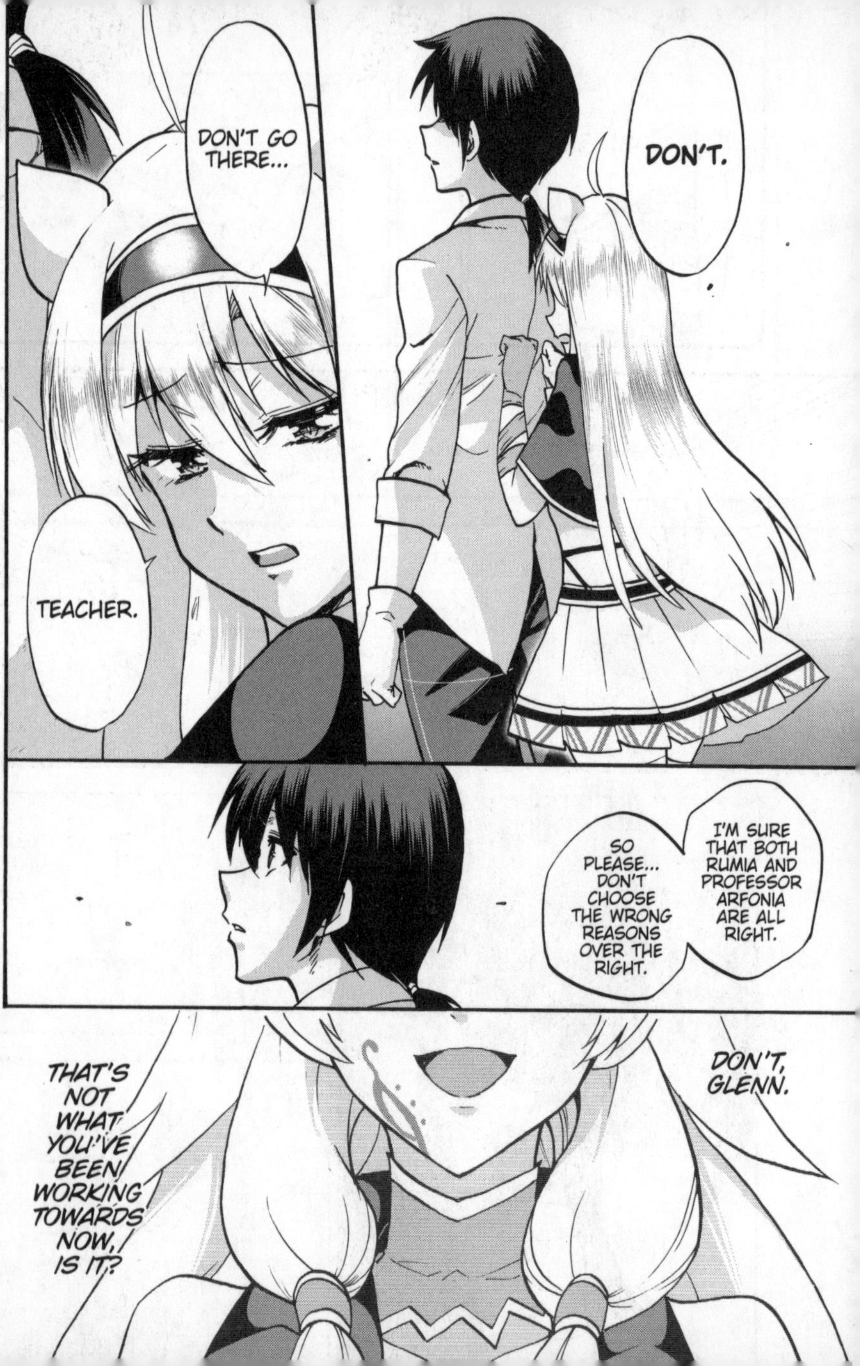
DON'T.
DON'T GO THERE...
TEACHER.
I'M SURE THAT BOTH RUMIA AND PROFESSOR ARFONIA ARE ALL RIGHT.
SO PLEASE... DON'T CHOOSE THE WRONG REASONS OVER THE RIGHT.
DON'T, GLENN.
THAT'S NOT WHAT YOU'VE BEEN WORKING TOWARDS NOW, IS IT?

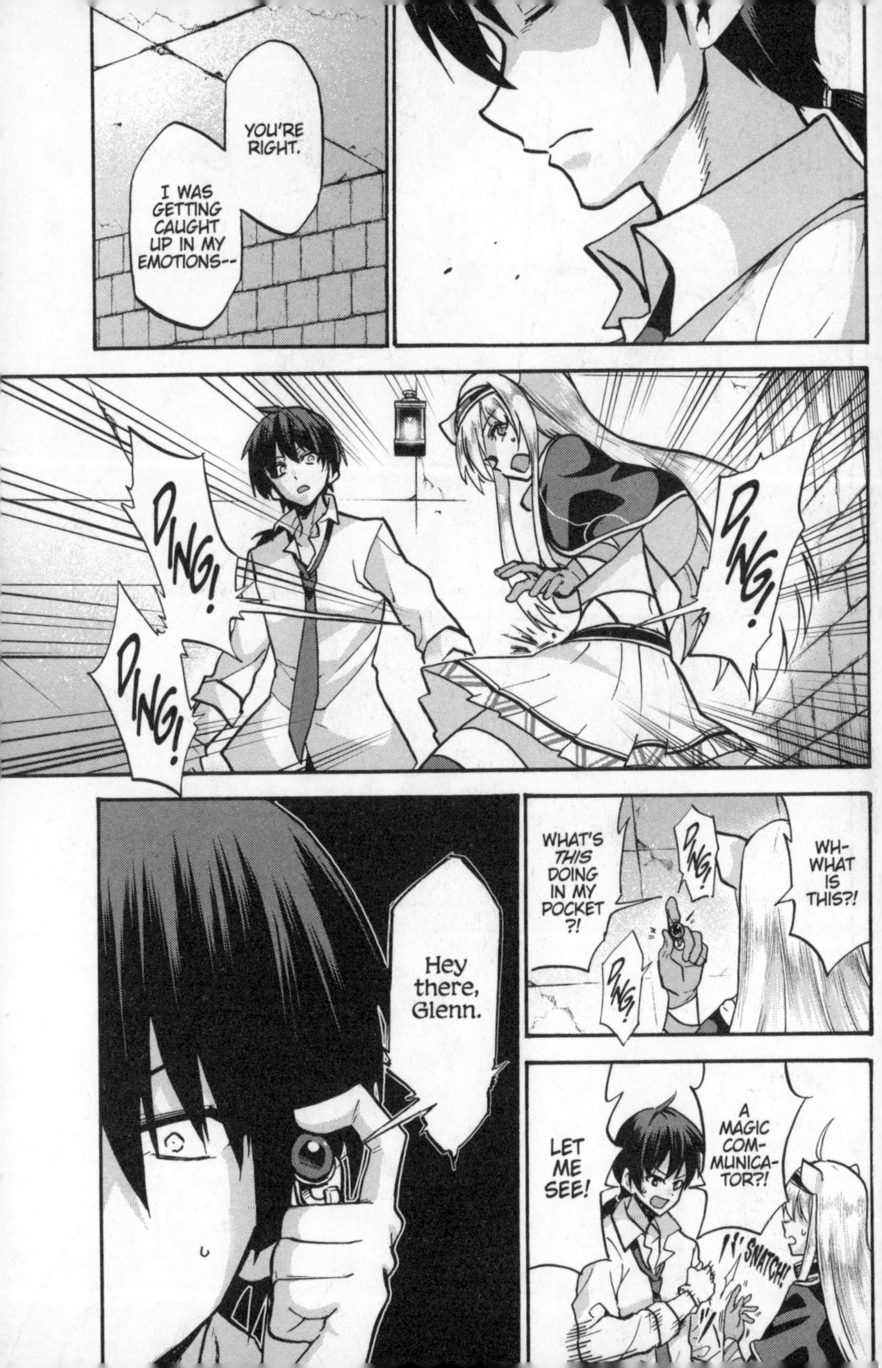
YOU'RE RIGHT.
I WAS GETTING CAUGHT UP IN MY EMOTIONS--
DING!
DING!
DING!
WH-WHAT IS THIS?!
DING!
WHAT'S *THIS* DOING IN MY POCKET?!
DING!
A MAGIC COM-MUNICA-TOR?!
LET ME SEE!
SNATCH!
Hey there, Glenn.

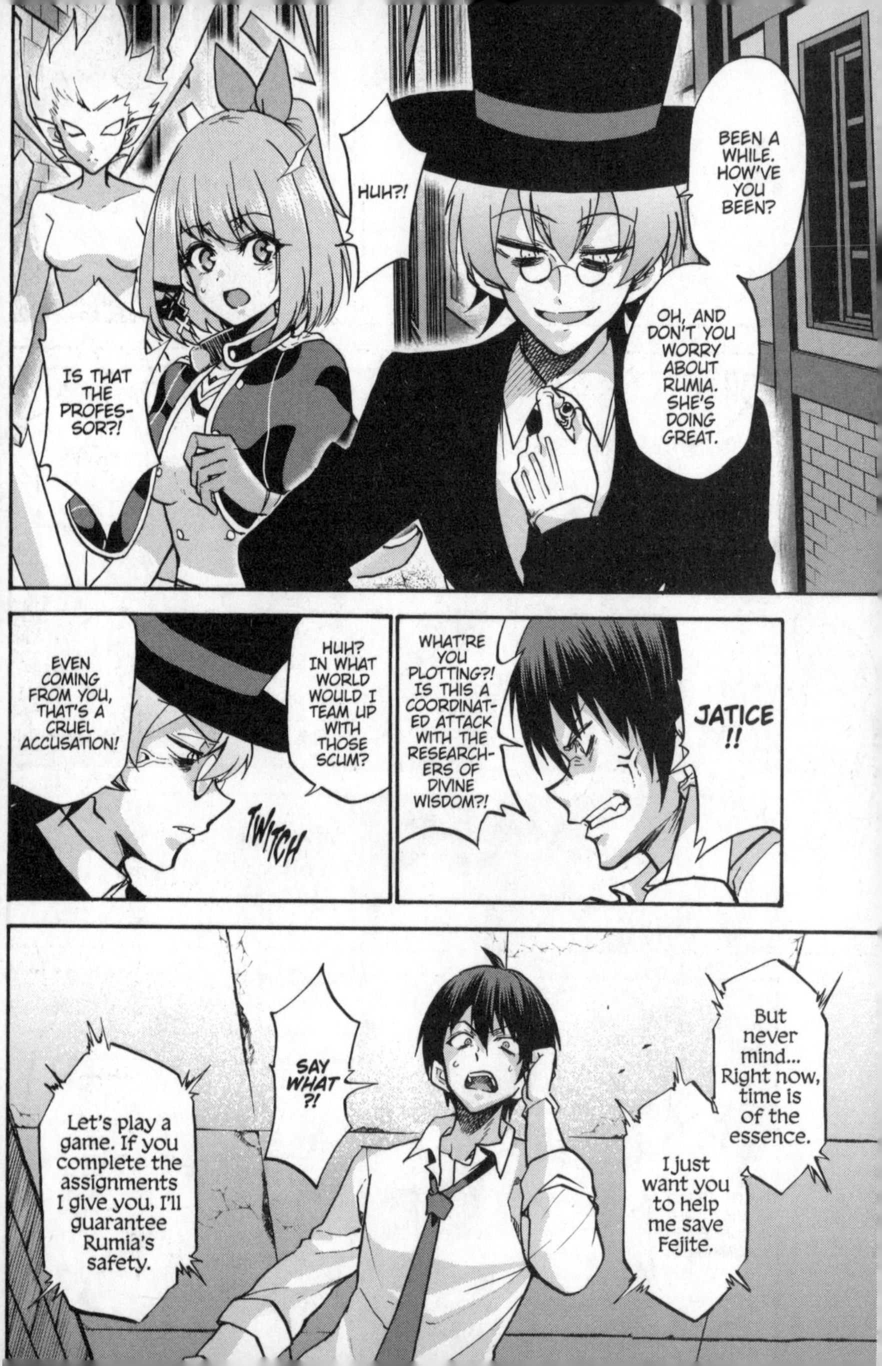

BEEN A WHILE. HOW'VE YOU BEEN?
OH, AND DON'T YOU WORRY ABOUT RUMIA. SHE'S DOING GREAT.
HUH?!
IS THAT THE PROFESSOR?!
JATICE !!
WHAT'RE YOU PLOTTING?! IS THIS A COORDINATED ATTACK WITH THE RESEARCHERS OF DIVINE WISDOM?!
HUH? IN WHAT WORLD WOULD I TEAM UP WITH THOSE SCUM?
EVEN COMING FROM YOU, THAT'S A CRUEL ACCUSATION!
TWITCH
But never mind... Right now, time is of the essence.
I just want you to help me save Fejite.
SAY WHAT?!
Let's play a game. If you complete the assignments I give you, I'll guarantee Rumia's safety.

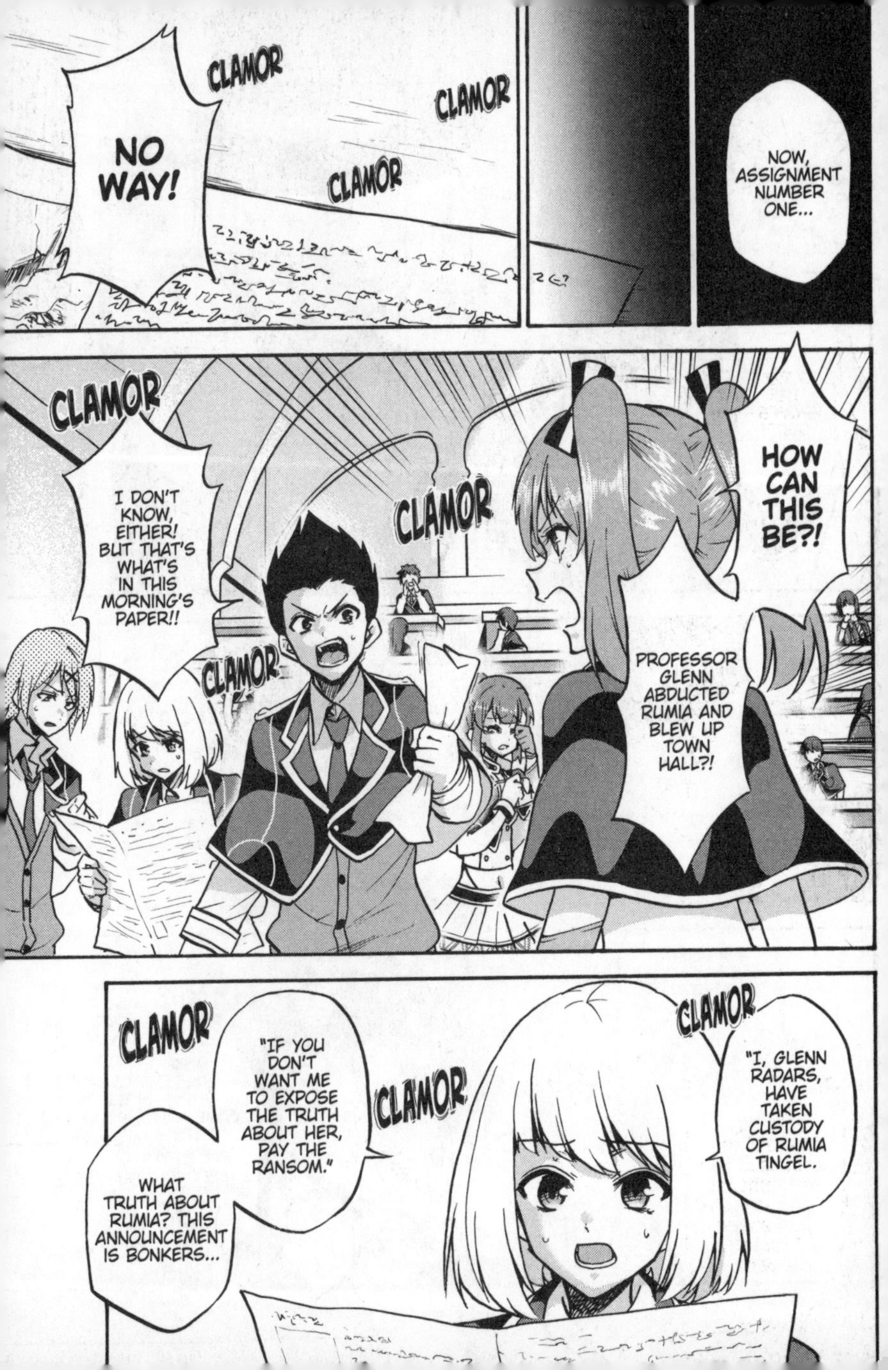
NOW, ASSIGNMENT NUMBER ONE...
CLAMOR
CLAMOR
CLAMOR
NO WAY!
HOW CAN THIS BE?!
PROFESSOR GLENN ABDUCTED RUMIA AND BLEW UP TOWN HALL?!
CLAMOR
CLAMOR
CLAMOR
I DON'T KNOW, EITHER! BUT THAT'S WHAT'S IN THIS MORNING'S PAPER!!
CLAMOR
"I, GLENN RADARS, HAVE TAKEN CUSTODY OF RUMIA TINGEL.
CLAMOR
"IF YOU DON'T WANT ME TO EXPOSE THE TRUTH ABOUT HER, PAY THE RANSOM."
CLAMOR
WHAT TRUTH ABOUT RUMIA? THIS ANNOUNCEMENT IS BONKERS...

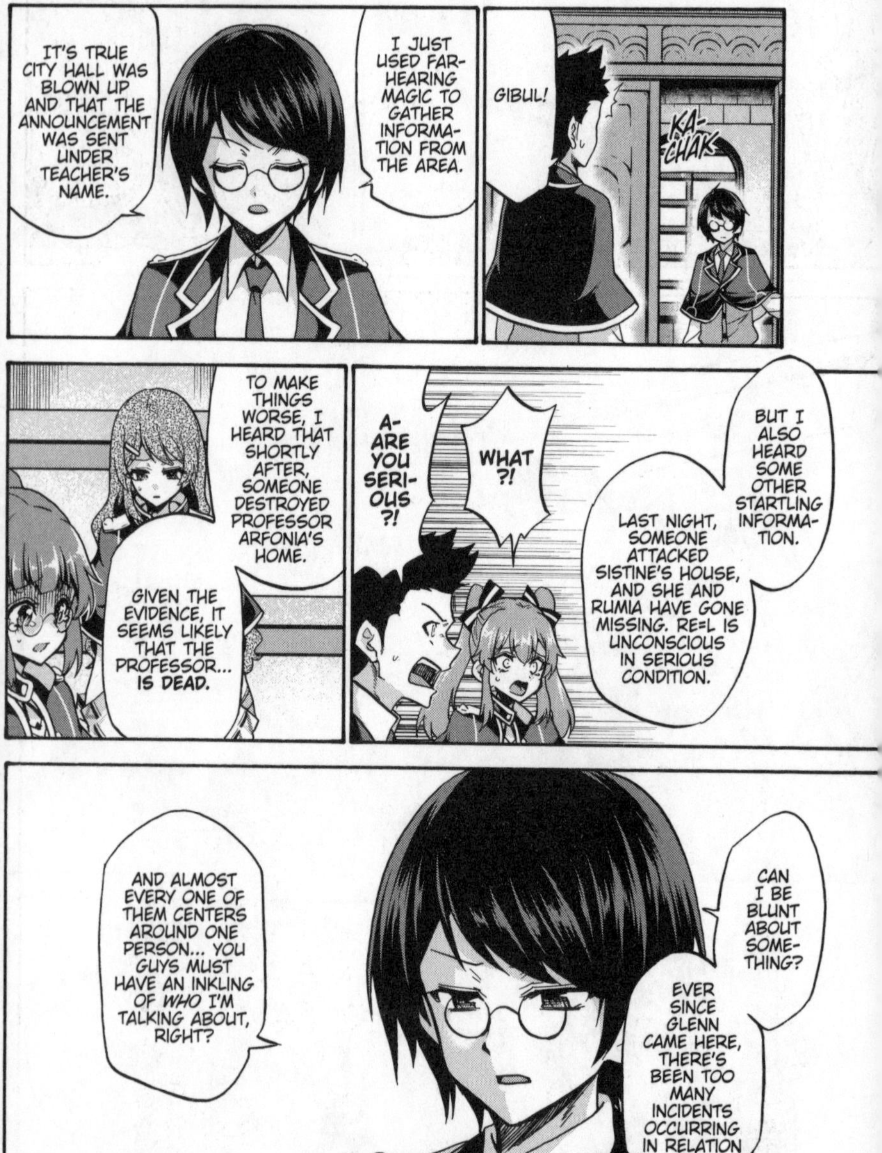
GIBUL!
KA-CHAK
I JUST USED FAR-HEARING MAGIC TO GATHER INFORMATION FROM THE AREA.
IT'S TRUE CITY HALL WAS BLOWN UP AND THAT THE ANNOUNCEMENT WAS SENT UNDER TEACHER'S NAME.
BUT I ALSO HEARD SOME OTHER STARTLING INFORMATION.
LAST NIGHT, SOMEONE ATTACKED SISTINE'S HOUSE, AND SHE AND RUMIA HAVE GONE MISSING. RE=L IS UNCONSCIOUS IN SERIOUS CONDITION.
WHAT?!
A-ARE YOU SERI-OUS?!
TO MAKE THINGS WORSE, I HEARD THAT SHORTLY AFTER, SOMEONE DESTROYED PROFESSOR ARFONIA'S HOME.
GIVEN THE EVIDENCE, IT SEEMS LIKELY THAT THE PROFESSOR... **IS DEAD.**
CAN I BE BLUNT ABOUT SOME-THING?
EVER SINCE GLENN CAME HERE, THERE'S BEEN TOO MANY INCIDENTS OCCURRING IN RELATION TO US.
AND ALMOST EVERY ONE OF THEM CENTERS AROUND ONE PERSON... YOU GUYS MUST HAVE AN INKLING OF *WHO* I'M TALKING ABOUT, RIGHT?

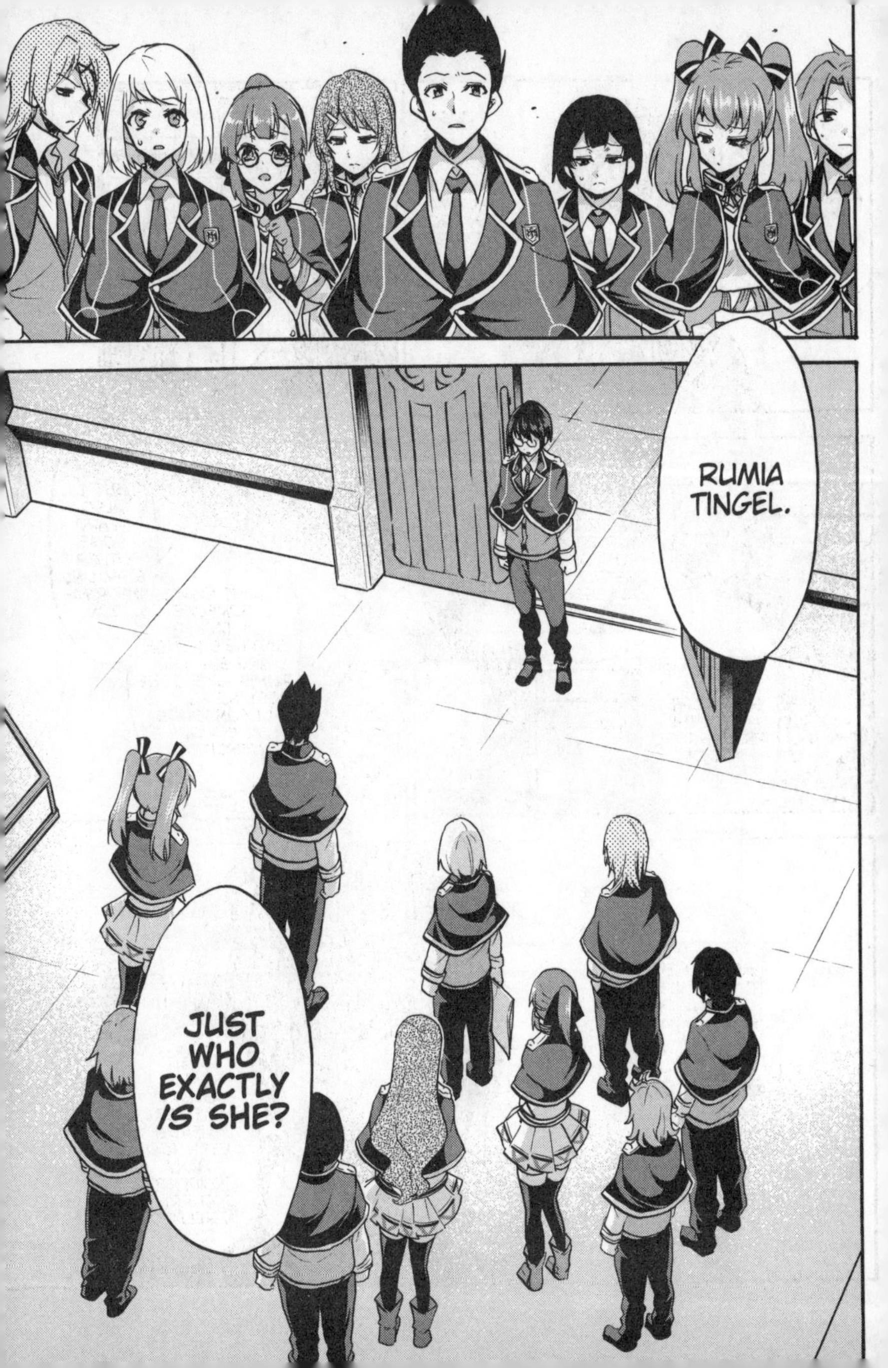
RUMIA TINGEL.
JUST WHO EXACTLY IS SHE?

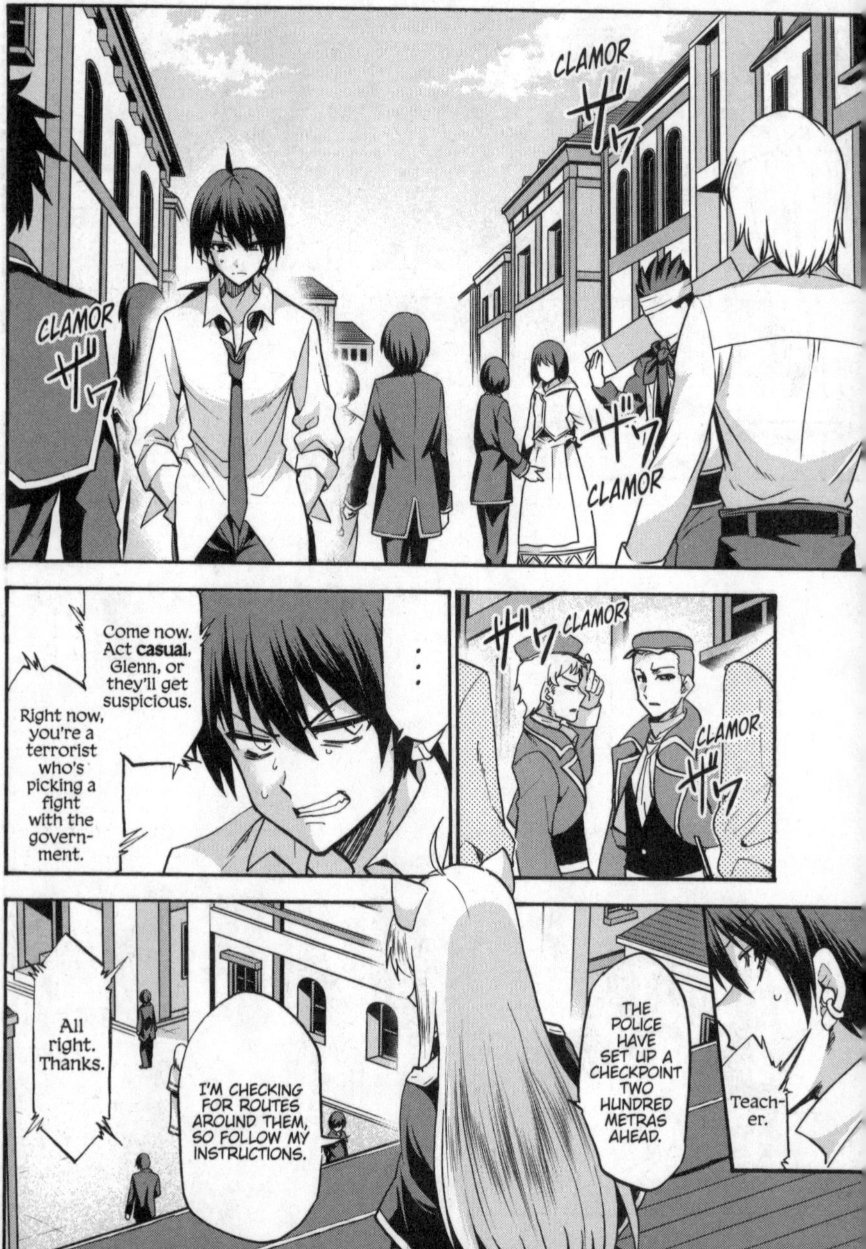
CLAMOR
ザワ
CLAMOR
ザワ
ザワ
CLAMOR
ザワ CLAMOR
CLAMOR
ザワ
...
Come now. Act **casual**, Glenn, or they'll get suspicious.
Right now, you're a terrorist who's picking a fight with the government.
Teacher.
THE POLICE HAVE SET UP A CHECKPOINT TWO HUNDRED METRAS AHEAD.
I'M CHECKING FOR ROUTES AROUND THEM, SO FOLLOW MY INSTRUCTIONS.
All right. Thanks.

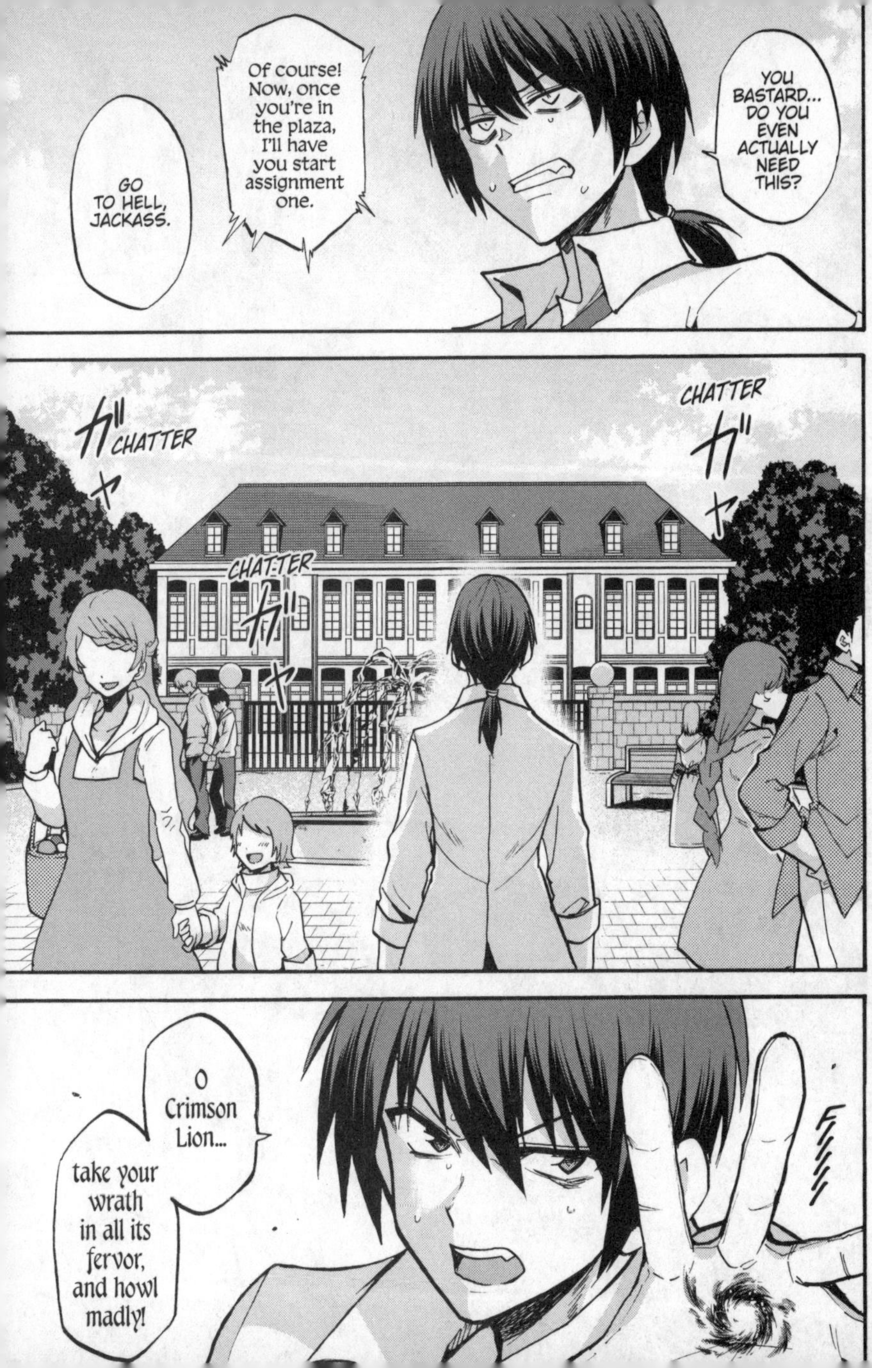

YOU BASTARD... DO YOU EVEN ACTUALLY NEED THIS?
Of course! Now, once you're in the plaza, I'll have you start assignment one.
GO TO HELL, JACKASS.
CHATTER
ガヤ
ガヤ
CHATTER
CHATTER
ガヤ
O Crimson Lion...
take your wrath in all its fervor, and howl madly!

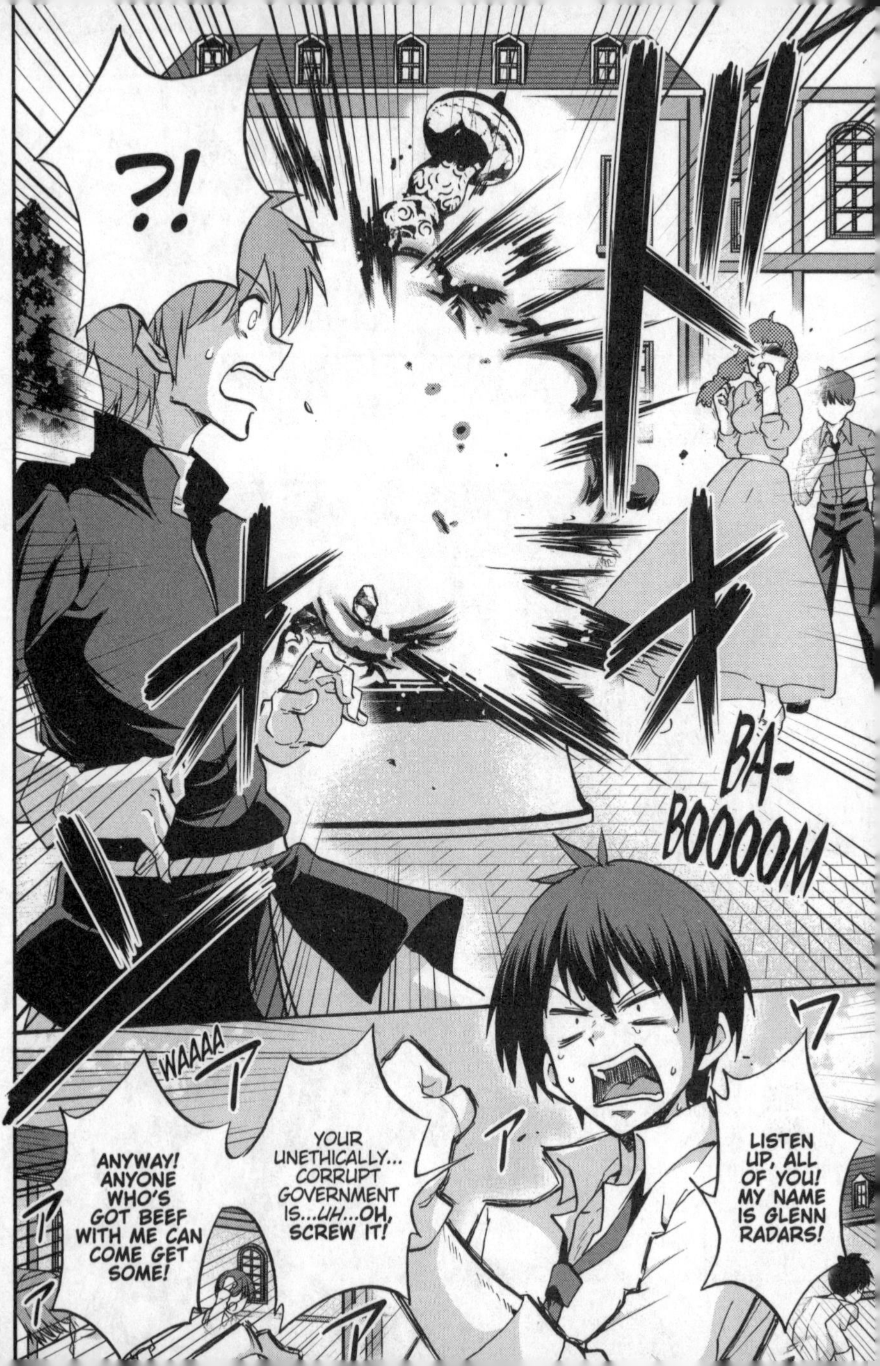
?!
BA-BOOOOM
WAAAA
LISTEN UP, ALL OF YOU! MY NAME IS GLENN RADARS!
YOUR UNETHICALLY... CORRUPT GOVERNMENT IS...UH...OH, SCREW IT!
ANYWAY! ANYONE WHO'S GOT BEEF WITH ME CAN COME GET SOME!

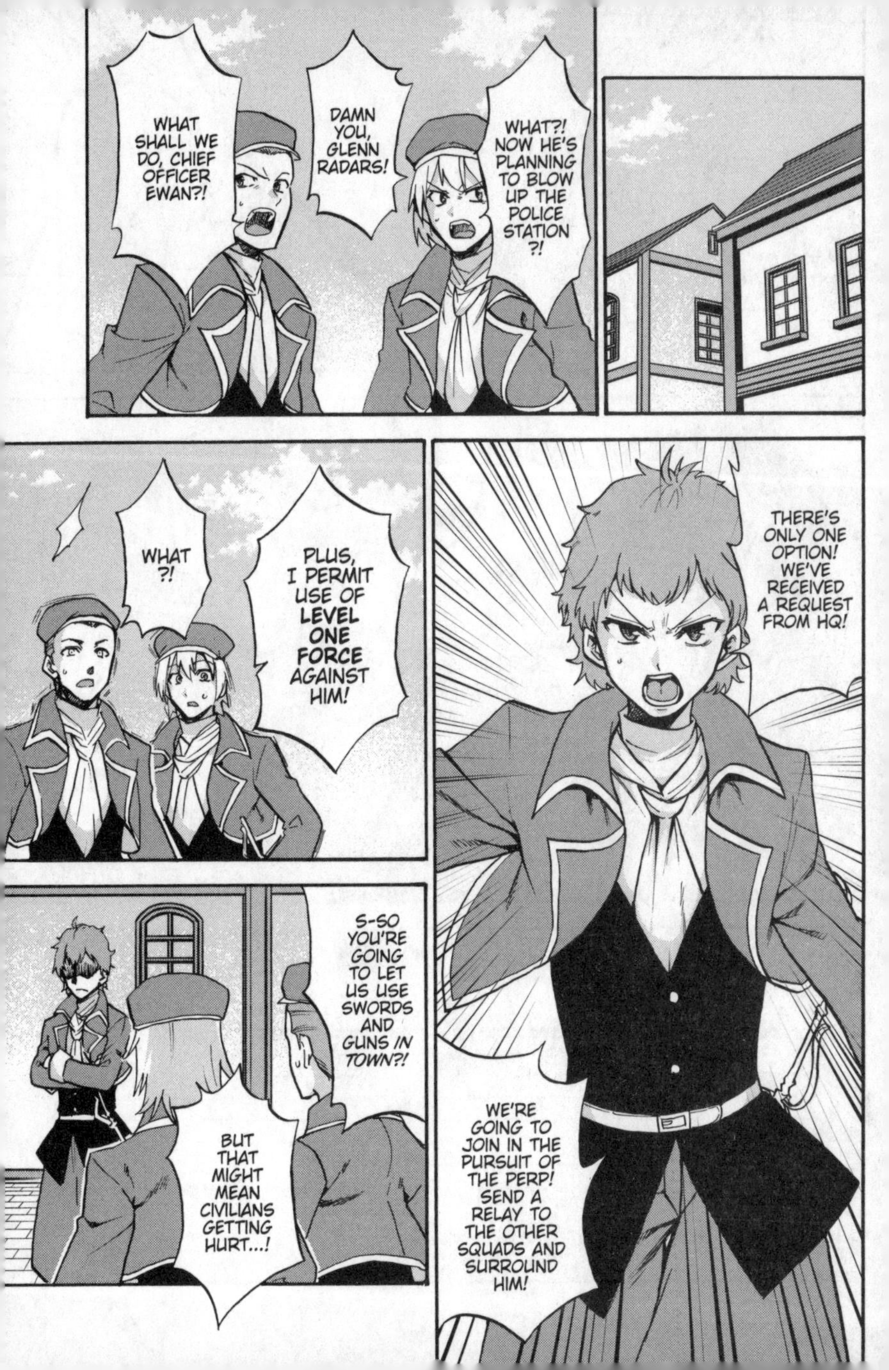
WHAT?! NOW HE'S PLANNING TO BLOW UP THE POLICE STATION?!
DAMN YOU, GLENN RADARS!
WHAT SHALL WE DO, CHIEF OFFICER EWAN?!
THERE'S ONLY ONE OPTION! WE'VE RECEIVED A REQUEST FROM HQ!
WE'RE GOING TO JOIN IN THE PURSUIT OF THE PERP! SEND A RELAY TO THE OTHER SQUADS AND SURROUND HIM!
PLUS, I PERMIT USE OF **LEVEL ONE FORCE** AGAINST HIM!
WHAT?!
S-SO YOU'RE GOING TO LET US USE SWORDS AND GUNS *IN TOWN*?!
BUT THAT MIGHT MEAN CIVILIANS GETTING HURT...!

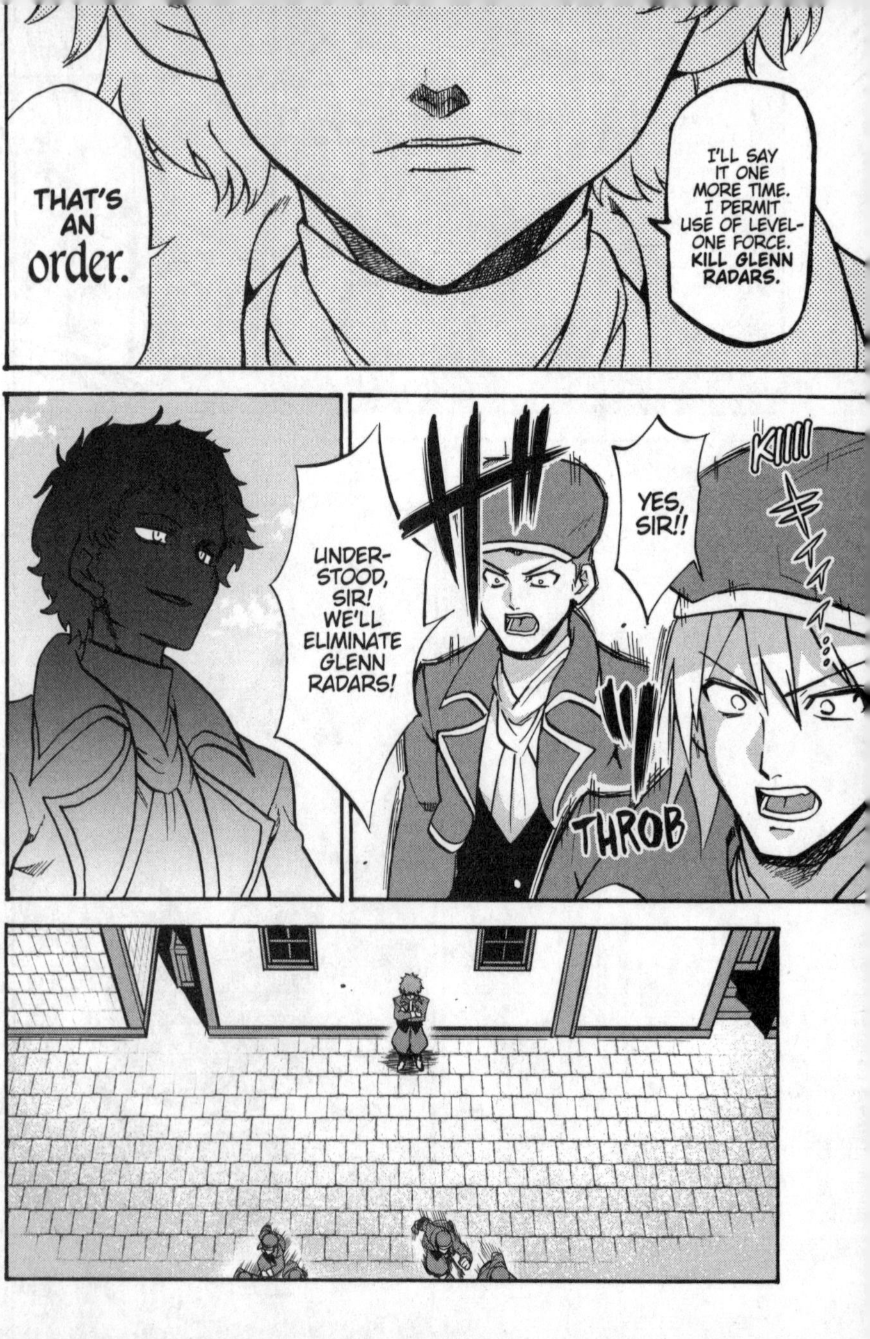
I'LL SAY IT ONE MORE TIME. I PERMIT USE OF LEVEL-ONE FORCE. KILL GLENN RADARS.
THAT'S AN order.
KIIII
YES, SIR!!
THROB
UNDER-STOOD, SIR! WE'LL ELIMINATE GLENN RADARS!

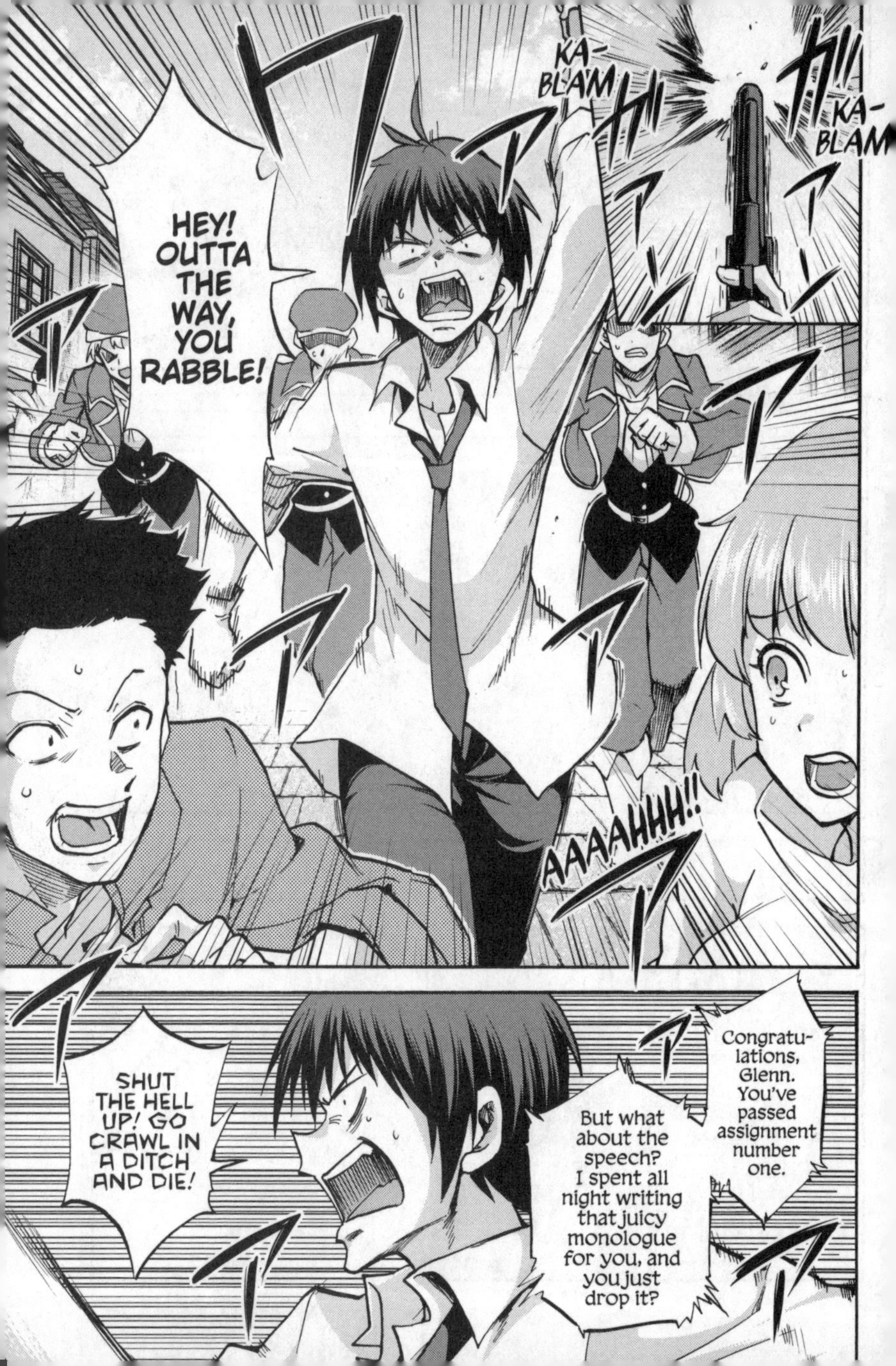
KA-BLAM
KA-BLAM
HEY! OUTTA THE WAY, YOU RABBLE!
AAAAHHH!!
Congratulations, Glenn. You've passed assignment number one.
But what about the speech? I spent all night writing that juicy monologue for you, and you just drop it?
SHUT THE HELL UP! GO CRAWL IN A DITCH AND DIE!

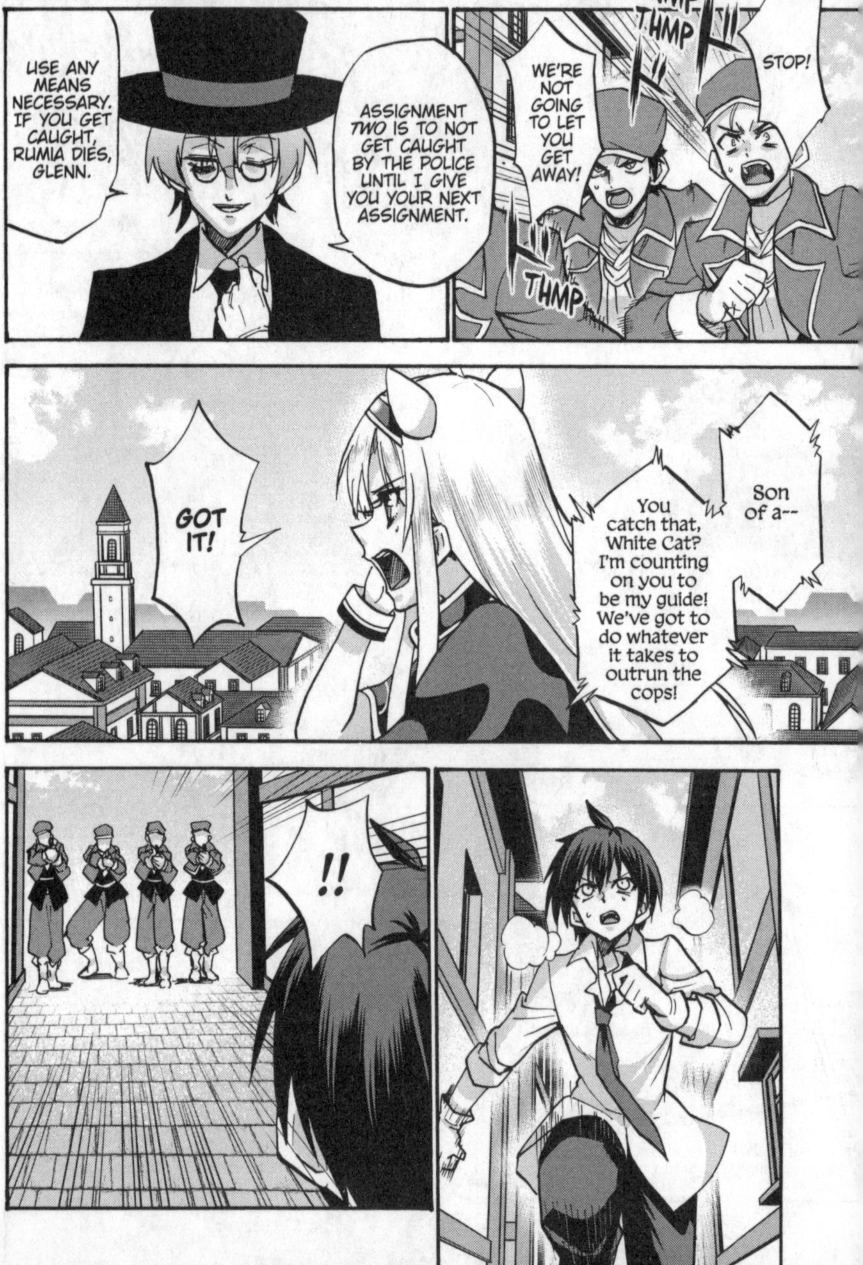
THMP THMP
STOP!
WE'RE NOT GOING TO LET YOU GET AWAY!
THMP
ASSIGNMENT *TWO* IS TO NOT GET CAUGHT BY THE POLICE UNTIL I GIVE YOU YOUR NEXT ASSIGNMENT.
USE ANY MEANS NECESSARY. IF YOU GET CAUGHT, RUMIA DIES, GLENN.
Son of a--
You catch that, White Cat? I'm counting on you to be my guide! We've got to do whatever it takes to outrun the cops!
GOT IT!
!!

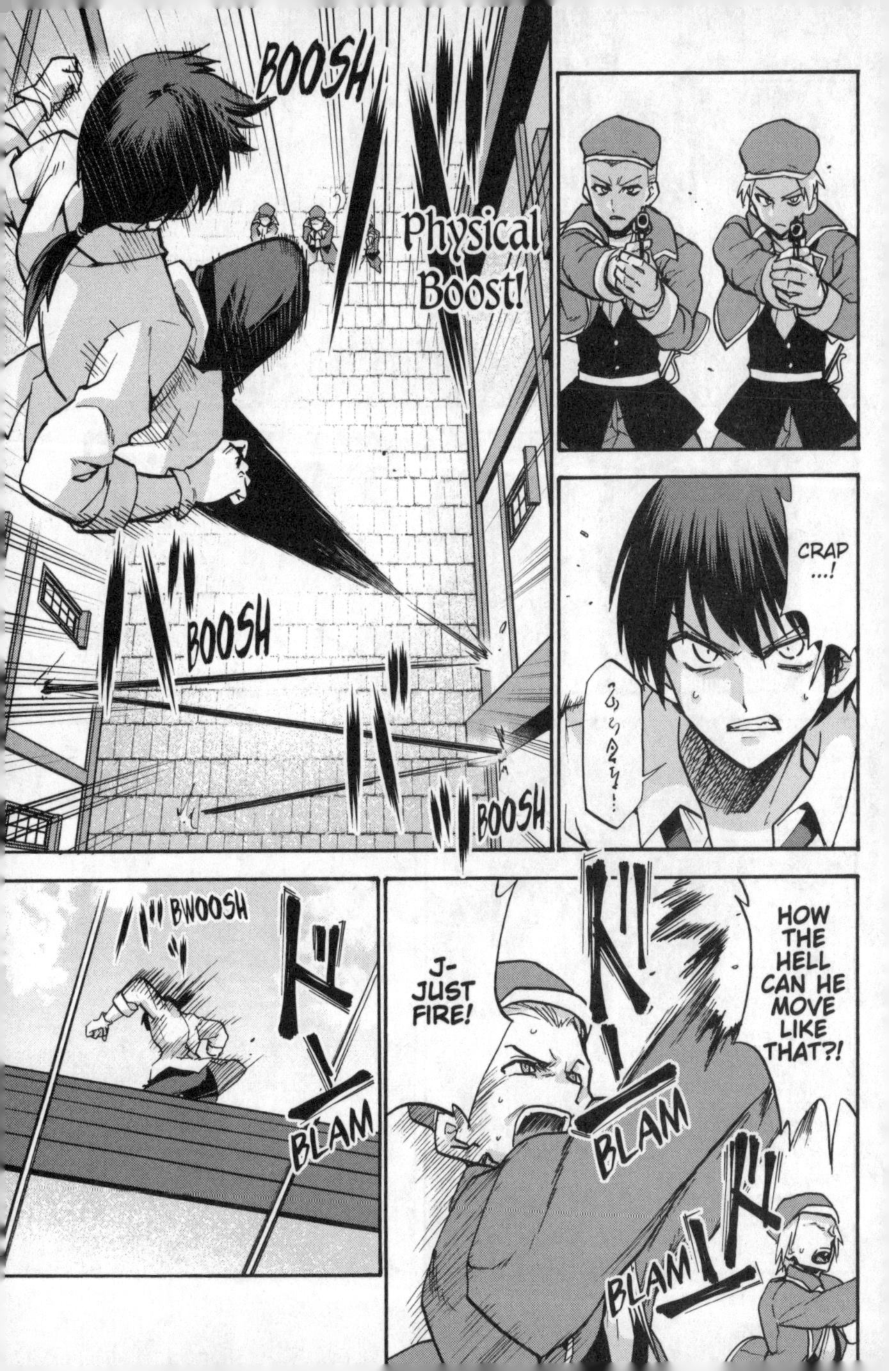
CRAP ...!
Physical Boost!
BOOSH
BOOSH
BOOSH
HOW THE HELL CAN HE MOVE LIKE THAT?!
J-JUST FIRE!
BLAM
BLAM
BWOOSH
BLAM

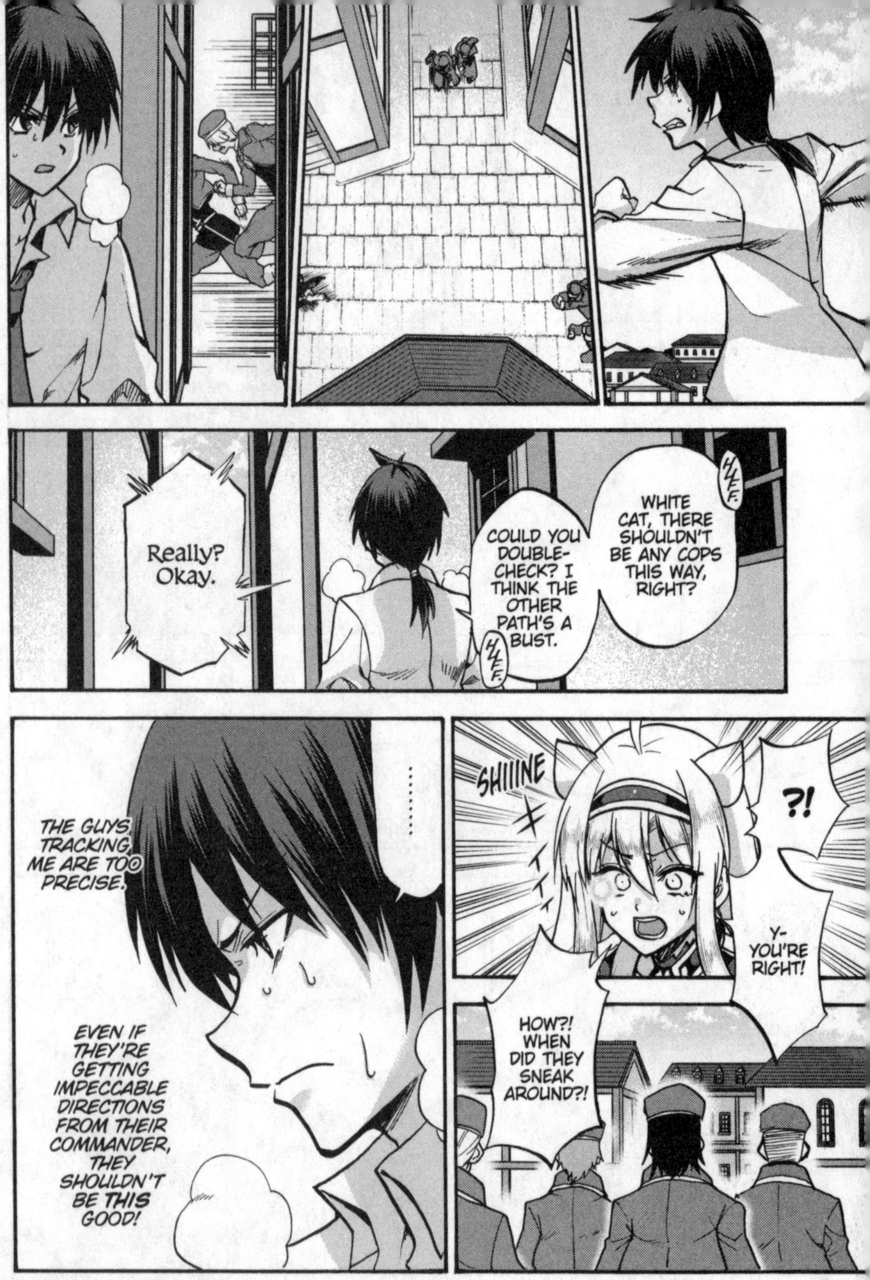
HUFF
WHITE CAT, THERE SHOULDN'T BE ANY COPS THIS WAY, RIGHT?
HUFF
COULD YOU DOUBLE-CHECK? I THINK THE OTHER PATH'S A BUST.
Really? Okay.
SHIIINE
?!
Y-YOU'RE RIGHT!
HOW?! WHEN DID THEY SNEAK AROUND?!
......
THE GUYS TRACKING ME ARE TOO PRECISE.
EVEN IF THEY'RE GETTING IMPECCABLE DIRECTIONS FROM THEIR COMMANDER, THEY SHOULDN'T BE THIS GOOD!

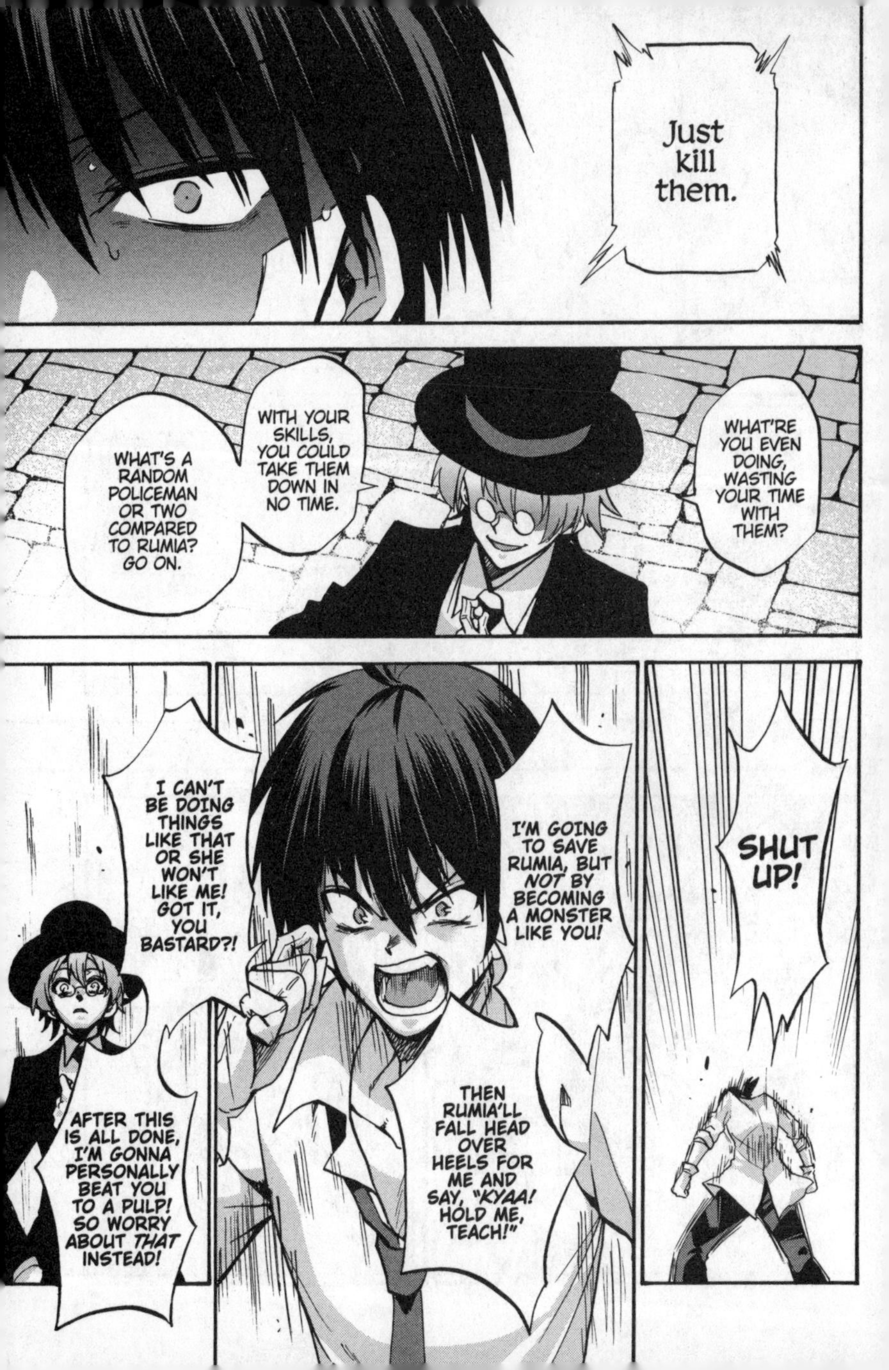
Just kill them.
WHAT'RE YOU EVEN DOING, WASTING YOUR TIME WITH THEM?
WITH YOUR SKILLS, YOU COULD TAKE THEM DOWN IN NO TIME.
WHAT'S A RANDOM POLICEMAN OR TWO COMPARED TO RUMIA? GO ON.
SHUT UP!
I'M GOING TO SAVE RUMIA, BUT *NOT* BY BECOMING A MONSTER LIKE YOU!
I CAN'T BE DOING THINGS LIKE THAT OR SHE WON'T LIKE ME! GOT IT, YOU BASTARD?!
THEN RUMIA'LL FALL HEAD OVER HEELS FOR ME AND SAY, "*KYAA!* HOLD ME, TEACH!"
AFTER THIS IS ALL DONE, I'M GONNA PERSONALLY BEAT YOU TO A PULP! SO WORRY ABOUT *THAT* INSTEAD!

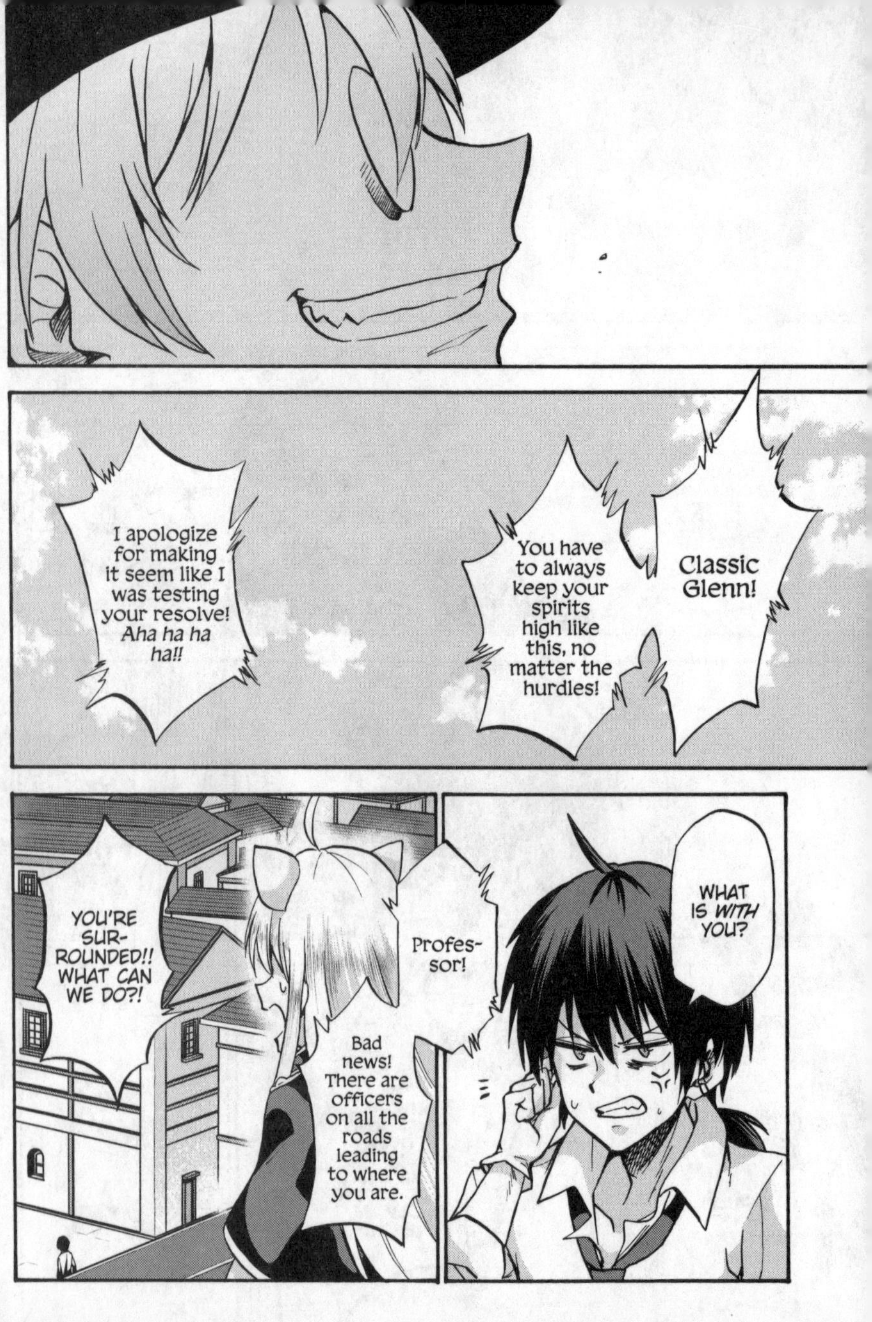
Classic Glenn!
You have to always keep your spirits high like this, no matter the hurdles!
I apologize for making it seem like I was testing your resolve! Aha ha ha ha!!
WHAT IS *WITH* YOU?
Profes-sor!
Bad news! There are officers on all the roads leading to where you are.
YOU'RE SUR-ROUNDED!! WHAT CAN WE DO?!

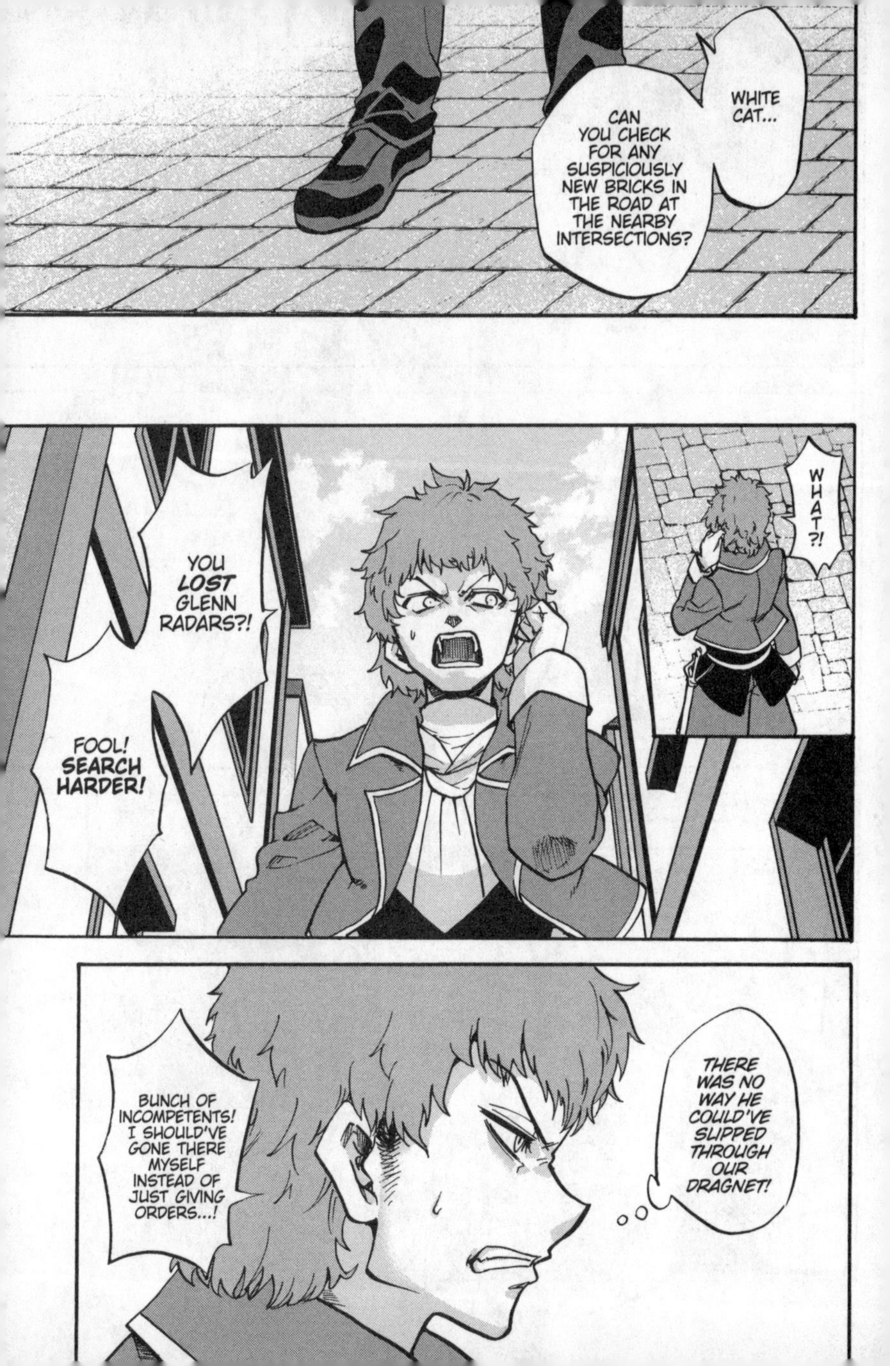
WHITE CAT...
CAN YOU CHECK FOR ANY SUSPICIOUSLY NEW BRICKS IN THE ROAD AT THE NEARBY INTERSECTIONS?
WHAT?!
YOU *LOST* GLENN RADARS?!
FOOL! **SEARCH HARDER!**
THERE WAS NO WAY HE COULD'VE SLIPPED THROUGH OUR DRAGNET!
BUNCH OF INCOMPETENTS! I SHOULD'VE GONE THERE MYSELF INSTEAD OF JUST GIVING ORDERS...!

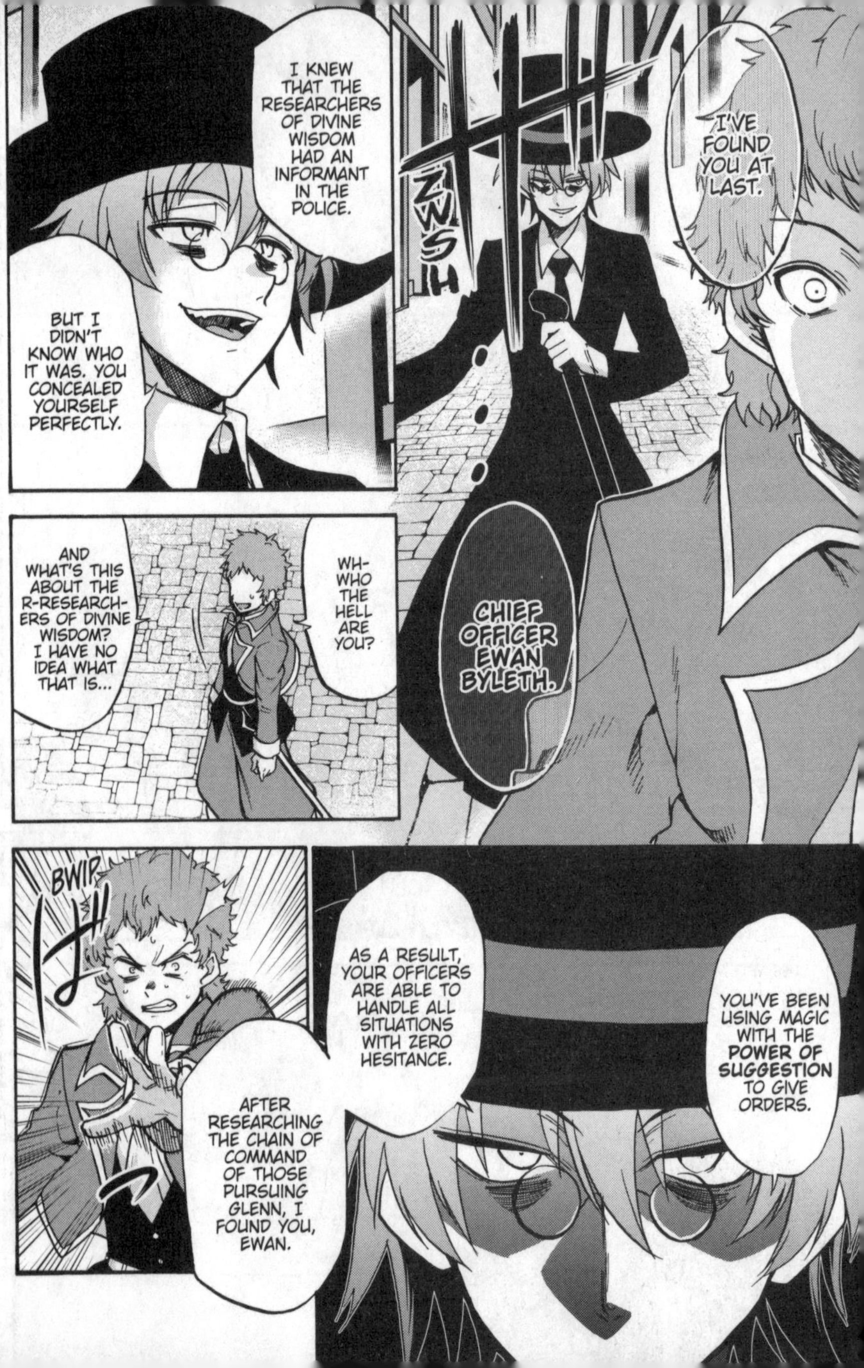

I'VE FOUND YOU AT LAST.
ZWSH
CHIEF OFFICER EWAN BYLETH.
I KNEW THAT THE RESEARCHERS OF DIVINE WISDOM HAD AN INFORMANT IN THE POLICE.
BUT I DIDN'T KNOW WHO IT WAS. YOU CONCEALED YOURSELF PERFECTLY.
WH-WHO THE HELL ARE YOU?
AND WHAT'S THIS ABOUT THE R-RESEARCHERS OF DIVINE WISDOM? I HAVE NO IDEA WHAT THAT IS...
YOU'VE BEEN USING MAGIC WITH THE POWER OF SUGGESTION TO GIVE ORDERS.
AS A RESULT, YOUR OFFICERS ARE ABLE TO HANDLE ALL SITUATIONS WITH ZERO HESITANCE.
AFTER RESEARCHING THE CHAIN OF COMMAND OF THOSE PURSUING GLENN, I FOUND YOU, EWAN.
BWIP

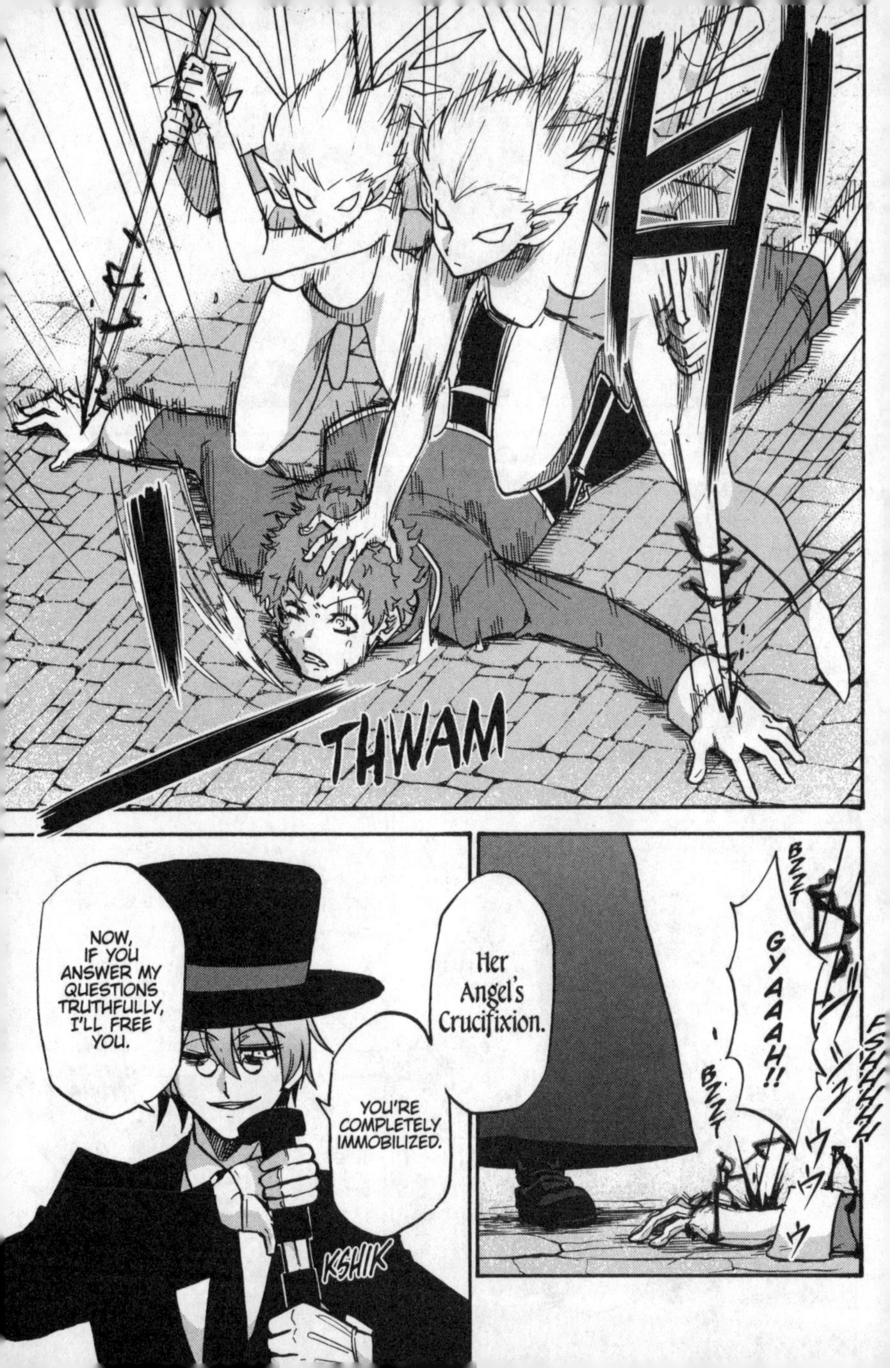
THWAM
BZZT
GYAAAAH!!
BZZT
FSHHHHH
Her Angel's Crucifixion.
YOU'RE COMPLETELY IMMOBILIZED.
NOW, IF YOU ANSWER MY QUESTIONS TRUTHFULLY, I'LL FREE YOU.
KSHIK

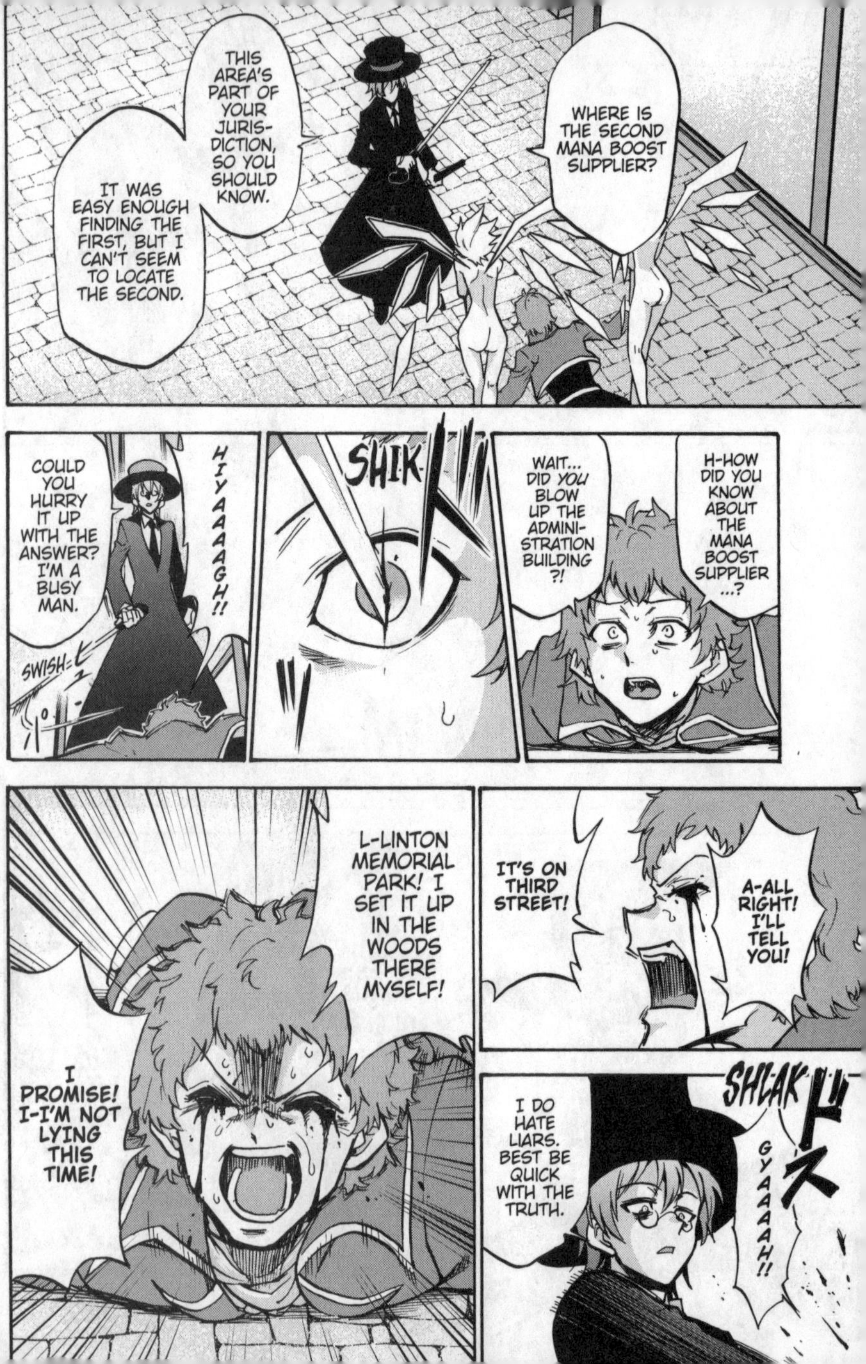
WHERE IS THE SECOND MANA BOOST SUPPLIER?
THIS AREA'S PART OF YOUR JURIS-DICTION, SO YOU SHOULD KNOW.
IT WAS EASY ENOUGH FINDING THE FIRST, BUT I CAN'T SEEM TO LOCATE THE SECOND.
H-HOW DID YOU KNOW ABOUT THE MANA BOOST SUPPLIER ...?
WAIT... DID YOU BLOW UP THE ADMINI-STRATION BUILDING ?!
SHIK
HIYAAAAAGH!!
COULD YOU HURRY IT UP WITH THE ANSWER? I'M A BUSY MAN.
SWISH
A-ALL RIGHT! I'LL TELL YOU!
IT'S ON THIRD STREET!
L-LINTON MEMORIAL PARK! I SET IT UP IN THE WOODS THERE MYSELF!
SHLAK
ドス
GYAAAAAH!!
I DO HATE LIARS. BEST BE QUICK WITH THE TRUTH.
I PROMISE! I-I'M NOT LYING THIS TIME!

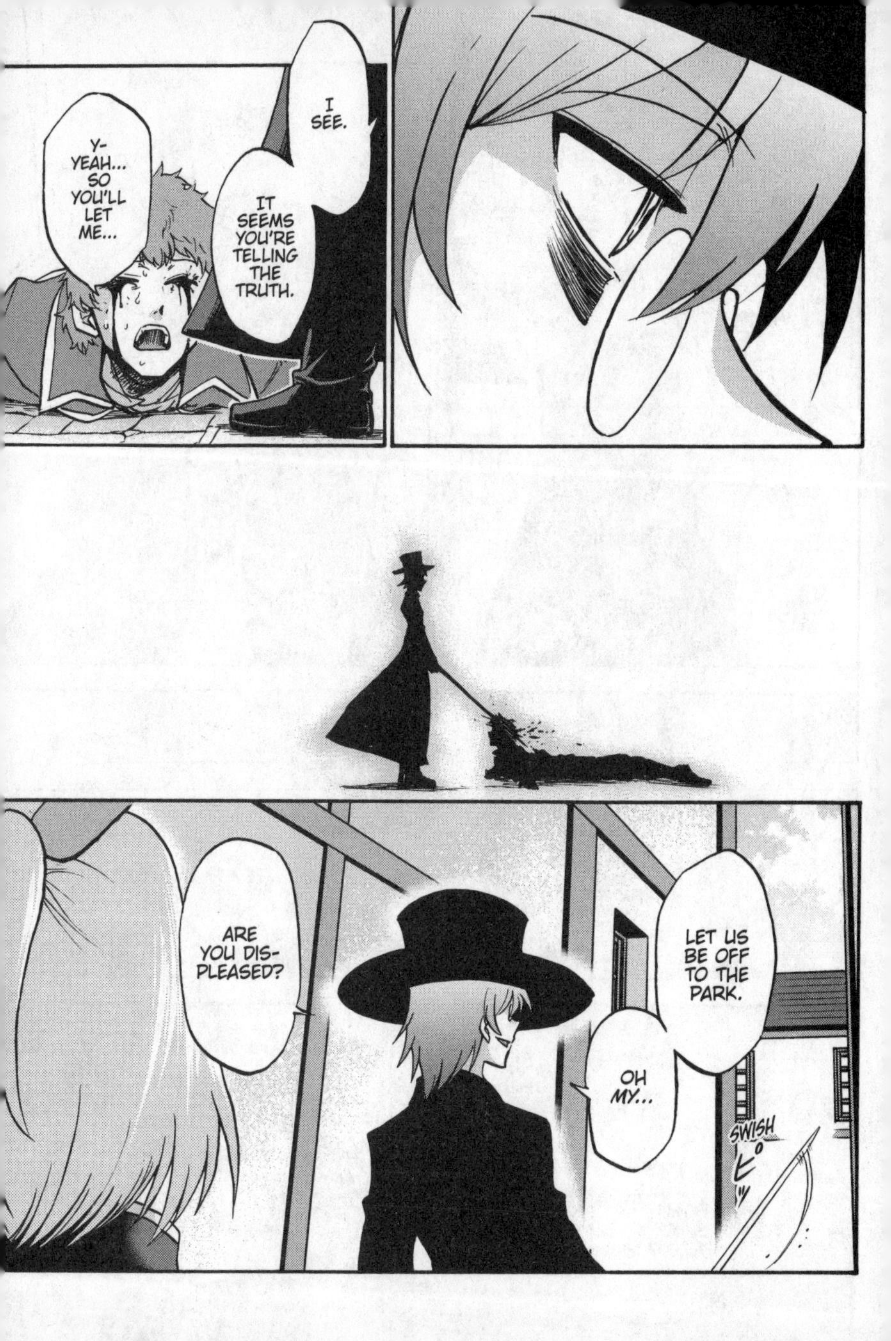
I SEE.
IT SEEMS YOU'RE TELLING THE TRUTH.
Y-YEAH... SO YOU'LL LET ME...
LET US BE OFF TO THE PARK.
OH MY...
SWISH
ARE YOU DIS-PLEASED?

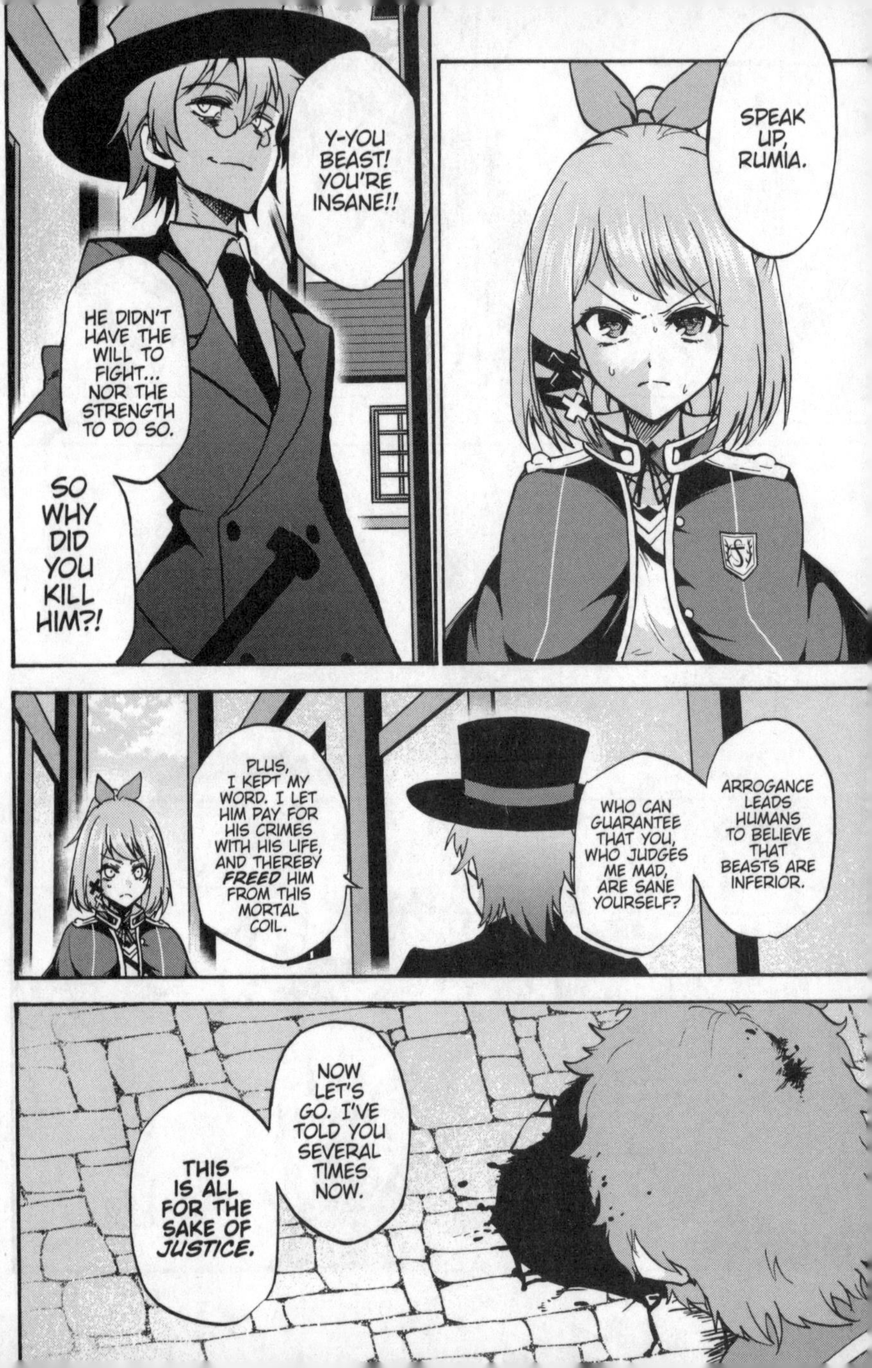
SPEAK UP, RUMIA.
Y-YOU BEAST! YOU'RE INSANE!!
HE DIDN'T HAVE THE WILL TO FIGHT... NOR THE STRENGTH TO DO SO.
SO WHY DID YOU KILL HIM?!
ARROGANCE LEADS HUMANS TO BELIEVE THAT BEASTS ARE INFERIOR.
WHO CAN GUARANTEE THAT YOU, WHO JUDGES ME MAD, ARE SANE YOURSELF?
PLUS, I KEPT MY WORD. I LET HIM PAY FOR HIS CRIMES WITH HIS LIFE, AND THEREBY *FREED* HIM FROM THIS MORTAL COIL.
NOW LET'S GO. I'VE TOLD YOU SEVERAL TIMES NOW.
THIS IS ALL FOR THE SAKE OF *JUSTICE*.

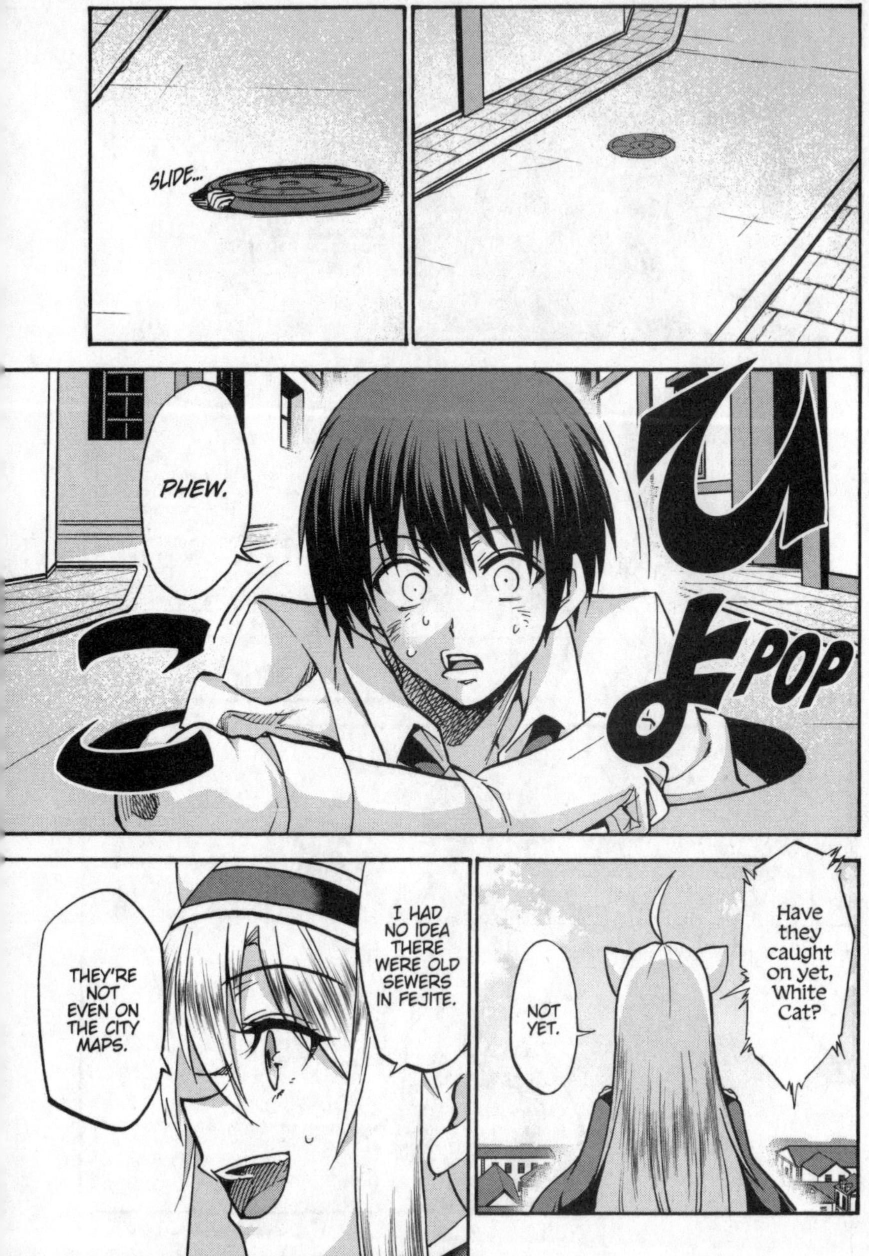
SLIDE...
POP
PHEW.
Have they caught on yet, White Cat?
NOT YET.
I HAD NO IDEA THERE WERE OLD SEWERS IN FEJITE.
THEY'RE NOT EVEN ON THE CITY MAPS.

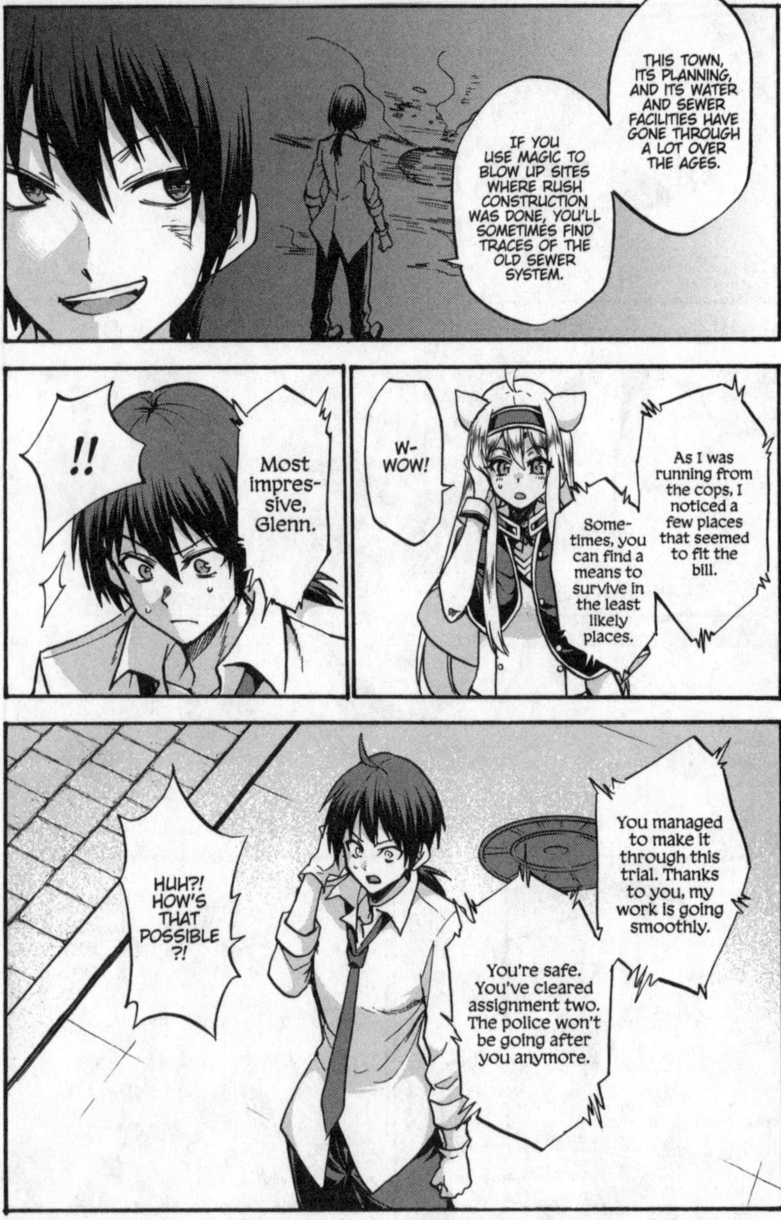

THIS TOWN, ITS PLANNING, AND ITS WATER AND SEWER FACILITIES HAVE GONE THROUGH A LOT OVER THE AGES.
IF YOU USE MAGIC TO BLOW UP SITES WHERE RUSH CONSTRUCTION WAS DONE, YOU'LL SOMETIMES FIND TRACES OF THE OLD SEWER SYSTEM.
As I was running from the cops, I noticed a few places that seemed to fit the bill.
Sometimes, you can find a means to survive in the least likely places.
W-WOW!
Most impressive, Glenn.
!!
You managed to make it through this trial. Thanks to you, my work is going smoothly.
You're safe. You've cleared assignment two. The police won't be going after you anymore.
HUH?! HOW'S THAT POSSIBLE?!

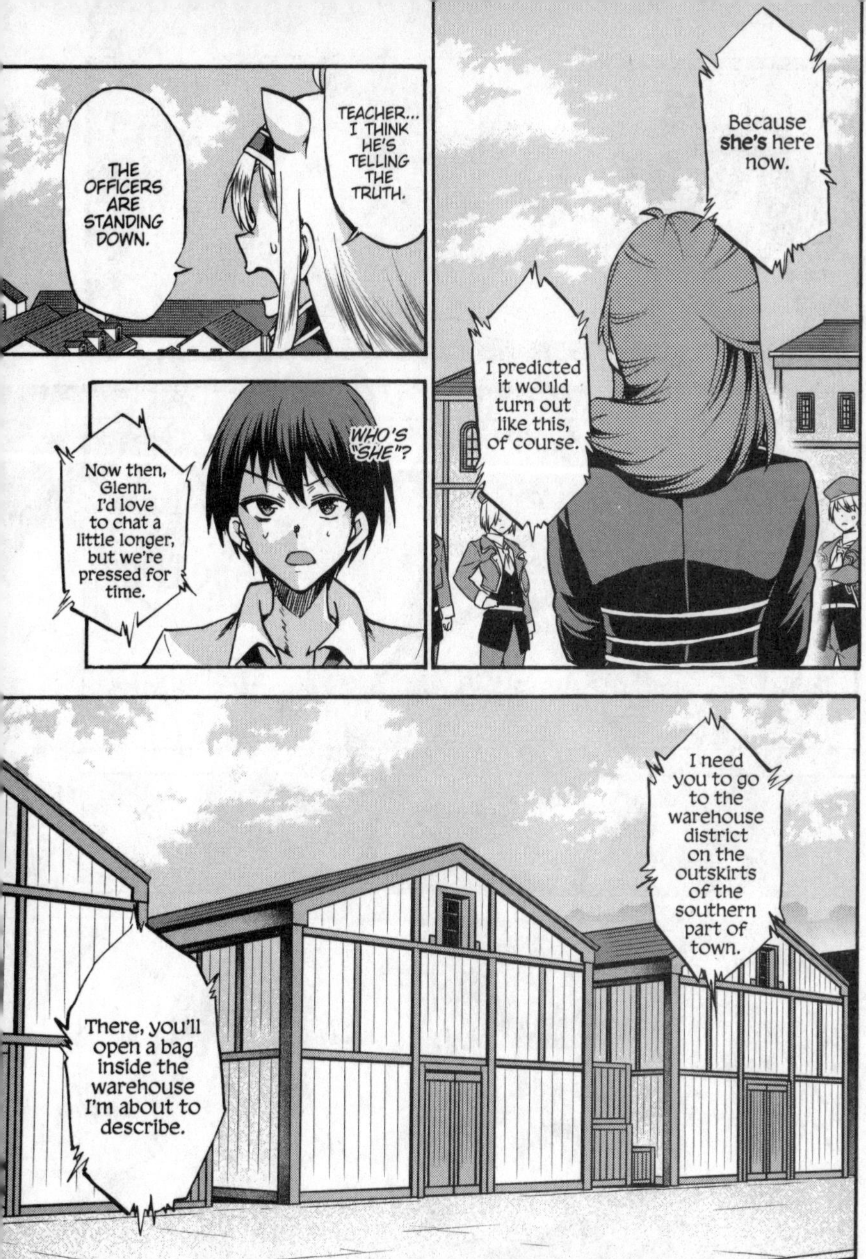
Because **she's** here now.
I predicted it would turn out like this, of course.
TEACHER... I THINK HE'S TELLING THE TRUTH.
THE OFFICERS ARE STANDING DOWN.
WHO'S "SHE"?
Now then, Glenn. I'd love to chat a little longer, but we're pressed for time.
I need you to go to the warehouse district on the outskirts of the southern part of town.
There, you'll open a bag inside the warehouse I'm about to describe.

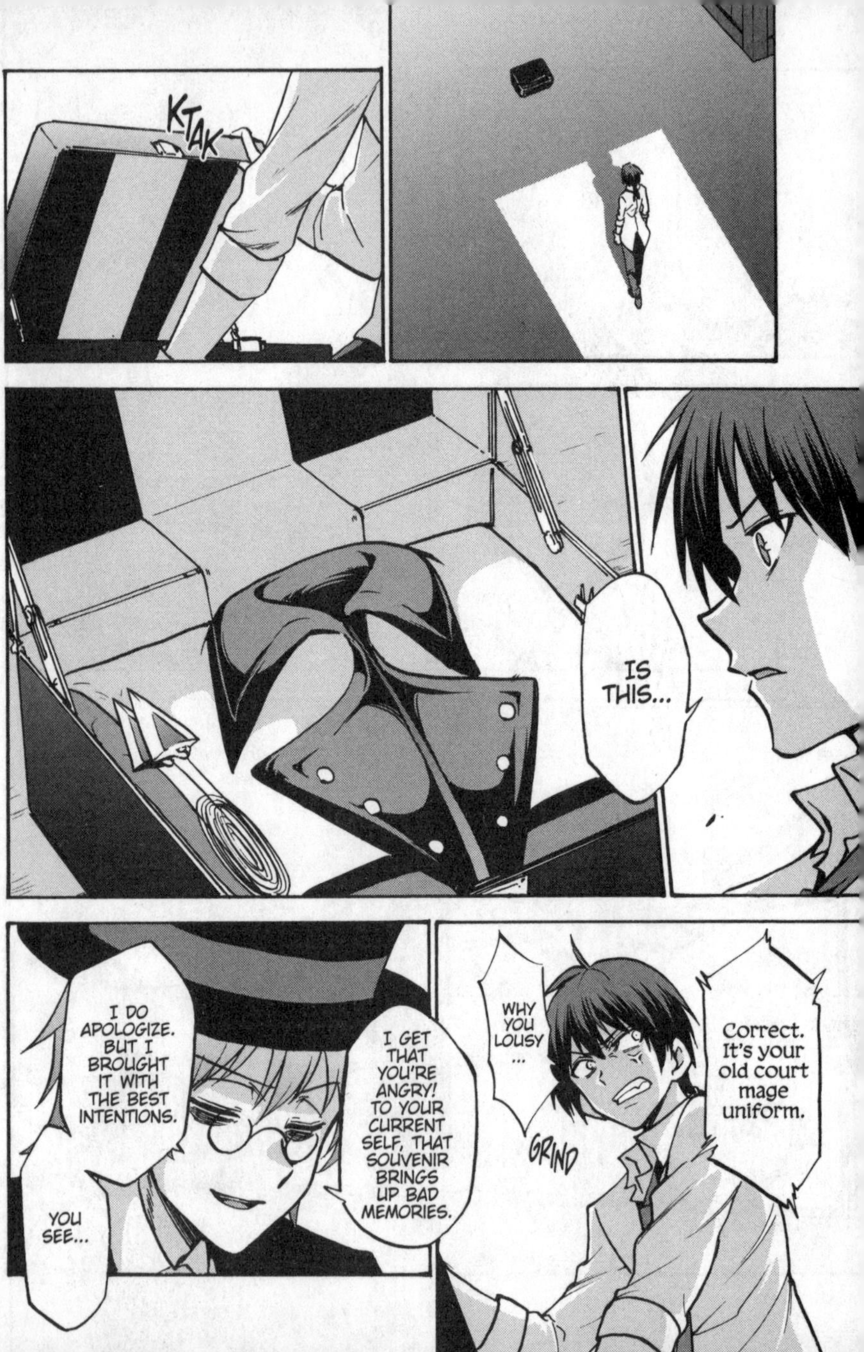
KTAK
IS THIS...
Correct. It's your old court mage uniform.
WHY YOU LOUSY ...
GRIND
I GET THAT YOU'RE ANGRY! TO YOUR CURRENT SELF, THAT SOUVENIR BRINGS UP BAD MEMORIES.
I DO APOLOGIZE. BUT I BROUGHT IT WITH THE BEST INTENTIONS.
YOU SEE...

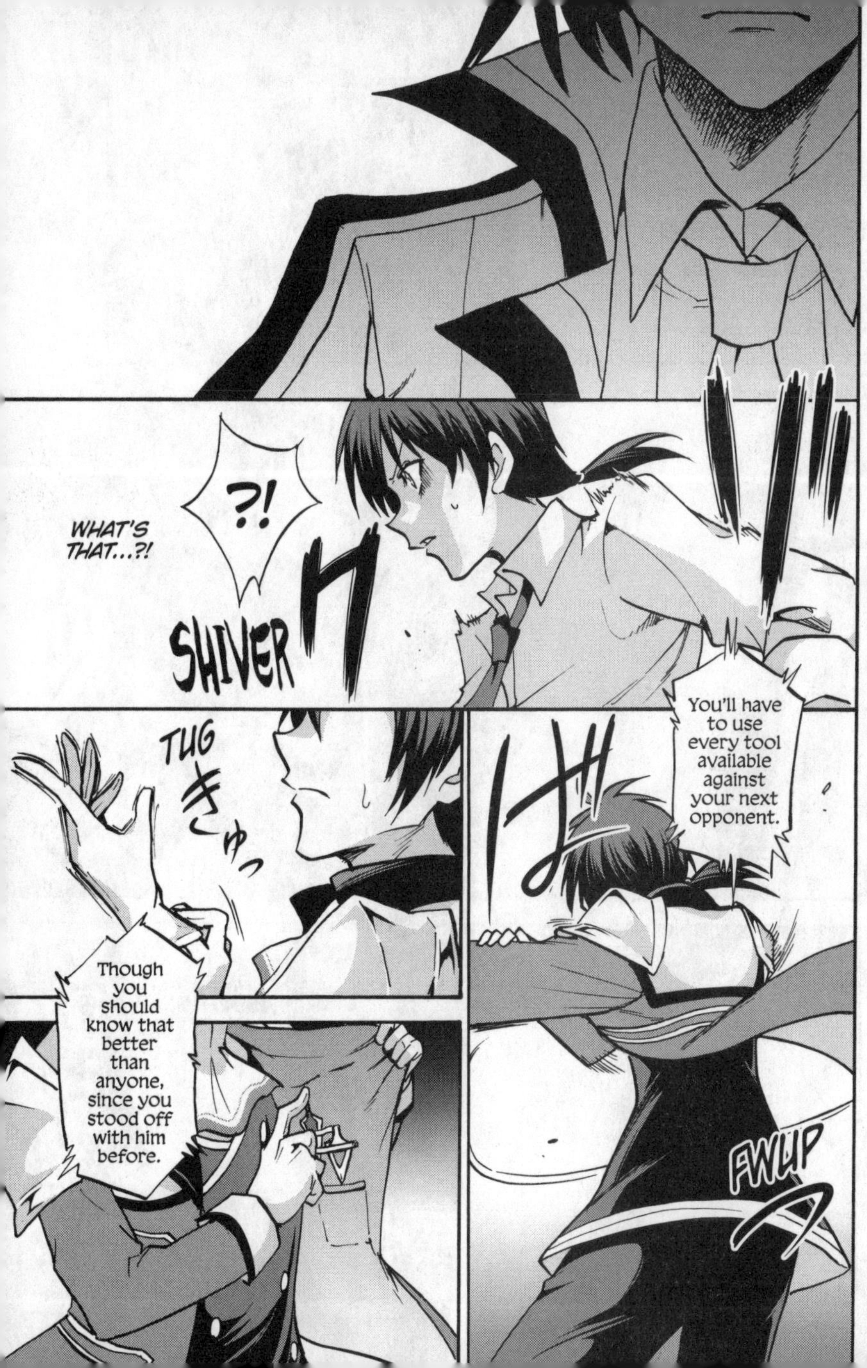
?!
WHAT'S THAT...?!
SHIVER
You'll have to use every tool available against your next opponent.
TUG
きゅっ
Though you should know that better than anyone, since you stood off with him before.
FWUP

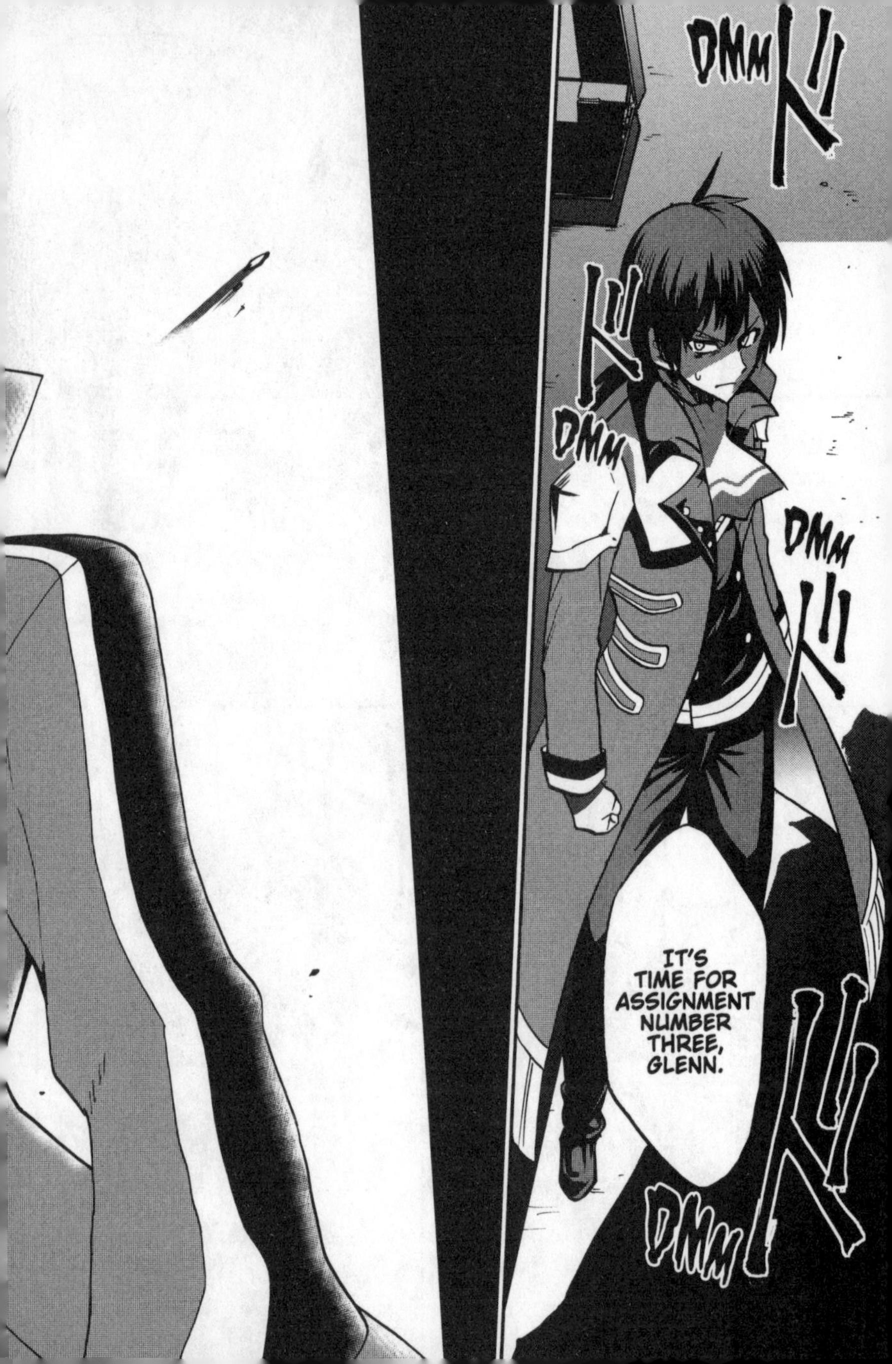

DMM
DMM
DMM
IT'S TIME FOR ASSIGNMENT NUMBER THREE, GLENN.
DMM

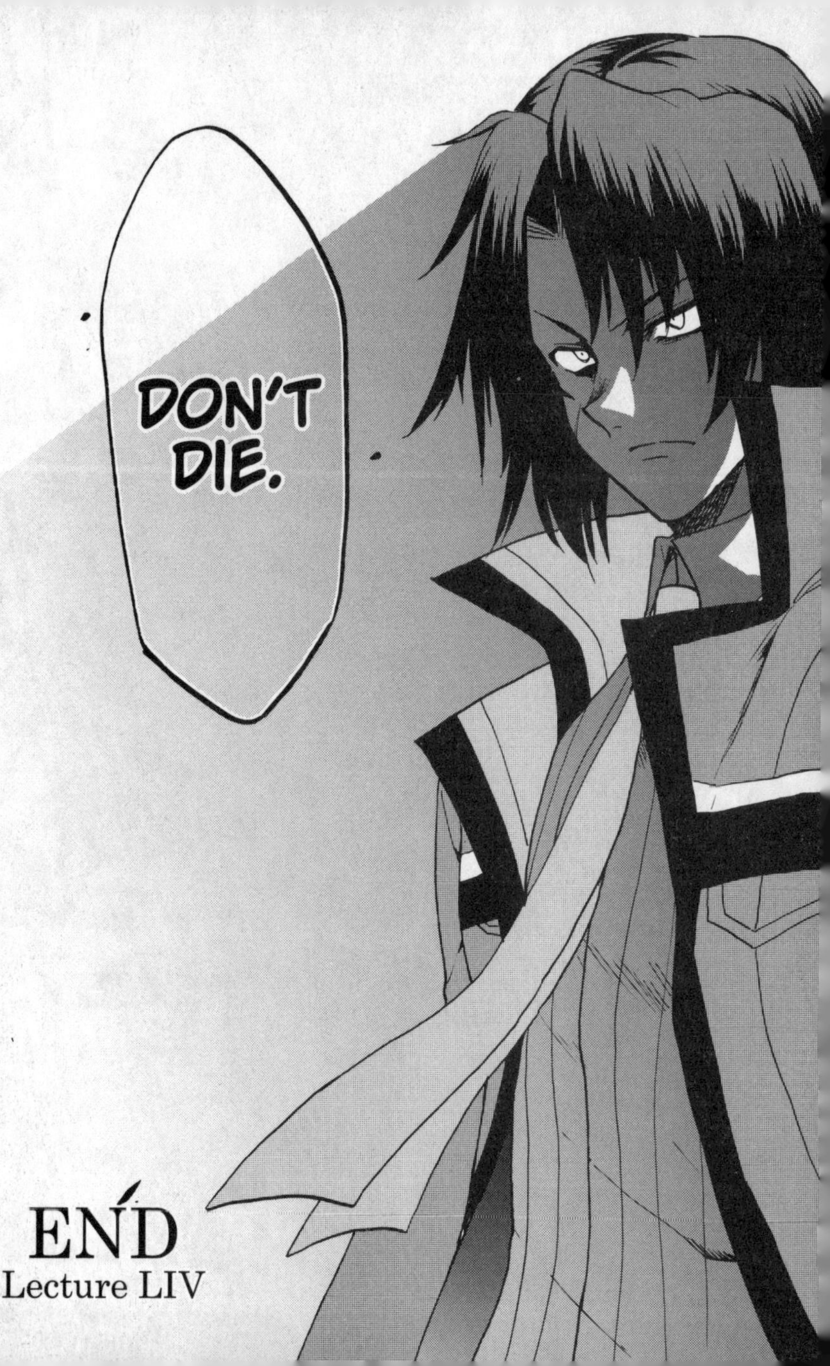
DON'T DIE.

END
Lecture LIV

Akashic Records
o f *Bastard* Magic *Instructor*

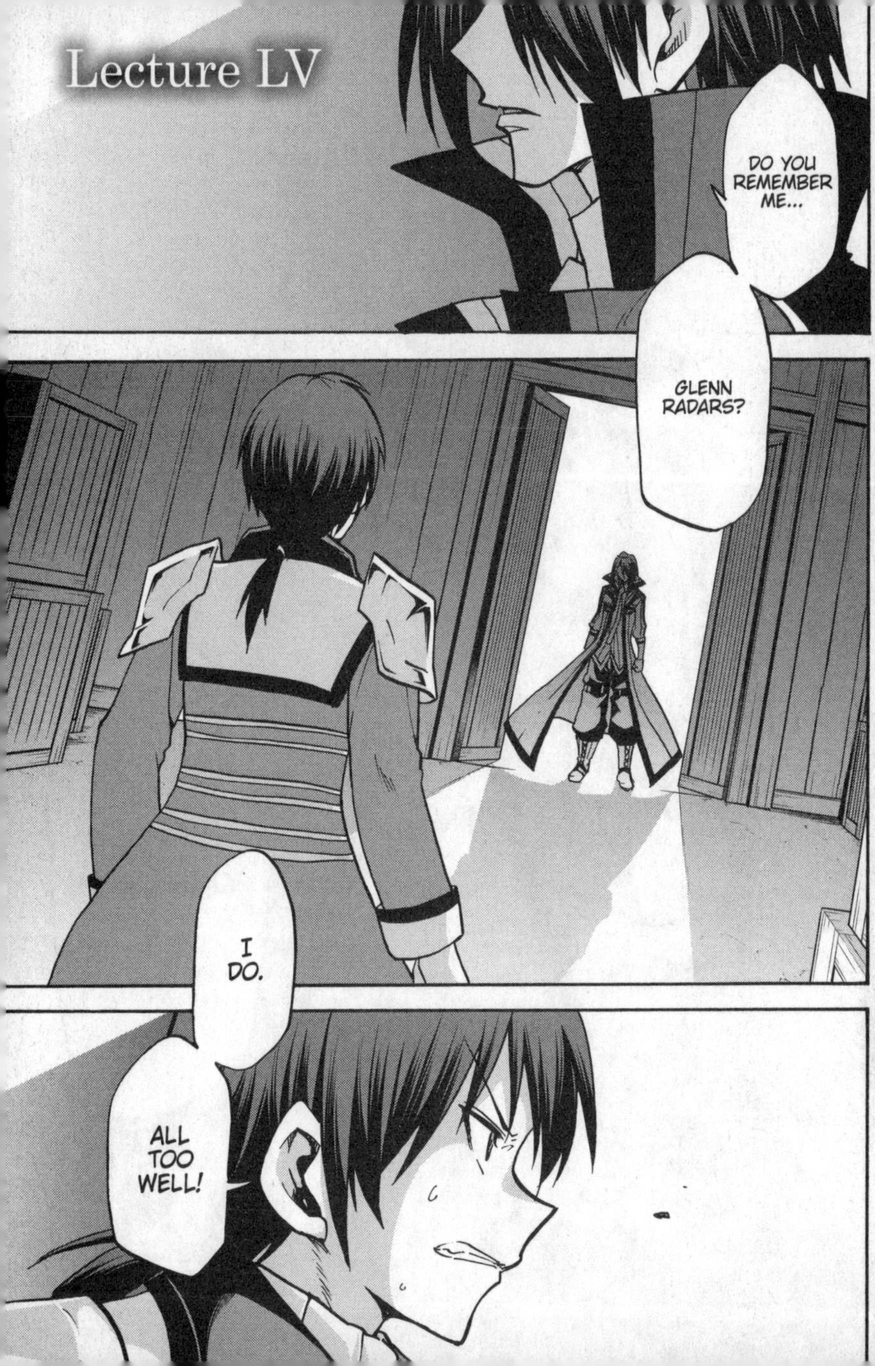

Lecture LV
DO YOU REMEMBER ME...
GLENN RADARS?
I DO.
ALL TOO WELL!

Lecture LV

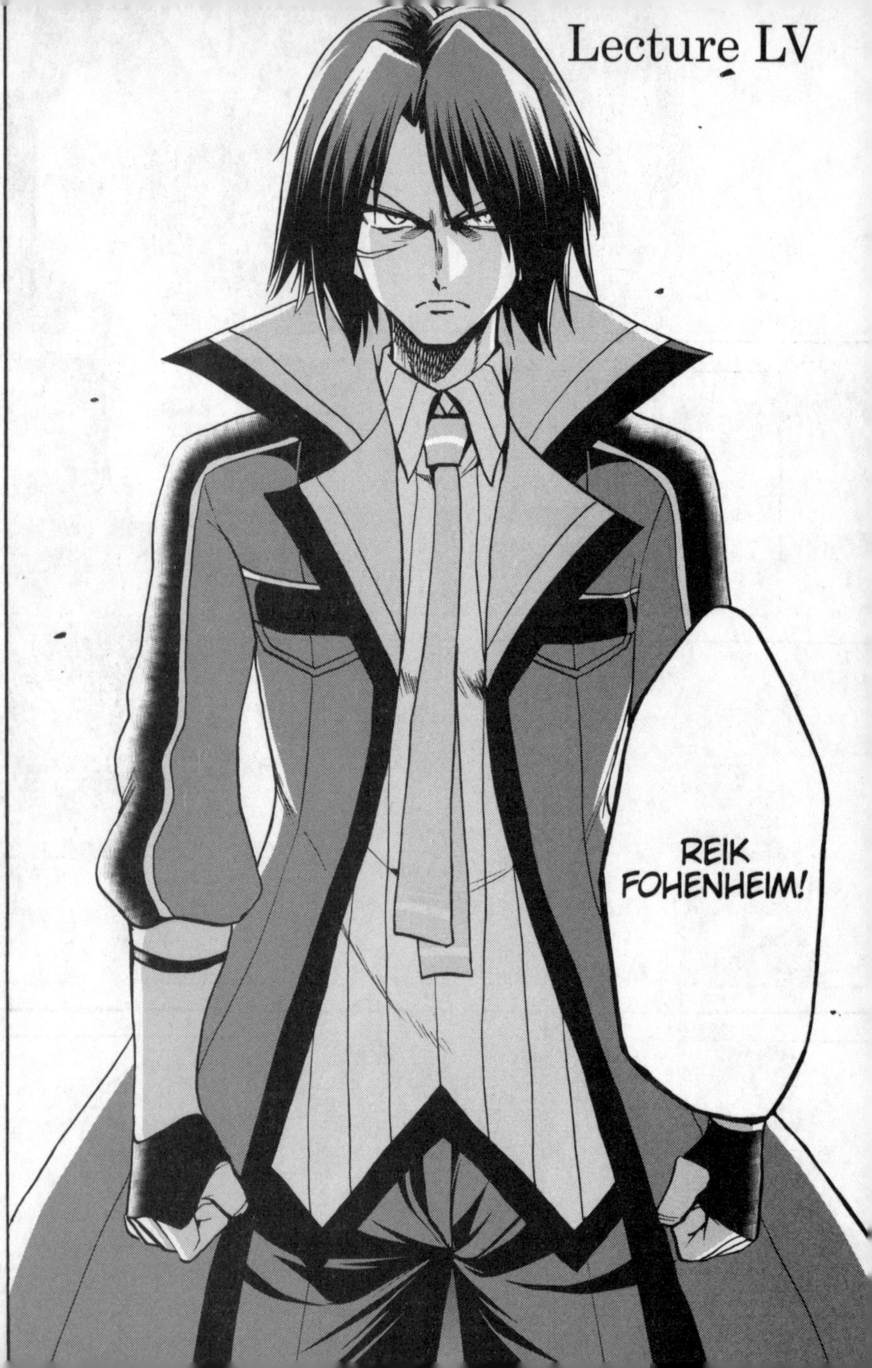
REIK FOHENHEIM!

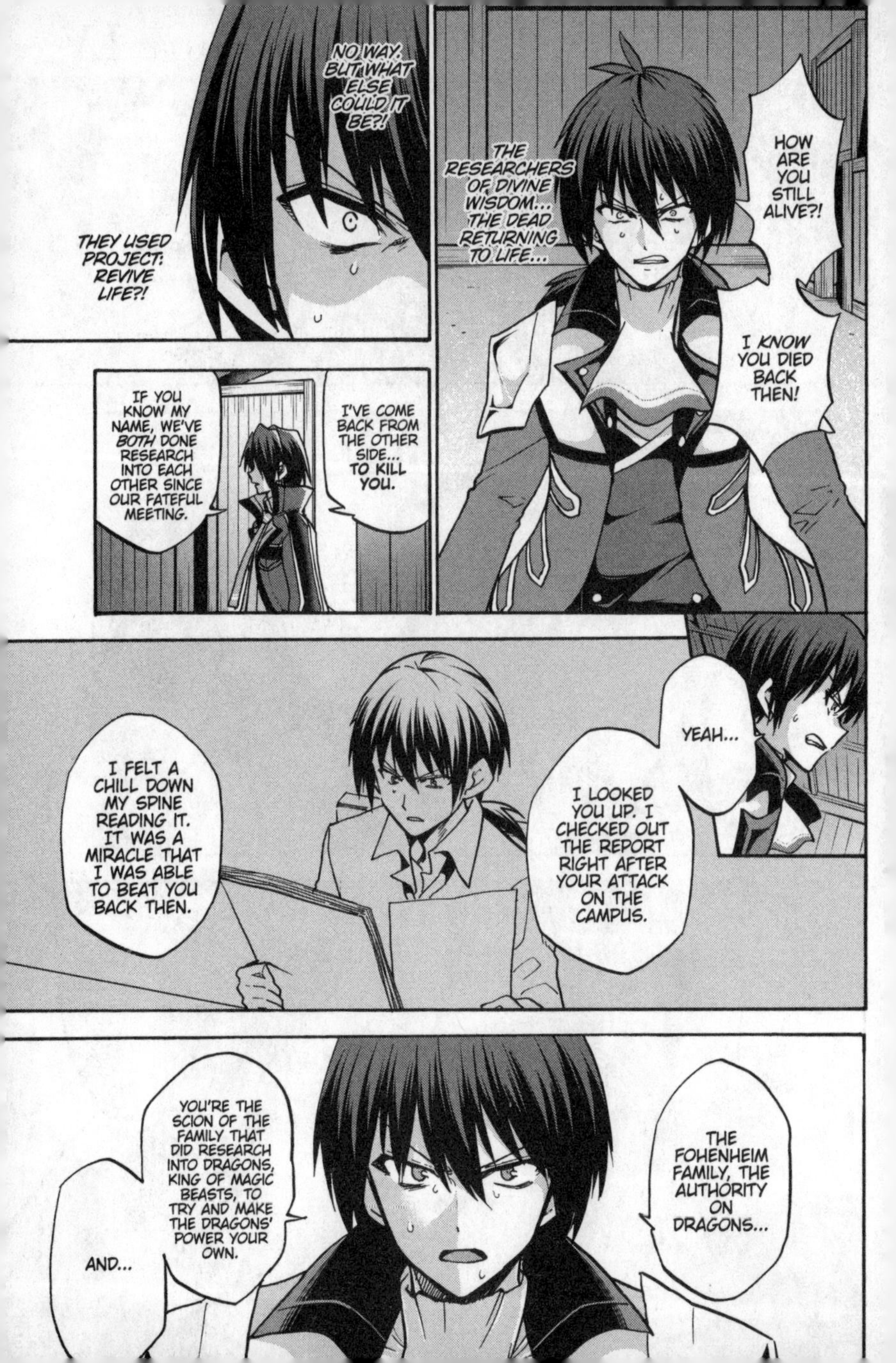
HOW ARE YOU STILL ALIVE?!
THE RESEARCHERS OF DIVINE WISDOM... THE DEAD RETURNING TO LIFE...
I *KNOW* YOU DIED BACK THEN!
NO WAY. BUT WHAT ELSE COULD IT BE?!
THEY USED PROJECT: REVIVE LIFE?!
I'VE COME BACK FROM THE OTHER SIDE... TO KILL YOU.
IF YOU KNOW MY NAME, WE'VE *BOTH* DONE RESEARCH INTO EACH OTHER SINCE OUR FATEFUL MEETING.
YEAH...
I LOOKED YOU UP. I CHECKED OUT THE REPORT RIGHT AFTER YOUR ATTACK ON THE CAMPUS.
I FELT A CHILL DOWN MY SPINE READING IT. IT WAS A MIRACLE THAT I WAS ABLE TO BEAT YOU BACK THEN.
THE FOHENHEIM FAMILY, THE AUTHORITY ON DRAGONS...
YOU'RE THE SCION OF THE FAMILY THAT DID RESEARCH INTO DRAGONS, KING OF MAGIC BEASTS, TO TRY AND MAKE THE DRAGONS' POWER YOUR OWN.
AND...

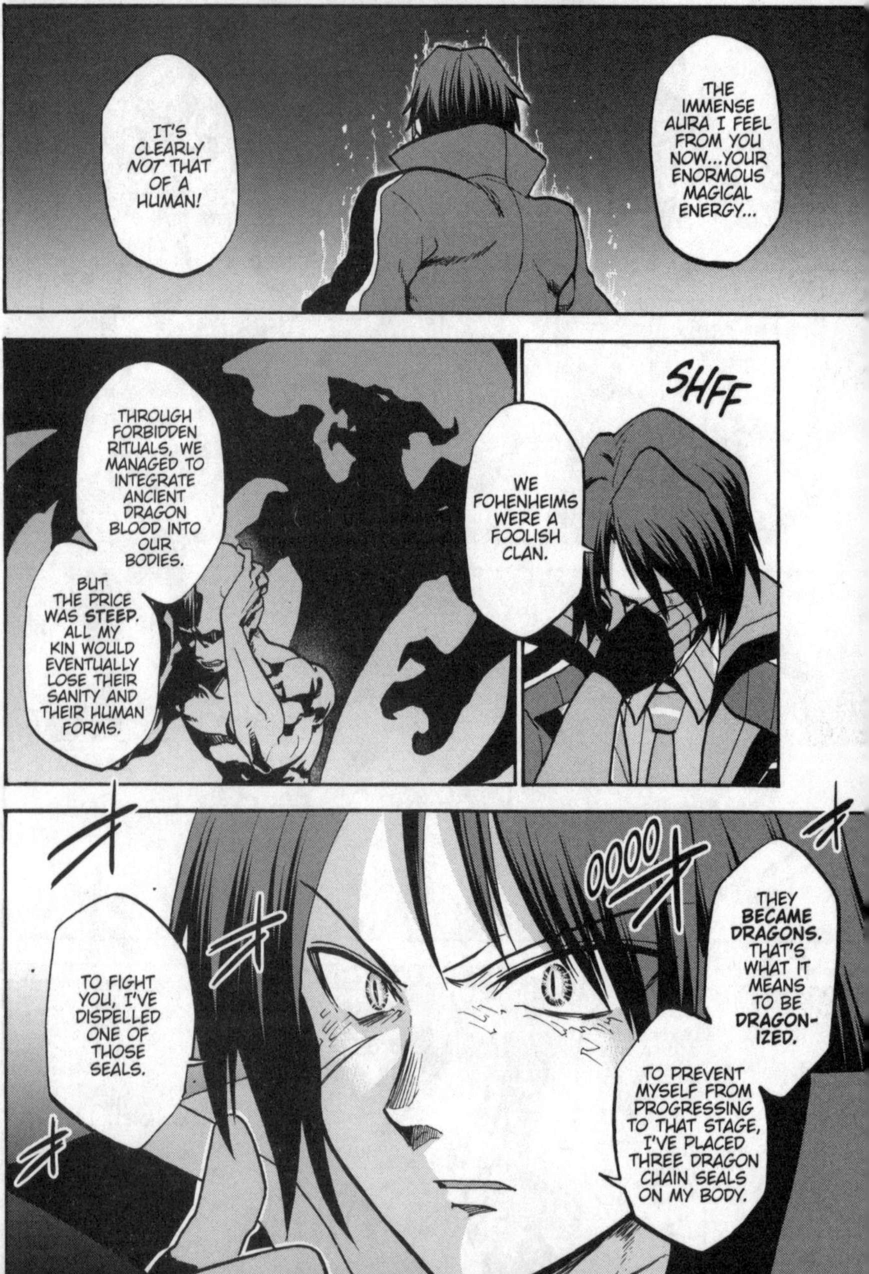
THE IMMENSE AURA I FEEL FROM YOU NOW...YOUR ENORMOUS MAGICAL ENERGY...
IT'S CLEARLY *NOT* THAT OF A HUMAN!
SHFF
WE FOHENHEIMS WERE A FOOLISH CLAN.
THROUGH FORBIDDEN RITUALS, WE MANAGED TO INTEGRATE ANCIENT DRAGON BLOOD INTO OUR BODIES.
BUT THE PRICE WAS **STEEP.** ALL MY KIN WOULD EVENTUALLY LOSE THEIR SANITY AND THEIR HUMAN FORMS.
THEY **BECAME DRAGONS.** THAT'S WHAT IT MEANS TO BE **DRAGON-IZED.**
TO PREVENT MYSELF FROM PROGRESSING TO THAT STAGE, I'VE PLACED THREE DRAGON CHAIN SEALS ON MY BODY.
OOOO
TO FIGHT YOU, I'VE DISPELLED ONE OF THOSE SEALS.

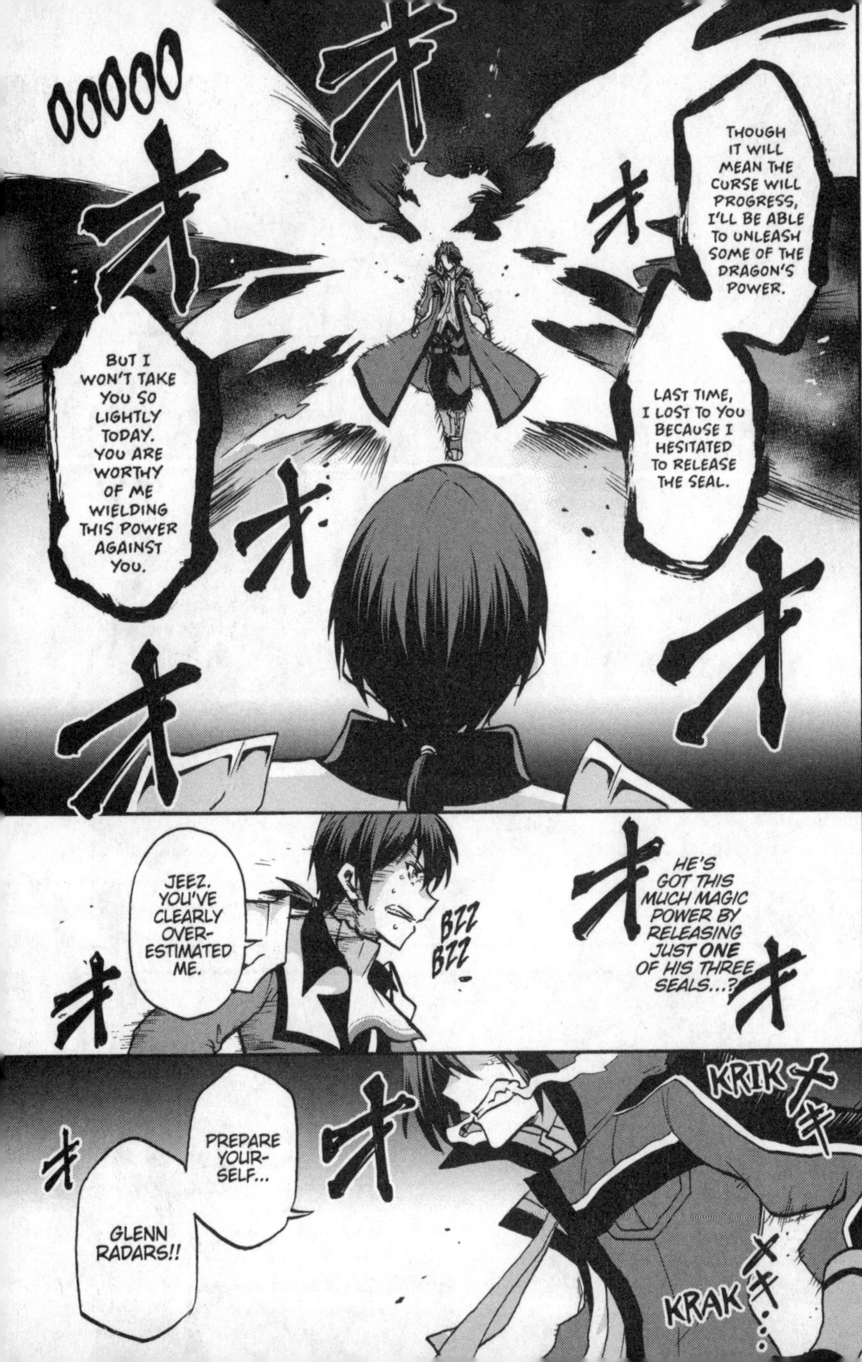
OOOOO
THOUGH IT WILL MEAN THE CURSE WILL PROGRESS, I'LL BE ABLE TO UNLEASH SOME OF THE DRAGON'S POWER.
LAST TIME, I LOST TO YOU BECAUSE I HESITATED TO RELEASE THE SEAL.
BUT I WON'T TAKE YOU SO LIGHTLY TODAY. YOU ARE WORTHY OF ME WIELDING THIS POWER AGAINST YOU.
HE'S GOT THIS MUCH MAGIC POWER BY RELEASING JUST ONE OF HIS THREE SEALS...?
BZZ BZZ
JEEZ. YOU'VE CLEARLY OVER-ESTIMATED ME.
KRIK
KRAK
PREPARE YOUR-SELF...
GLENN RADARS!!

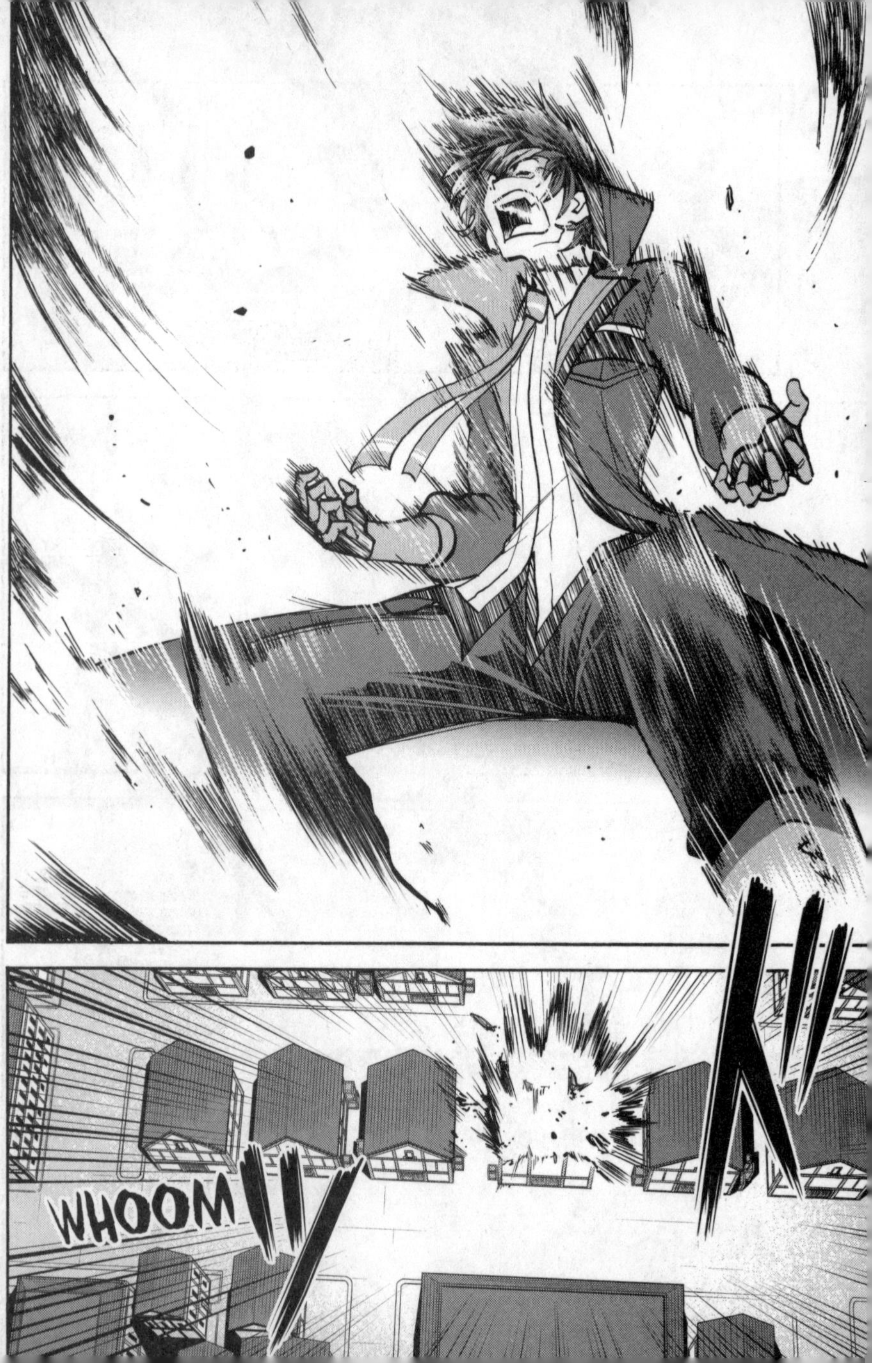
WHOOM

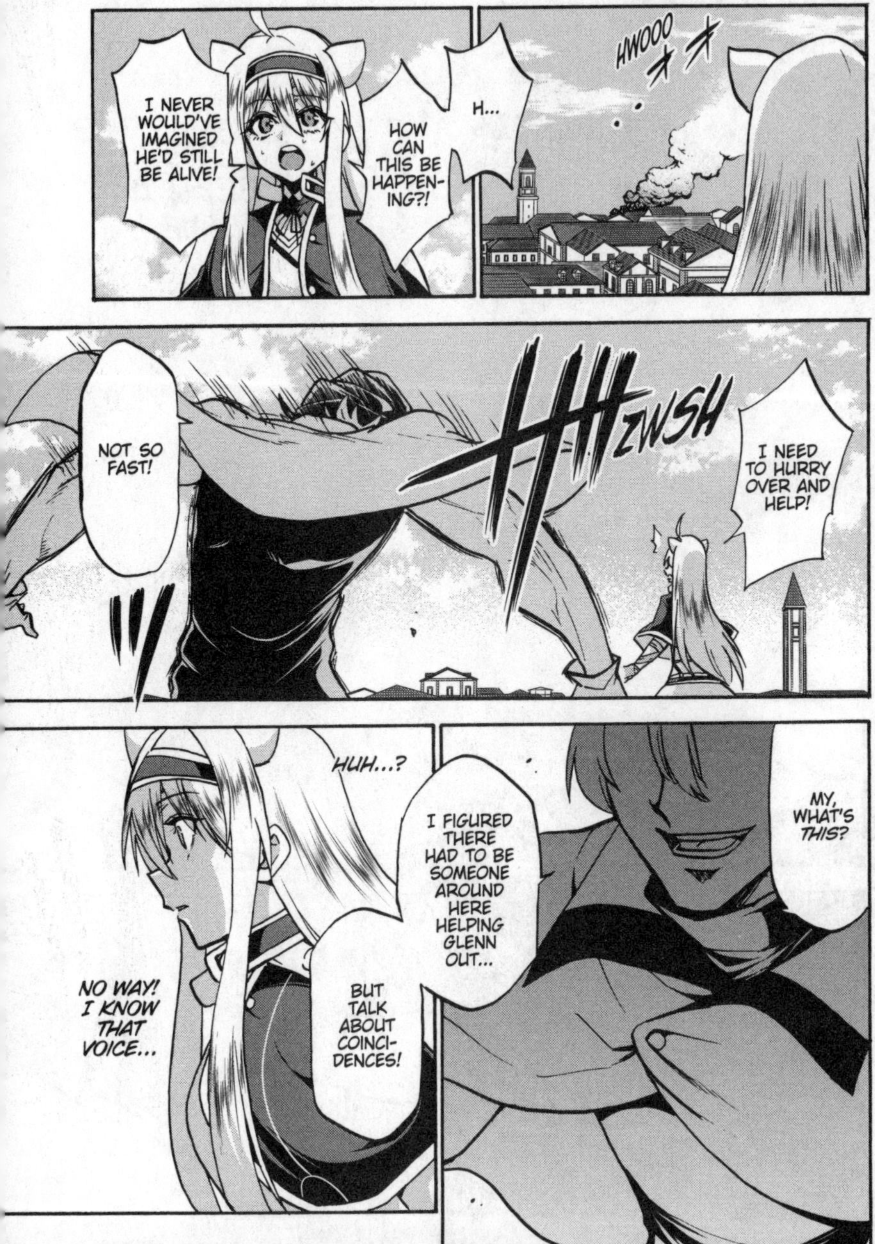
HWOOO
H...
HOW CAN THIS BE HAPPENING?!
I NEVER WOULD'VE IMAGINED HE'D STILL BE ALIVE!
I NEED TO HURRY OVER AND HELP!
ZWSH
NOT SO FAST!
MY, WHAT'S *THIS*?
I FIGURED THERE HAD TO BE SOMEONE AROUND HERE HELPING GLENN OUT...
BUT TALK ABOUT COINCIDENCES!
HUH...?
NO WAY! I KNOW THAT VOICE...

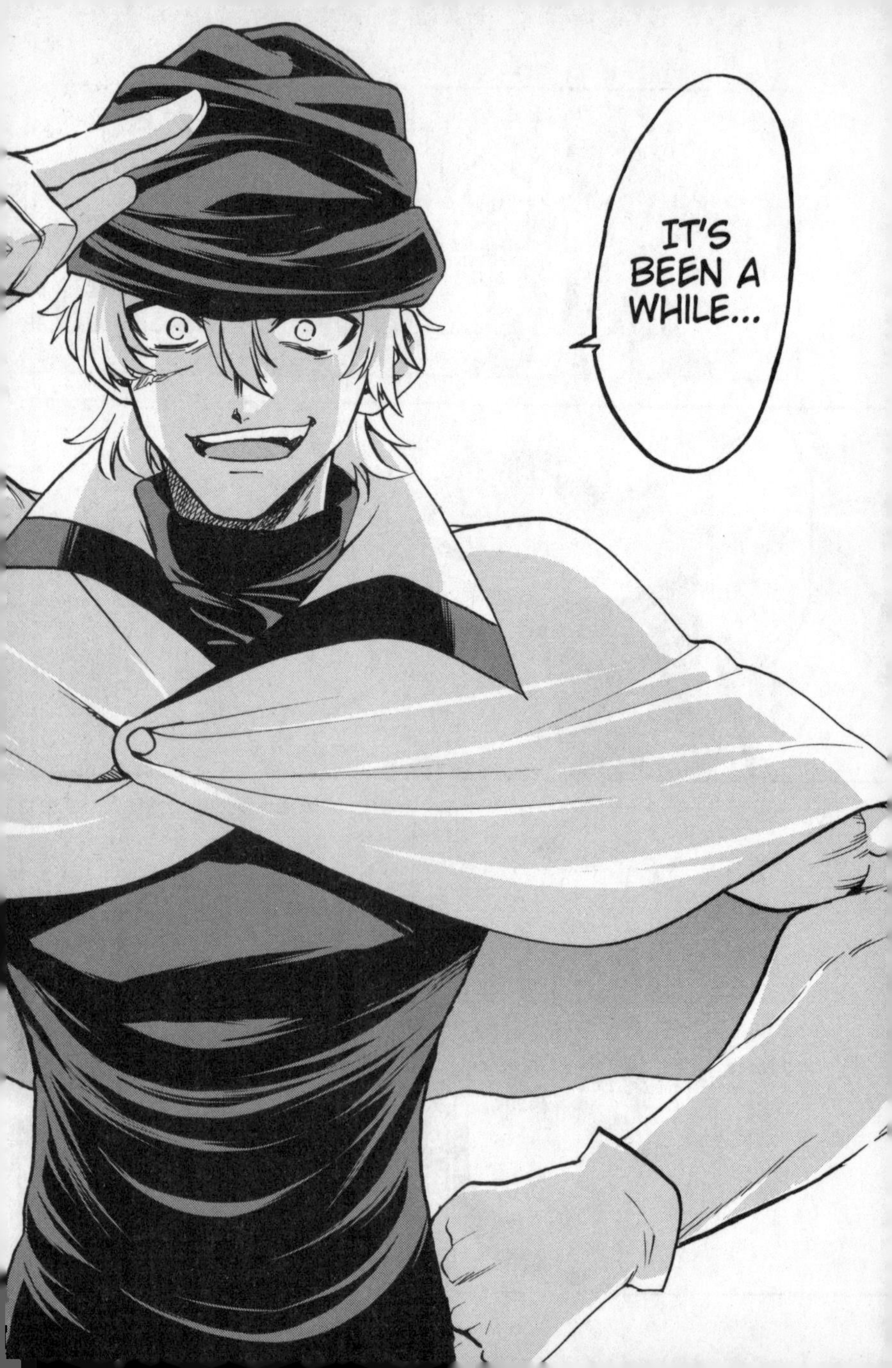
IT'S BEEN A WHILE...

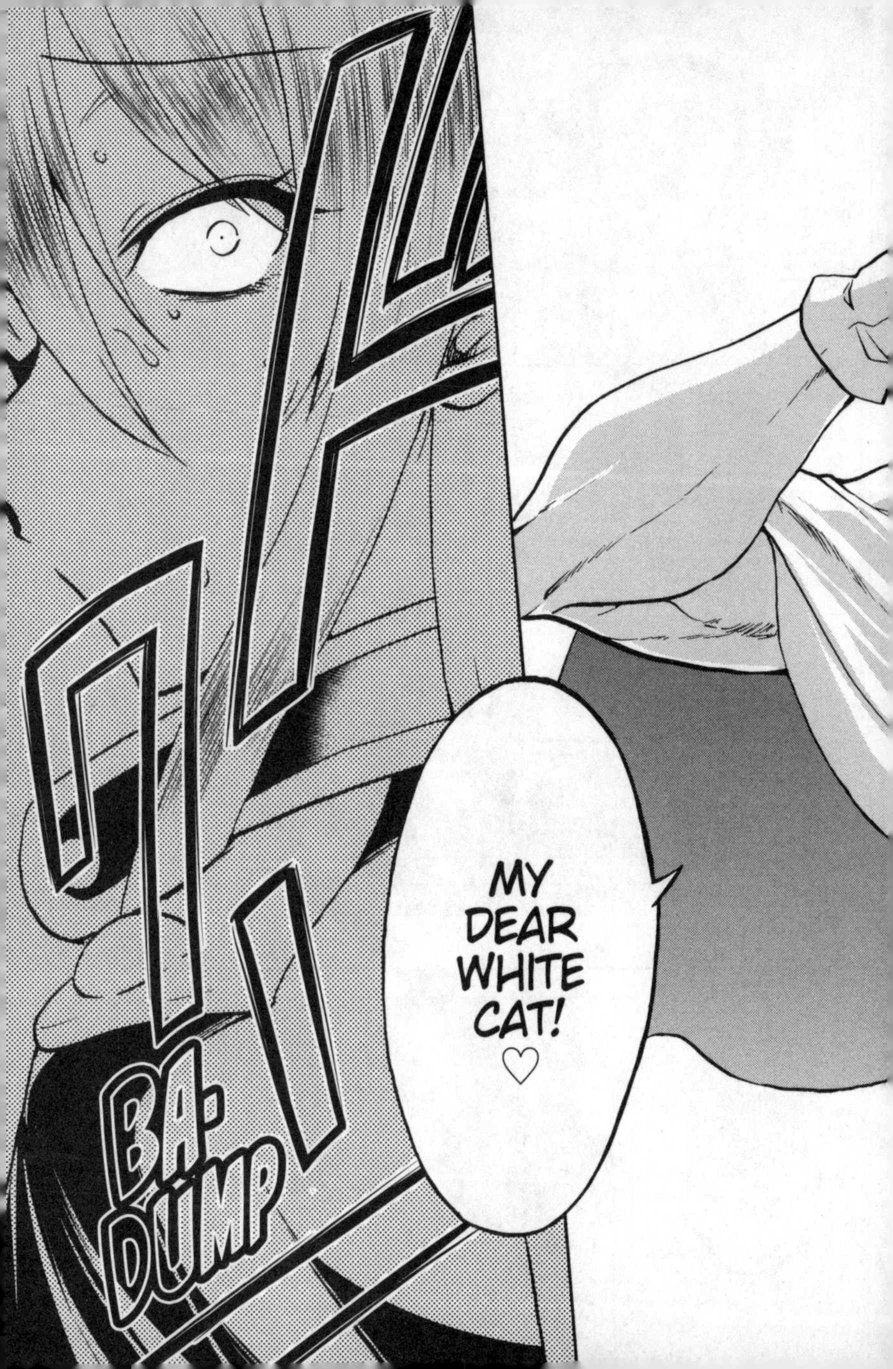
MY DEAR WHITE CAT! ♡
BA-DUMP

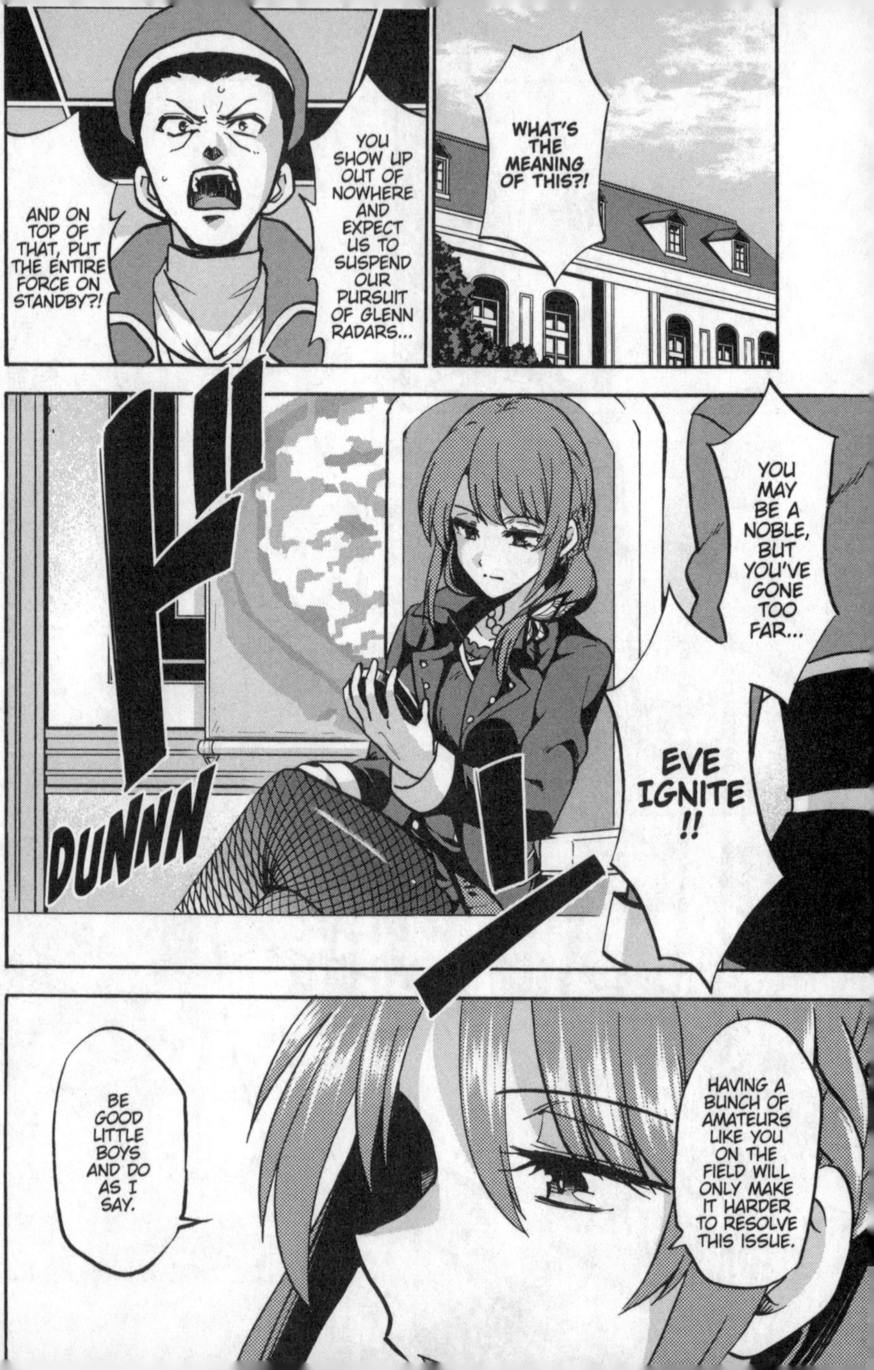
WHAT'S THE MEANING OF THIS?!
YOU SHOW UP OUT OF NOWHERE AND EXPECT US TO SUSPEND OUR PURSUIT OF GLENN RADARS...
AND ON TOP OF THAT, PUT THE ENTIRE FORCE ON STANDBY?!
YOU MAY BE A NOBLE, BUT YOU'VE GONE TOO FAR...
DUNNN
EVE IGNITE !!
HAVING A BUNCH OF AMATEURS LIKE YOU ON THE FIELD WILL ONLY MAKE IT HARDER TO RESOLVE THIS ISSUE.
BE GOOD LITTLE BOYS AND DO AS I SAY.

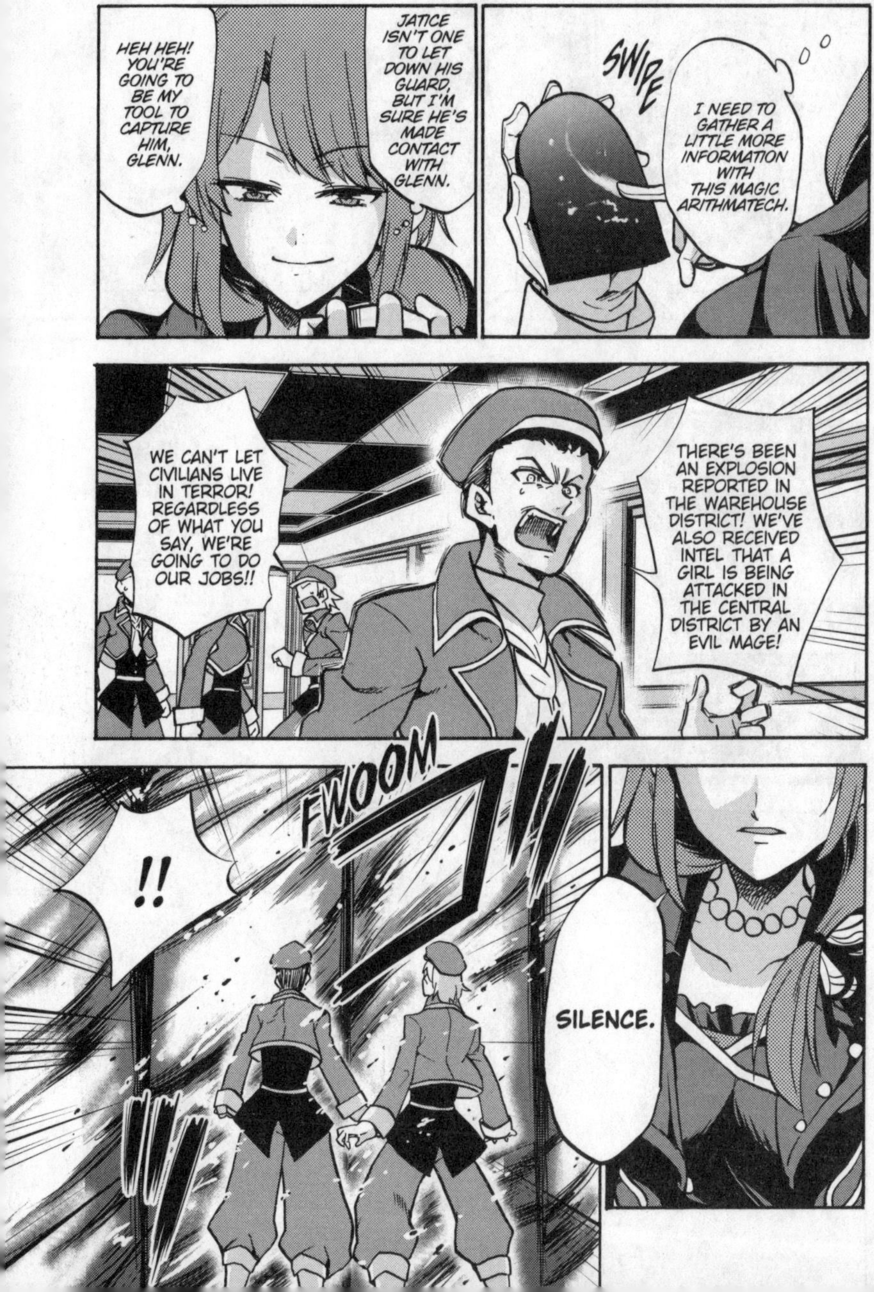
SWIPE
I NEED TO GATHER A LITTLE MORE INFORMATION WITH THIS MAGIC ARITHMATECH.
JATICE ISN'T ONE TO LET DOWN HIS GUARD, BUT I'M SURE HE'S MADE CONTACT WITH GLENN.
HEH HEH! YOU'RE GOING TO BE MY TOOL TO CAPTURE HIM, GLENN.
THERE'S BEEN AN EXPLOSION REPORTED IN THE WAREHOUSE DISTRICT! WE'VE ALSO RECEIVED INTEL THAT A GIRL IS BEING ATTACKED IN THE CENTRAL DISTRICT BY AN EVIL MAGE!
WE CAN'T LET CIVILIANS LIVE IN TERROR! REGARDLESS OF WHAT YOU SAY, WE'RE GOING TO DO OUR JOBS!!
SILENCE.
FWOOM
!!

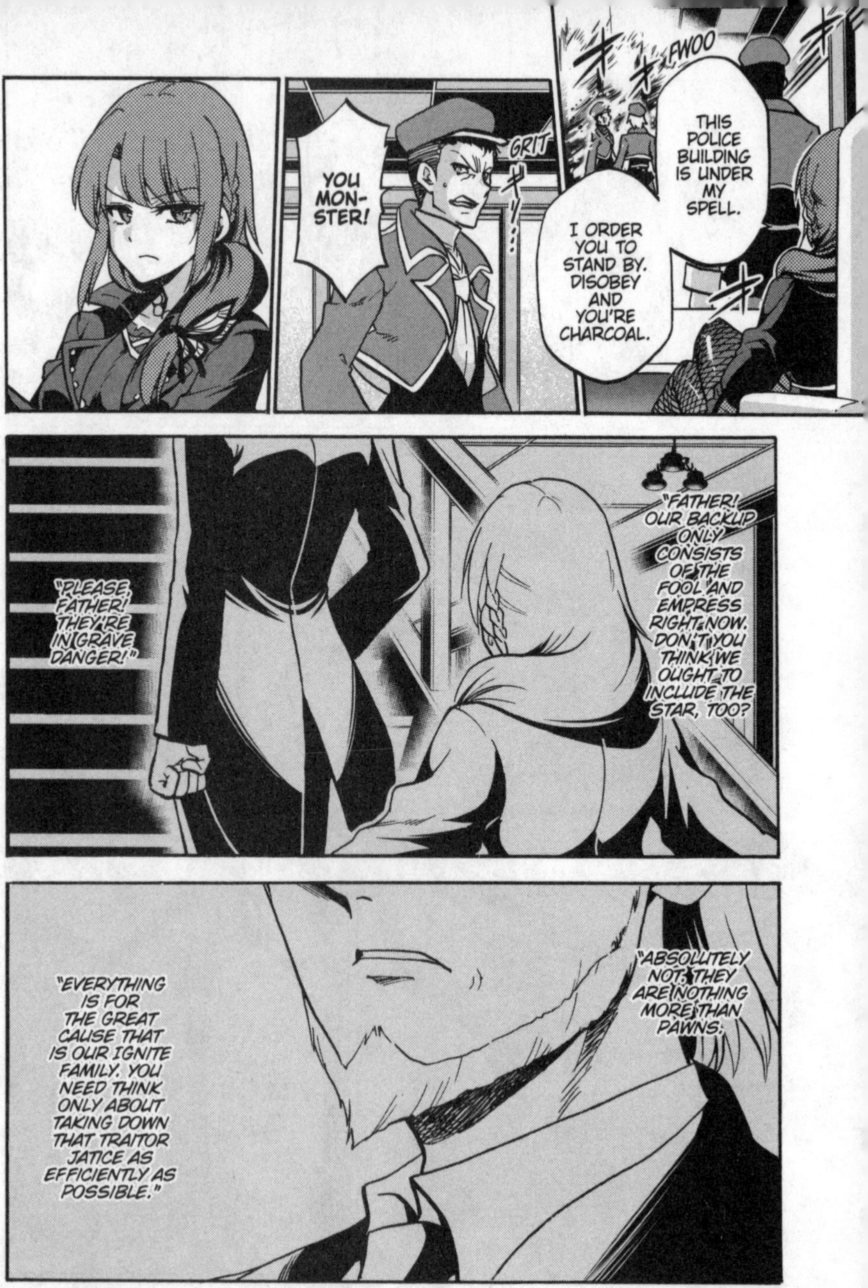
FWOO
THIS POLICE BUILDING IS UNDER MY SPELL.
I ORDER YOU TO STAND BY. DISOBEY AND YOU'RE CHARCOAL.
GRIT
YOU MON-STER!
"FATHER! OUR BACKUP ONLY CONSISTS OF THE FOOL AND EMPRESS RIGHT NOW. DON'T YOU THINK WE OUGHT TO INCLUDE THE STAR, TOO?
"PLEASE, FATHER! THEY'RE IN GRAVE DANGER!"
"ABSOLUTELY NOT. THEY ARE NOTHING MORE THAN PAWNS.
"EVERYTHING IS FOR THE GREAT CAUSE THAT IS OUR IGNITE FAMILY. YOU NEED THINK ONLY ABOUT TAKING DOWN THAT TRAITOR JATICE AS EFFICIENTLY AS POSSIBLE."

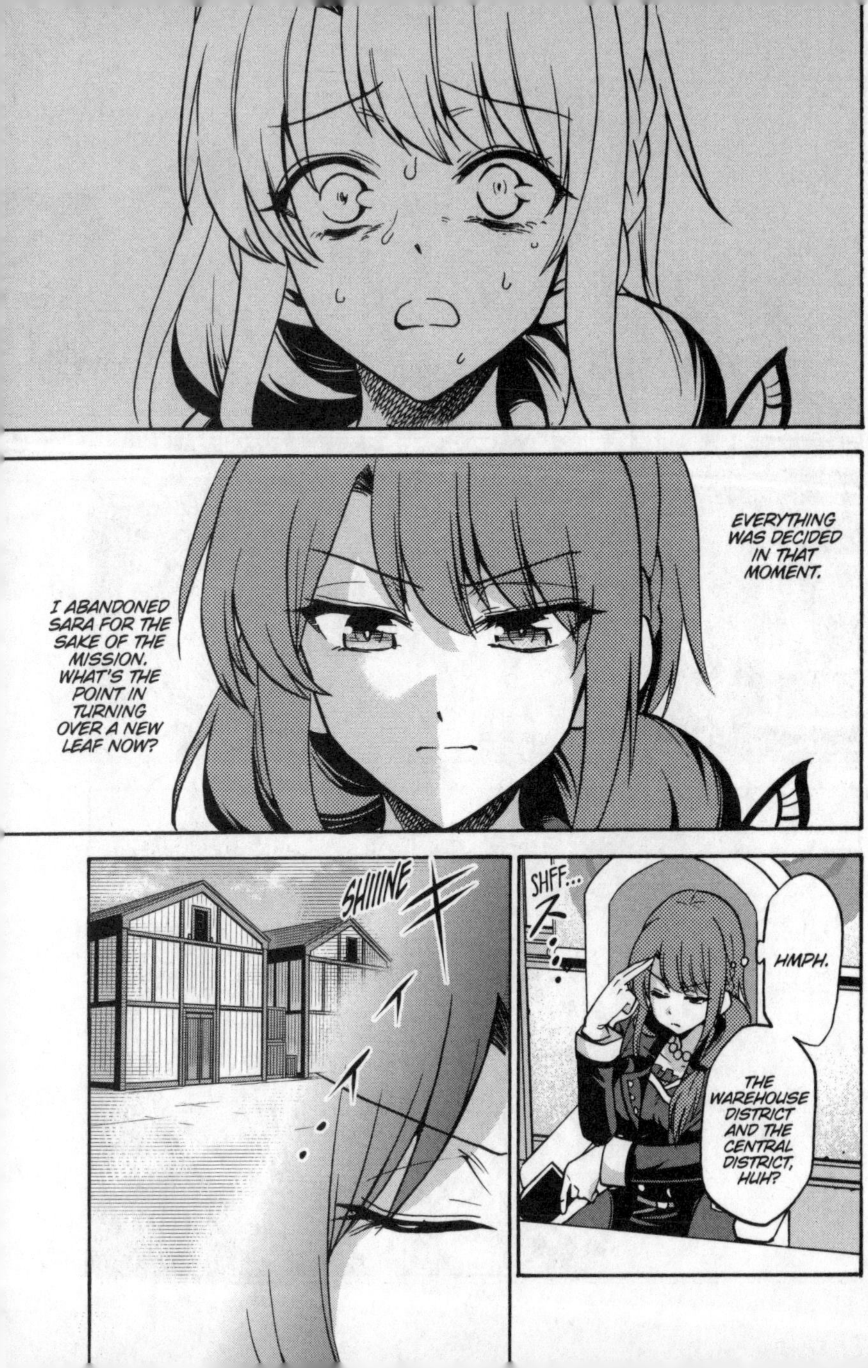
EVERYTHING WAS DECIDED IN THAT MOMENT.
I ABANDONED SARA FOR THE SAKE OF THE MISSION. WHAT'S THE POINT IN TURNING OVER A NEW LEAF NOW?
SHFF...
HMPH.
THE WAREHOUSE DISTRICT AND THE CENTRAL DISTRICT, HUH?
SHIIINE

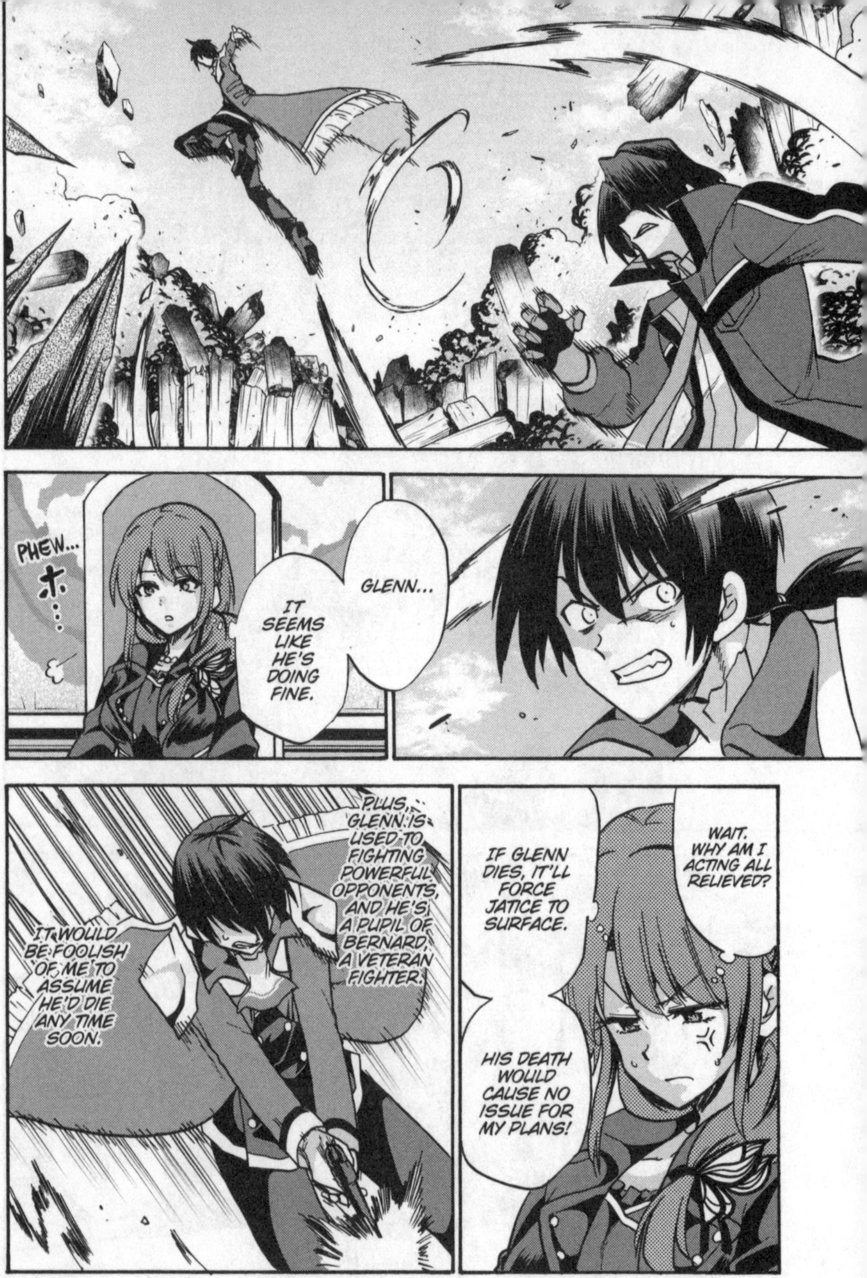
GLENN...
IT SEEMS LIKE HE'S DOING FINE.
PHEW...
WAIT. WHY AM I ACTING ALL RELIEVED?
IF GLENN DIES, IT'LL FORCE JATICE TO SURFACE.
HIS DEATH WOULD CAUSE NO ISSUE FOR MY PLANS!
PLUS, GLENN IS USED TO FIGHTING POWERFUL OPPONENTS, AND HE'S A PUPIL OF BERNARD, A VETERAN FIGHTER.
IT WOULD BE FOOLISH OF ME TO ASSUME HE'D DIE ANY TIME SOON.

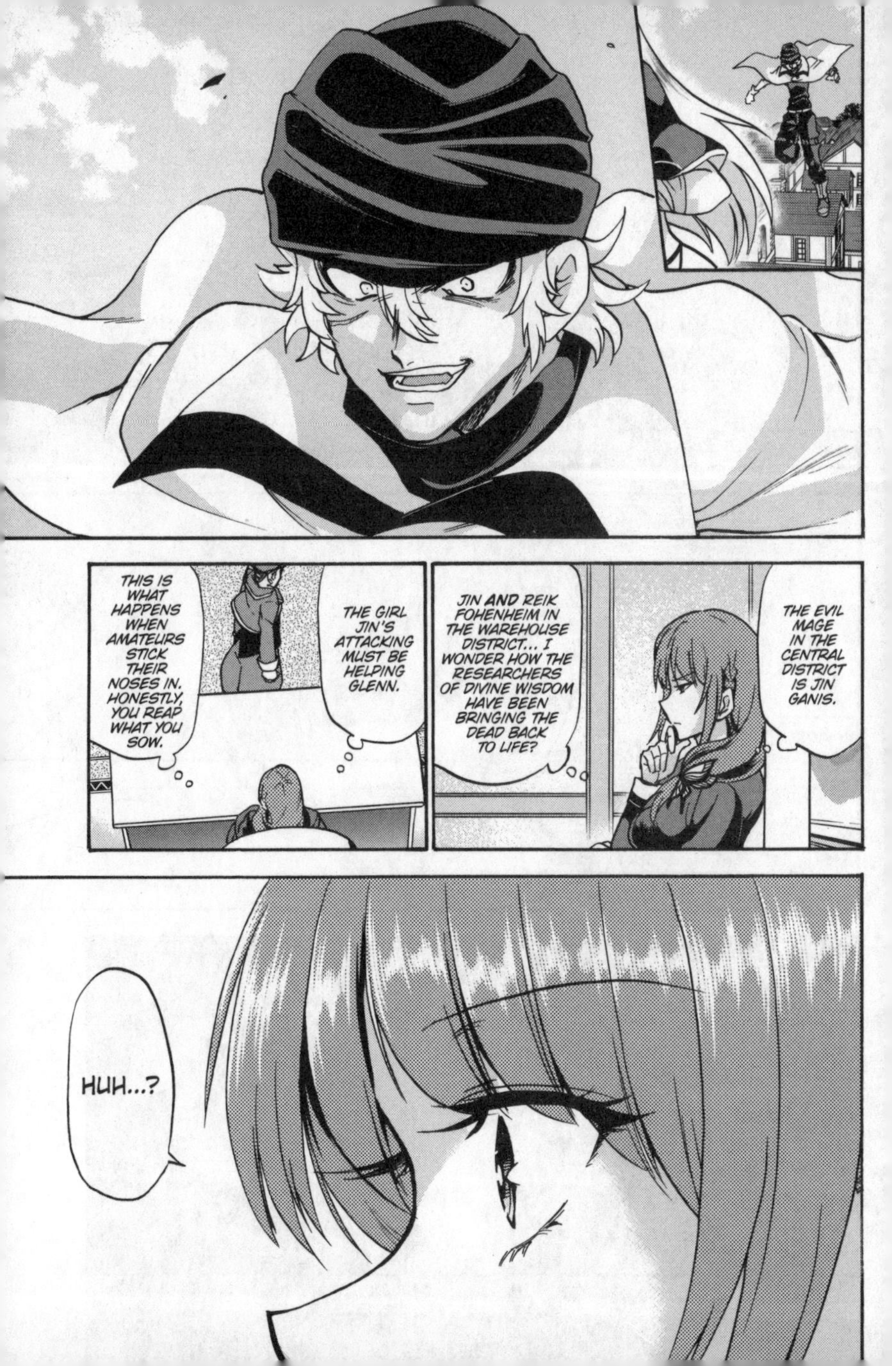
THE EVIL MAGE IN THE CENTRAL DISTRICT IS JIN GANIS.
JIN AND REIK FOHENHEIM IN THE WAREHOUSE DISTRICT... I WONDER HOW THE RESEARCHERS OF DIVINE WISDOM HAVE BEEN BRINGING THE DEAD BACK TO LIFE?
THE GIRL JIN'S ATTACKING MUST BE HELPING GLENN.
THIS IS WHAT HAPPENS WHEN AMATEURS STICK THEIR NOSES IN. HONESTLY, YOU REAP WHAT YOU SOW.
HUH...?

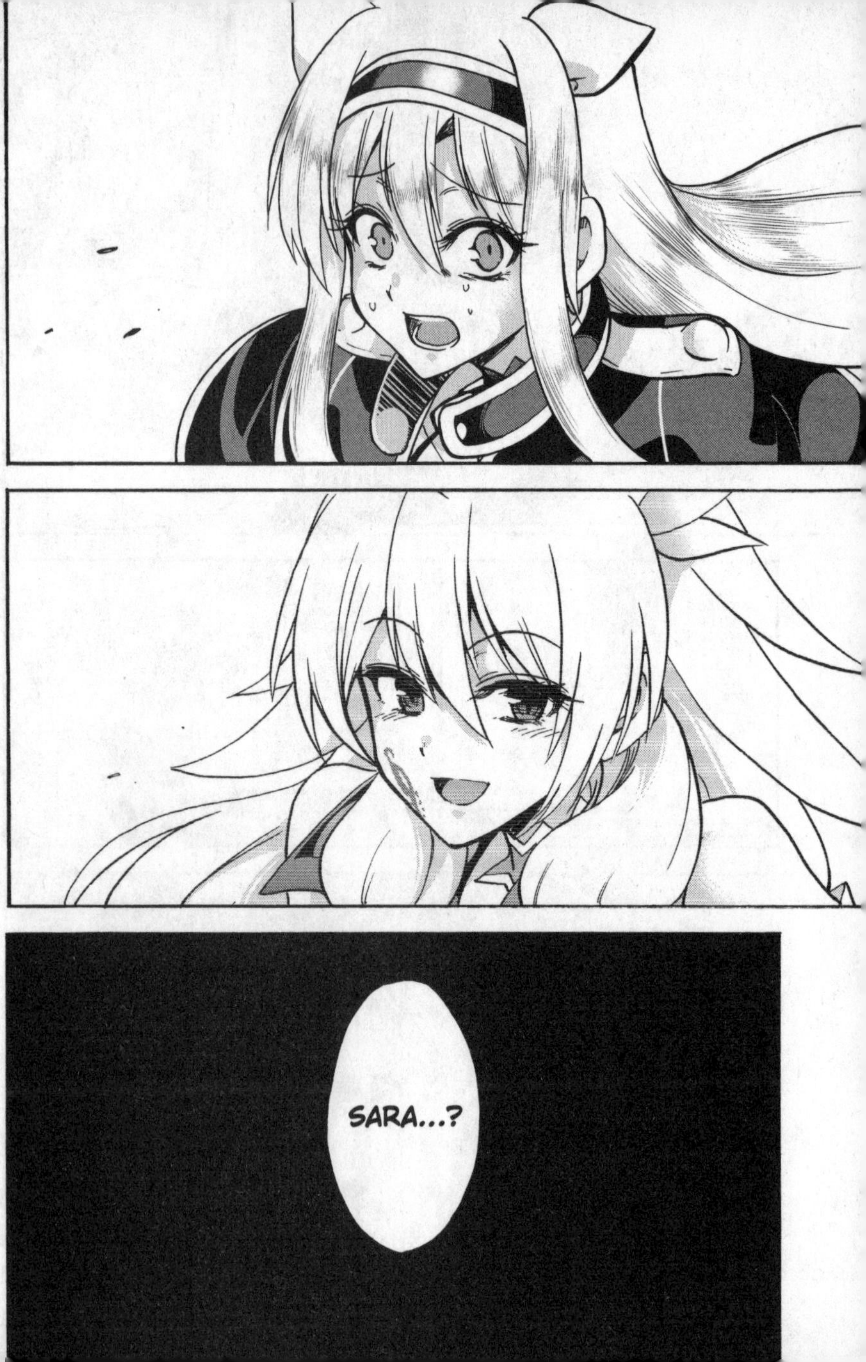
SARA...?

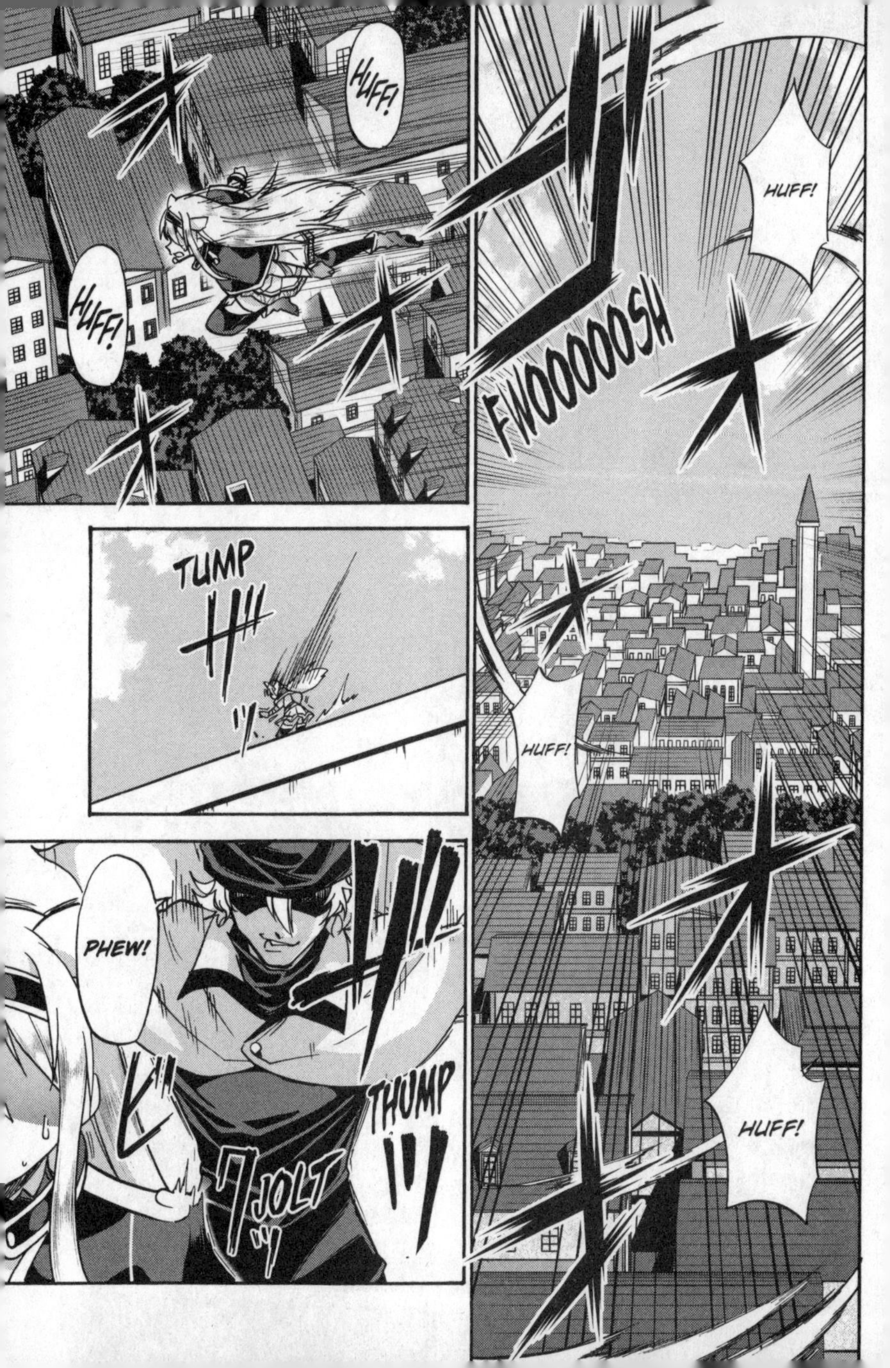

HUFF!
HUFF!
FWOOOOOSH
HUFF!
HUFF!
HUFF!
TUMP
PHEW!
THUMP
JOLT

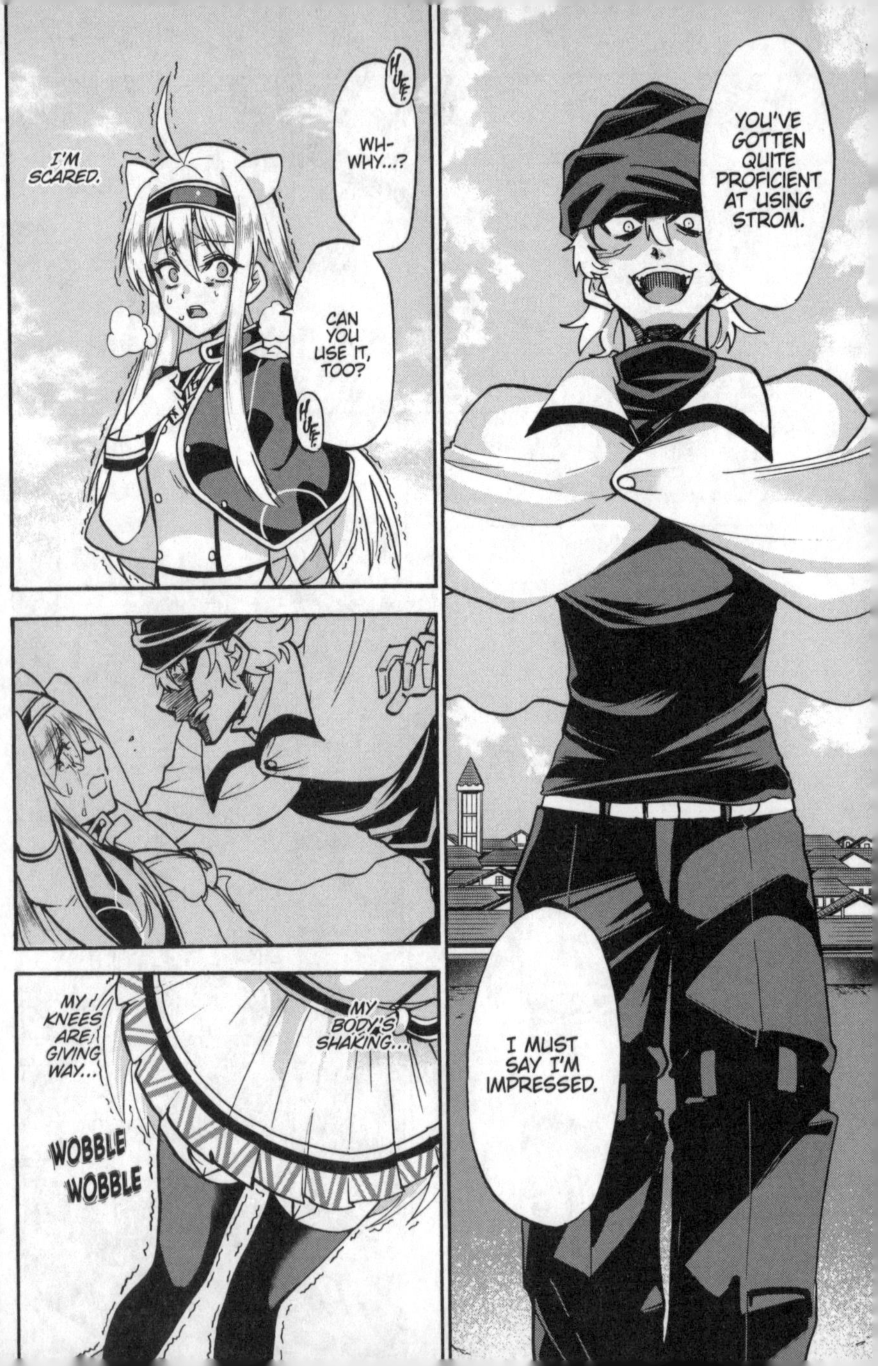
YOU'VE GOTTEN QUITE PROFICIENT AT USING STROM.
I MUST SAY I'M IMPRESSED.
HUFF
WH- WHY...?
I'M SCARED.
CAN YOU USE IT, TOO?
HUFF
MY BODY'S SHAKING...
MY KNEES ARE GIVING WAY...
WOBBLE WOBBLE

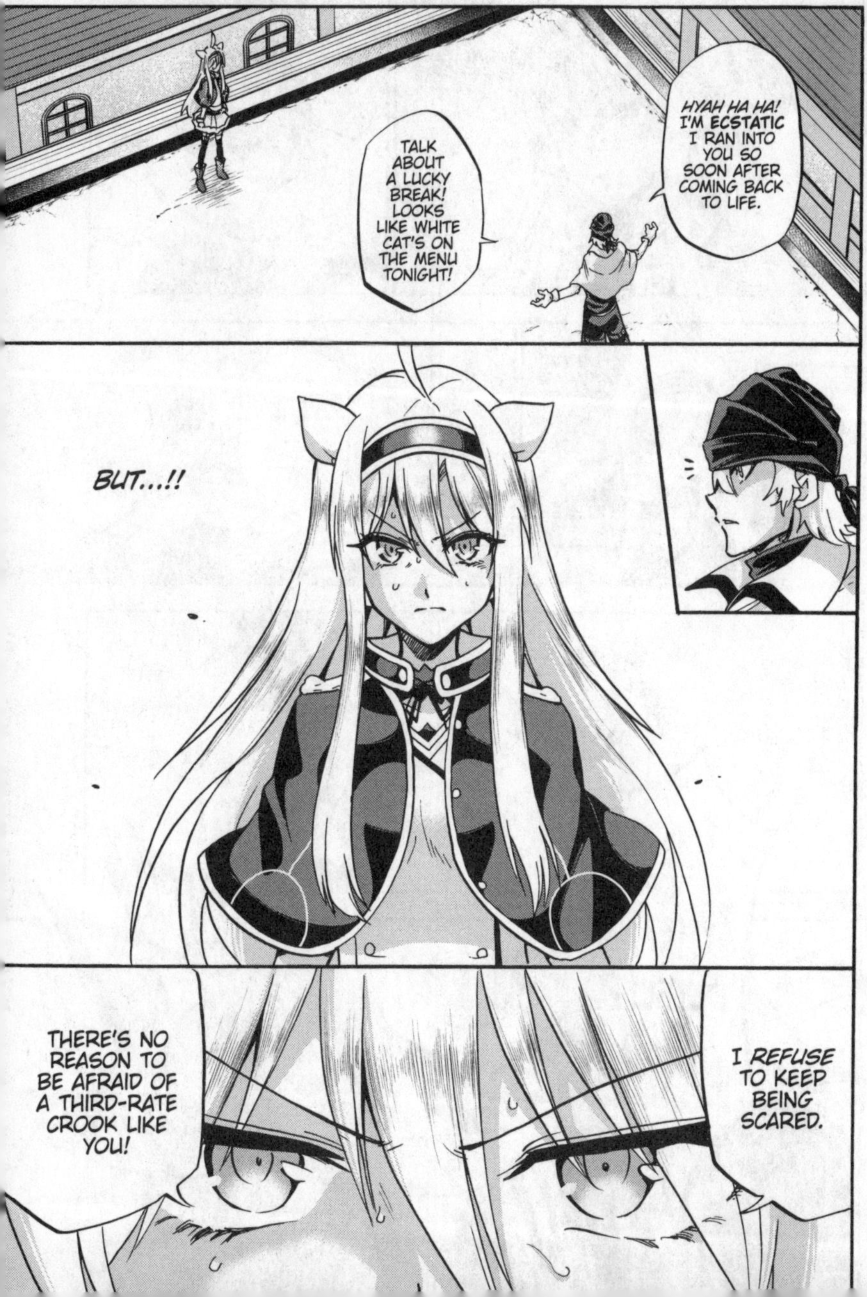
HYAH HA HA! I'M ECSTATIC I RAN INTO YOU SO SOON AFTER COMING BACK TO LIFE.
TALK ABOUT A LUCKY BREAK! LOOKS LIKE WHITE CAT'S ON THE MENU TONIGHT!
BUT...!!
I REFUSE TO KEEP BEING SCARED.
THERE'S NO REASON TO BE AFRAID OF A THIRD-RATE CROOK LIKE YOU!

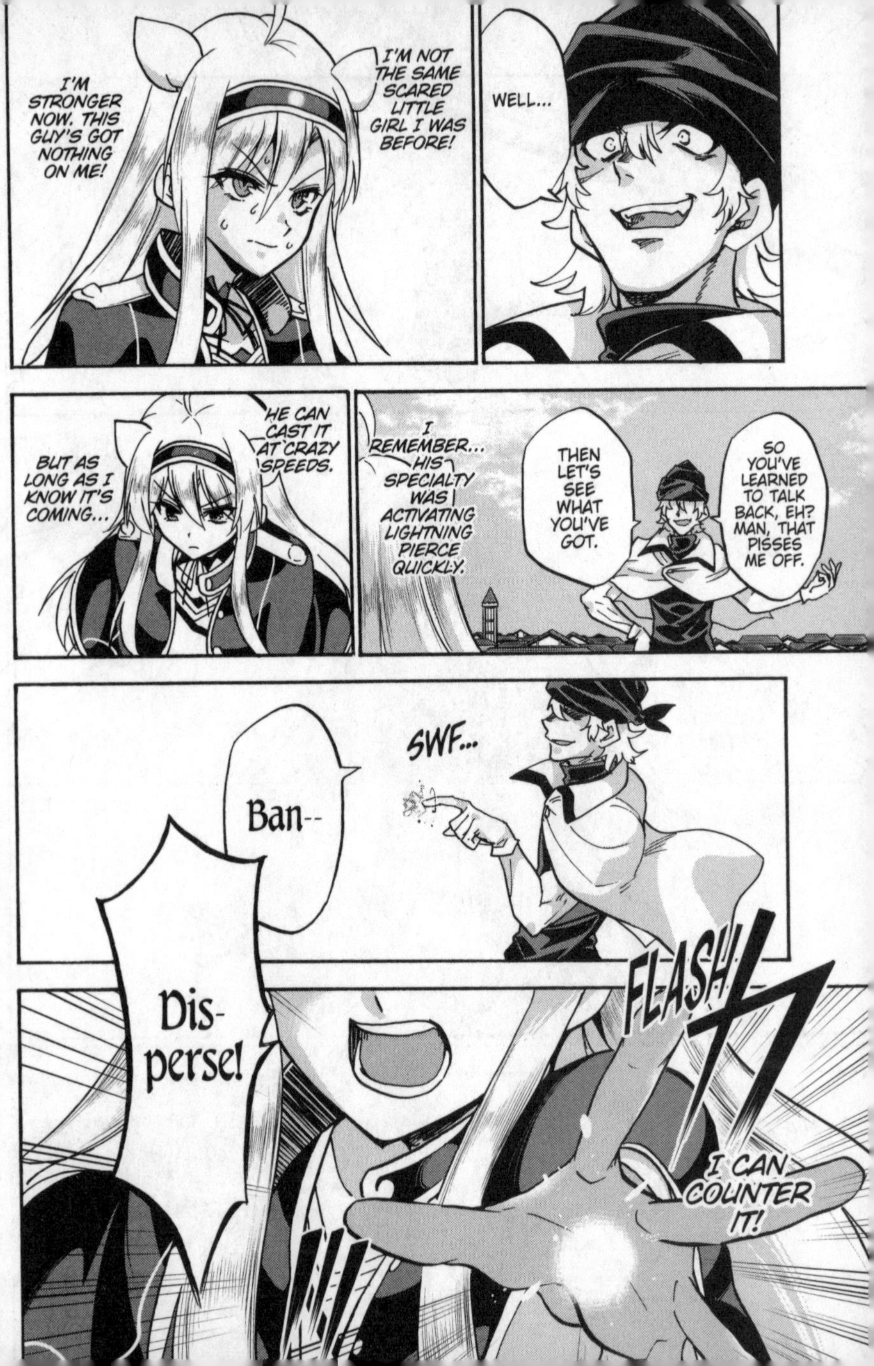
I'M NOT THE SAME SCARED LITTLE GIRL I WAS BEFORE!
I'M STRONGER NOW. THIS GUY'S GOT NOTHING ON ME!
WELL...
HE CAN CAST IT AT CRAZY SPEEDS.
BUT AS LONG AS I KNOW IT'S COMING...
SO YOU'VE LEARNED TO TALK BACK, EH? MAN, THAT PISSES ME OFF.
THEN LET'S SEE WHAT YOU'VE GOT.
I REMEMBER... HIS SPECIALTY WAS ACTIVATING LIGHTNING PIERCE QUICKLY.
SWF...
Ban--
Dis-perse!
FLASH
I CAN COUNTER IT!

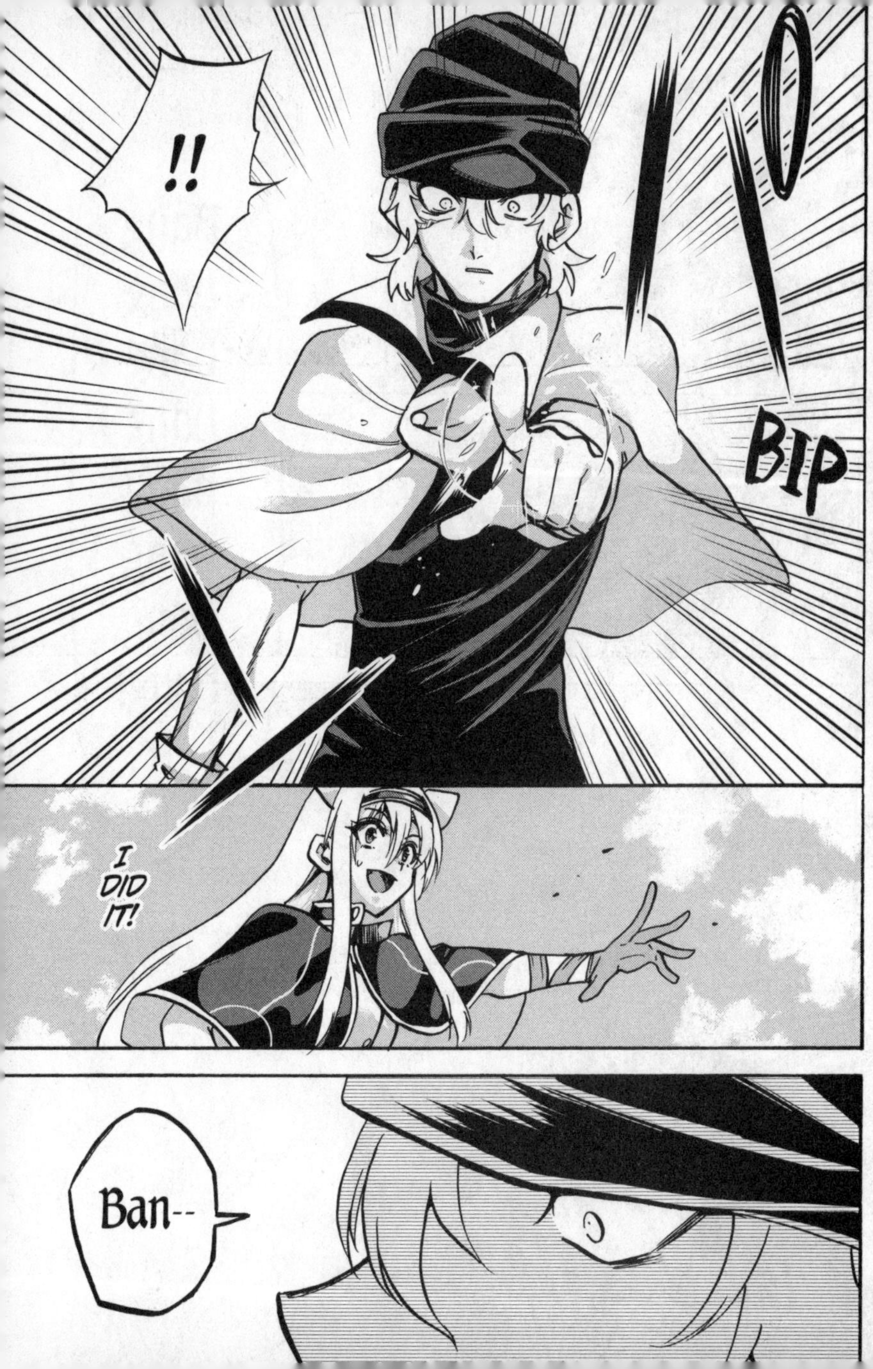
!!
BIP
I DID IT!
Ban--

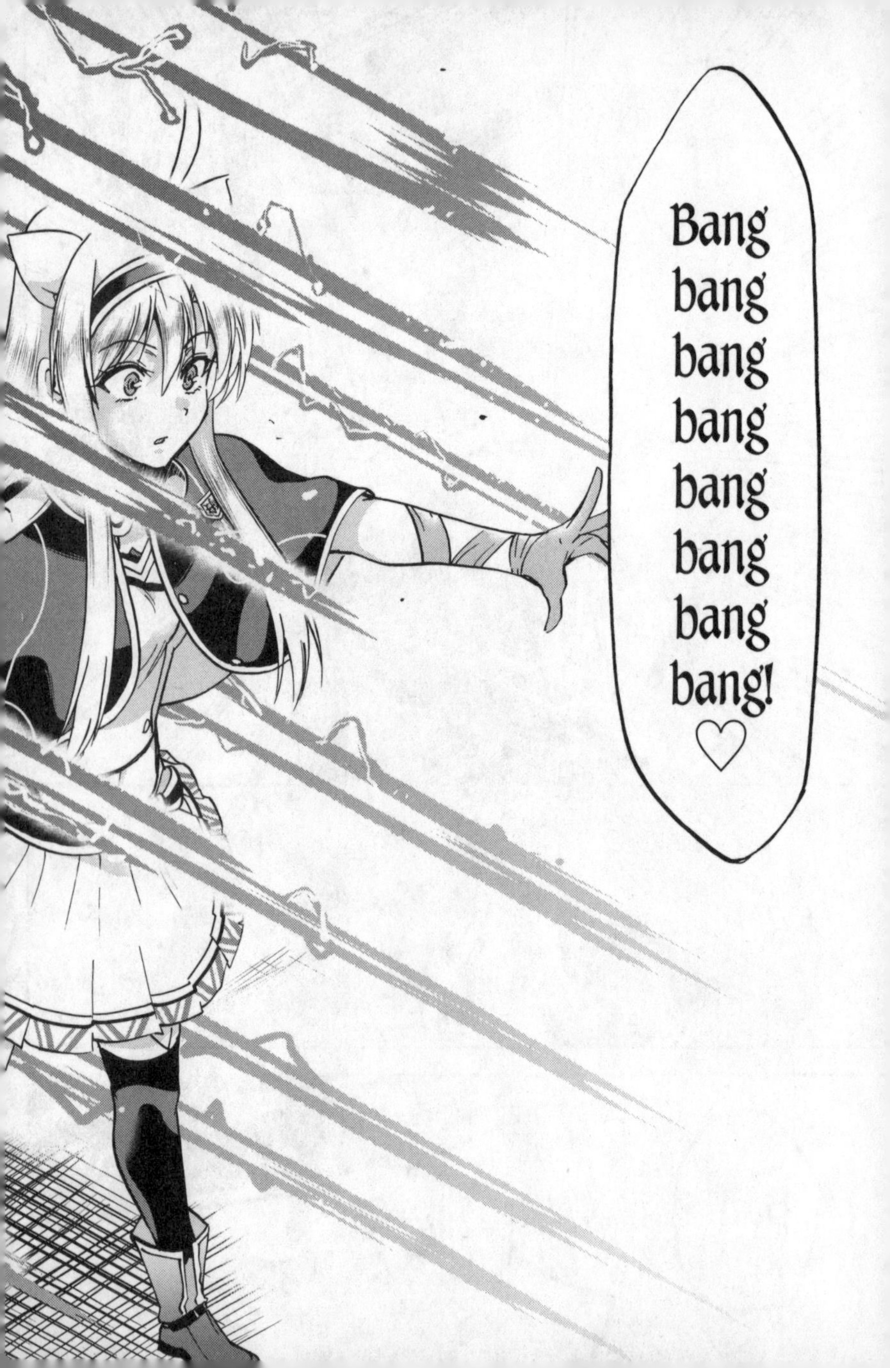
Bang bang bang bang bang bang bang bang! ♡

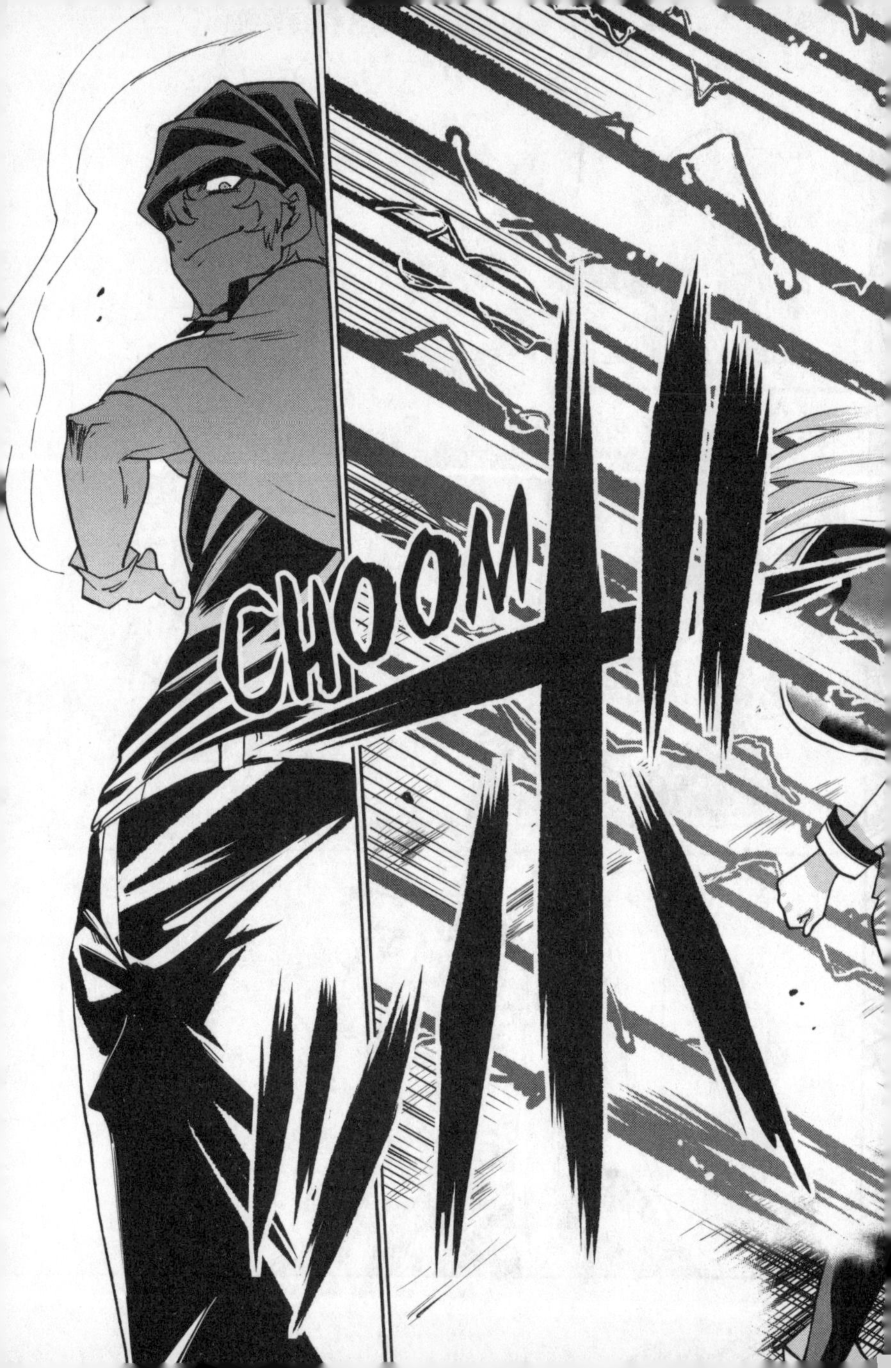
CHOOM

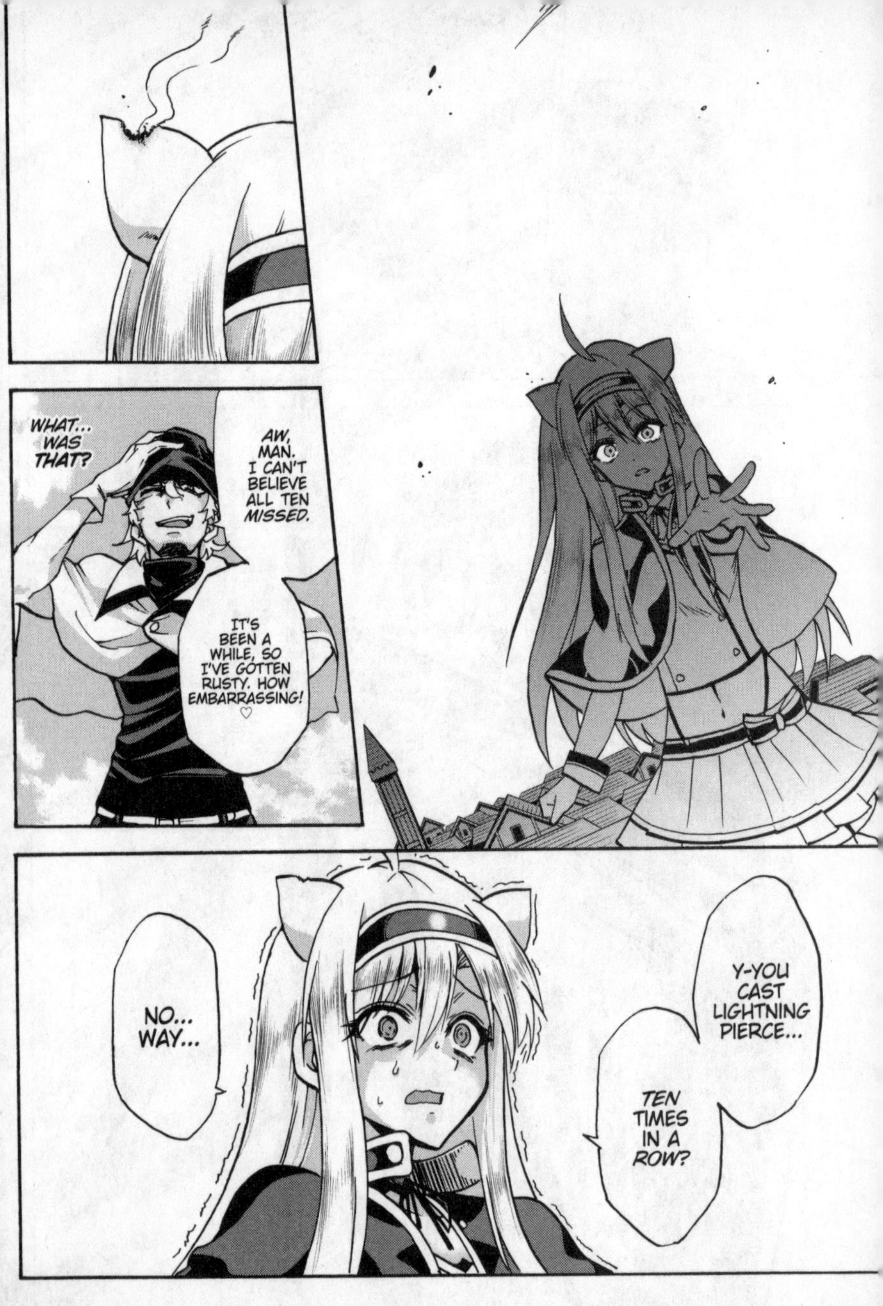
AW, MAN. I CAN'T BELIEVE ALL TEN MISSED.
WHAT... WAS THAT?
IT'S BEEN A WHILE, SO I'VE GOTTEN RUSTY. HOW EMBARRASSING! ♡
Y-YOU CAST LIGHTNING PIERCE...
TEN TIMES IN A ROW?
NO... WAY...

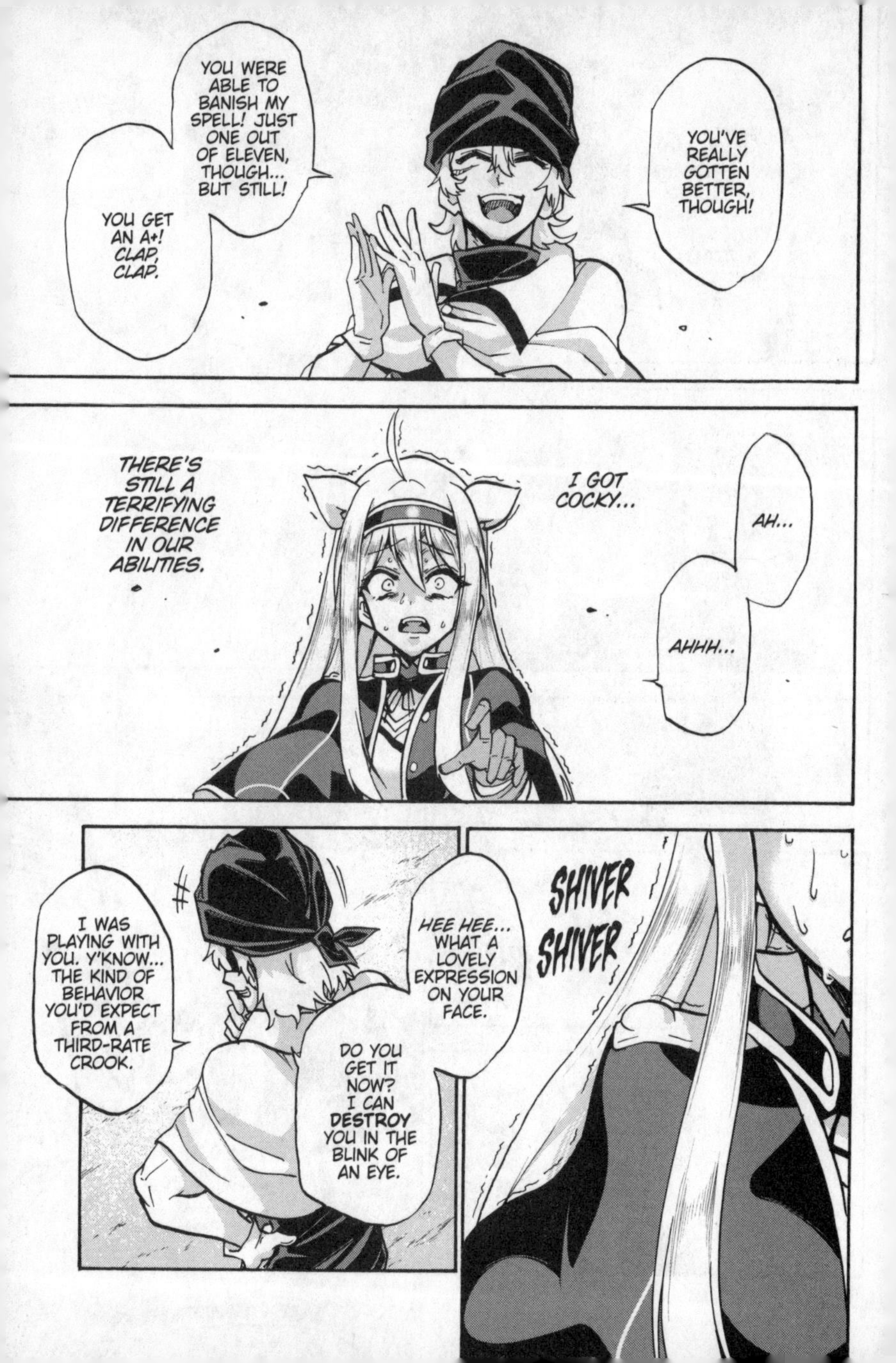
YOU'VE REALLY GOTTEN BETTER, THOUGH!
YOU WERE ABLE TO BANISH MY SPELL! JUST ONE OUT OF ELEVEN, THOUGH... BUT STILL!
YOU GET AN A+! CLAP, CLAP.
AH...
AHHH...
I GOT COCKY...
THERE'S STILL A TERRIFYING DIFFERENCE IN OUR ABILITIES.
SHIVER
SHIVER
HEE HEE... WHAT A LOVELY EXPRESSION ON YOUR FACE.
DO YOU GET IT NOW? I CAN DESTROY YOU IN THE BLINK OF AN EYE.
I WAS PLAYING WITH YOU. Y'KNOW... THE KIND OF BEHAVIOR YOU'D EXPECT FROM A THIRD-RATE CROOK.

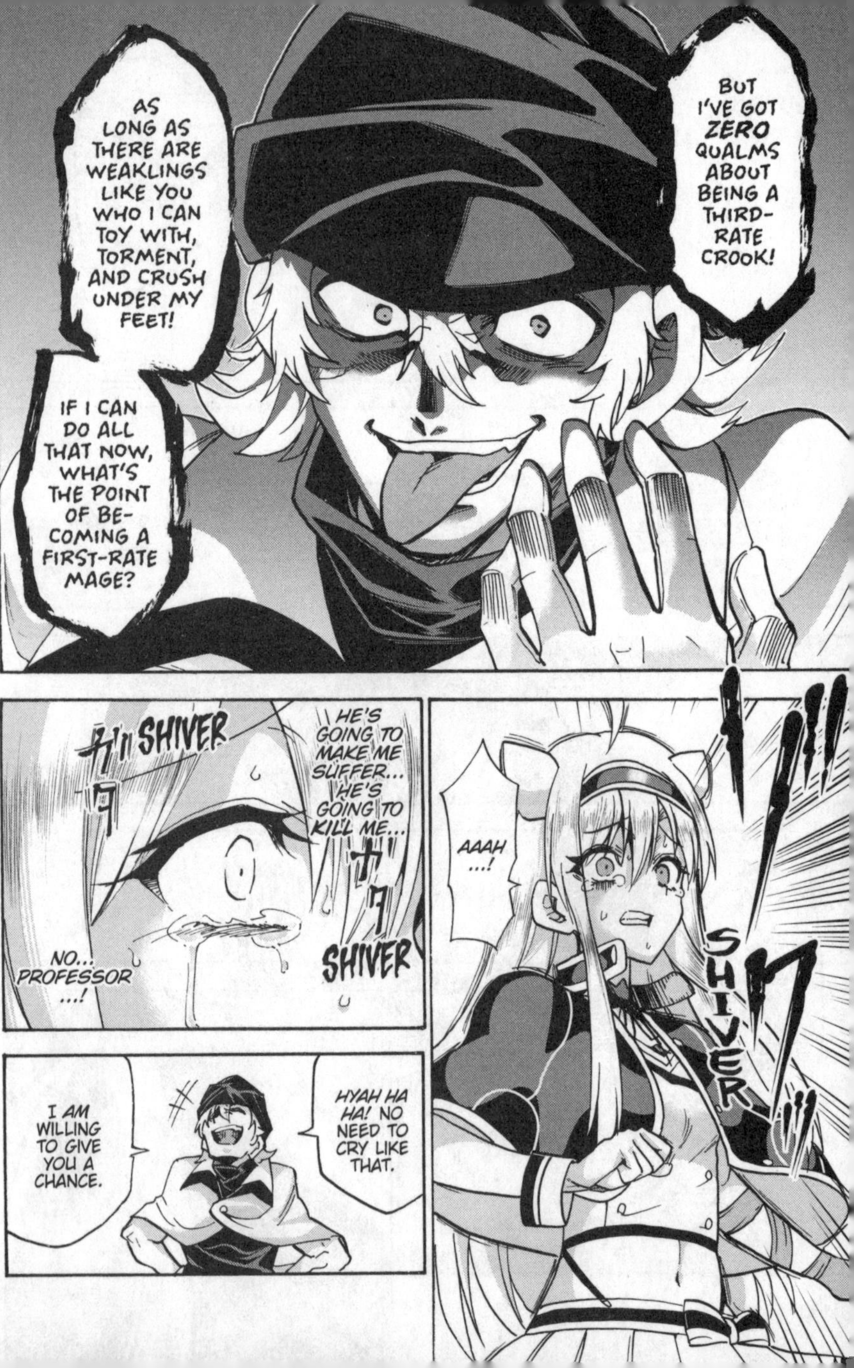
BUT I'VE GOT ZERO QUALMS ABOUT BEING A THIRD-RATE CROOK!
AS LONG AS THERE ARE WEAKLINGS LIKE YOU WHO I CAN TOY WITH, TORMENT, AND CRUSH UNDER MY FEET!
IF I CAN DO ALL THAT NOW, WHAT'S THE POINT OF BE-COMING A FIRST-RATE MAGE?
AAAH ...!
SHIVER
HE'S GOING TO MAKE ME SUFFER... HE'S GOING TO KILL ME...
SHIVER
SHIVER
NO... PROFESSOR ...!
HYAH HA HA! NO NEED TO CRY LIKE THAT.
I AM WILLING TO GIVE YOU A CHANCE.

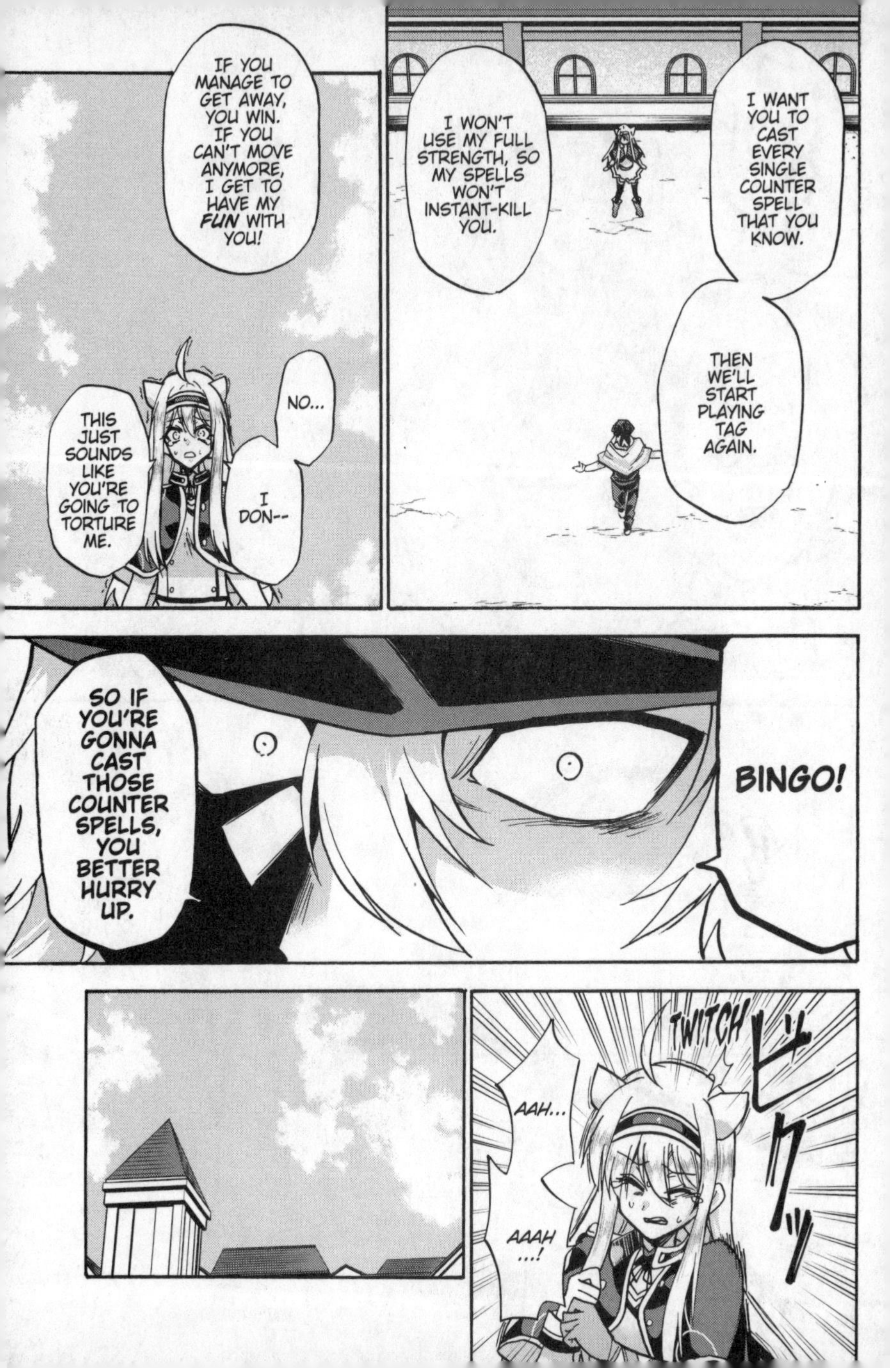
I WANT YOU TO CAST EVERY SINGLE COUNTER SPELL THAT YOU KNOW.
THEN WE'LL START PLAYING TAG AGAIN.
I WON'T USE MY FULL STRENGTH, SO MY SPELLS WON'T INSTANT-KILL YOU.
IF YOU MANAGE TO GET AWAY, YOU WIN. IF YOU CAN'T MOVE ANYMORE, I GET TO HAVE MY FUN WITH YOU!
NO...
I DON--
THIS JUST SOUNDS LIKE YOU'RE GOING TO TORTURE ME.
BINGO!
SO IF YOU'RE GONNA CAST THOSE COUNTER SPELLS, YOU BETTER HURRY UP.
TWITCH
AAH...
AAAH ...!

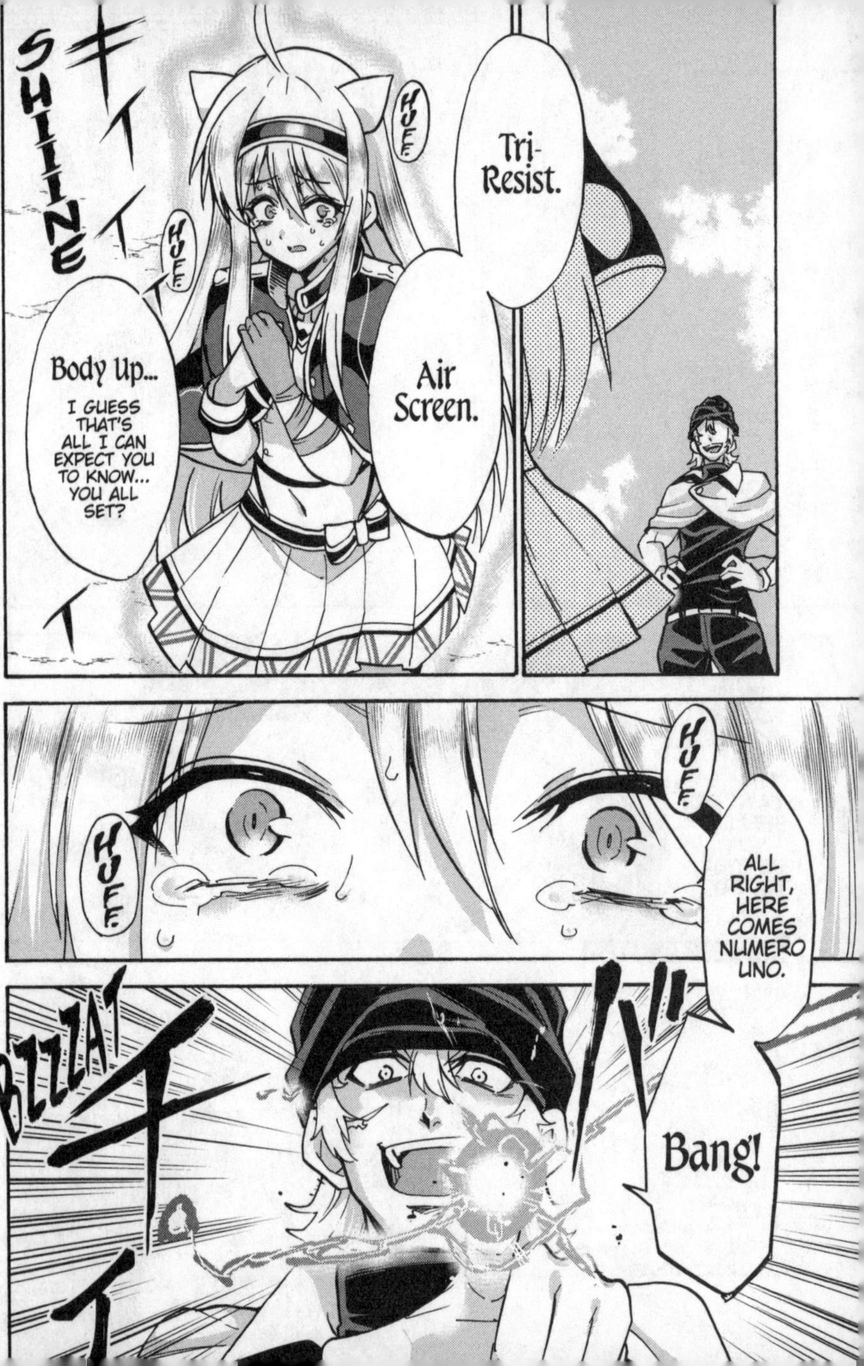
Tri-Resist.
Air Screen.
HUFF.
HUFF.
Body Up... I GUESS THAT'S ALL I CAN EXPECT YOU TO KNOW... YOU ALL SET?
SHIIINE
HUFF.
HUFF.
ALL RIGHT, HERE COMES NUMERO UNO.
Bang!
BZZZAT

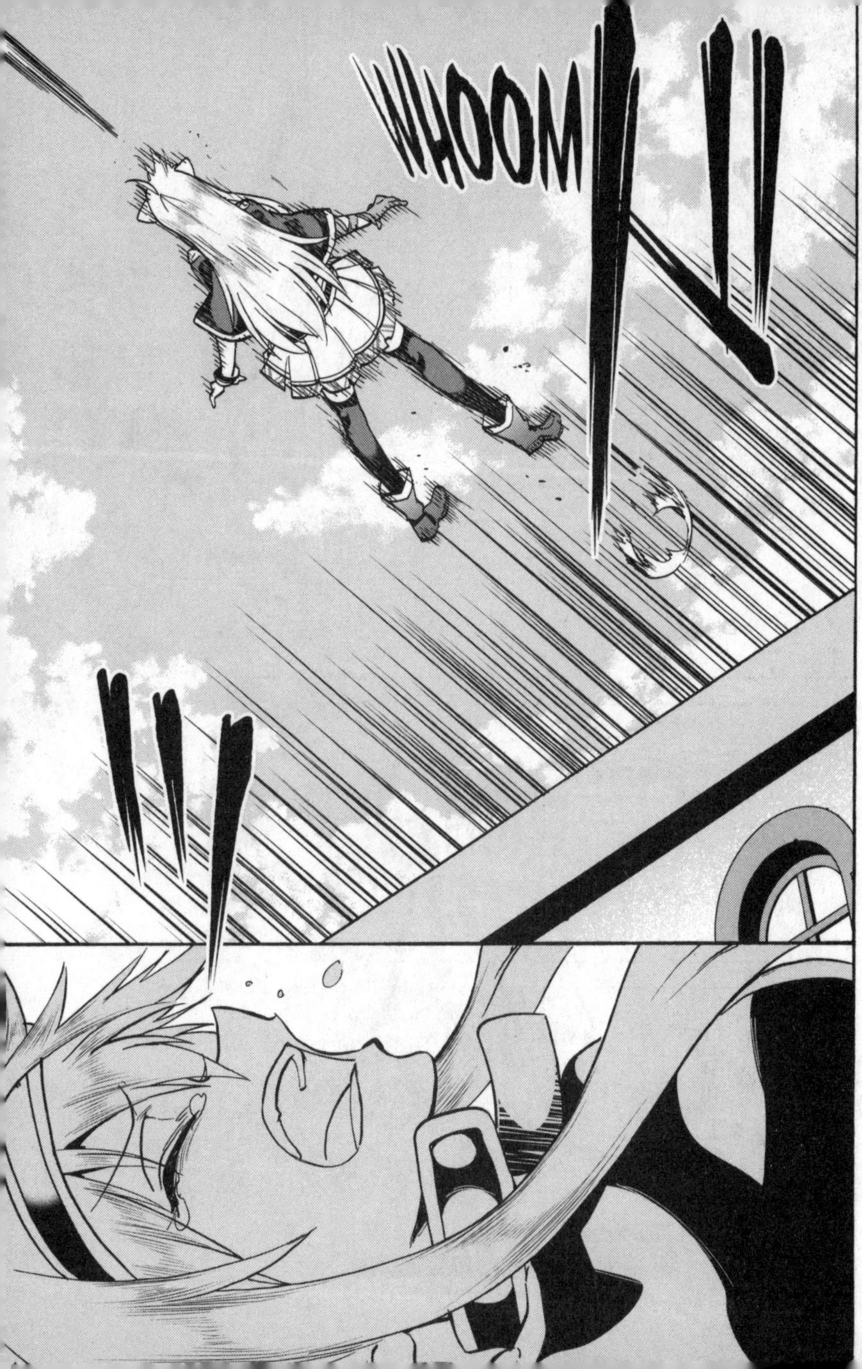
WHOOM!!

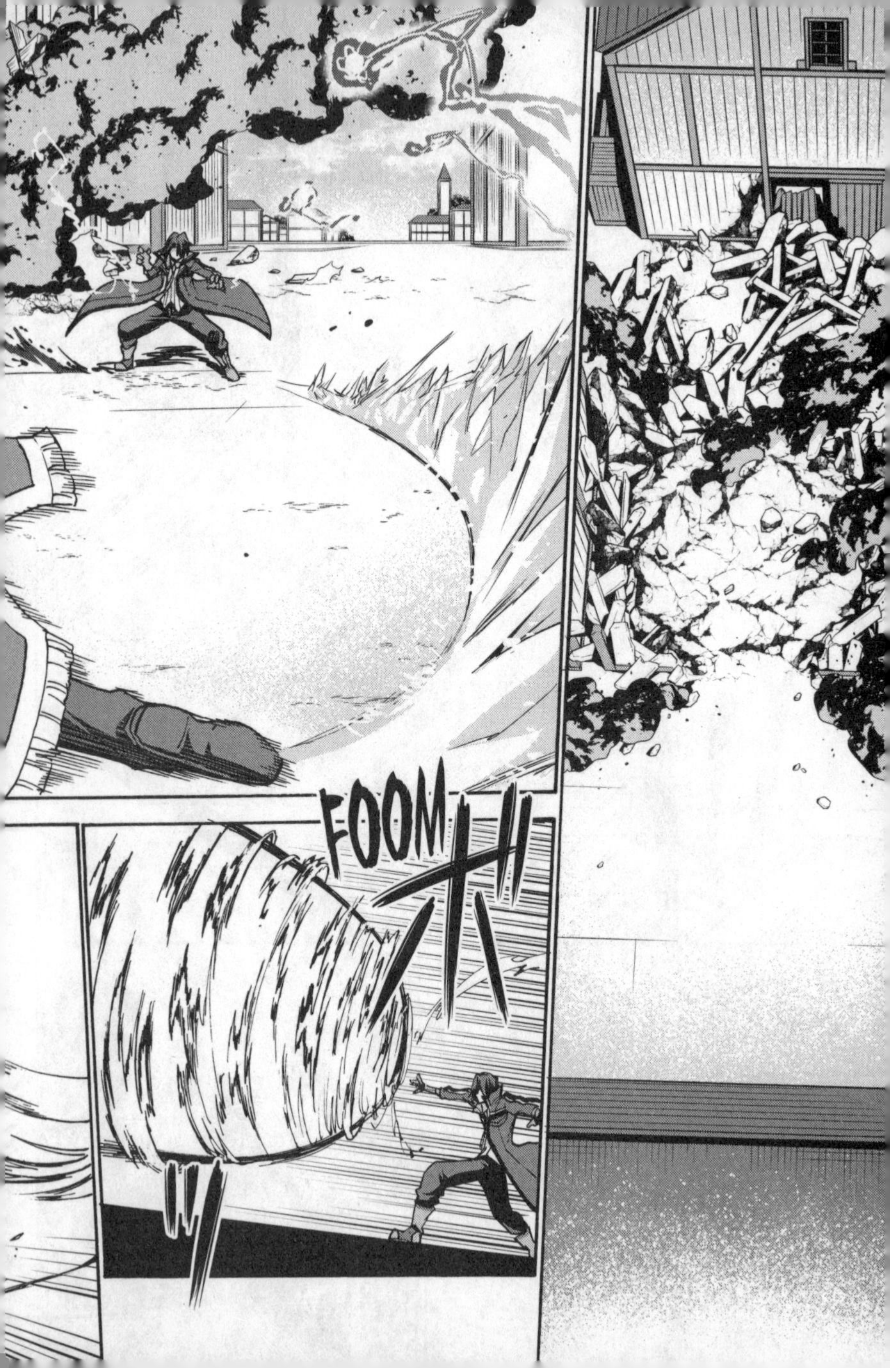
FOOM

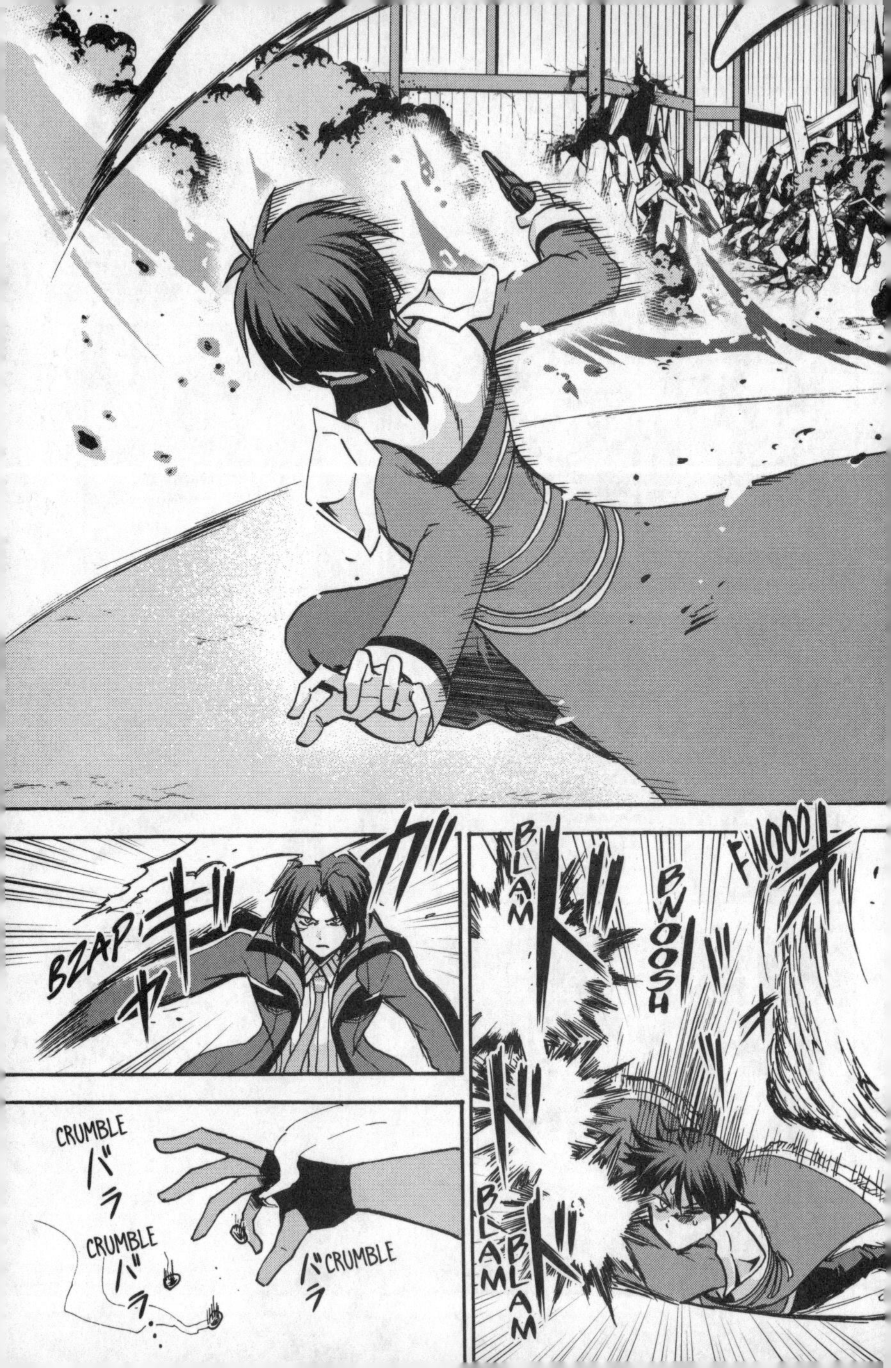
FWOOO
BWOOSH
BLAM
BLAM
BLAM
BLAM
BZAP
CRUMBLE
バラ
CRUMBLE
バラ
CRUMBLE
バラ

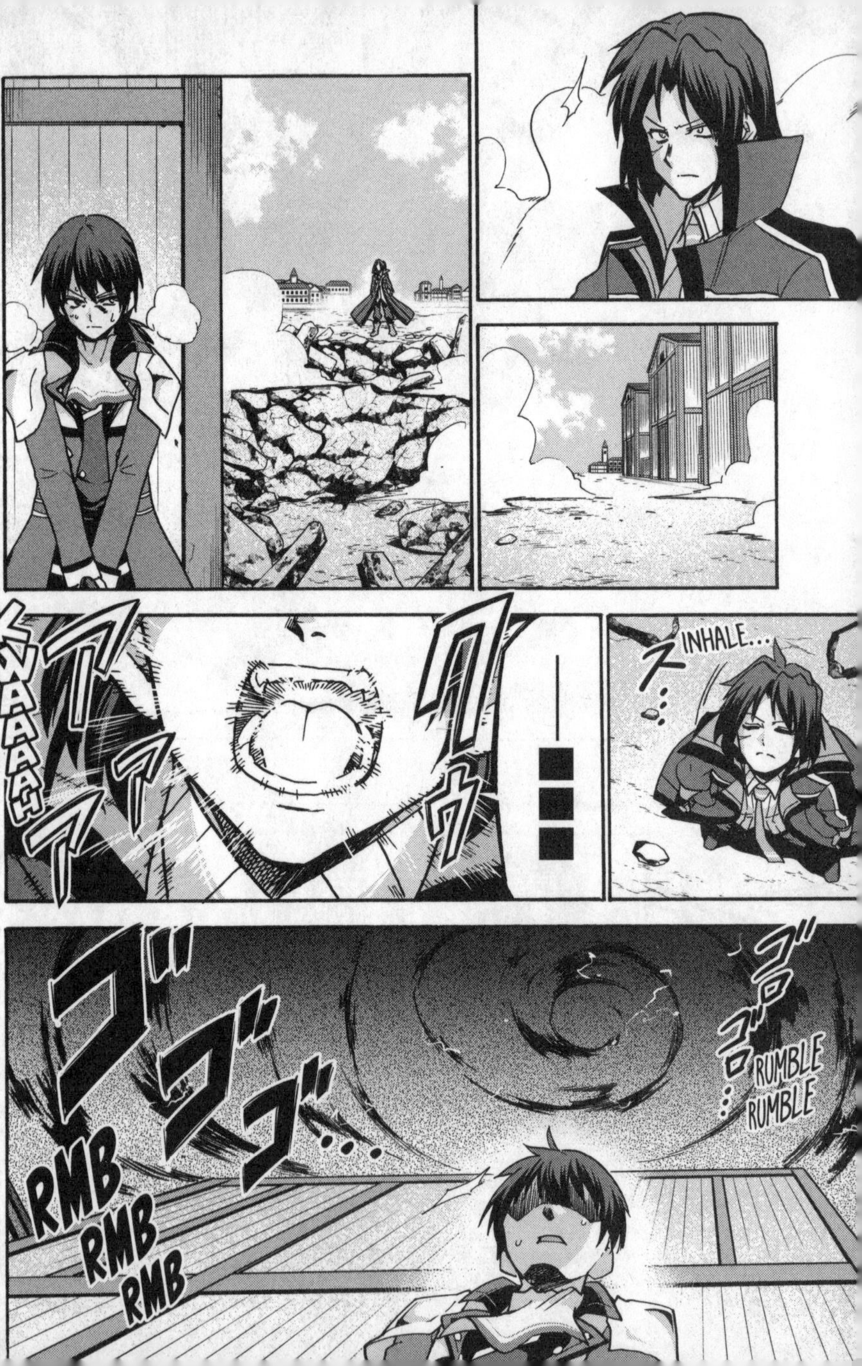

ス…
INHALE...
クゥ
アアア
KWAAAAAH
ゴロゴロ…
RUMBLE RUMBLE
ゴゴゴ…
RMB RMB RMB

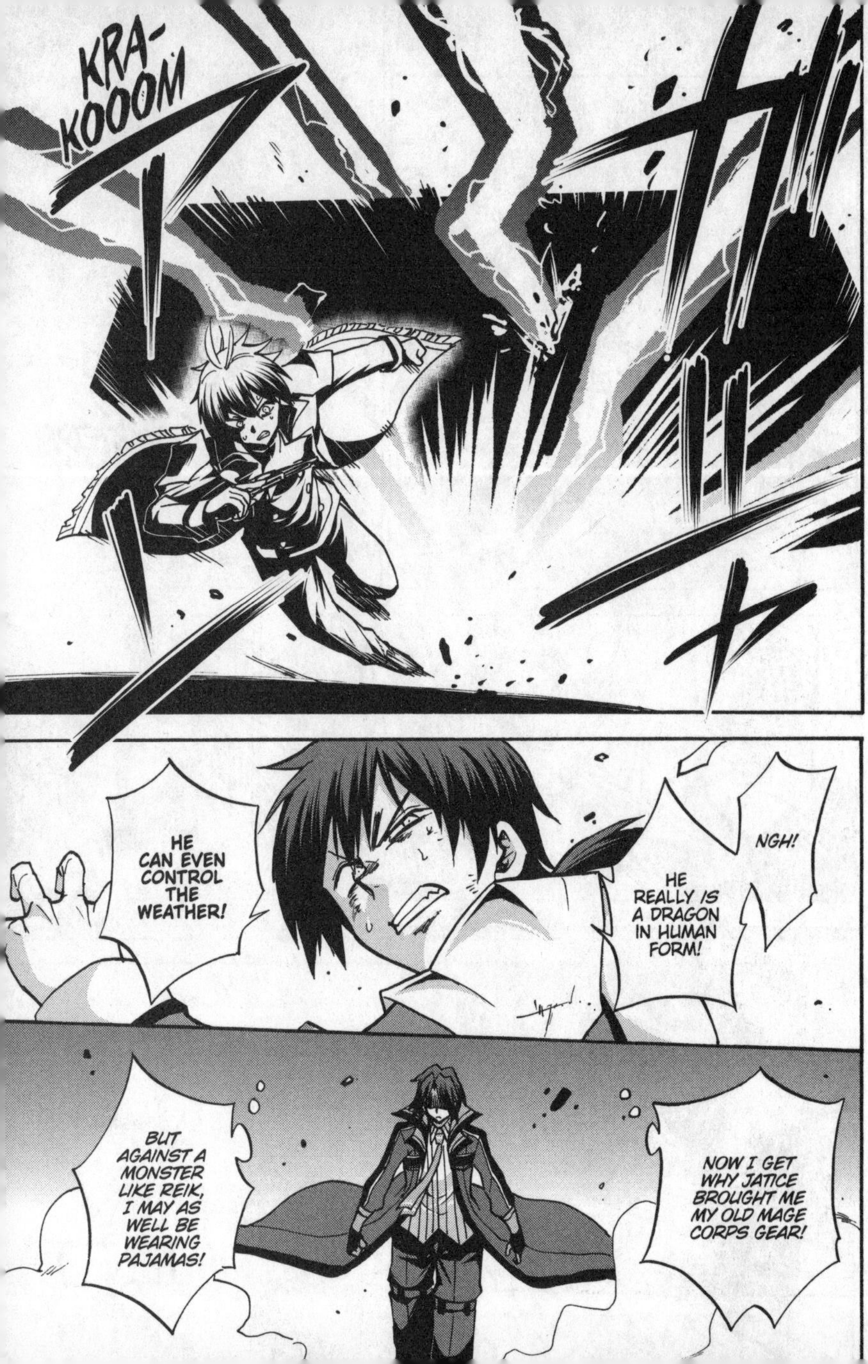
KRA-KOOOM
NGH!
HE REALLY IS A DRAGON IN HUMAN FORM!
HE CAN EVEN CONTROL THE WEATHER!
NOW I GET WHY JATICE BROUGHT ME MY OLD MAGE CORPS GEAR!
BUT AGAINST A MONSTER LIKE REIK, I MAY AS WELL BE WEARING PAJAMAS!

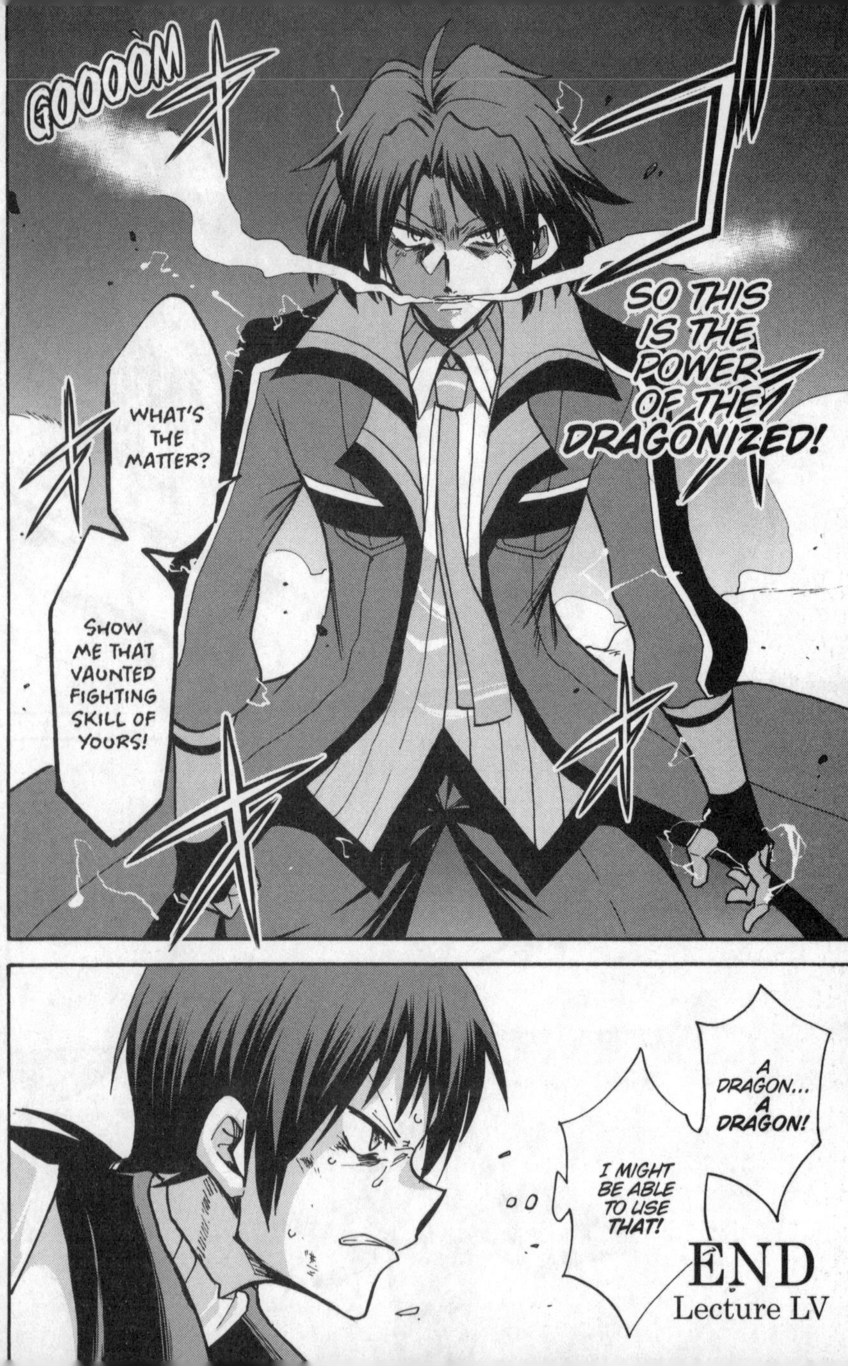
GOOOÒM
SO THIS IS THE POWER OF THE DRAGONIZED!
WHAT'S THE MATTER?
SHOW ME THAT VAUNTED FIGHTING SKILL OF YOURS!
A DRAGON... A DRAGON!
I MIGHT BE ABLE TO USE THAT!
END
Lecture LV

Akashic Records
o f *Bastard* Magic *Instructor*

Akashic Records
o f *Bastard* Magic *Instructor*

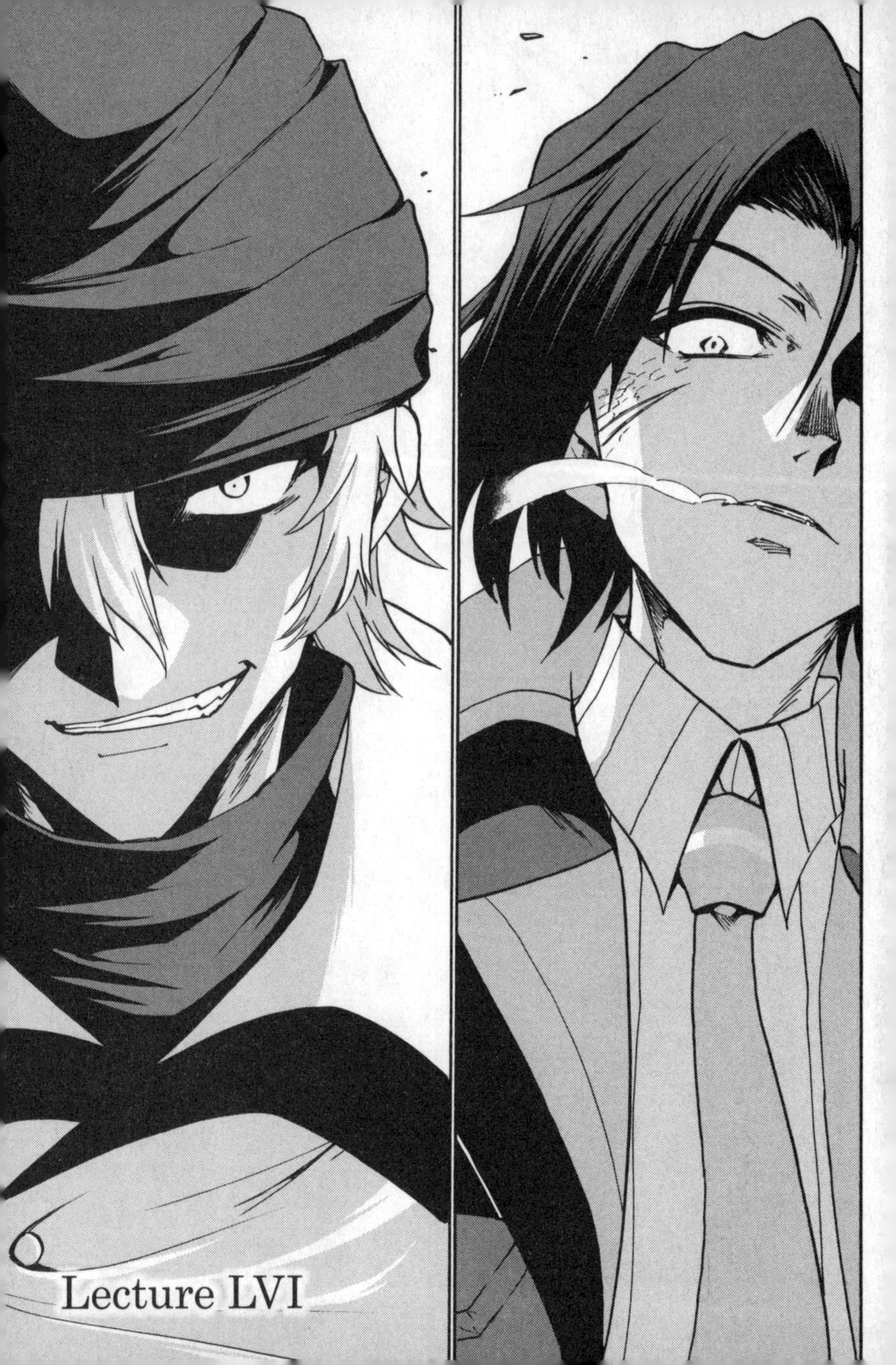

Lecture LVI

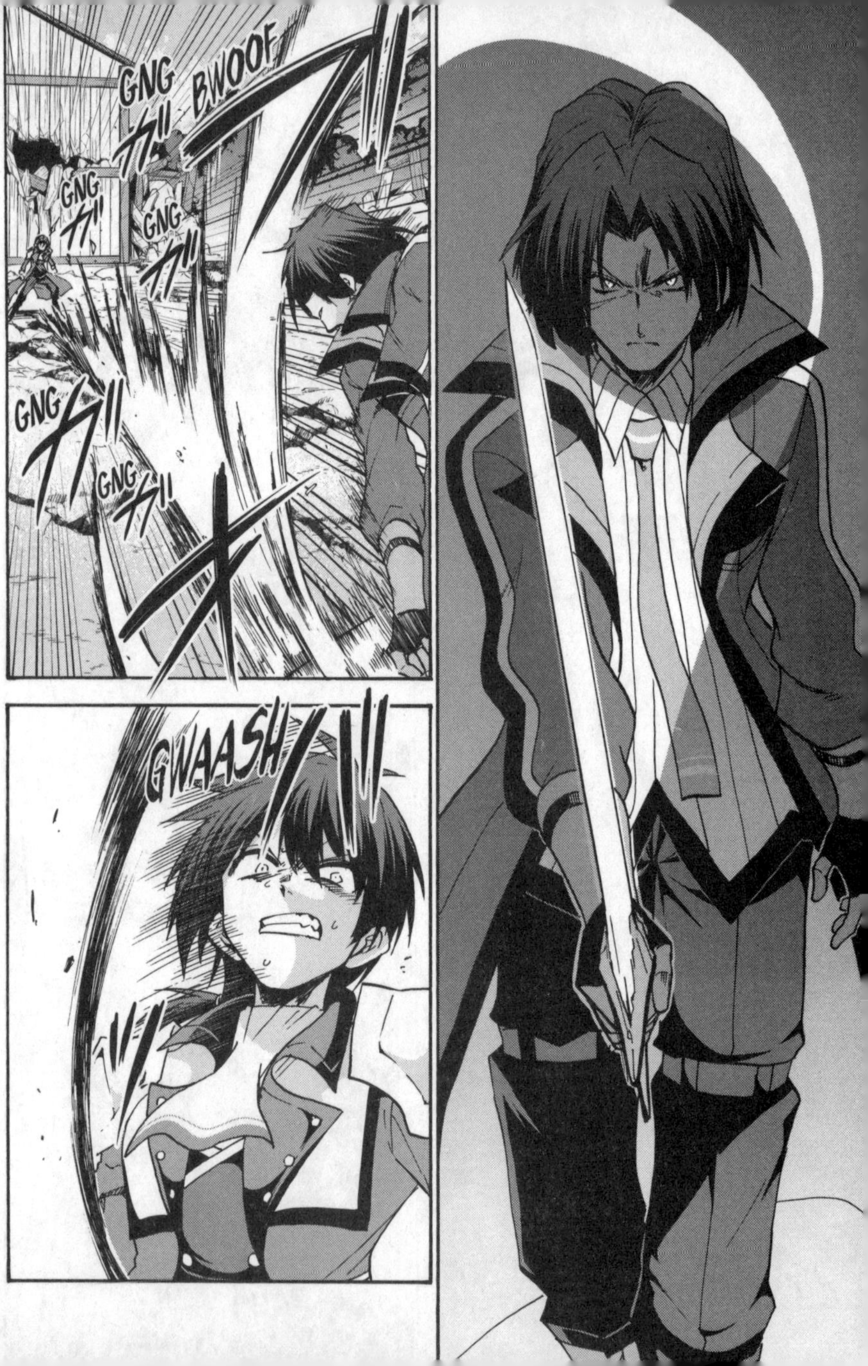

GNG ガ
BWOOF
GNG ガ
GNG ガ
GNG ガ
GNG ガ
GWAASH

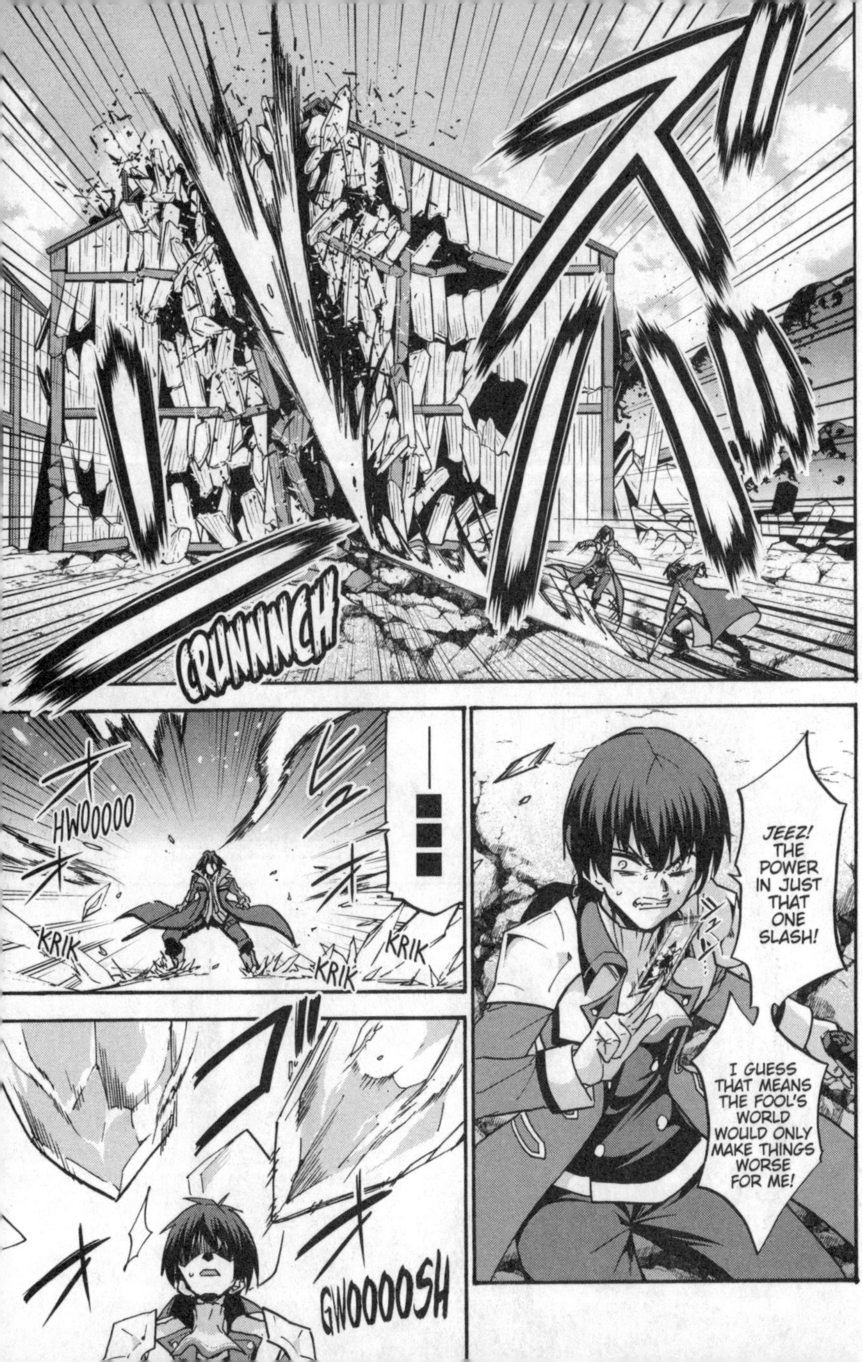
CRUNNNCH
JEEZ! THE POWER IN JUST THAT ONE SLASH!
I GUESS THAT MEANS THE FOOL'S WORLD WOULD ONLY MAKE THINGS WORSE FOR ME!
HWOOOOO
KRIK
KRIK
KRIK
GWOOOOSH

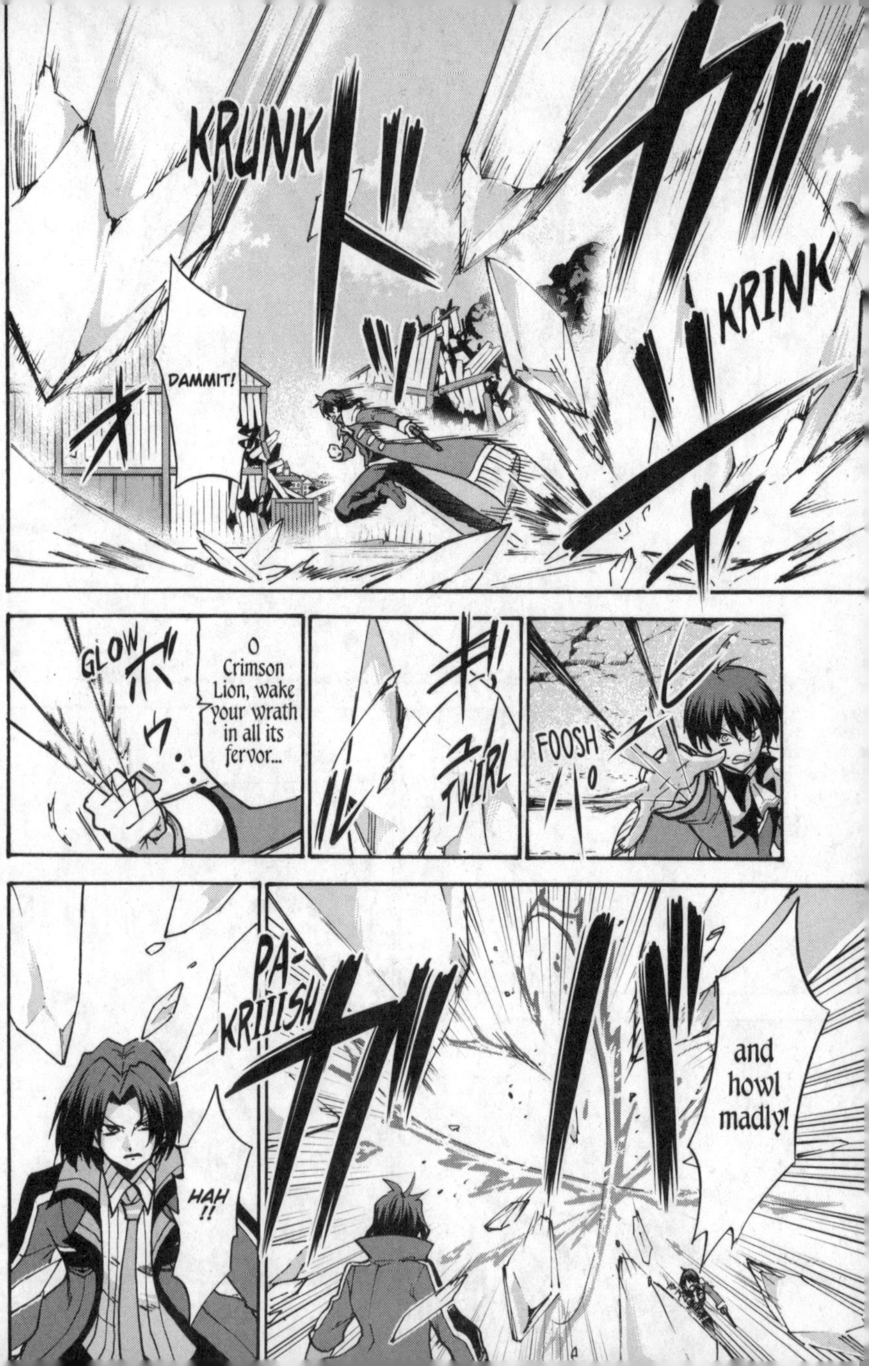

KRUNK
KRINK
DAMMIT!
FOOSH
TWIRL
GLOW
O Crimson Lion, wake your wrath in all its fervor...
and howl madly!
PA-KRIIISH
HAH!!

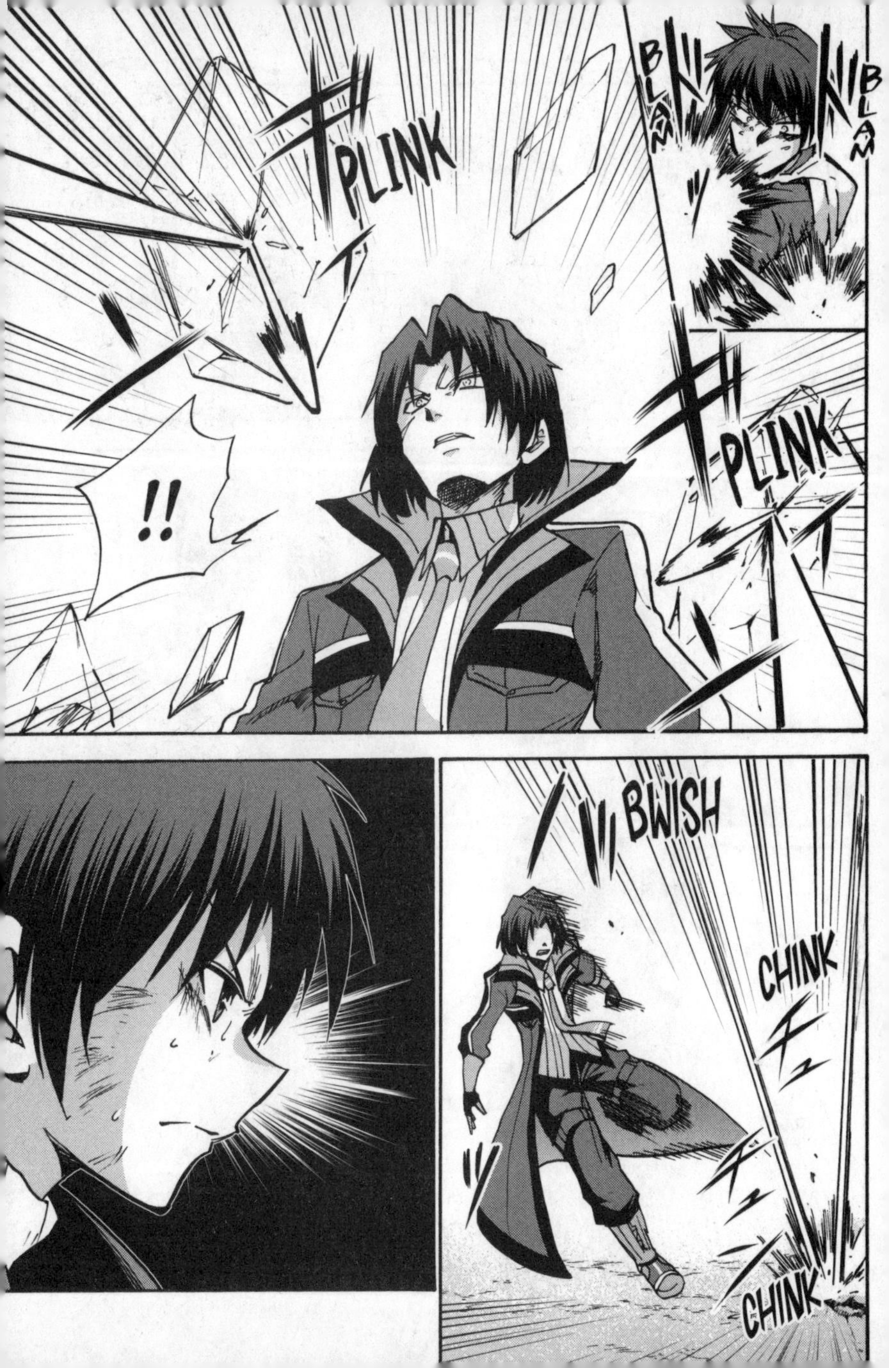
BLAM
BLAM
PLINK
PLINK
!!
BWISH
CHINK
CHINK

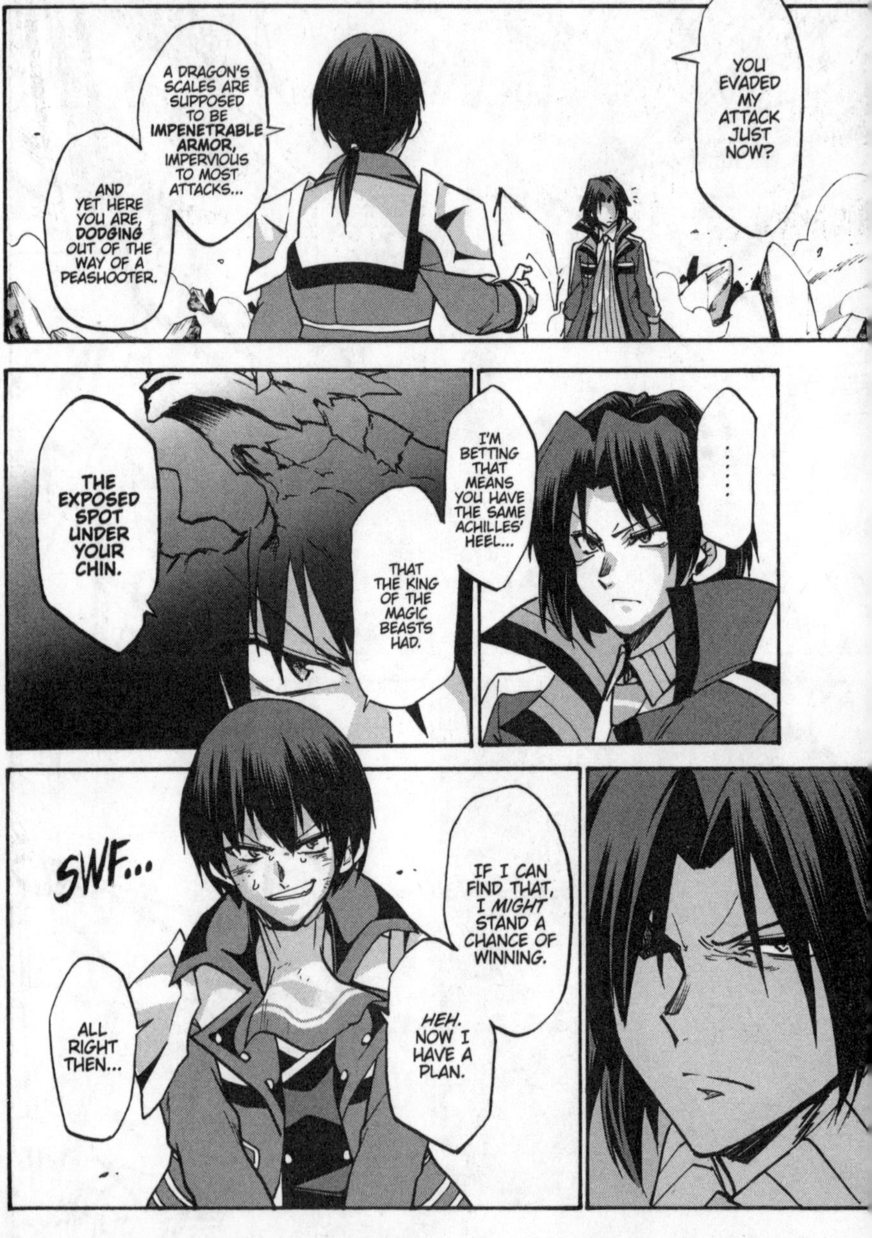
YOU EVADED MY ATTACK JUST NOW?
A DRAGON'S SCALES ARE SUPPOSED TO BE IMPENETRABLE ARMOR, IMPERVIOUS TO MOST ATTACKS...
AND YET HERE YOU ARE, DODGING OUT OF THE WAY OF A PEASHOOTER.
......
I'M BETTING THAT MEANS YOU HAVE THE SAME ACHILLES' HEEL...
THAT THE KING OF THE MAGIC BEASTS HAD.
THE EXPOSED SPOT UNDER YOUR CHIN.
IF I CAN FIND THAT, I MIGHT STAND A CHANCE OF WINNING.
HEH. NOW I HAVE A PLAN.
SWF...
ALL RIGHT THEN...

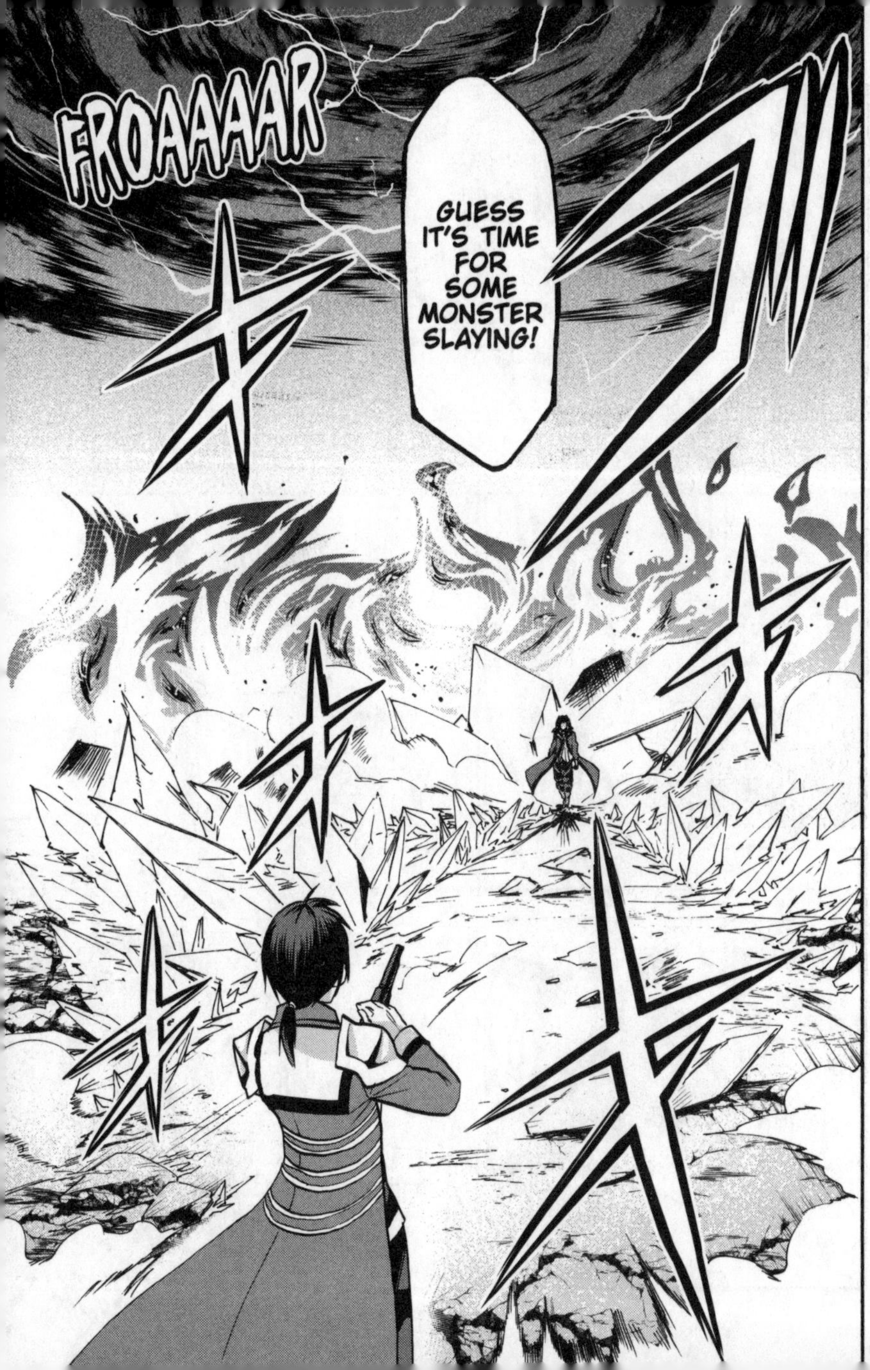
FROAAAAR
GUESS IT'S TIME FOR SOME MONSTER SLAYING!

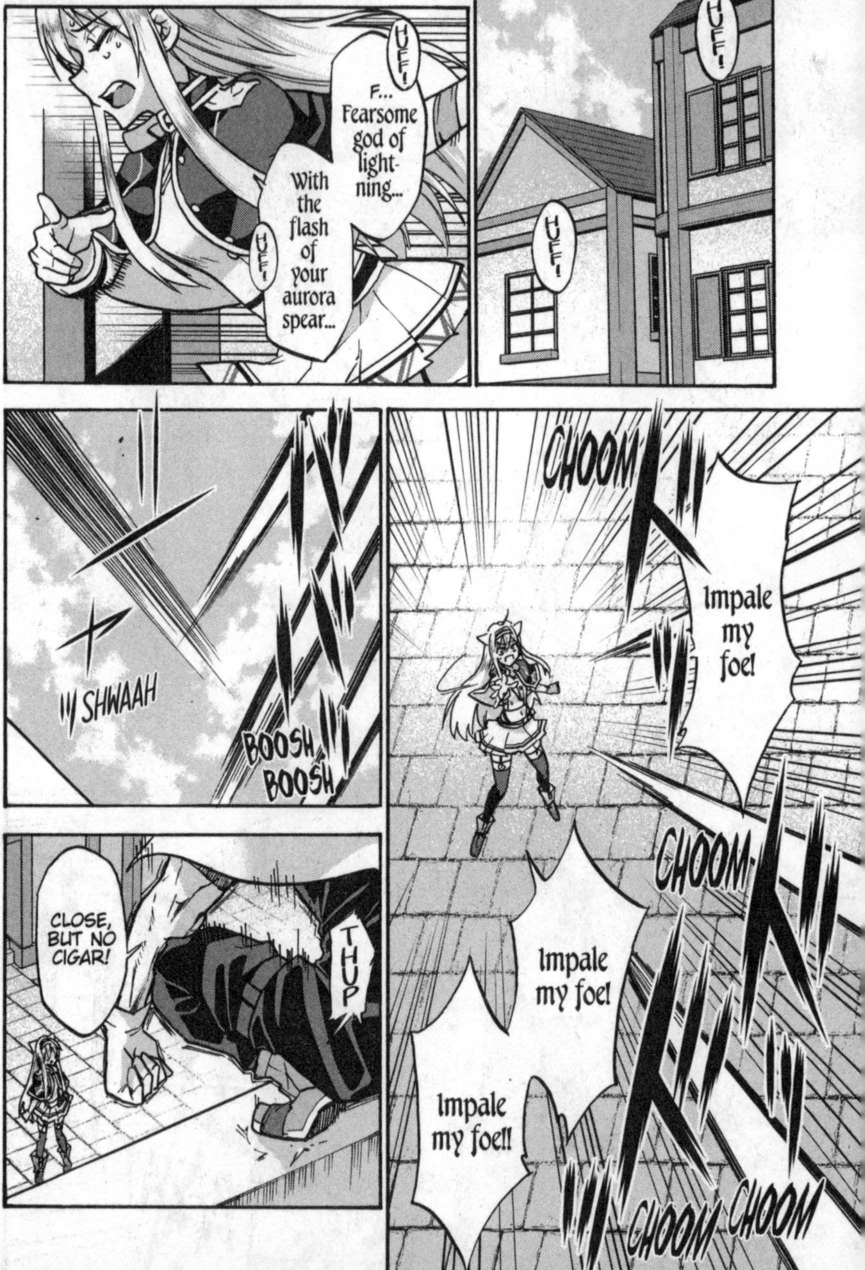
HUFF!
HUFF!
HUFF!
F... Fearsome god of lightning...
With the flash of your aurora spear...
HUFF!
CHOOM
Impale my foe!
CHOOM
Impale my foe!
Impale my foe!!
CHOOM CHOOM
SHWAAH
BOOSH BOOSH
CLOSE, BUT NO CIGAR!
THUP

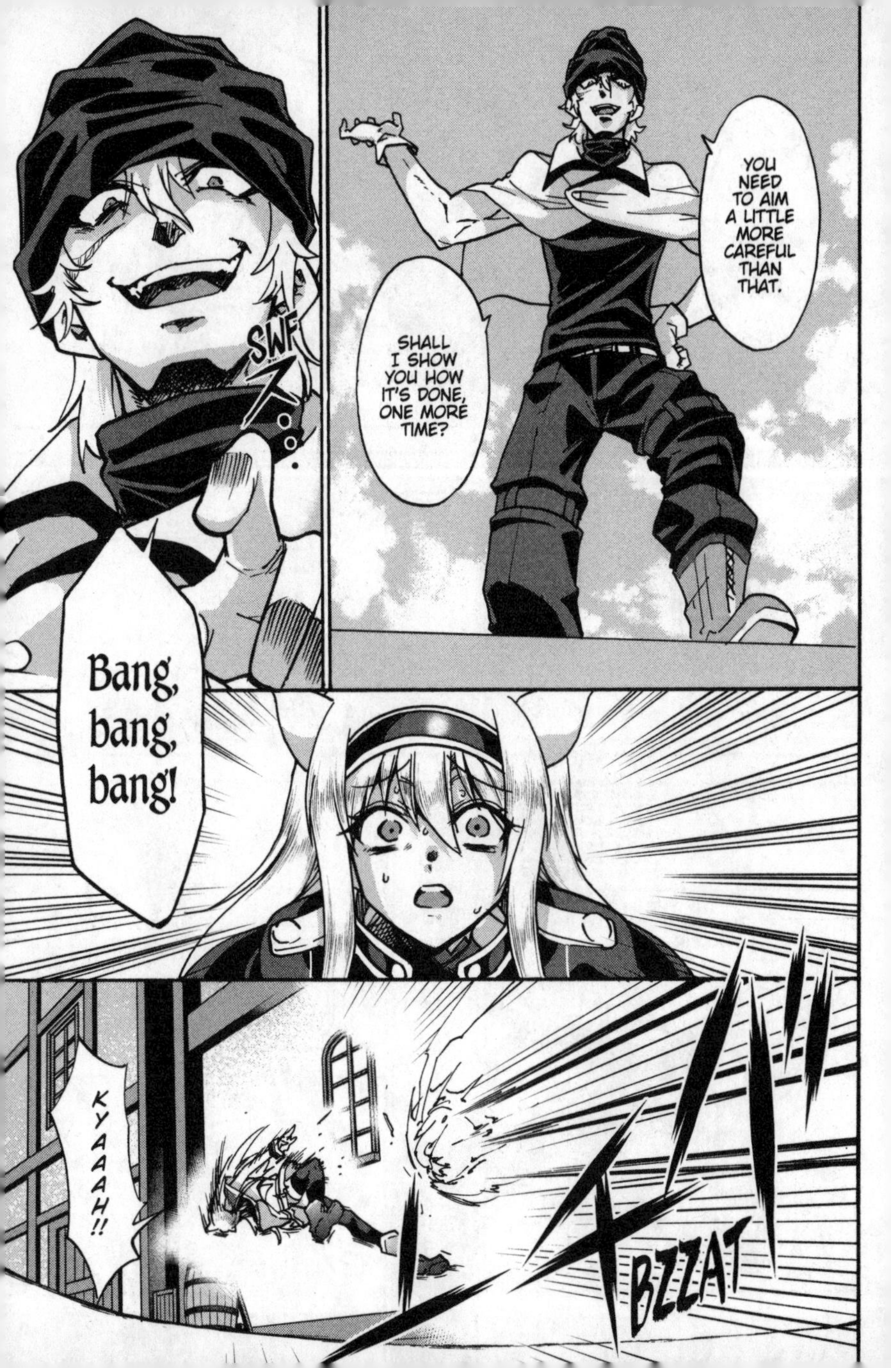
YOU NEED TO AIM A LITTLE MORE CAREFUL THAN THAT.
SHALL I SHOW YOU HOW IT'S DONE, ONE MORE TIME?
SWF
Bang, bang, bang!
BZZAT
KYAAAAH!!

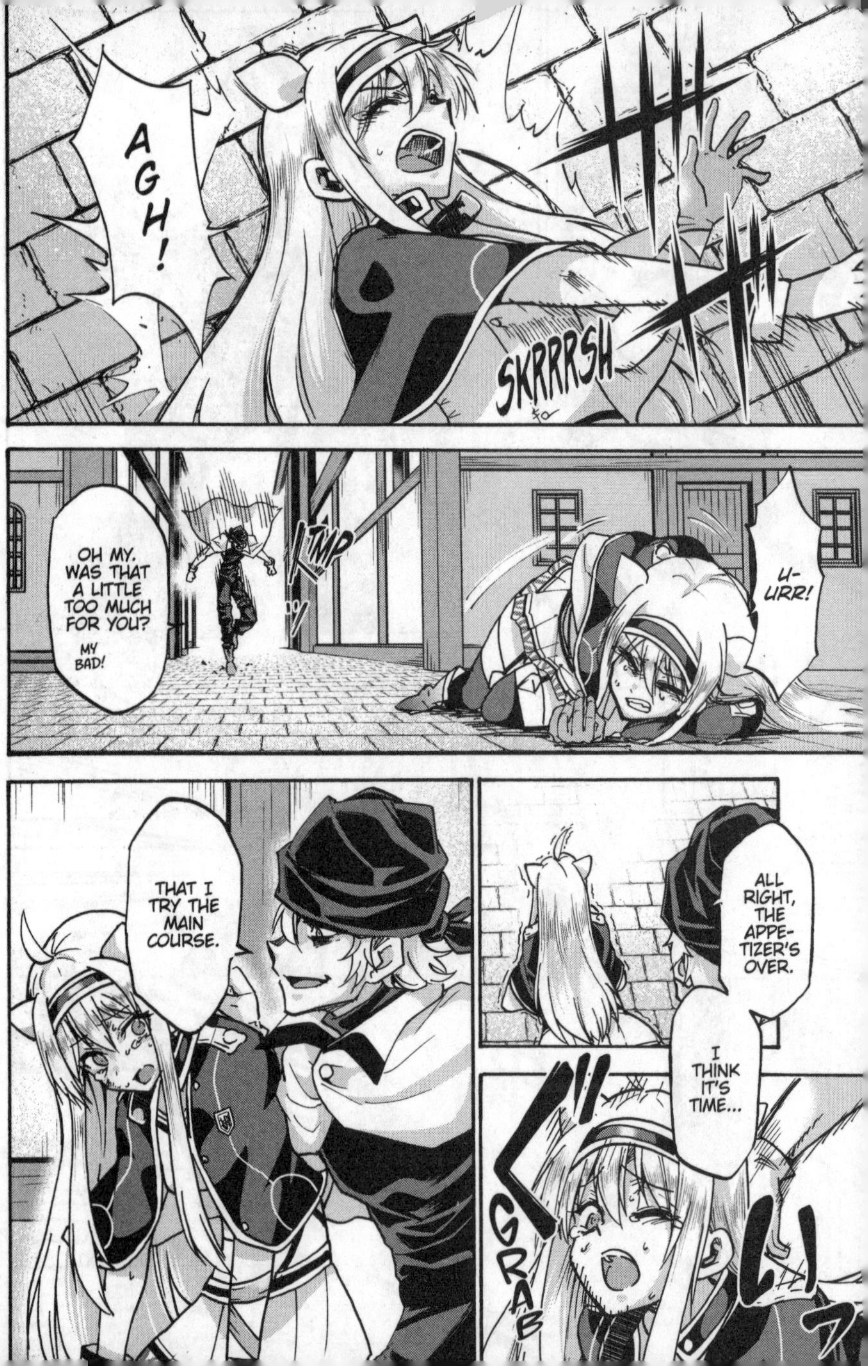
AGH!
SKRRRSH
U-URR!
TMP
OH MY. WAS THAT A LITTLE TOO MUCH FOR YOU?
MY BAD!
ALL RIGHT, THE APPETIZER'S OVER.
I THINK IT'S TIME...
THAT I TRY THE MAIN COURSE.
GRAB

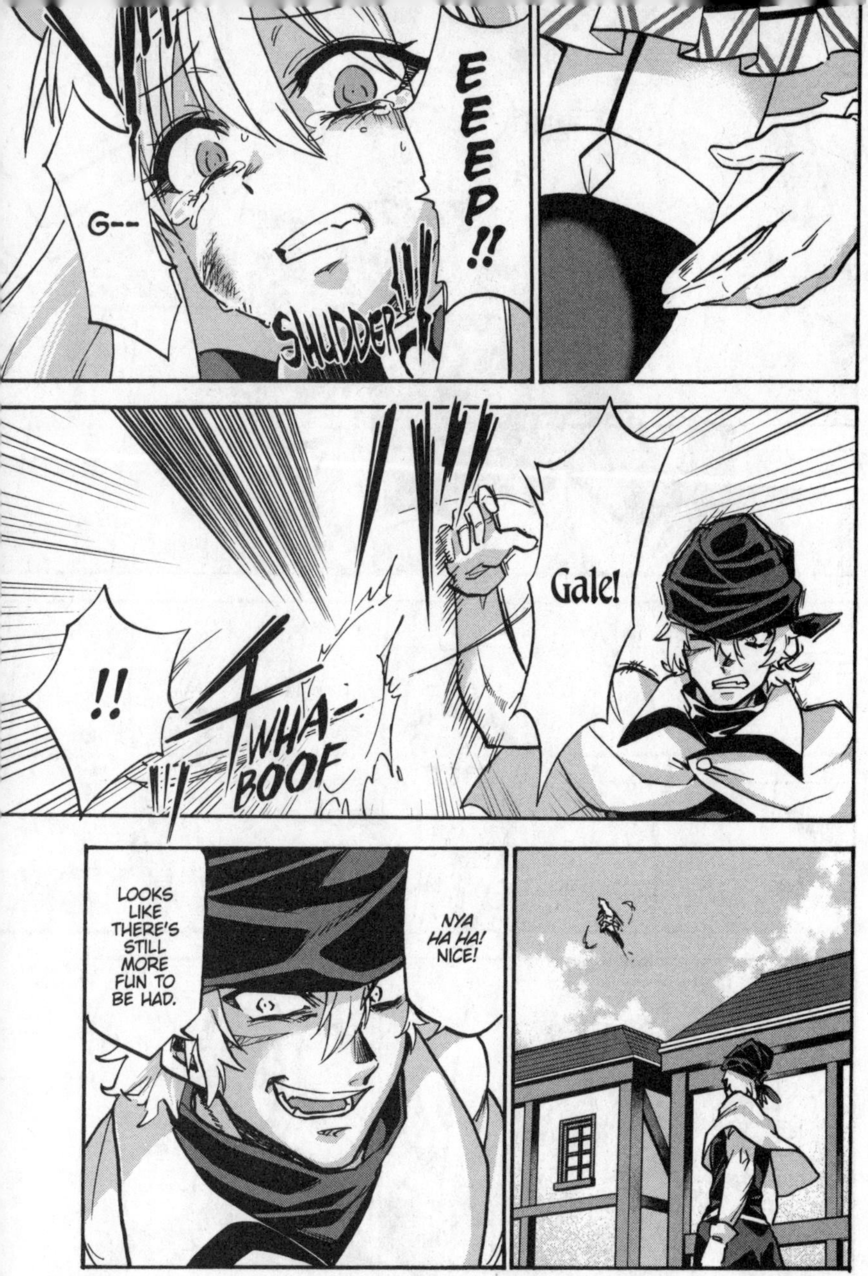
EEEEP!!
G---
SHUDDER
Gale!
!!
WHA BOOF
NYA HA HA! NICE!
LOOKS LIKE THERE'S STILL MORE FUN TO BE HAD.

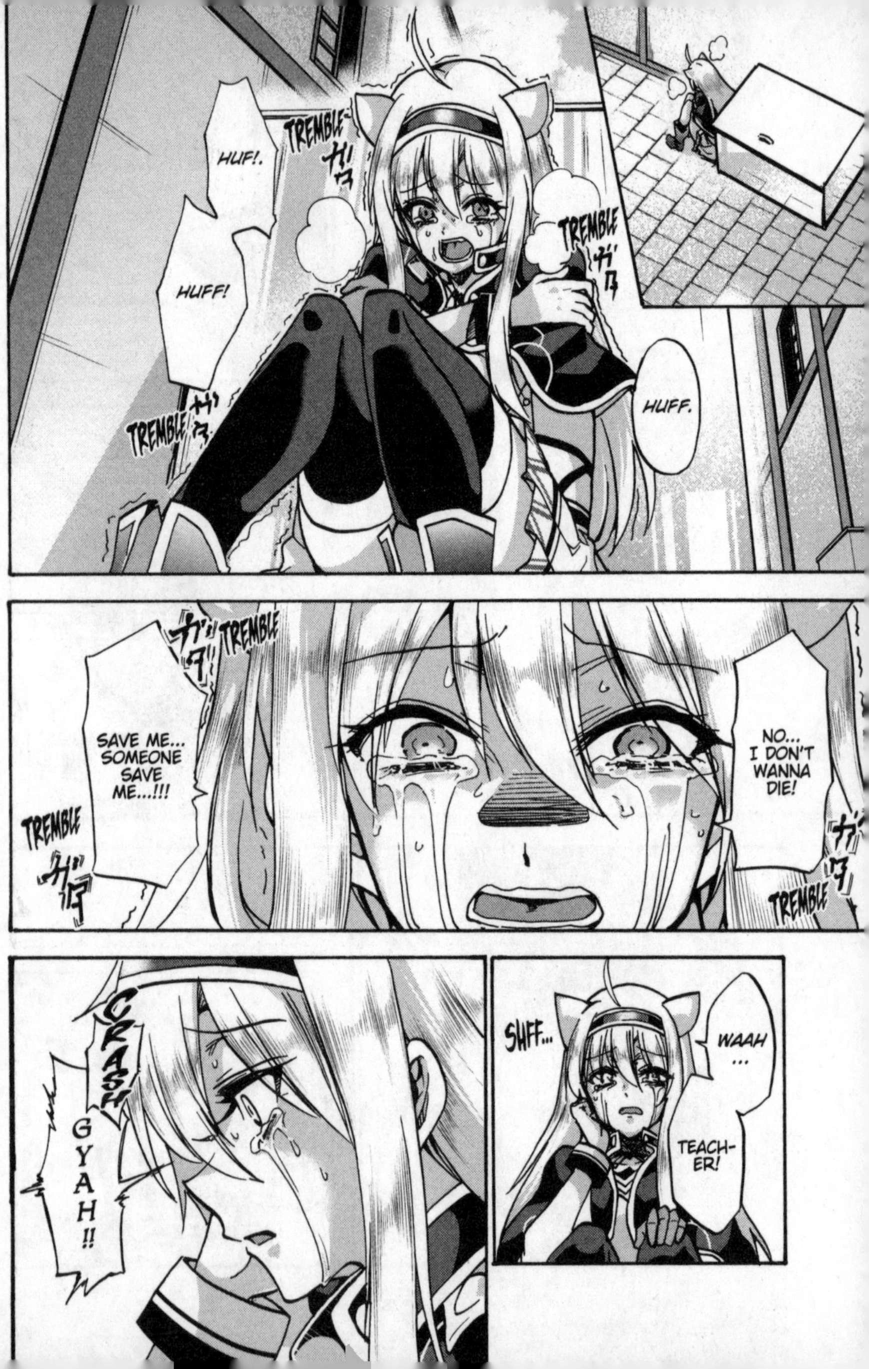
HUFF.
TREMBLE
HUFF!
HUF!.
TREMBLE
TREMBLE
NO... I DON'T WANNA DIE!
TREMBLE
SAVE ME... SOMEONE SAVE ME...!!!
TREMBLE
TREMBLE
WAAH ...
TEACH-ER!
SNIFF...
CRASH
GYAH!!

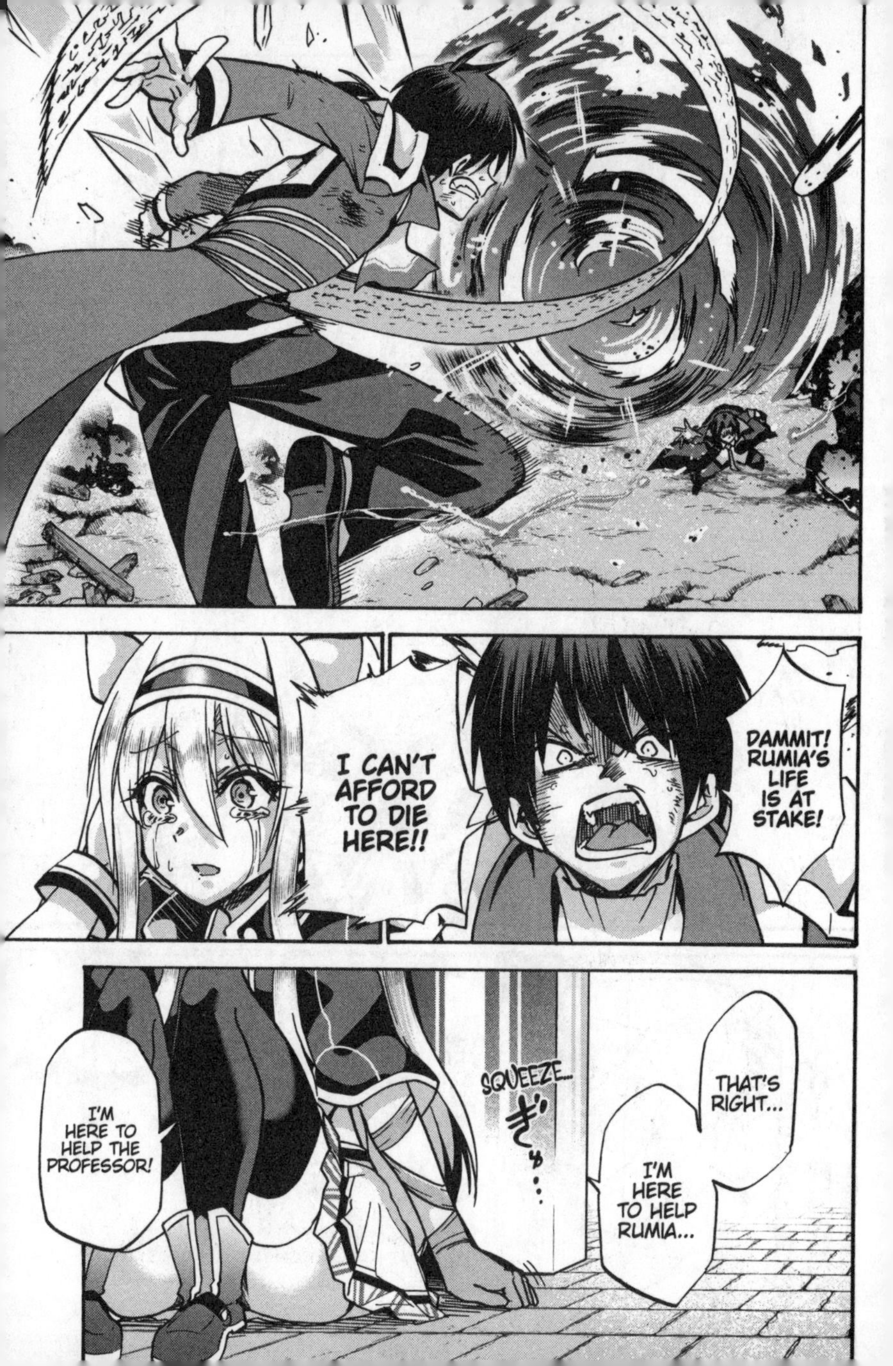
DAMMIT! RUMIA'S LIFE IS AT STAKE!
I CAN'T AFFORD TO DIE HERE!!
THAT'S RIGHT...
I'M HERE TO HELP RUMIA...
SQUEEZE...
I'M HERE TO HELP THE PROFESSOR!

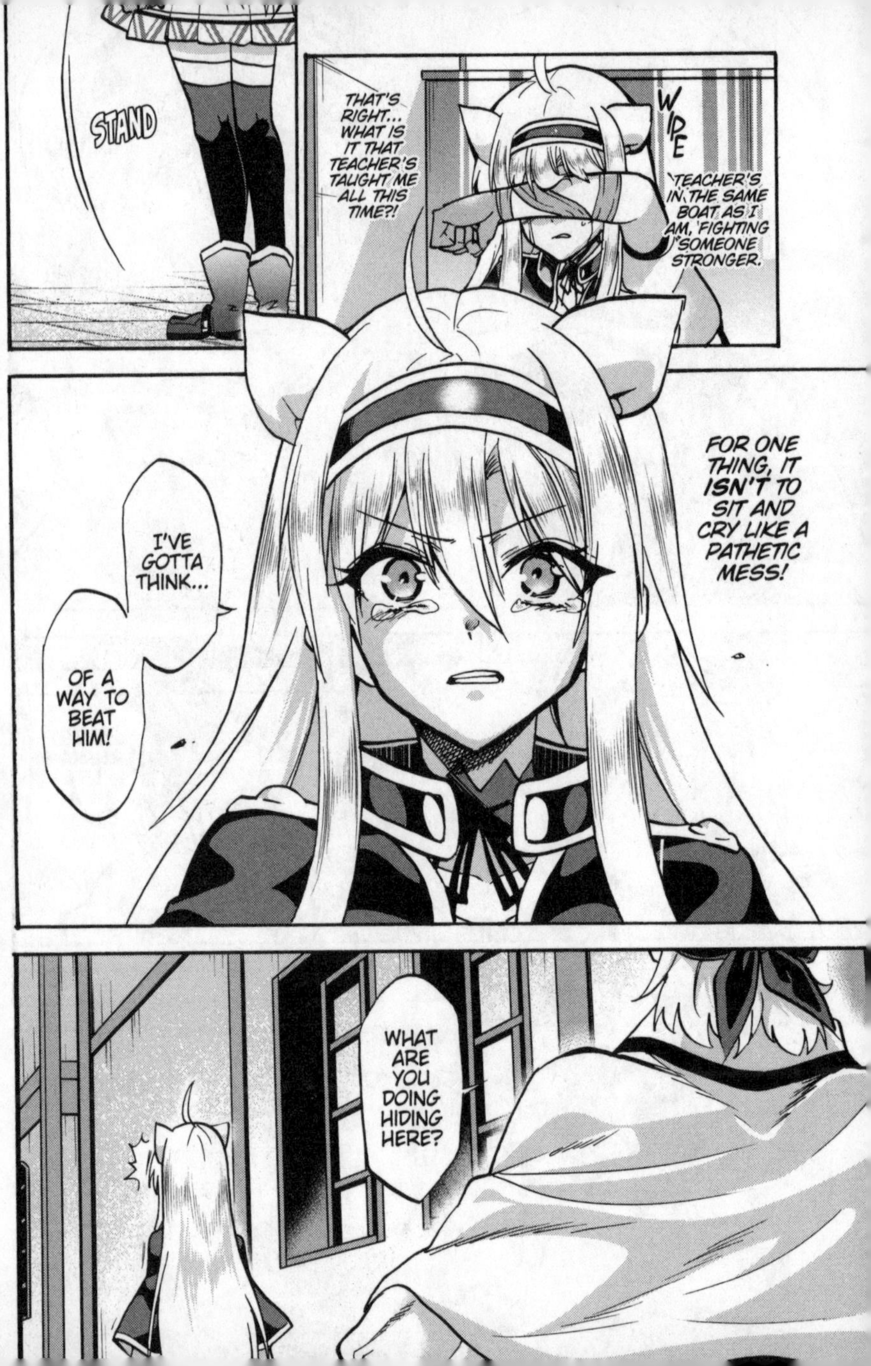
STAND
THAT'S RIGHT... WHAT IS IT THAT TEACHER'S TAUGHT ME ALL THIS TIME?!
WIPE
TEACHER'S IN THE SAME BOAT AS I AM, FIGHTING SOMEONE STRONGER.
FOR ONE THING, IT ISN'T TO SIT AND CRY LIKE A PATHETIC MESS!
I'VE GOTTA THINK...
OF A WAY TO BEAT HIM!
WHAT ARE YOU DOING HIDING HERE?

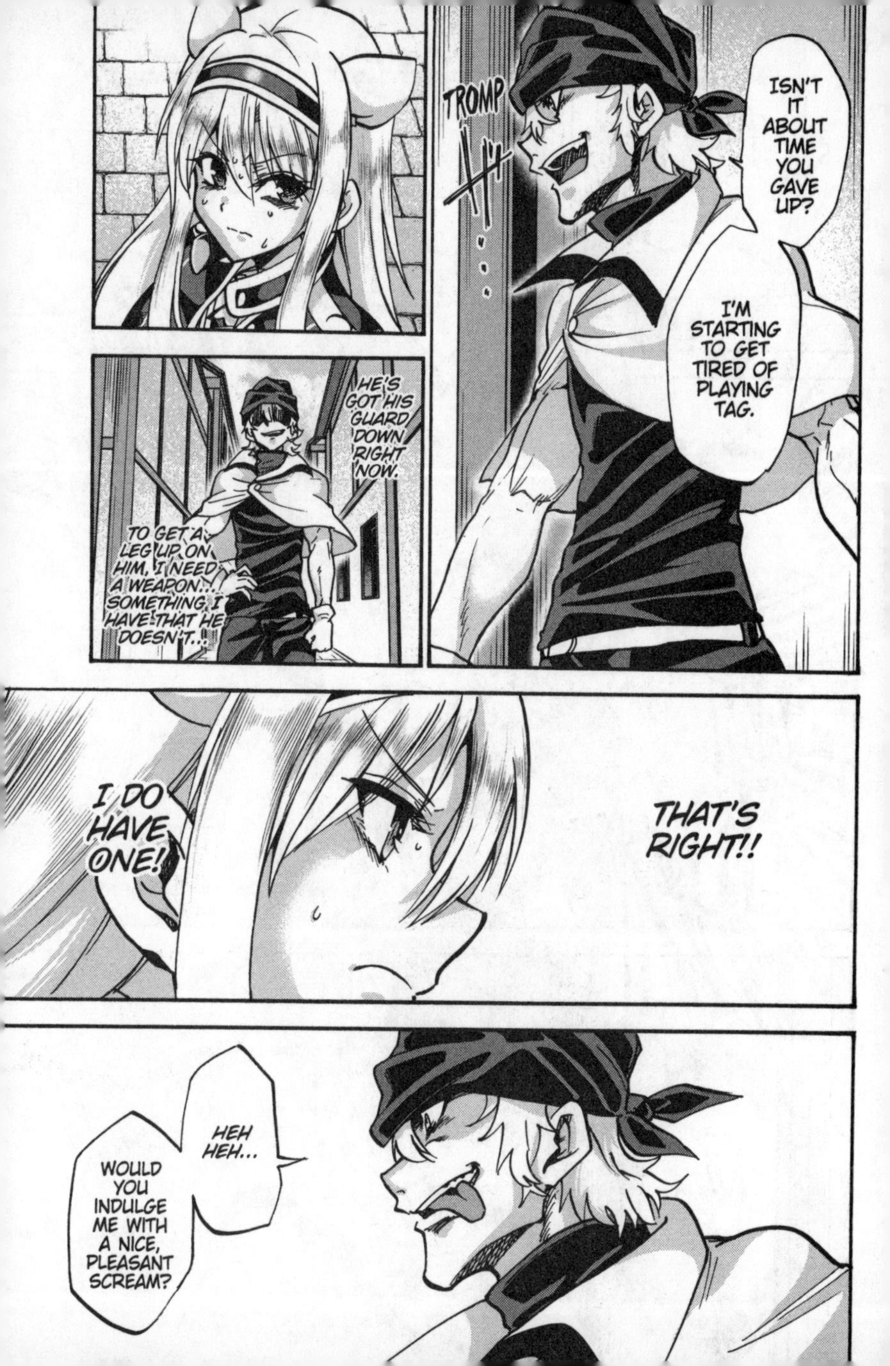
TROMP
ISN'T IT ABOUT TIME YOU GAVE UP?
I'M STARTING TO GET TIRED OF PLAYING TAG.
HE'S GOT HIS GUARD DOWN RIGHT NOW.
TO GET A LEG UP ON HIM, I NEED A WEAPON... SOMETHING I HAVE THAT HE DOESN'T...
THAT'S RIGHT!!
I DO HAVE ONE!
HEH HEH...
WOULD YOU INDULGE ME WITH A NICE, PLEASANT SCREAM?

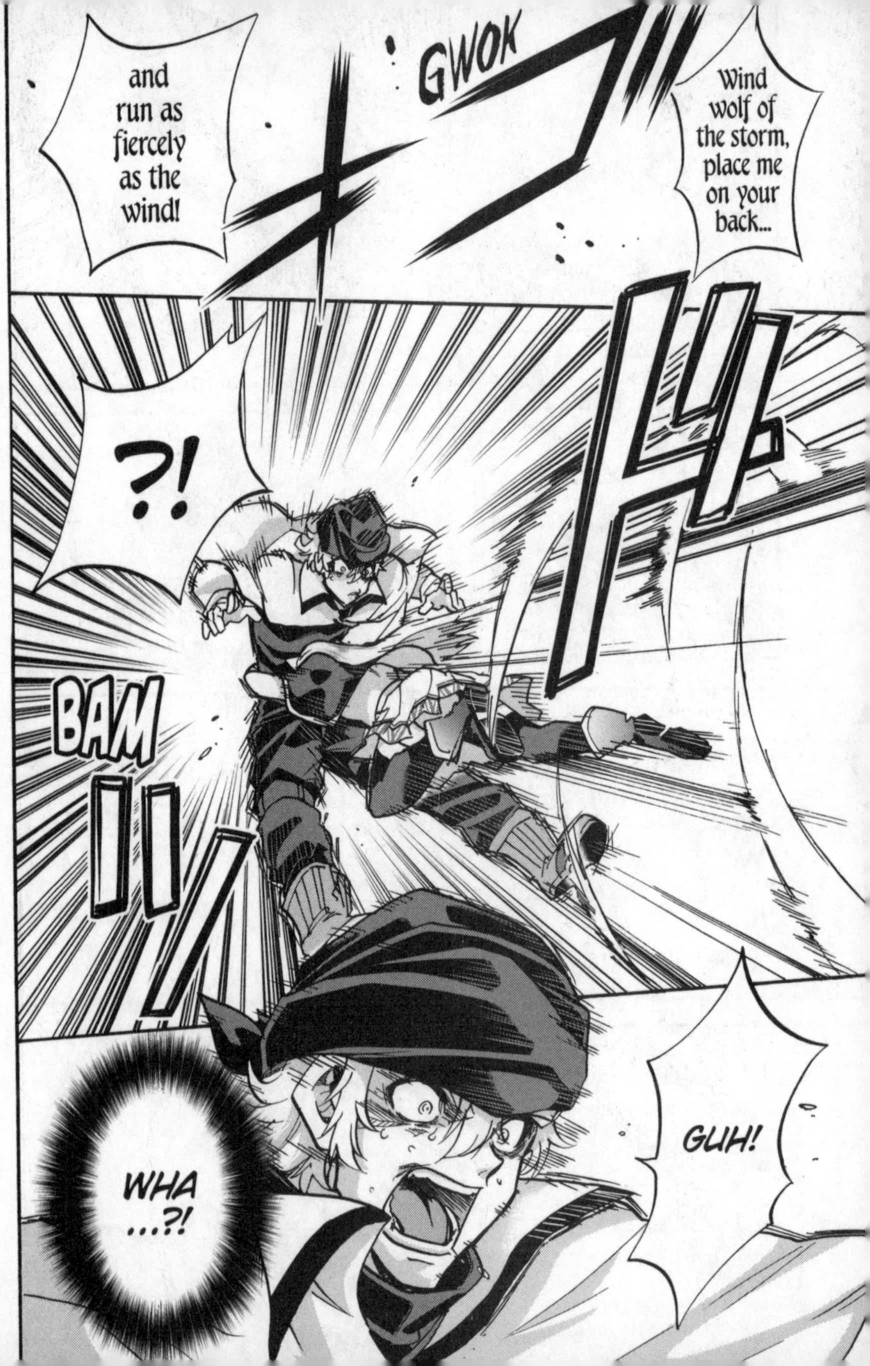
GWOK
Wind wolf of the storm, place me on your back...
and run as fiercely as the wind!
?!
BAM
GUH!
WHA ...?!

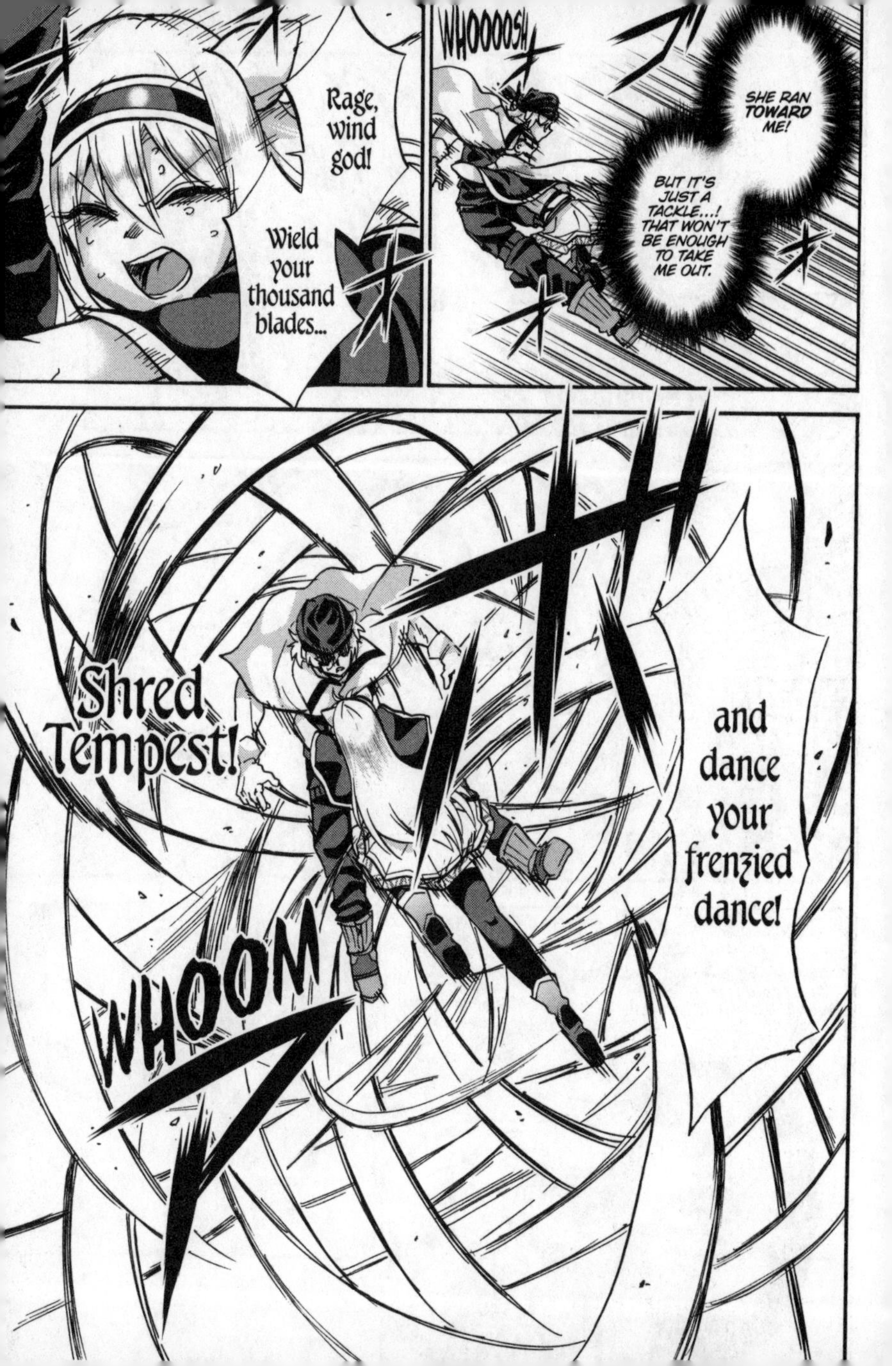
WHOOOOSH
SHE RAN TOWARD ME!
BUT IT'S JUST A TACKLE...! THAT WON'T BE ENOUGH TO TAKE ME OUT.
Rage, wind god!
Wield your thousand blades...
and dance your frenzied dance!
Shred Tempest!
WHOOM

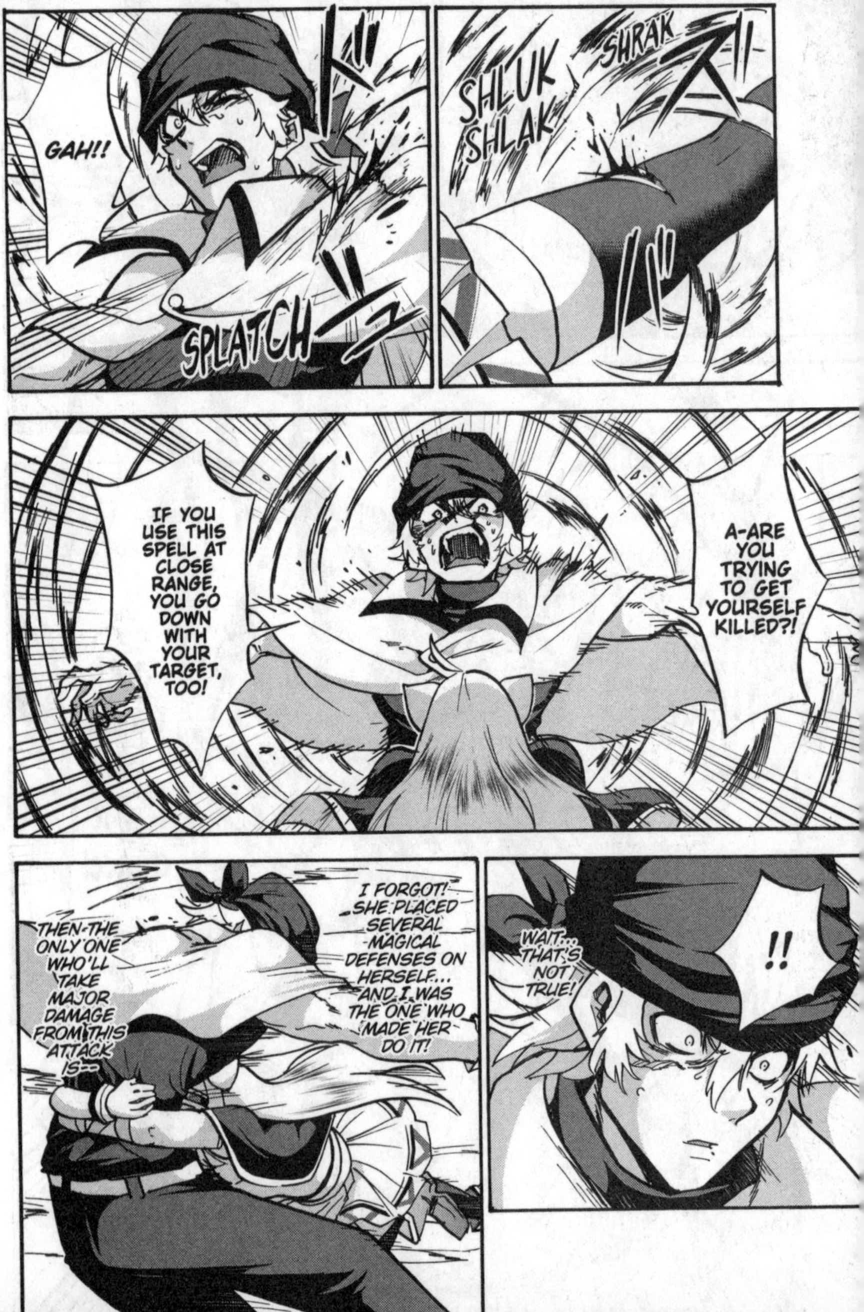
SHLUK
SHLAK
SHRAK
GAH!!
SPLATCH
A-ARE YOU TRYING TO GET YOURSELF KILLED?!
IF YOU USE THIS SPELL AT CLOSE RANGE, YOU GO DOWN WITH YOUR TARGET, TOO!
!!
WAIT... THAT'S NOT TRUE!
I FORGOT! SHE PLACED SEVERAL MAGICAL DEFENSES ON HERSELF... AND I WAS THE ONE WHO MADE HER DO IT!
THEN THE ONLY ONE WHO'LL TAKE MAJOR DAMAGE FROM THIS ATTACK IS--

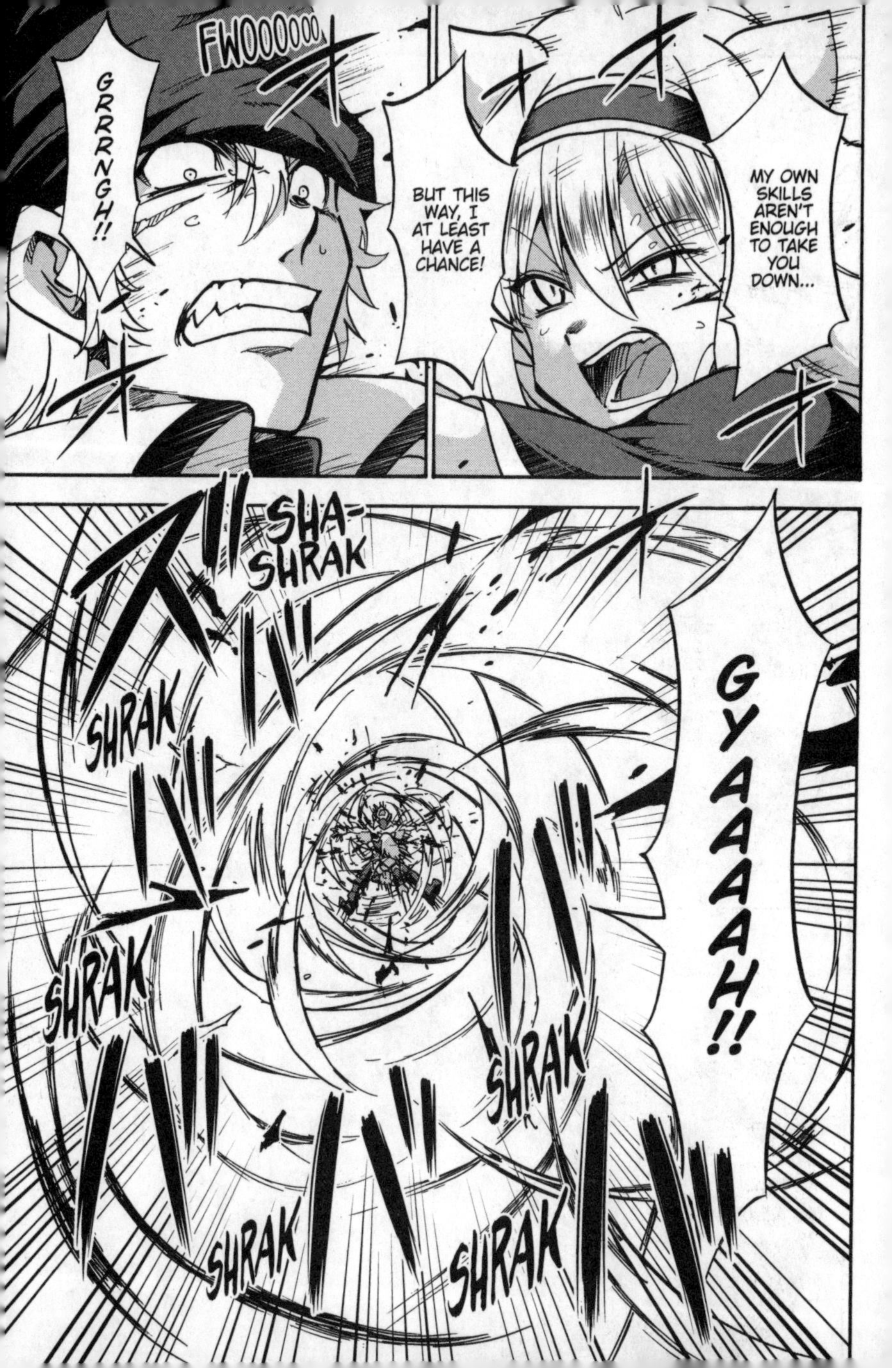
MY OWN SKILLS AREN'T ENOUGH TO TAKE YOU DOWN...
BUT THIS WAY, I AT LEAST HAVE A CHANCE!
FWOOOOOO
GRRRNGH!!
GYAAAAAH!!
SHA-SHRAK
SHRAK
SHRAK
SHRAK
SHRAK
SHRAK

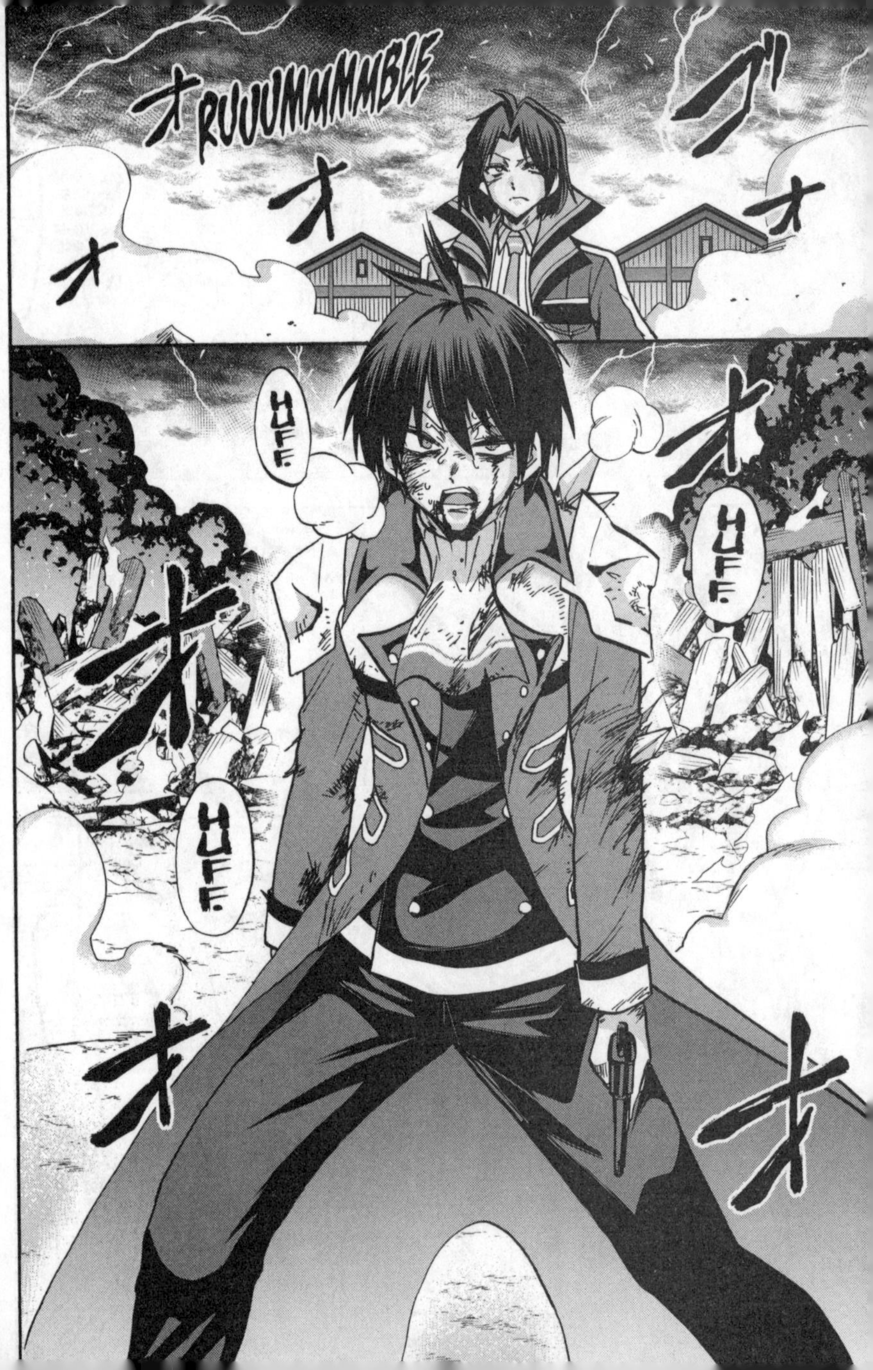
ゴ
オ
オ
RUUUMMMMBLE
オ
オ
HUFF.
HUFF.
オ
HUFF.
オ
オ
オ

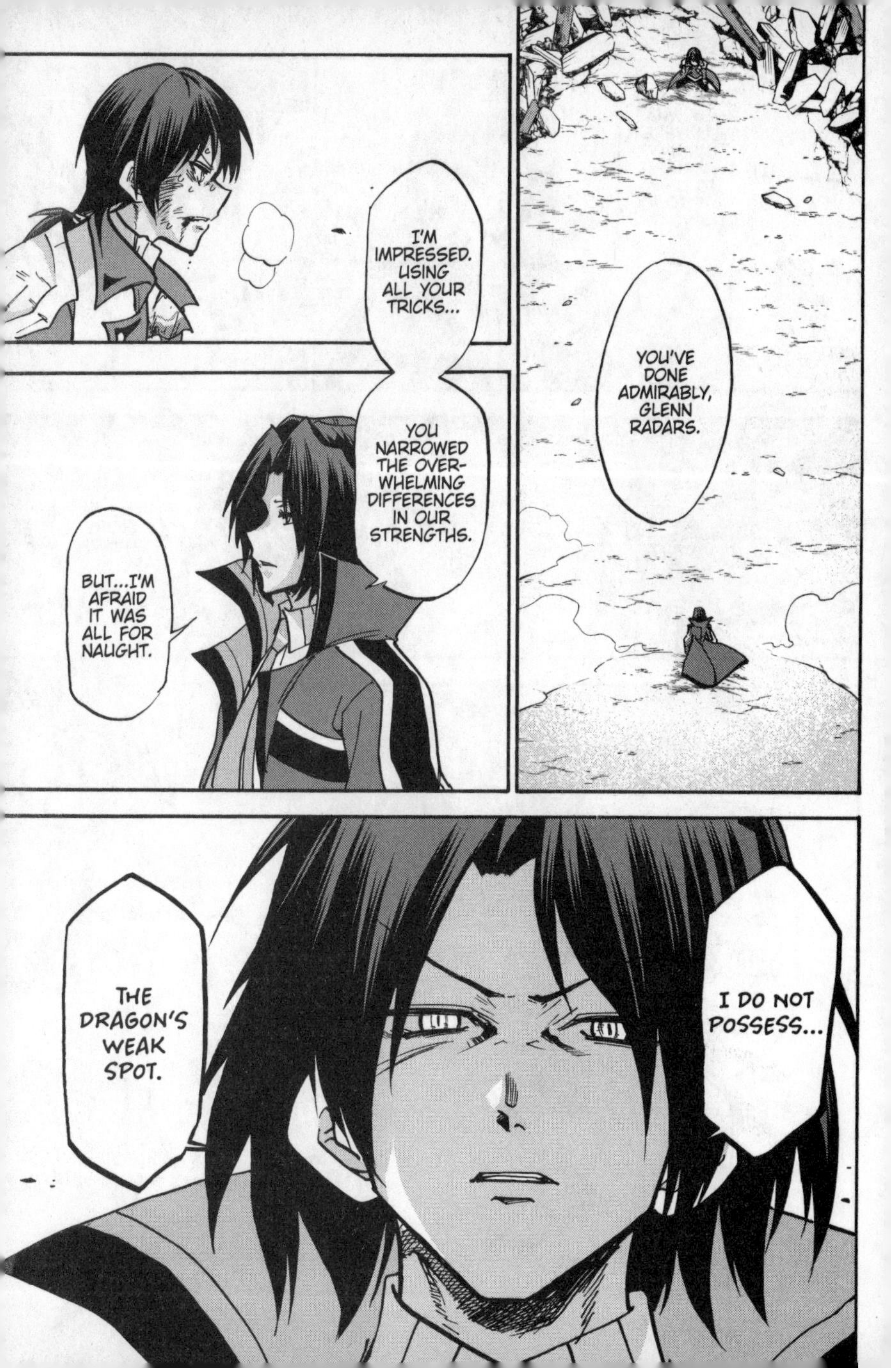
YOU'VE DONE ADMIRABLY, GLENN RADARS.
I'M IMPRESSED. USING ALL YOUR TRICKS...
YOU NARROWED THE OVER-WHELMING DIFFERENCES IN OUR STRENGTHS.
BUT...I'M AFRAID IT WAS ALL FOR NAUGHT.
I DO NOT POSSESS...
THE DRAGON'S WEAK SPOT.

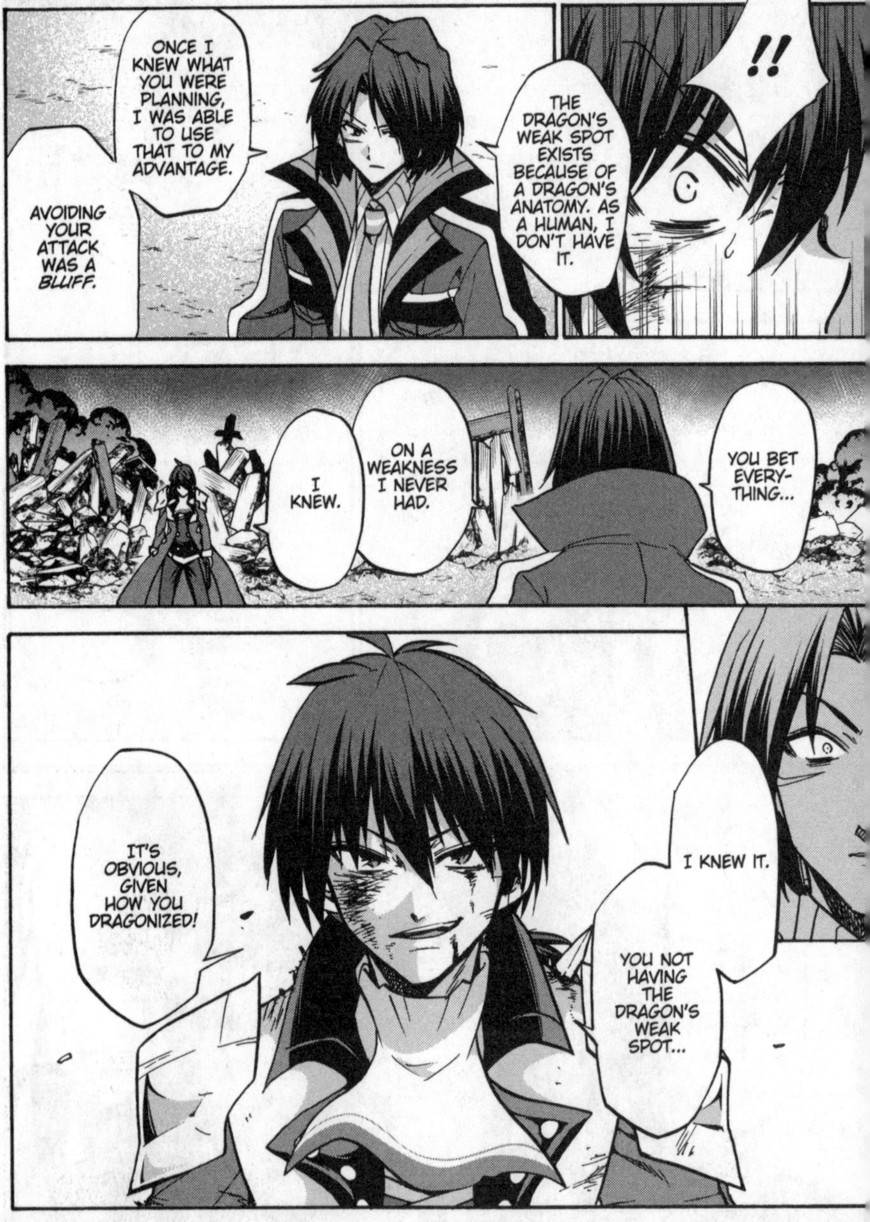
!!
THE DRAGON'S WEAK SPOT EXISTS BECAUSE OF A DRAGON'S ANATOMY. AS A HUMAN, I DON'T HAVE IT.
ONCE I KNEW WHAT YOU WERE PLANNING, I WAS ABLE TO USE THAT TO MY ADVANTAGE.
AVOIDING YOUR ATTACK WAS A *BLUFF*.
YOU BET EVERYTHING...
ON A WEAKNESS I NEVER HAD.
I KNEW.
I KNEW IT.
YOU NOT HAVING THE DRAGON'S WEAK SPOT...
IT'S OBVIOUS, GIVEN HOW YOU DRAGONIZED!

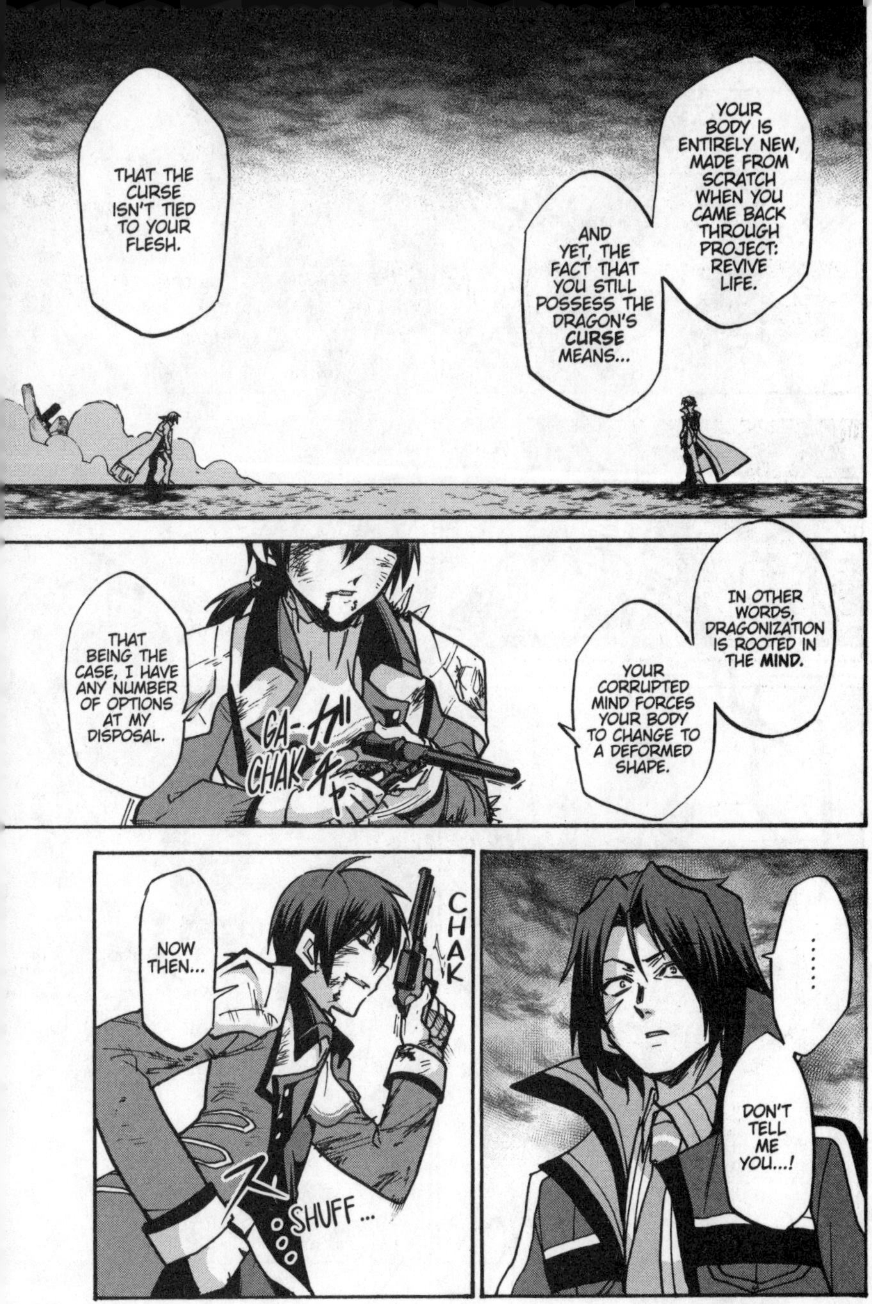
YOUR BODY IS ENTIRELY NEW, MADE FROM SCRATCH WHEN YOU CAME BACK THROUGH PROJECT: REVIVE LIFE.
AND YET, THE FACT THAT YOU STILL POSSESS THE DRAGON'S CURSE MEANS...
THAT THE CURSE ISN'T TIED TO YOUR FLESH.
IN OTHER WORDS, DRAGONIZATION IS ROOTED IN THE MIND.
YOUR CORRUPTED MIND FORCES YOUR BODY TO CHANGE TO A DEFORMED SHAPE.
GA-CHAK
THAT BEING THE CASE, I HAVE ANY NUMBER OF OPTIONS AT MY DISPOSAL.
NOW THEN...
CHAK
SHUFF...
......
DON'T TELL ME YOU...!

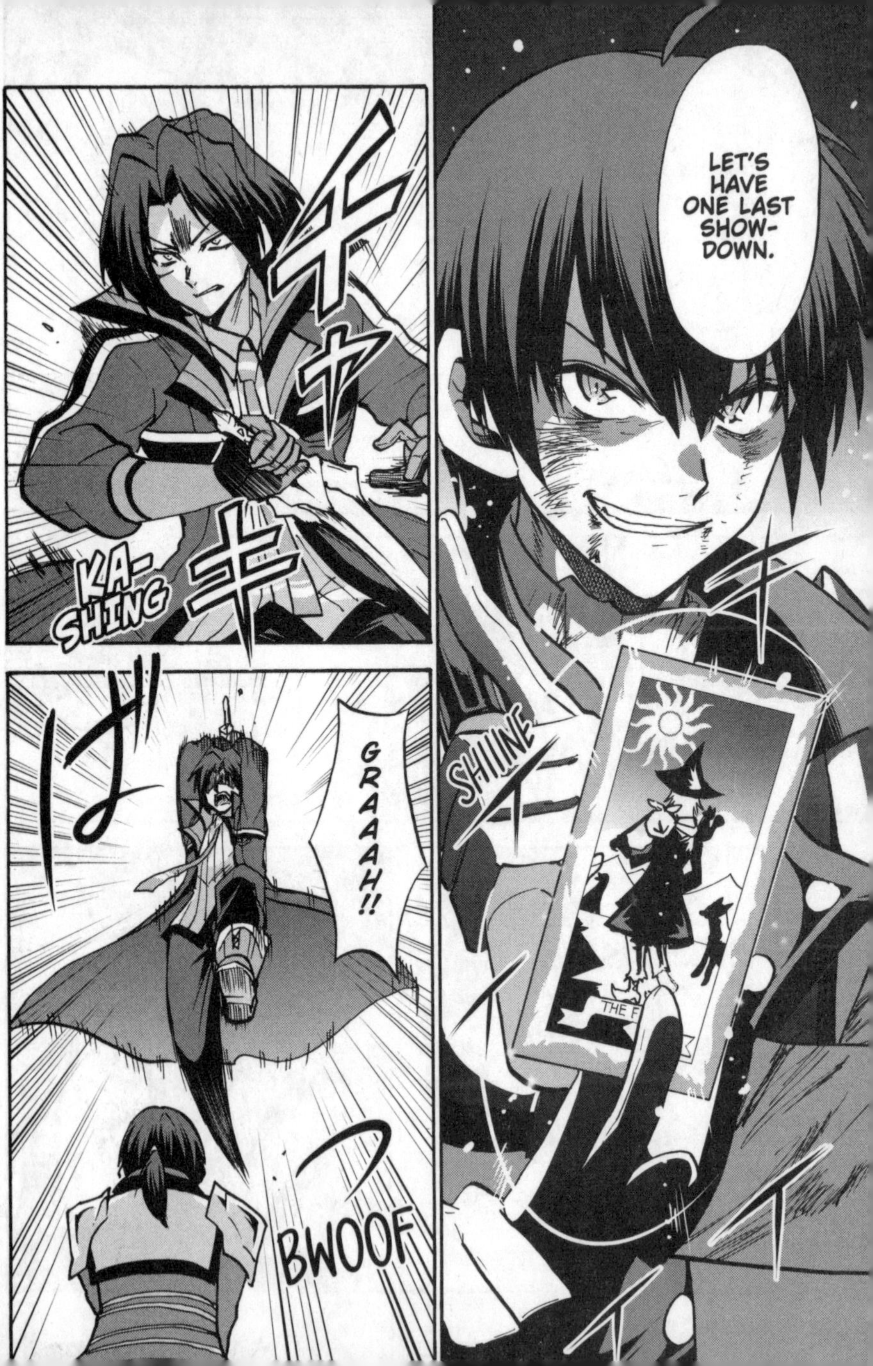

LET'S HAVE ONE LAST SHOW-DOWN.
SHIINE
THE F
KA-SHING
GRAAAAH!!
BWOOF

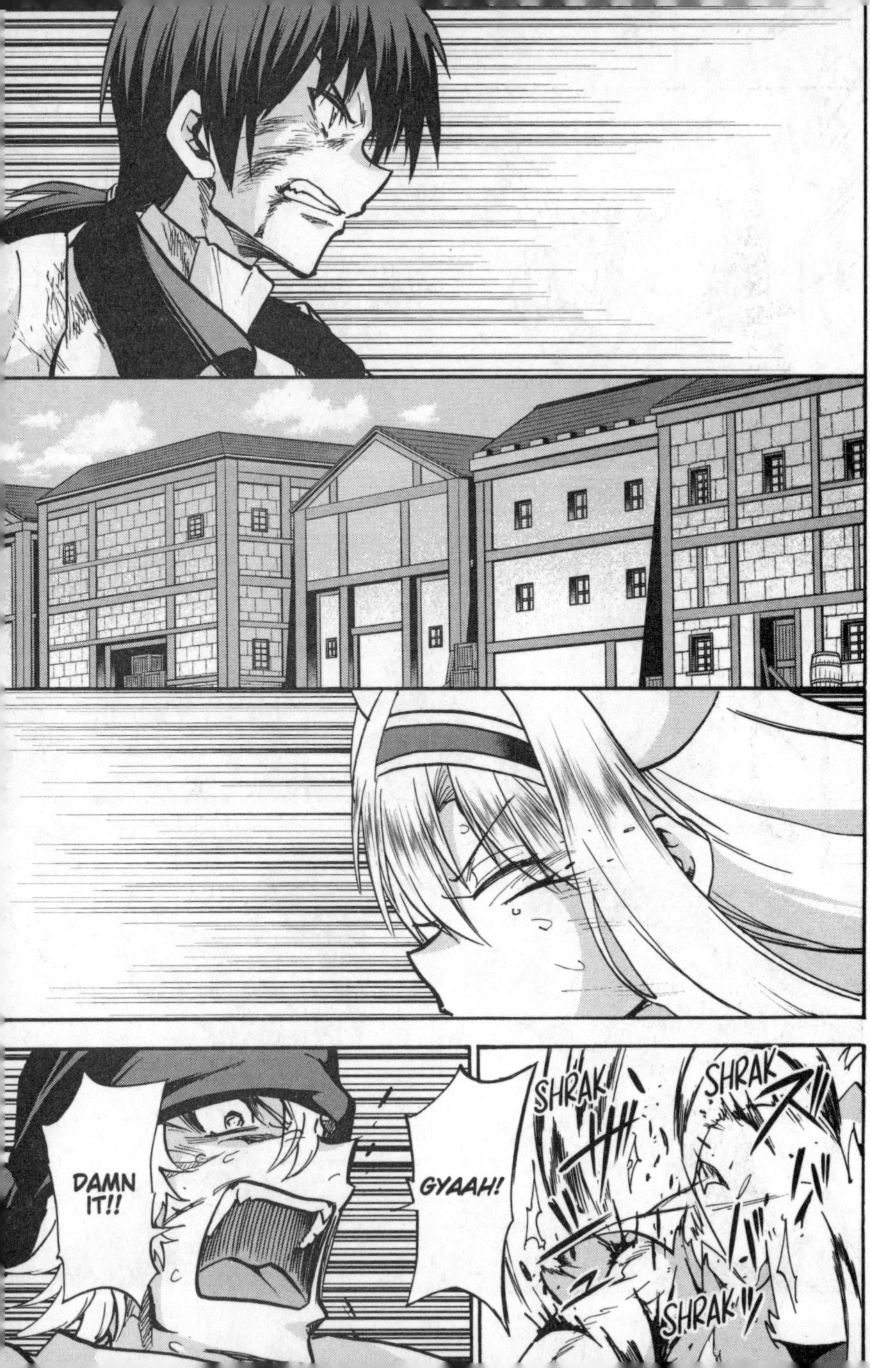
SHRAK
SHRAK
SHRAK!!
GYAAH!
DAMN IT!!

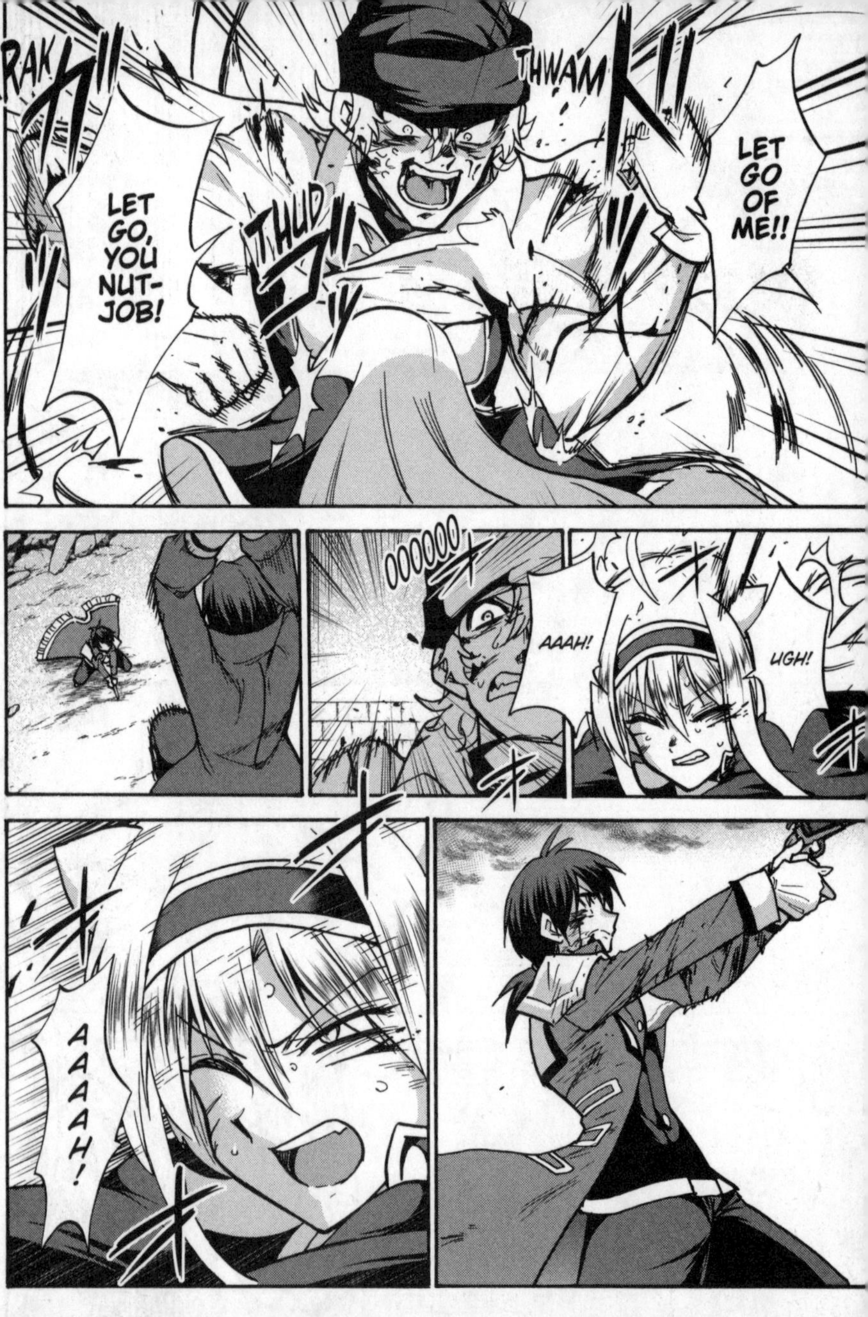
THWAM
LET GO OF ME!!
KRAK
THUD
LET GO, YOU NUT-JOB!
OOOOOO
UGH!
AAAH!
AAAAAH!

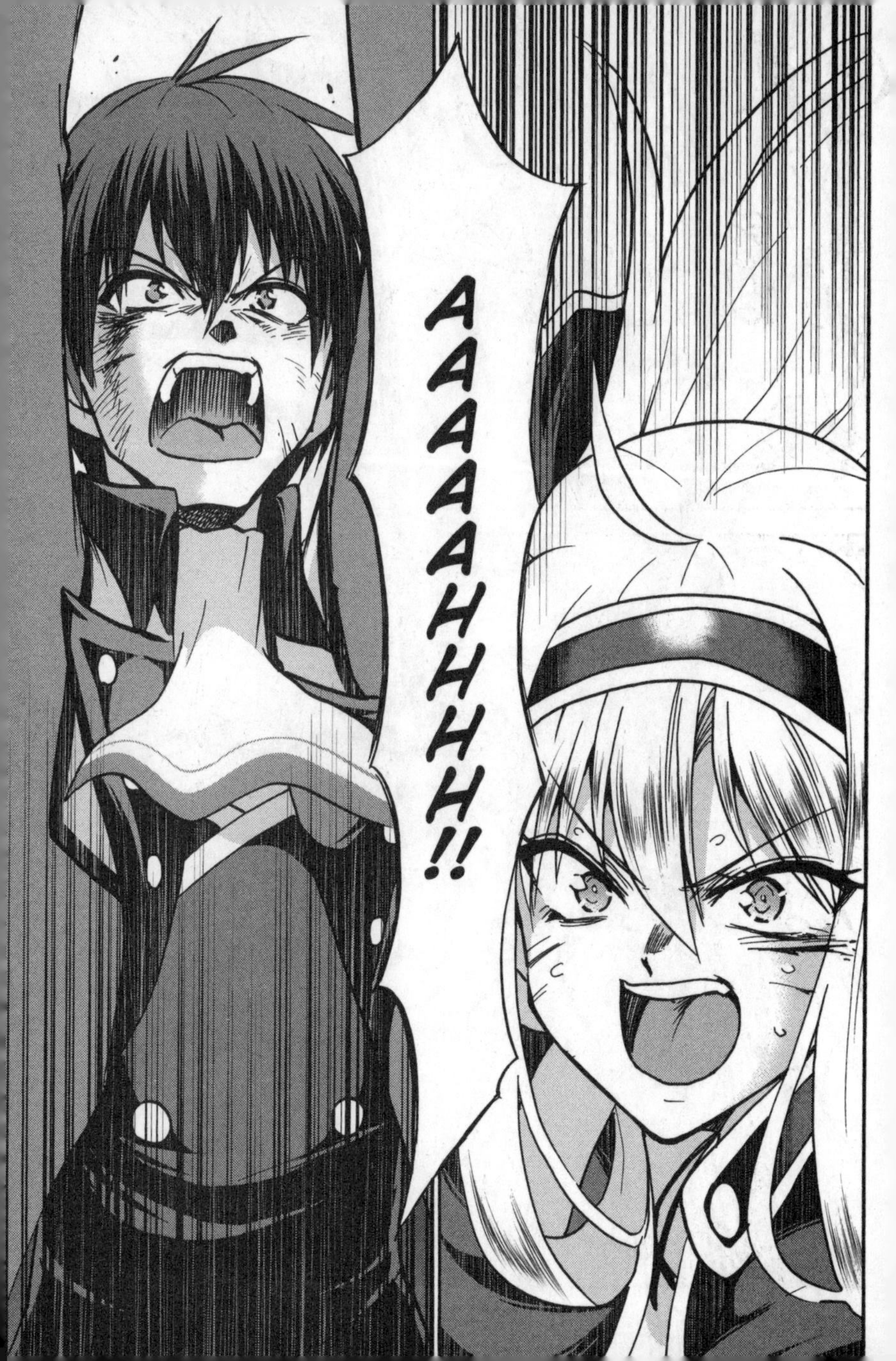
AAAAAHHHH!!

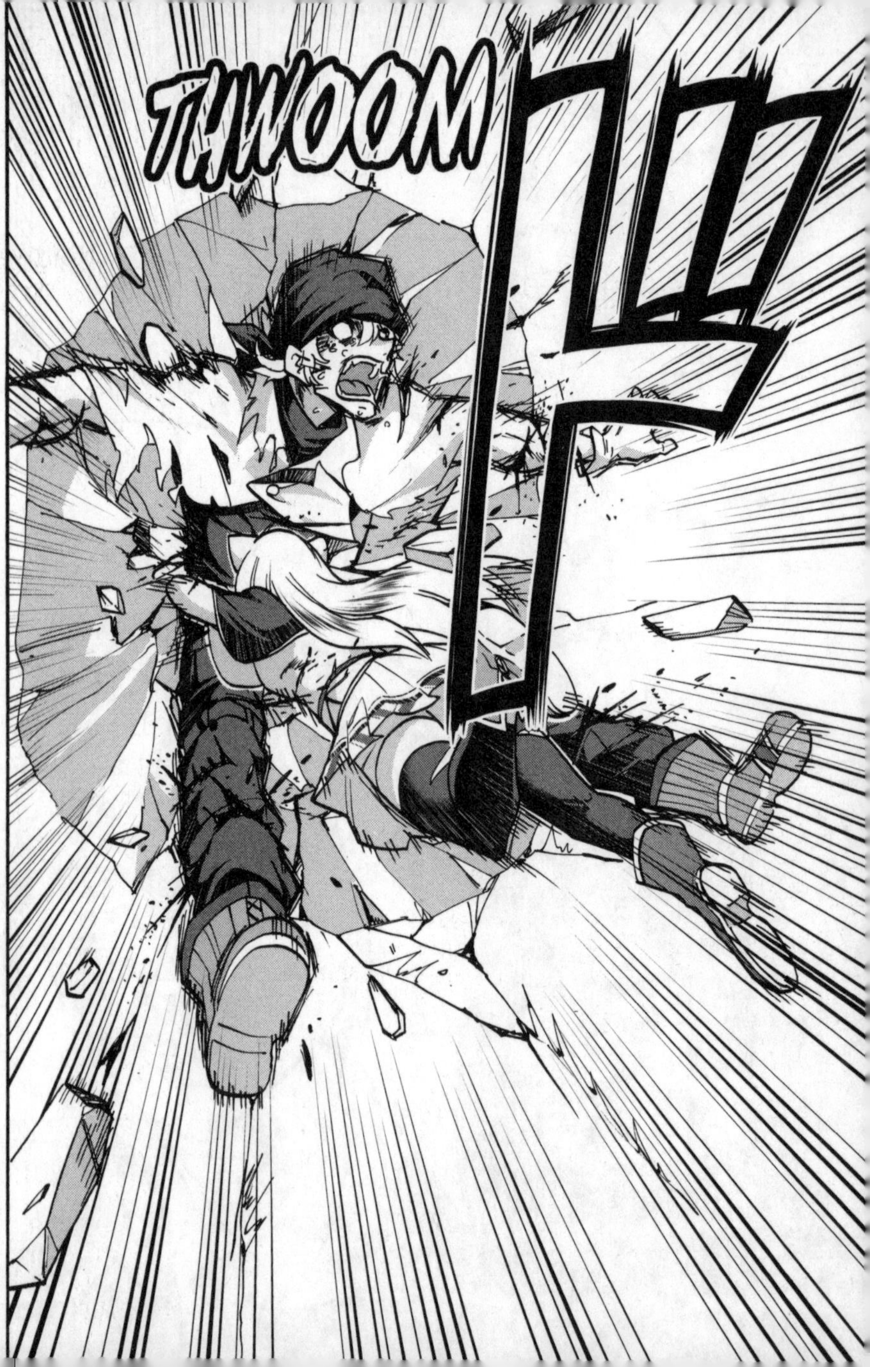
THWOOM

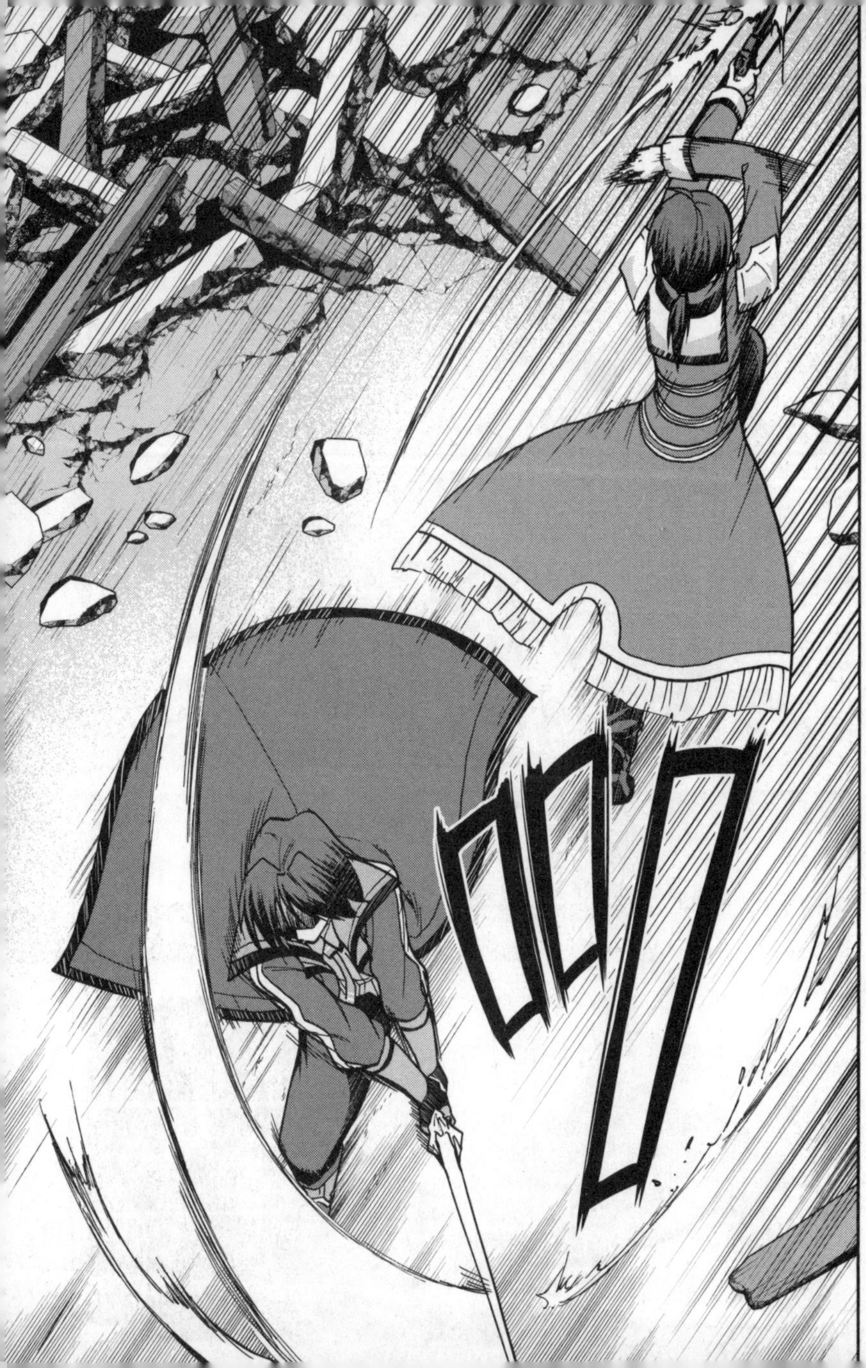

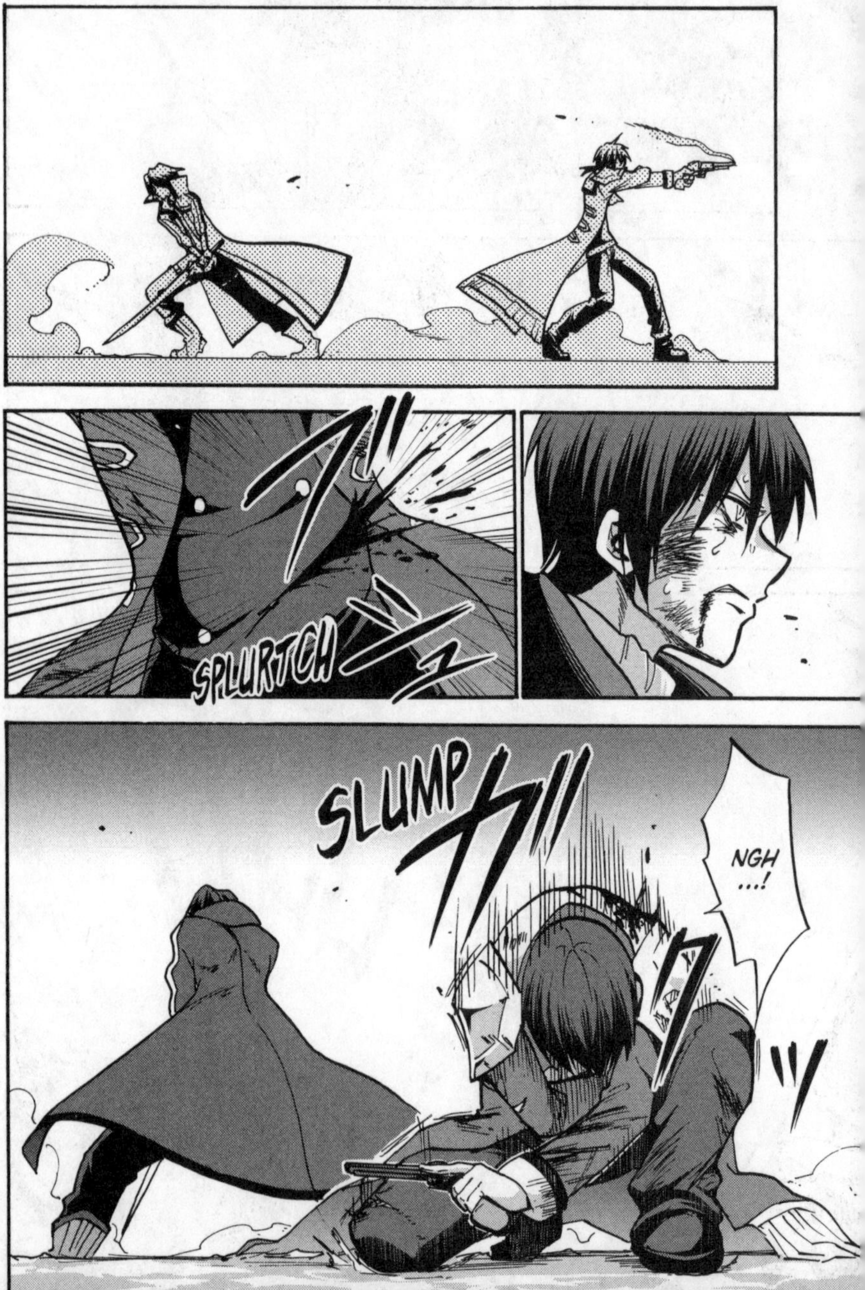
SPLURTCH
SLUMP
NGH ...!

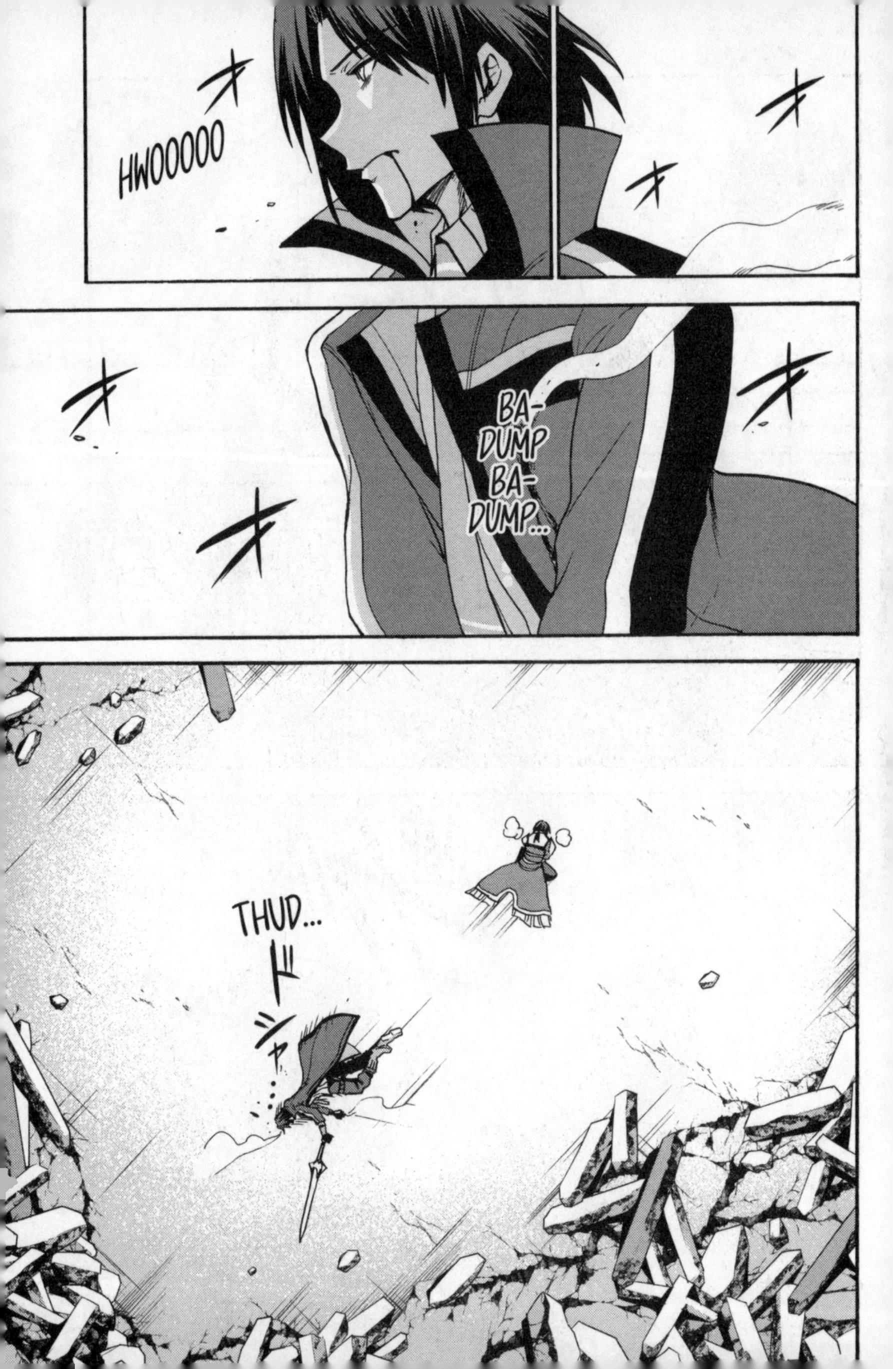

オ
HWOOOOO
オ
オ
オ
オ
BA-
DUMP
BA-
DUMP...
オ
THUD...
ドシャ

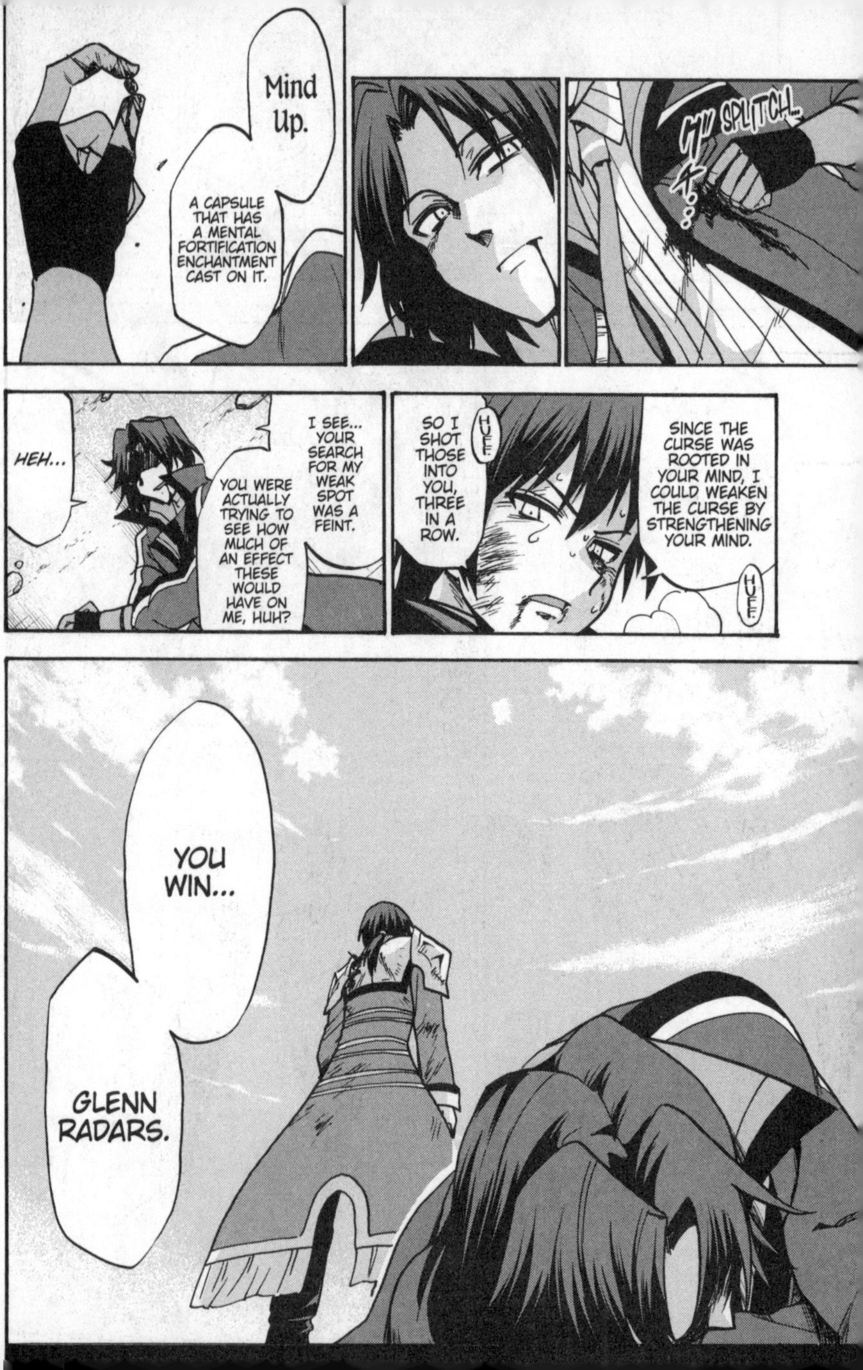
SPLITCH...
Mind Up.
A CAPSULE THAT HAS A MENTAL FORTIFICATION ENCHANTMENT CAST ON IT.
SINCE THE CURSE WAS ROOTED IN YOUR MIND, I COULD WEAKEN THE CURSE BY STRENGTHENING YOUR MIND.
HUFF
HUFF
SO I SHOT THOSE INTO YOU, THREE IN A ROW.
I SEE... YOUR SEARCH FOR MY WEAK SPOT WAS A FEINT.
YOU WERE ACTUALLY TRYING TO SEE HOW MUCH OF AN EFFECT THESE WOULD HAVE ON ME, HUH?
HEH...
YOU WIN...
GLENN RADARS.

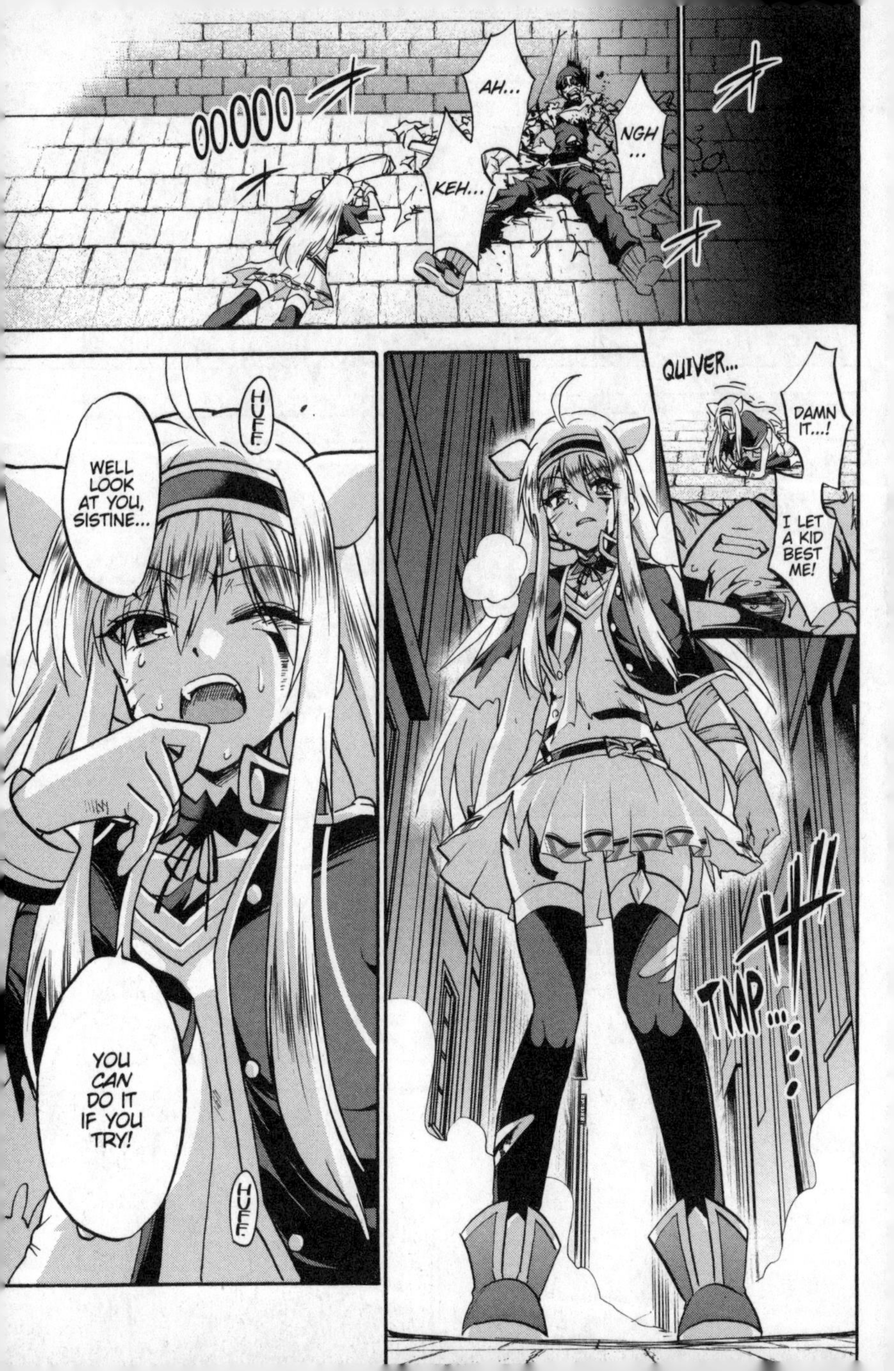
NGH ...
AH...
KEH...
OOOOO
DAMN IT...!
I LET A KID BEST ME!
QUIVER...
TMP...
HUFF
WELL LOOK AT YOU, SISTINE...
YOU CAN DO IT IF YOU TRY!
HUFF

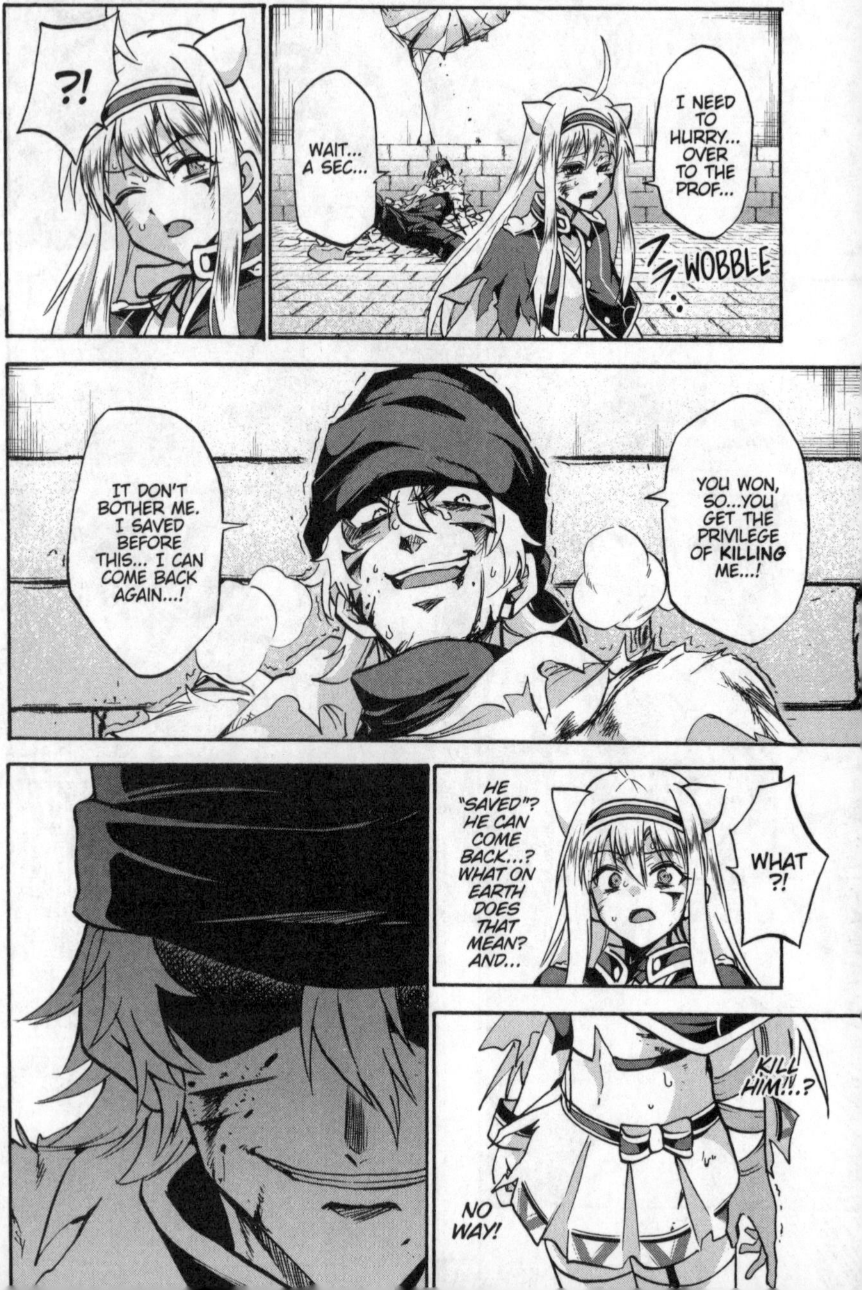
I NEED TO HURRY... OVER TO THE PROF...
WOBBLE
WAIT... A SEC...
?!
YOU WON, SO...YOU GET THE PRIVILEGE OF KILLING ME...!
IT DON'T BOTHER ME. I SAVED BEFORE THIS... I CAN COME BACK AGAIN...!
WHAT ?!
HE "SAVED"? HE CAN COME BACK...? WHAT ON EARTH DOES THAT MEAN? AND...
KILL HIM!!..?
NO WAY!

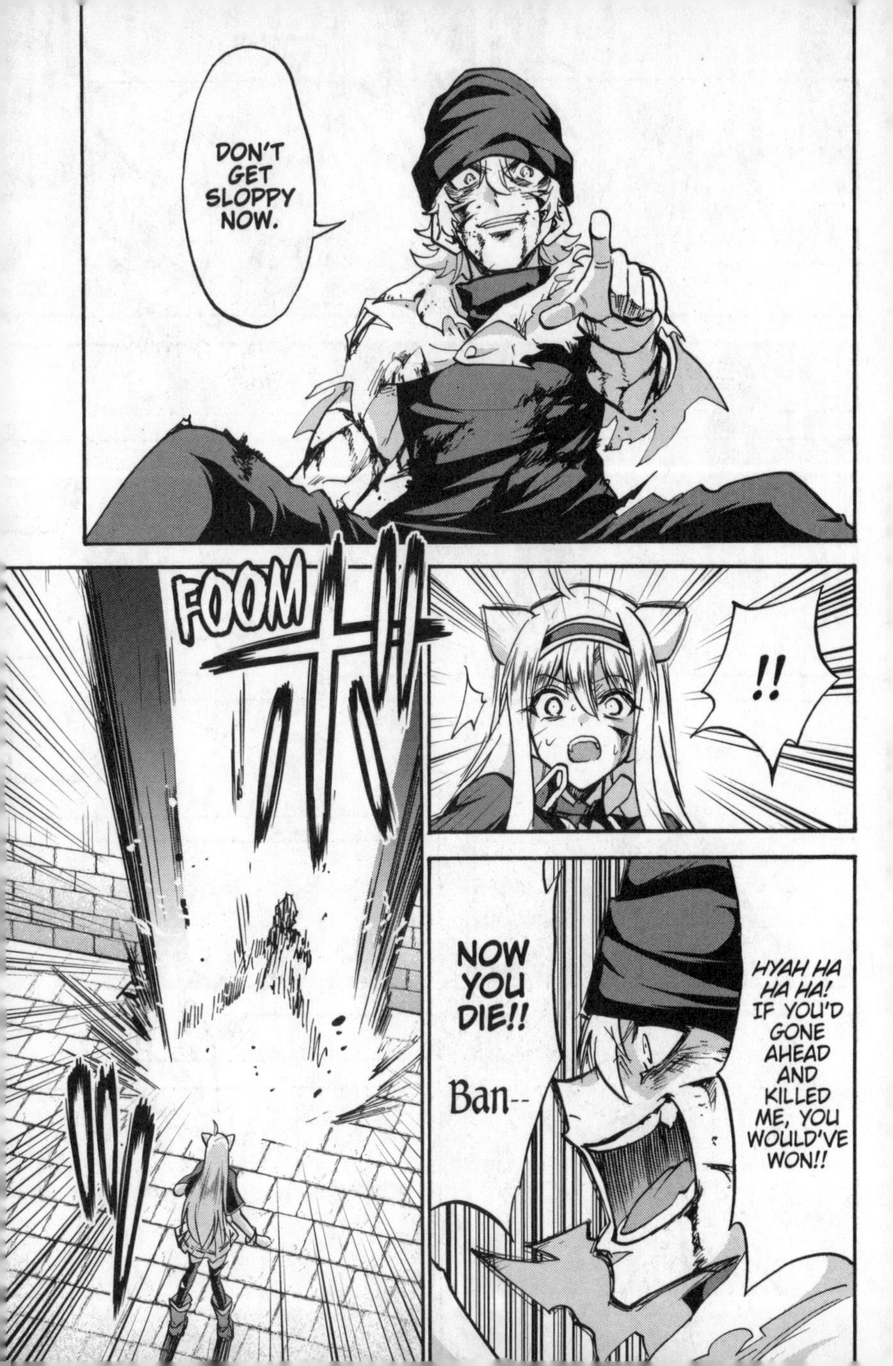

DON'T GET SLOPPY NOW.
!!
FOOM
NOW YOU DIE!!
HYAH HA HA HA! IF YOU'D GONE AHEAD AND KILLED ME, YOU WOULD'VE WON!!
Ban--

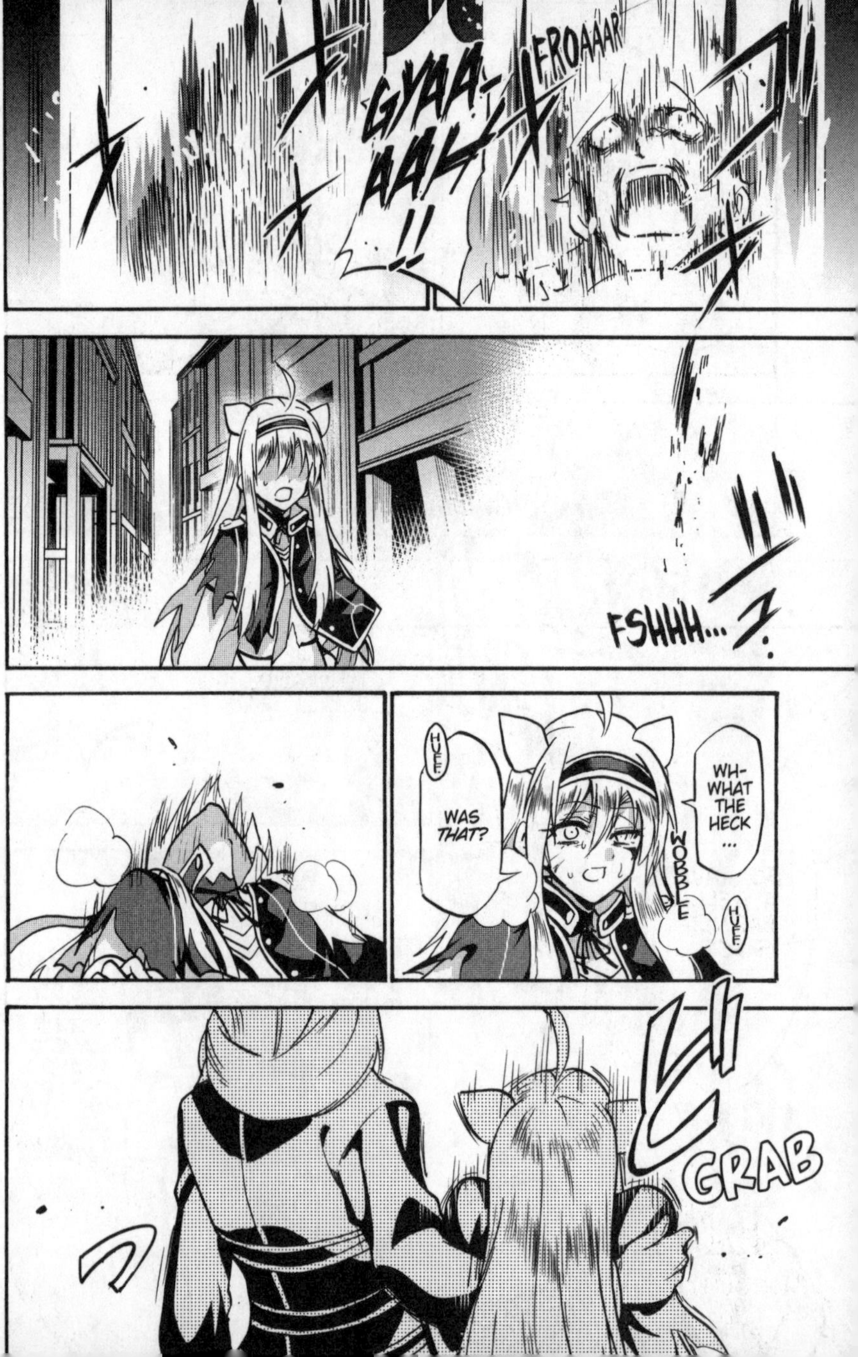
FROAAAR
GYAA-AAH-!!
FSHHH...
HUFF
WAS THAT?
WH-WHAT THE HECK...
WOBBLE
HUFF
GRAB

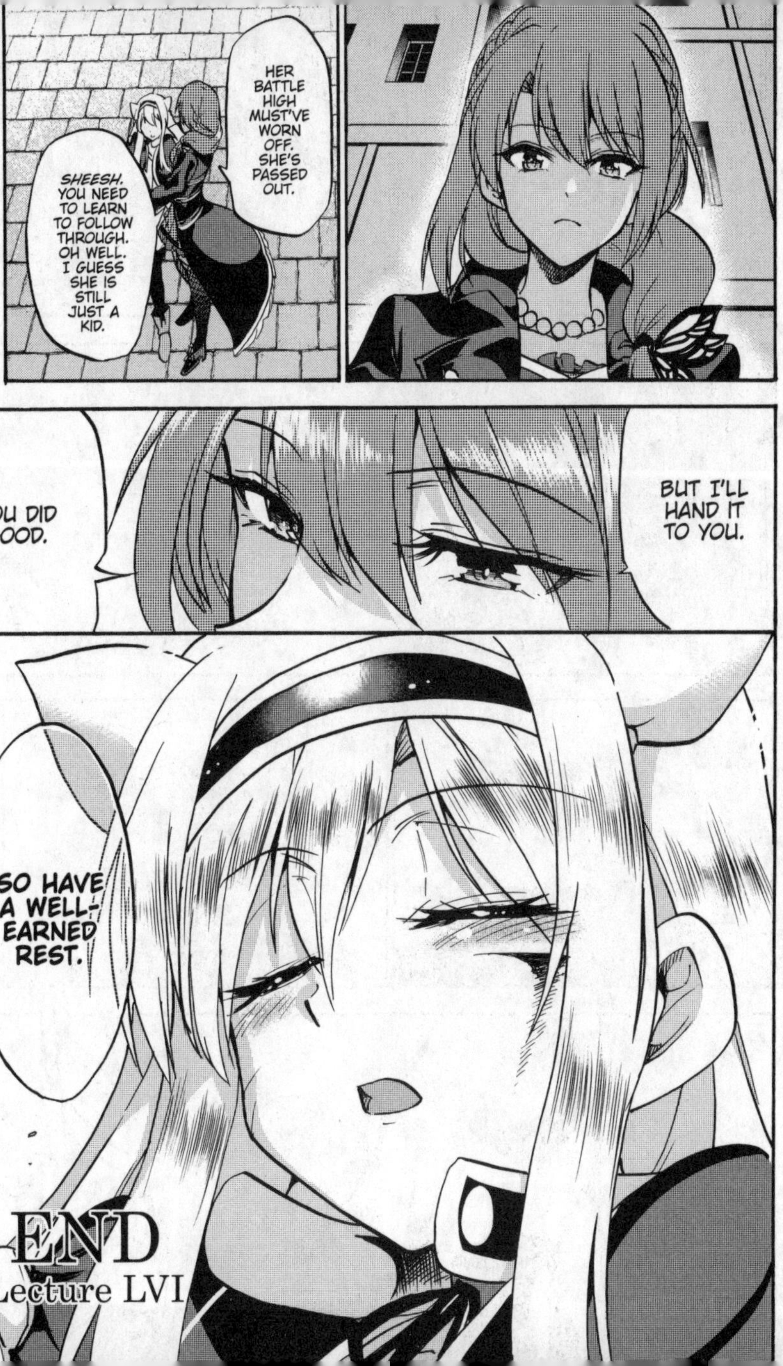
HER BATTLE HIGH MUST'VE WORN OFF. SHE'S PASSED OUT.
SHEESH. YOU NEED TO LEARN TO FOLLOW THROUGH. OH WELL. I GUESS SHE IS STILL JUST A KID.
BUT I'LL HAND IT TO YOU.
YOU DID GOOD.
SO HAVE A WELL-EARNED REST.
END
Lecture LVI

Akashic Records

o f **Bastard** Magic **Instructor**

Lecture LVII

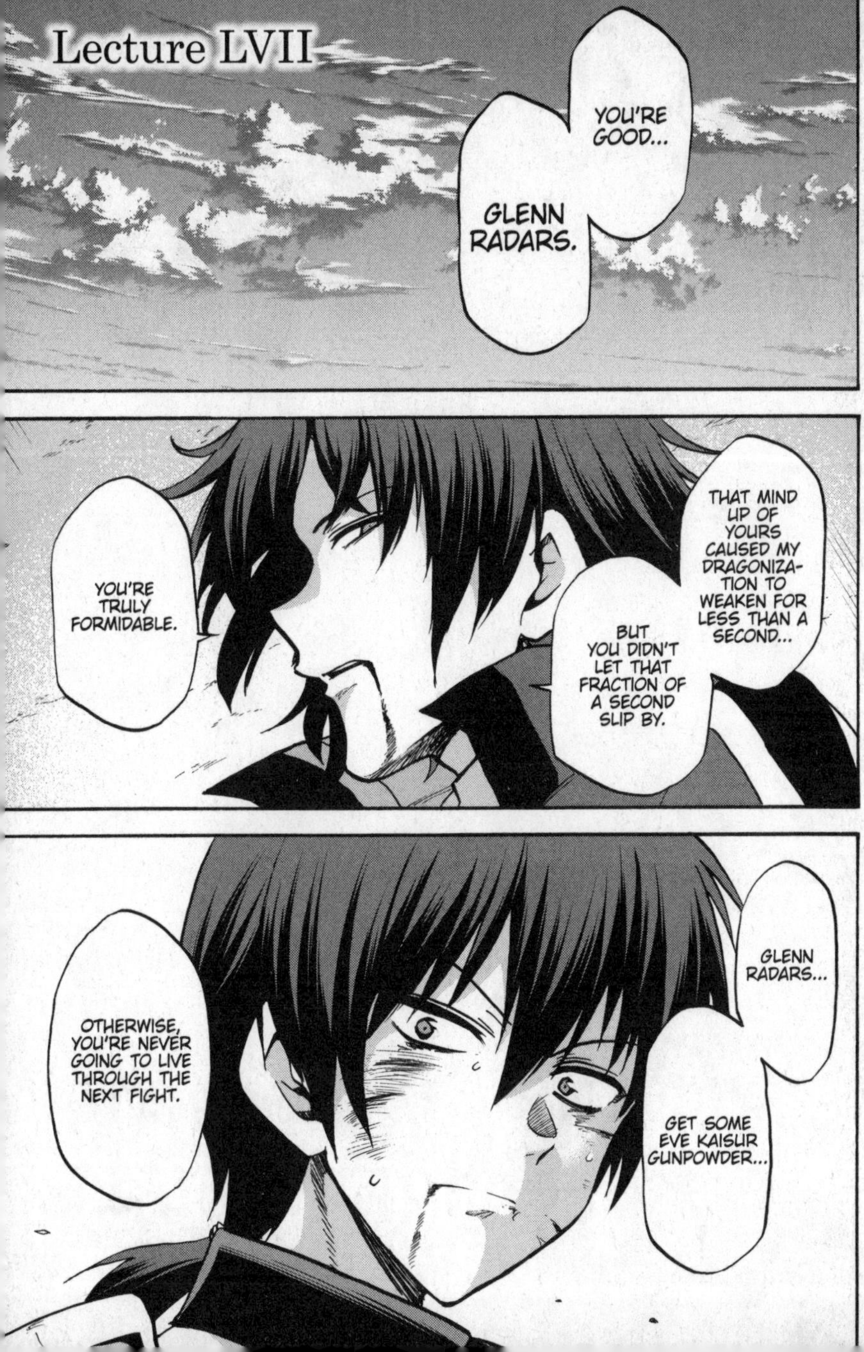
YOU'RE GOOD...
GLENN RADARS.
THAT MIND UP OF YOURS CAUSED MY DRAGONIZATION TO WEAKEN FOR LESS THAN A SECOND...
BUT YOU DIDN'T LET THAT FRACTION OF A SECOND SLIP BY.
YOU'RE TRULY FORMIDABLE.
GLENN RADARS...
GET SOME EVE KAISUR GUNPOWDER...
OTHERWISE, YOU'RE NEVER GOING TO LIVE THROUGH THE NEXT FIGHT.

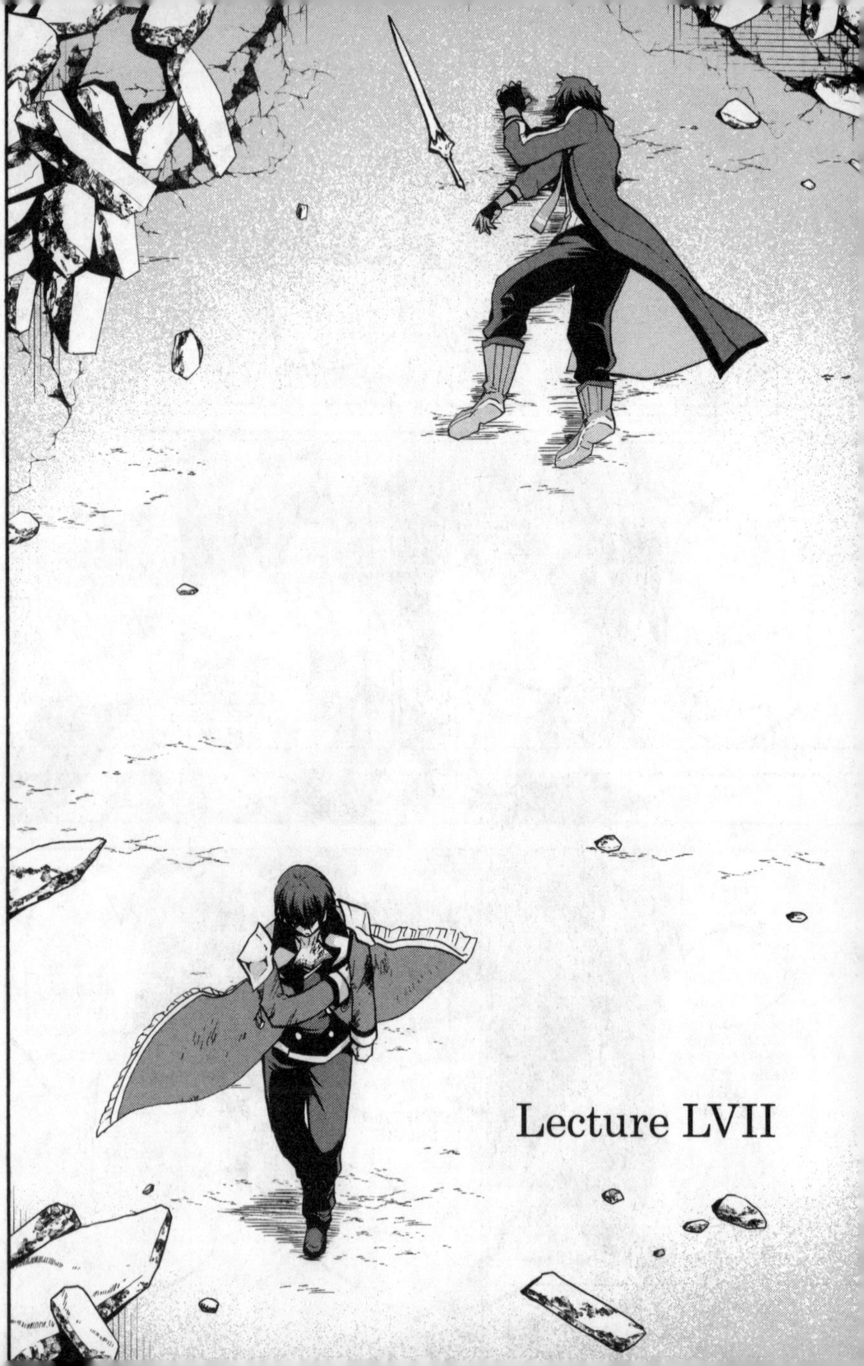

Lecture LVII

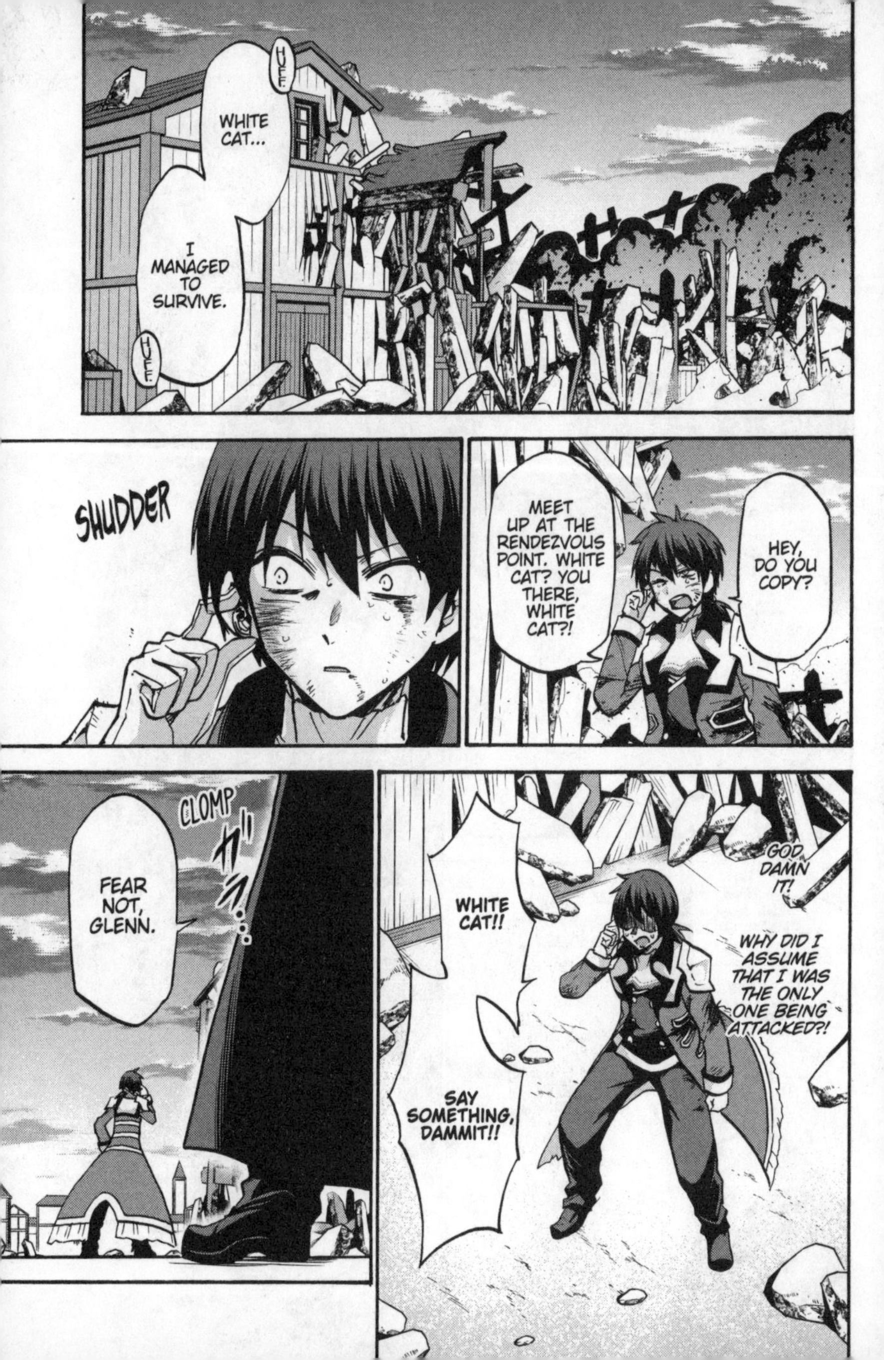
HUFF.
WHITE CAT...
I MANAGED TO SURVIVE.
HUFF.
HEY, DO YOU COPY?
MEET UP AT THE RENDEZVOUS POINT. WHITE CAT? YOU THERE, WHITE CAT?!
SHUDDER
GOD DAMN IT!
WHY DID I ASSUME THAT I WAS THE ONLY ONE BEING ATTACKED?!
WHITE CAT!!
SAY SOMETHING, DAMMIT!!
CLOMP
FEAR NOT, GLENN.

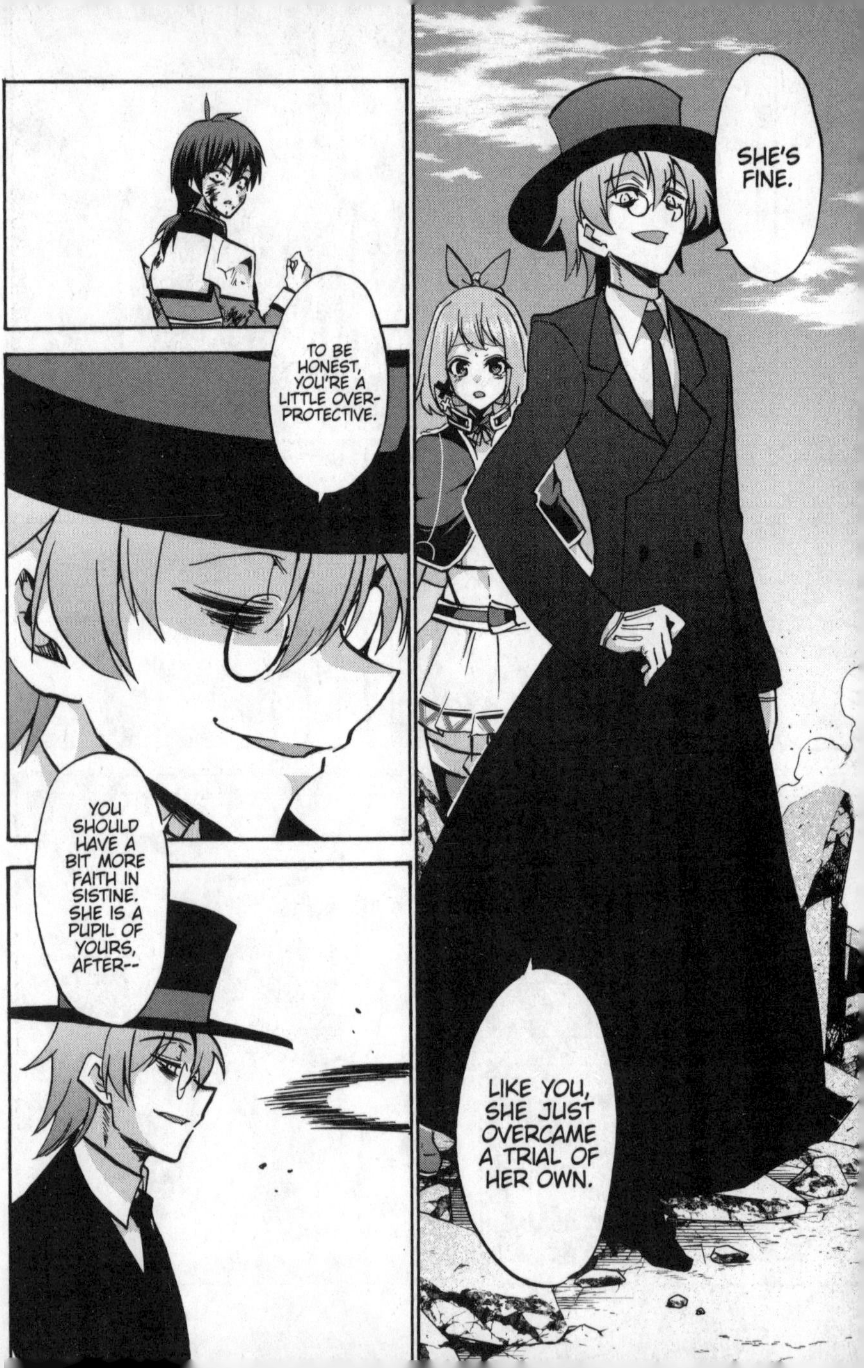
SHE'S FINE.
LIKE YOU, SHE JUST OVERCAME A TRIAL OF HER OWN.
TO BE HONEST, YOU'RE A LITTLE OVER-PROTECTIVE.
YOU SHOULD HAVE A BIT MORE FAITH IN SISTINE. SHE IS A PUPIL OF YOURS, AFTER--

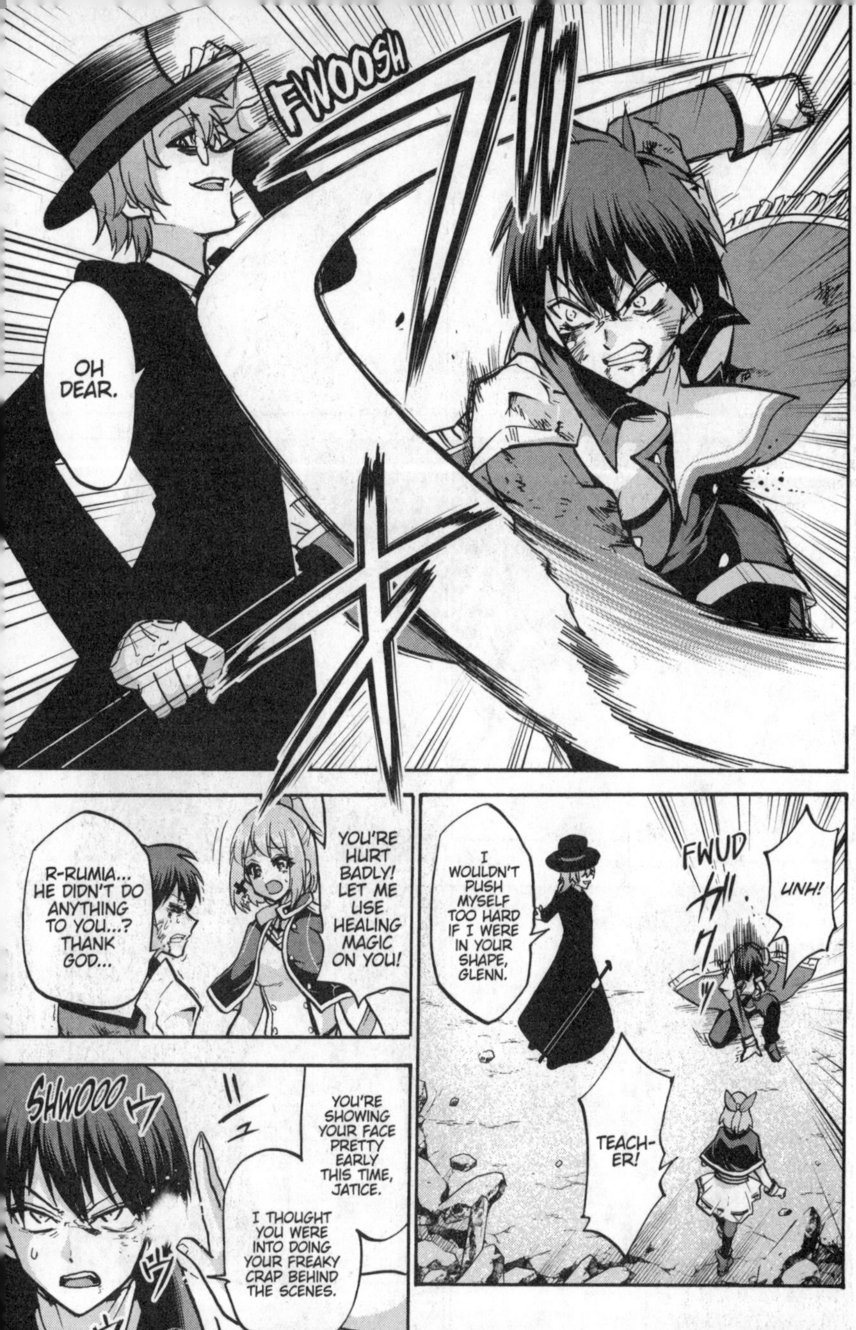
FWOOSH
OH DEAR.
FWUD
UNH!
I WOULDN'T PUSH MYSELF TOO HARD IF I WERE IN YOUR SHAPE, GLENN.
TEACHER!
YOU'RE HURT BADLY! LET ME USE HEALING MAGIC ON YOU!
R-RUMIA... HE DIDN'T DO ANYTHING TO YOU...? THANK GOD...
SHWOOO
YOU'RE SHOWING YOUR FACE PRETTY EARLY THIS TIME, JATICE.
I THOUGHT YOU WERE INTO DOING YOUR FREAKY CRAP BEHIND THE SCENES.

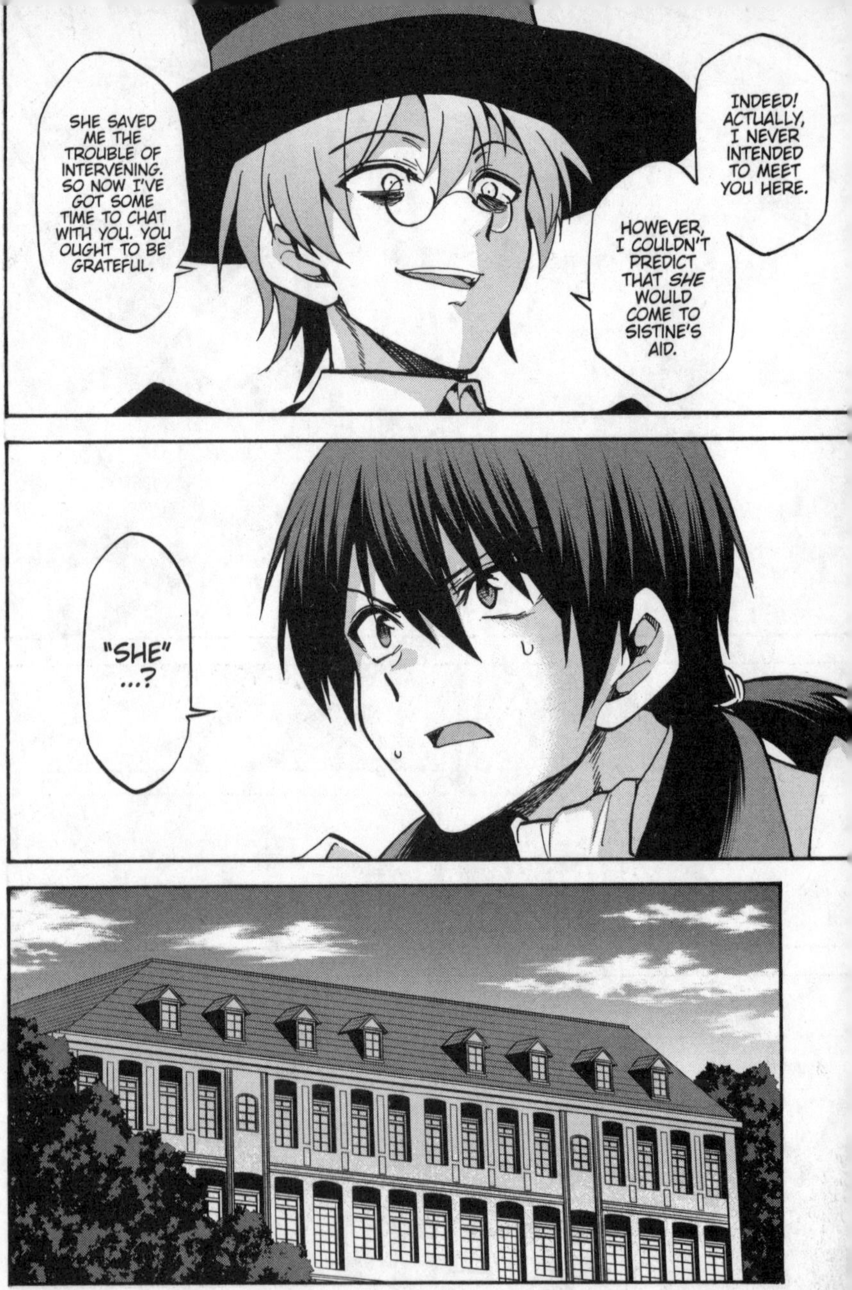
INDEED! ACTUALLY, I NEVER INTENDED TO MEET YOU HERE.
HOWEVER, I COULDN'T PREDICT THAT *SHE* WOULD COME TO SISTINE'S AID.
SHE SAVED ME THE TROUBLE OF INTERVENING. SO NOW I'VE GOT SOME TIME TO CHAT WITH YOU. YOU OUGHT TO BE GRATEFUL.
"SHE" ...?

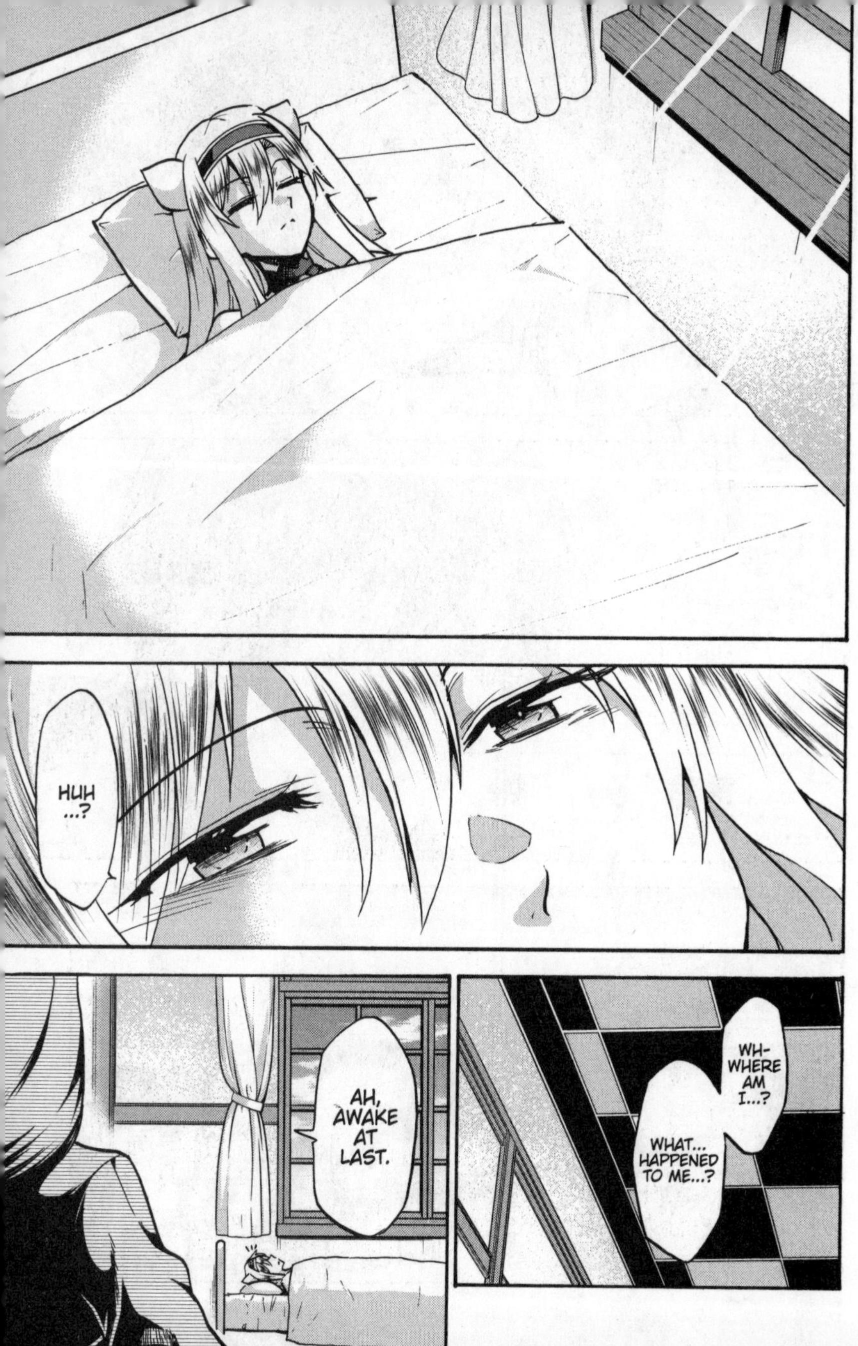
HUH ...?
WH- WHERE AM I...?
WHAT... HAPPENED TO ME...?
AH, AWAKE AT LAST.

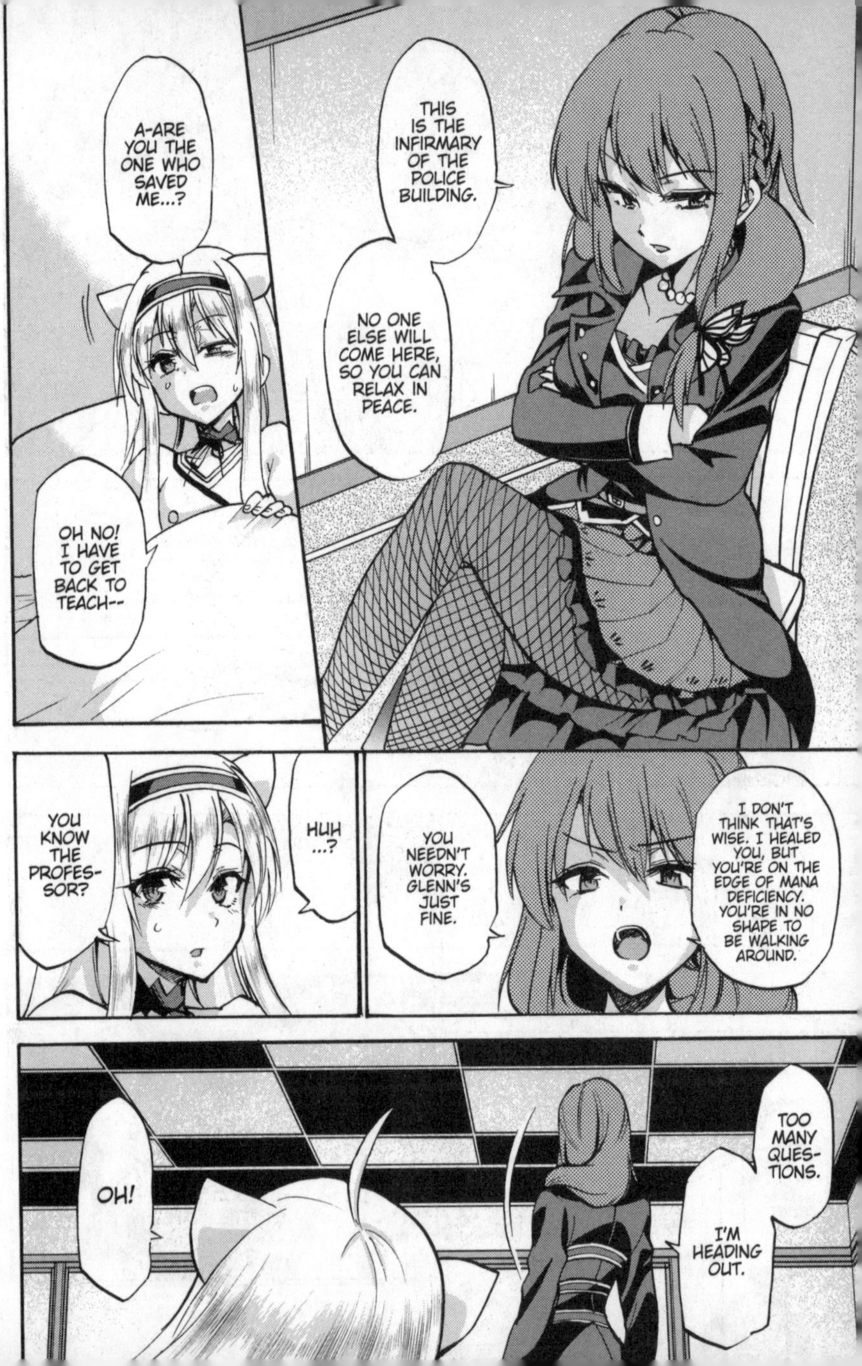
THIS IS THE INFIRMARY OF THE POLICE BUILDING.
NO ONE ELSE WILL COME HERE, SO YOU CAN RELAX IN PEACE.
A-ARE YOU THE ONE WHO SAVED ME...?
OH NO! I HAVE TO GET BACK TO TEACH--
I DON'T THINK THAT'S WISE. I HEALED YOU, BUT YOU'RE ON THE EDGE OF MANA DEFICIENCY. YOU'RE IN NO SHAPE TO BE WALKING AROUND.
YOU NEEDN'T WORRY. GLENN'S JUST FINE.
HUH ...?
YOU KNOW THE PROFES-SOR?
TOO MANY QUES-TIONS.
I'M HEADING OUT.
OH!

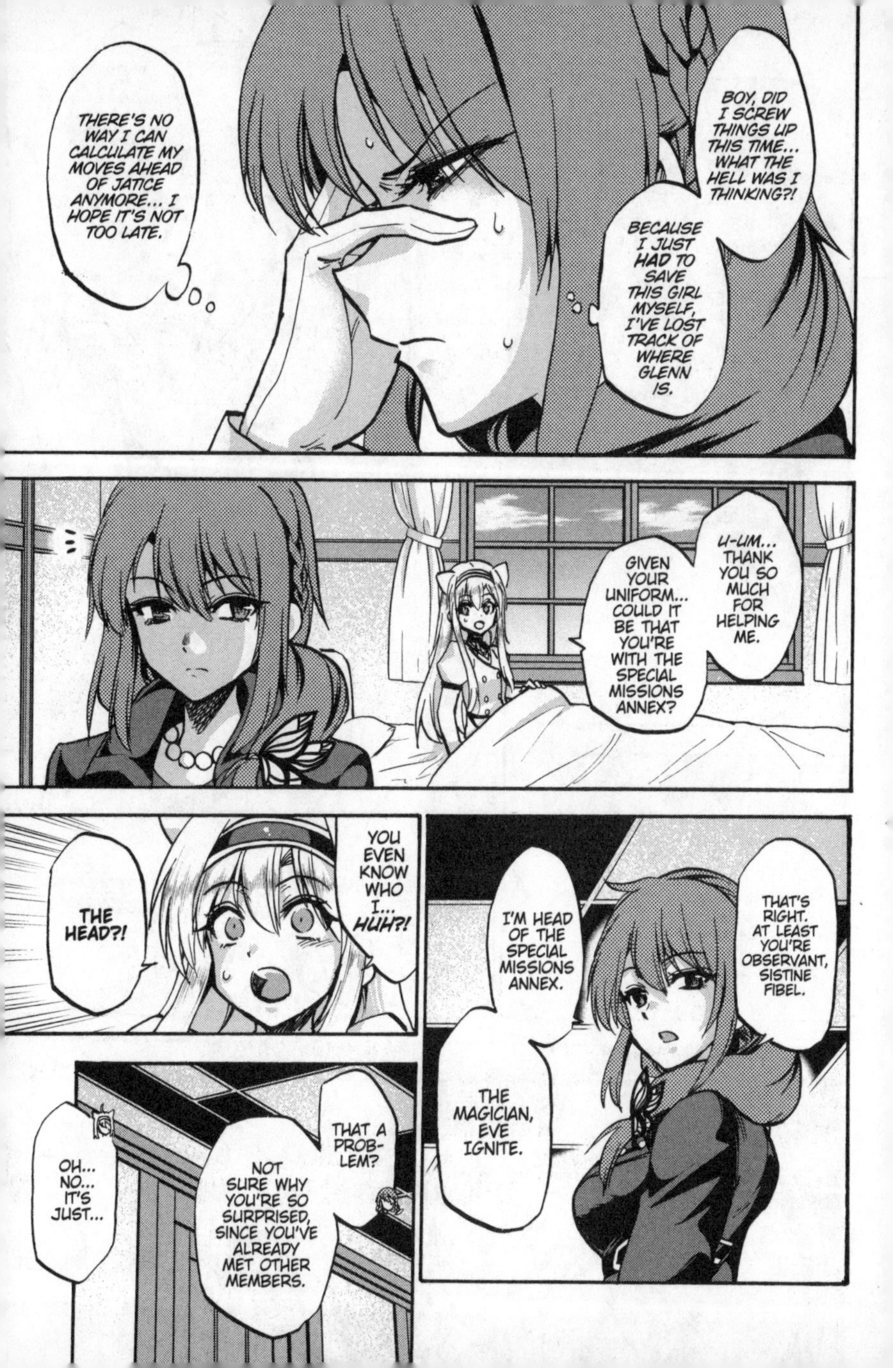
BOY, DID I SCREW THINGS UP THIS TIME... WHAT THE HELL WAS I THINKING?!
BECAUSE I JUST HAD TO SAVE THIS GIRL MYSELF, I'VE LOST TRACK OF WHERE GLENN IS.
THERE'S NO WAY I CAN CALCULATE MY MOVES AHEAD OF JATICE ANYMORE... I HOPE IT'S NOT TOO LATE.
U-UM... THANK YOU SO MUCH FOR HELPING ME.
GIVEN YOUR UNIFORM... COULD IT BE THAT YOU'RE WITH THE SPECIAL MISSIONS ANNEX?
THAT'S RIGHT. AT LEAST YOU'RE OBSERVANT, SISTINE FIBEL.
I'M HEAD OF THE SPECIAL MISSIONS ANNEX.
THE MAGICIAN, EVE IGNITE.
YOU EVEN KNOW WHO I... HUH?!
THE HEAD?!
THAT A PROB-LEM?
NOT SURE WHY YOU'RE SO SURPRISED, SINCE YOU'VE ALREADY MET OTHER MEMBERS.
OH... NO... IT'S JUST...

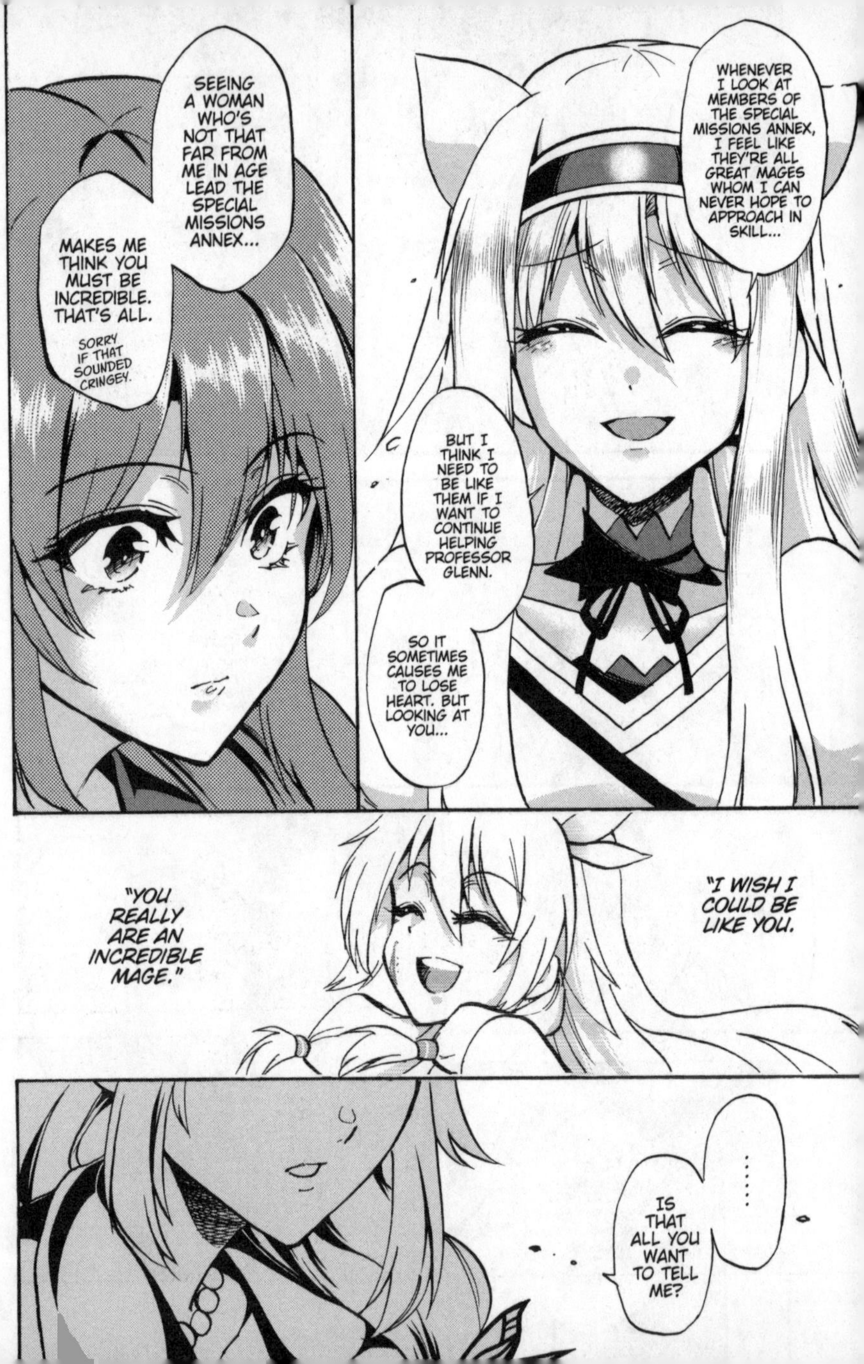
WHENEVER I LOOK AT MEMBERS OF THE SPECIAL MISSIONS ANNEX, I FEEL LIKE THEY'RE ALL GREAT MAGES WHOM I CAN NEVER HOPE TO APPROACH IN SKILL...
BUT I THINK I NEED TO BE LIKE THEM IF I WANT TO CONTINUE HELPING PROFESSOR GLENN.
SO IT SOMETIMES CAUSES ME TO LOSE HEART. BUT LOOKING AT YOU...
SEEING A WOMAN WHO'S NOT THAT FAR FROM ME IN AGE LEAD THE SPECIAL MISSIONS ANNEX...
MAKES ME THINK YOU MUST BE INCREDIBLE. THAT'S ALL.
SORRY IF THAT SOUNDED CRINGEY.
"I WISH I COULD BE LIKE YOU.
"YOU REALLY ARE AN INCREDIBLE MAGE."
......
IS THAT ALL YOU WANT TO TELL ME?

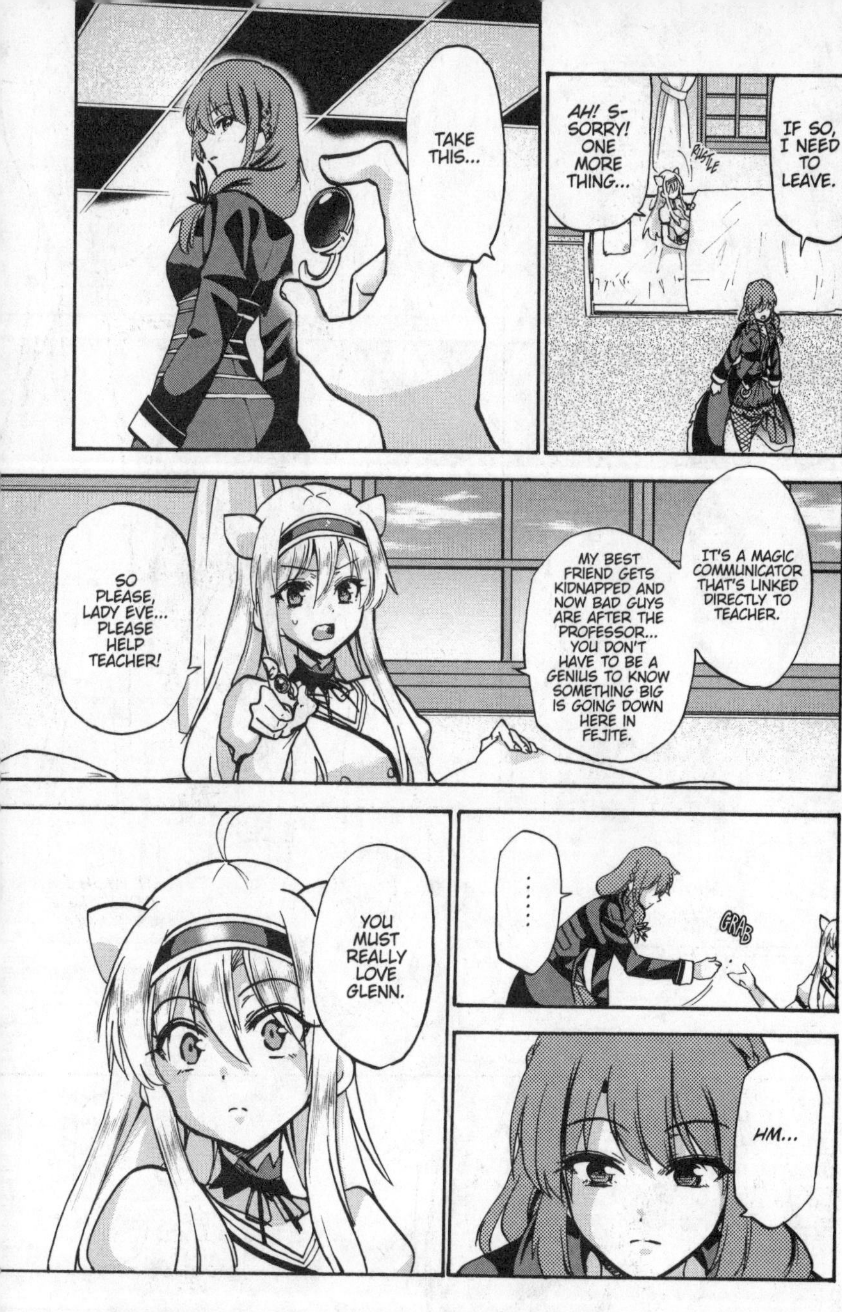
IF SO, I NEED TO LEAVE.
AH! S-SORRY! ONE MORE THING...
RUSTLE
TAKE THIS...
IT'S A MAGIC COMMUNICATOR THAT'S LINKED DIRECTLY TO TEACHER.
MY BEST FRIEND GETS KIDNAPPED AND NOW BAD GUYS ARE AFTER THE PROFESSOR... YOU DON'T HAVE TO BE A GENIUS TO KNOW SOMETHING BIG IS GOING DOWN HERE IN FEJITE.
SO PLEASE, LADY EVE... PLEASE HELP TEACHER!
......
GRAB
YOU MUST REALLY LOVE GLENN.
HM...

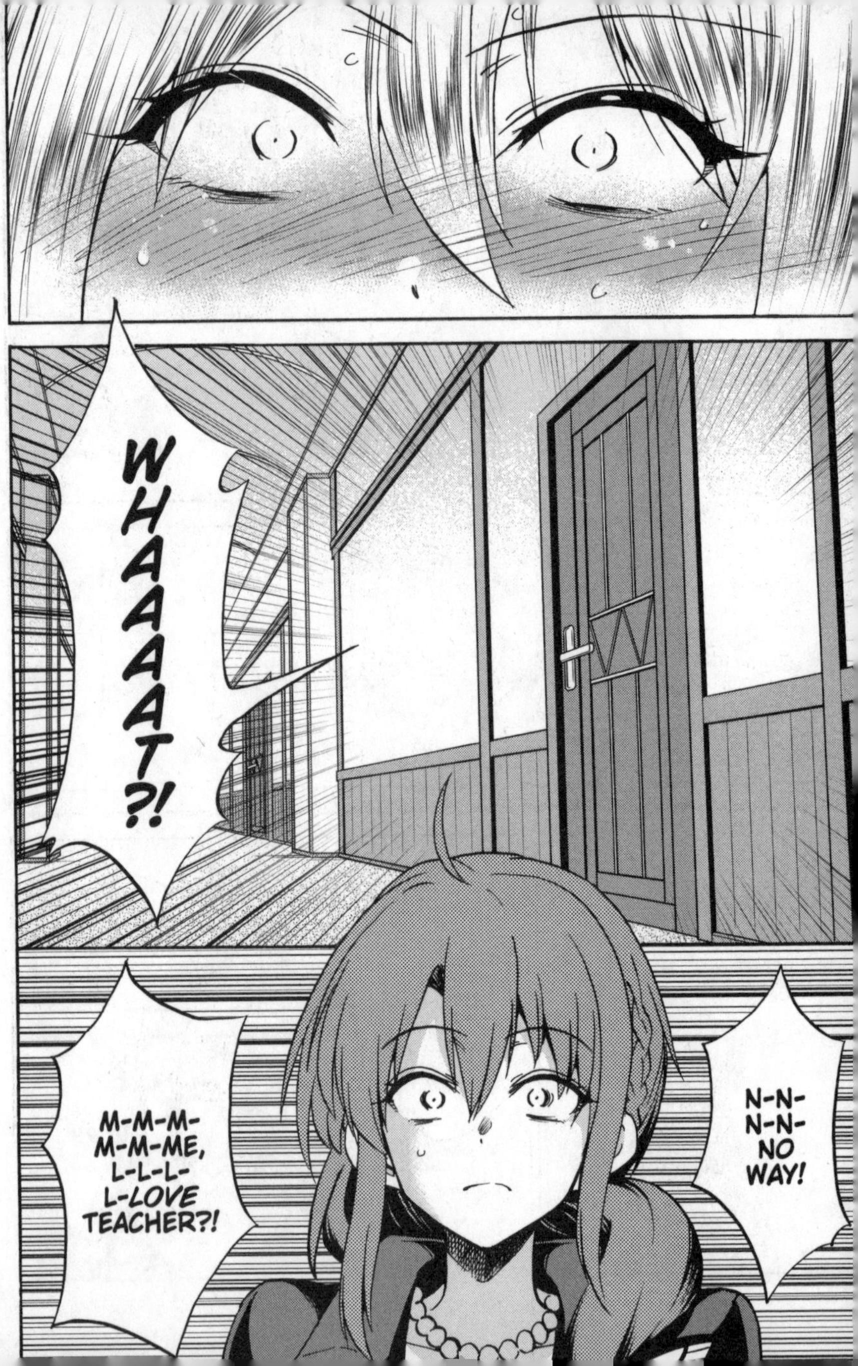
WHAAAAAT?!
N-N-N-N-NO WAY!
M-M-M-M-M-ME, L-L-L-L-LOVE TEACHER?!

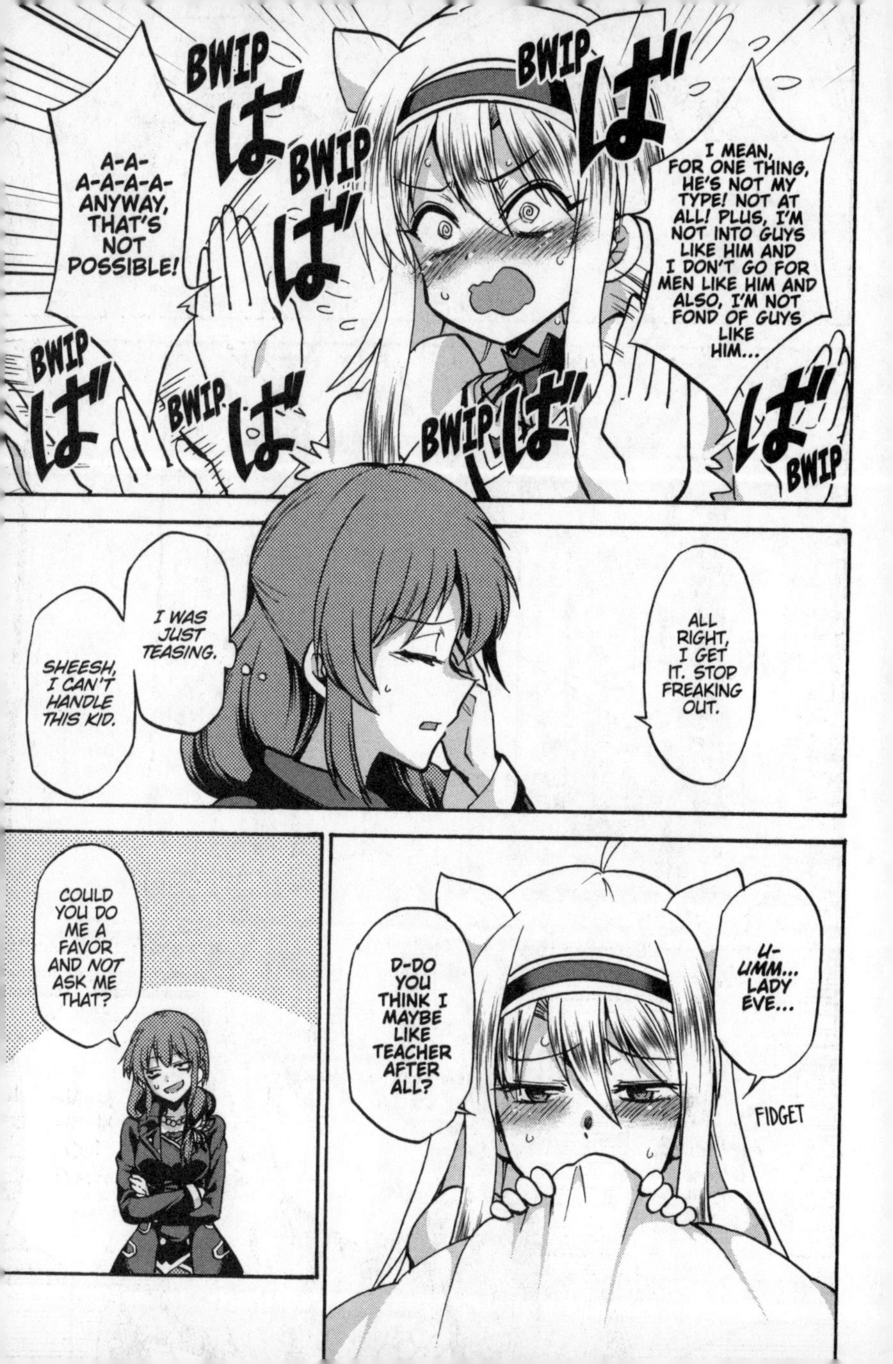
BWIP ば
BWIP ば
BWIP ば
I MEAN, FOR ONE THING, HE'S NOT MY TYPE! NOT AT ALL! PLUS, I'M NOT INTO GUYS LIKE HIM AND I DON'T GO FOR MEN LIKE HIM AND ALSO, I'M NOT FOND OF GUYS LIKE HIM...
A-A-A-A-A-A-ANYWAY, THAT'S NOT POSSIBLE!
BWIP ば
BWIP ば
BWIP ば
BWIP ば
ALL RIGHT, I GET IT. STOP FREAKING OUT.
I WAS JUST TEASING.
SHEESH, I CAN'T HANDLE THIS KID.
U-UMM... LADY EVE...
FIDGET
D-DO YOU THINK I MAYBE LIKE TEACHER AFTER ALL?
COULD YOU DO ME A FAVOR AND NOT ASK ME THAT?

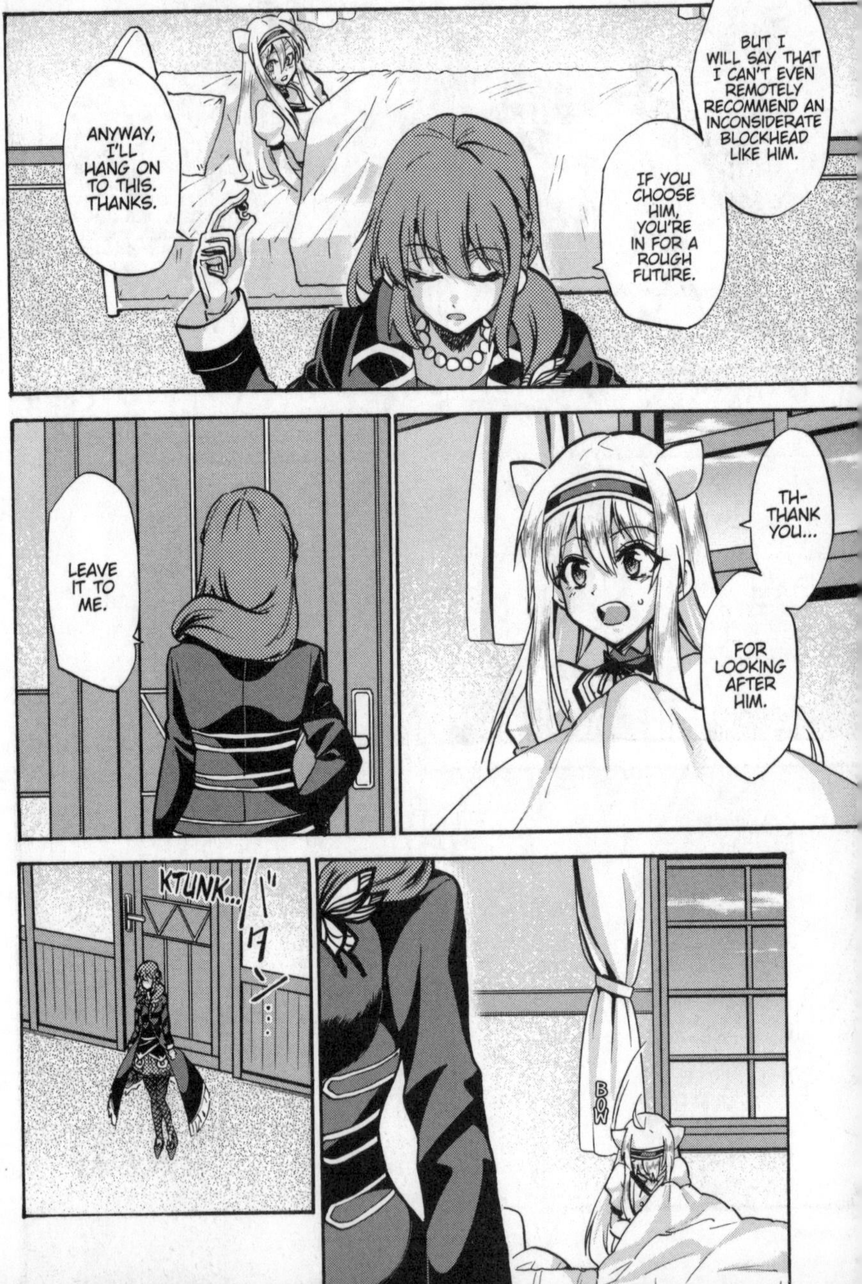

BUT I WILL SAY THAT I CAN'T EVEN REMOTELY RECOMMEND AN INCONSIDERATE BLOCKHEAD LIKE HIM.
IF YOU CHOOSE HIM, YOU'RE IN FOR A ROUGH FUTURE.
ANYWAY, I'LL HANG ON TO THIS. THANKS.
TH-THANK YOU...
FOR LOOKING AFTER HIM.
LEAVE IT TO ME.
KTUNK...
バタン
...
BOW

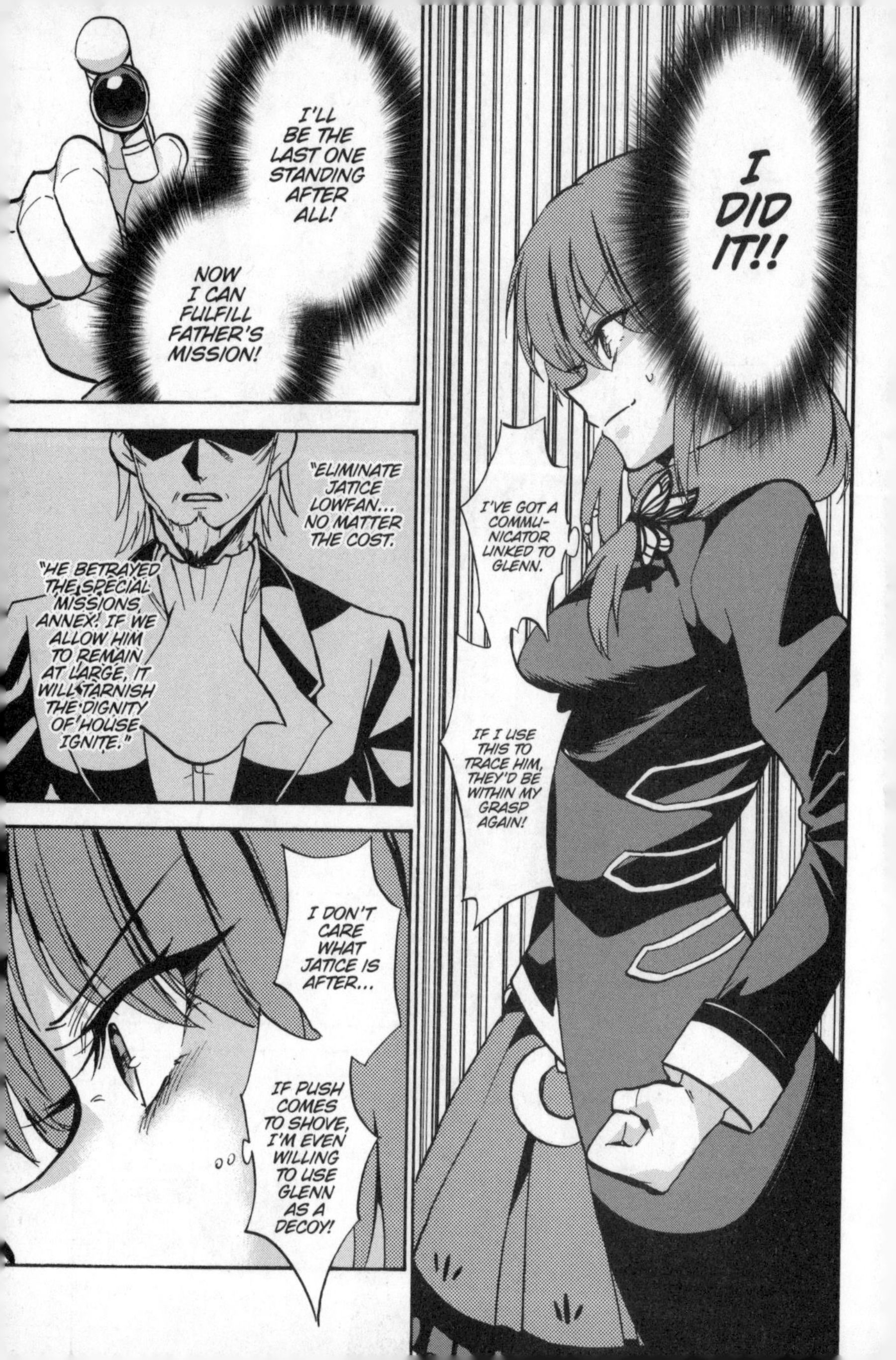
I DID IT!!
I'VE GOT A COMMUNICATOR LINKED TO GLENN.
IF I USE THIS TO TRACE HIM, THEY'D BE WITHIN MY GRASP AGAIN!
I'LL BE THE LAST ONE STANDING AFTER ALL!
NOW I CAN FULFILL FATHER'S MISSION!
"ELIMINATE JATICE LOWFAN... NO MATTER THE COST.
"HE BETRAYED THE SPECIAL MISSIONS ANNEX! IF WE ALLOW HIM TO REMAIN AT LARGE, IT WILL TARNISH THE DIGNITY OF HOUSE IGNITE."
I DON'T CARE WHAT JATICE IS AFTER...
IF PUSH COMES TO SHOVE, I'M EVEN WILLING TO USE GLENN AS A DECOY!

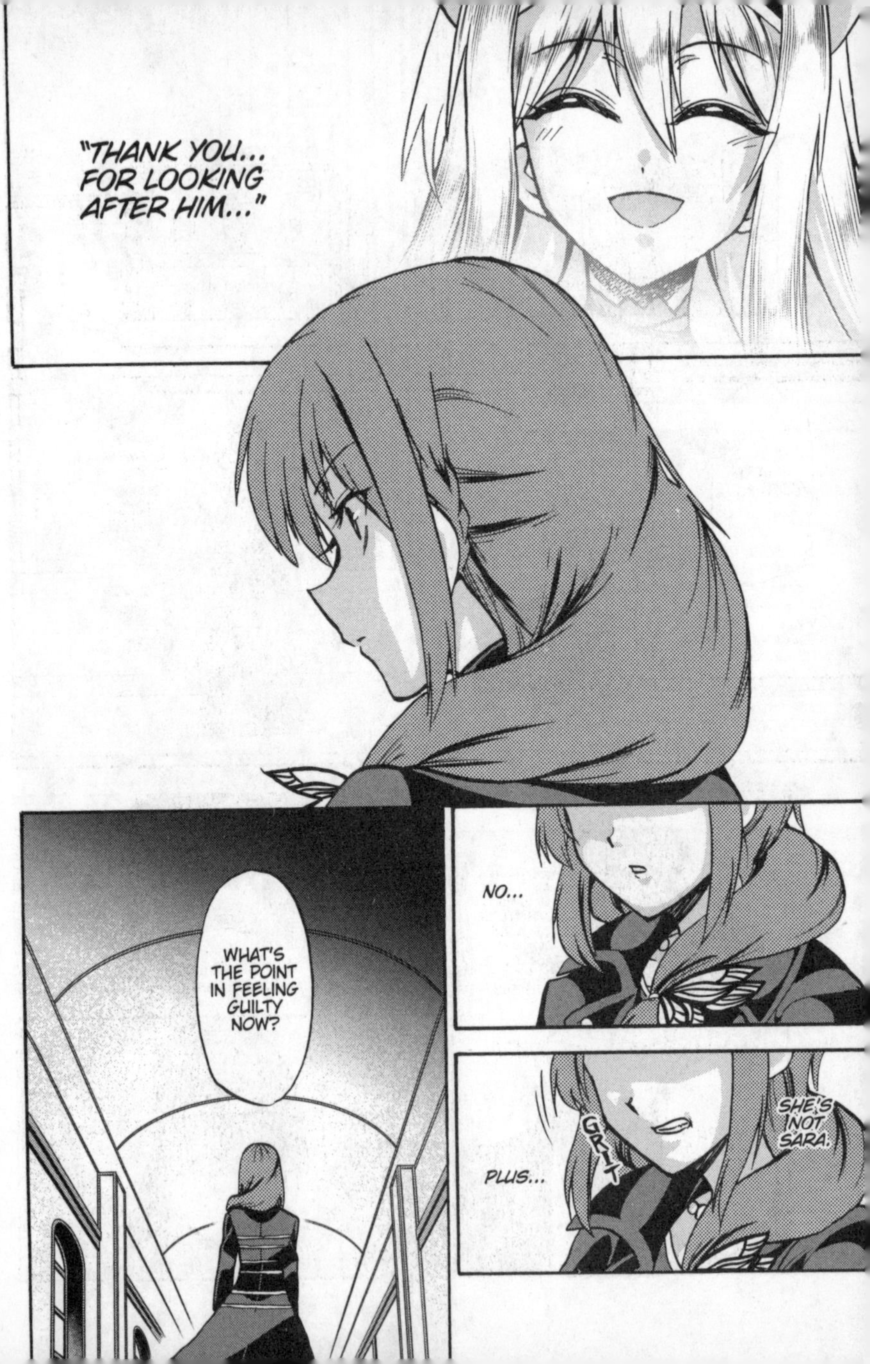
"THANK YOU... FOR LOOKING AFTER HIM..."
NO...
SHE'S NOT SARA.
GRIT
PLUS...
WHAT'S THE POINT IN FEELING GUILTY NOW?

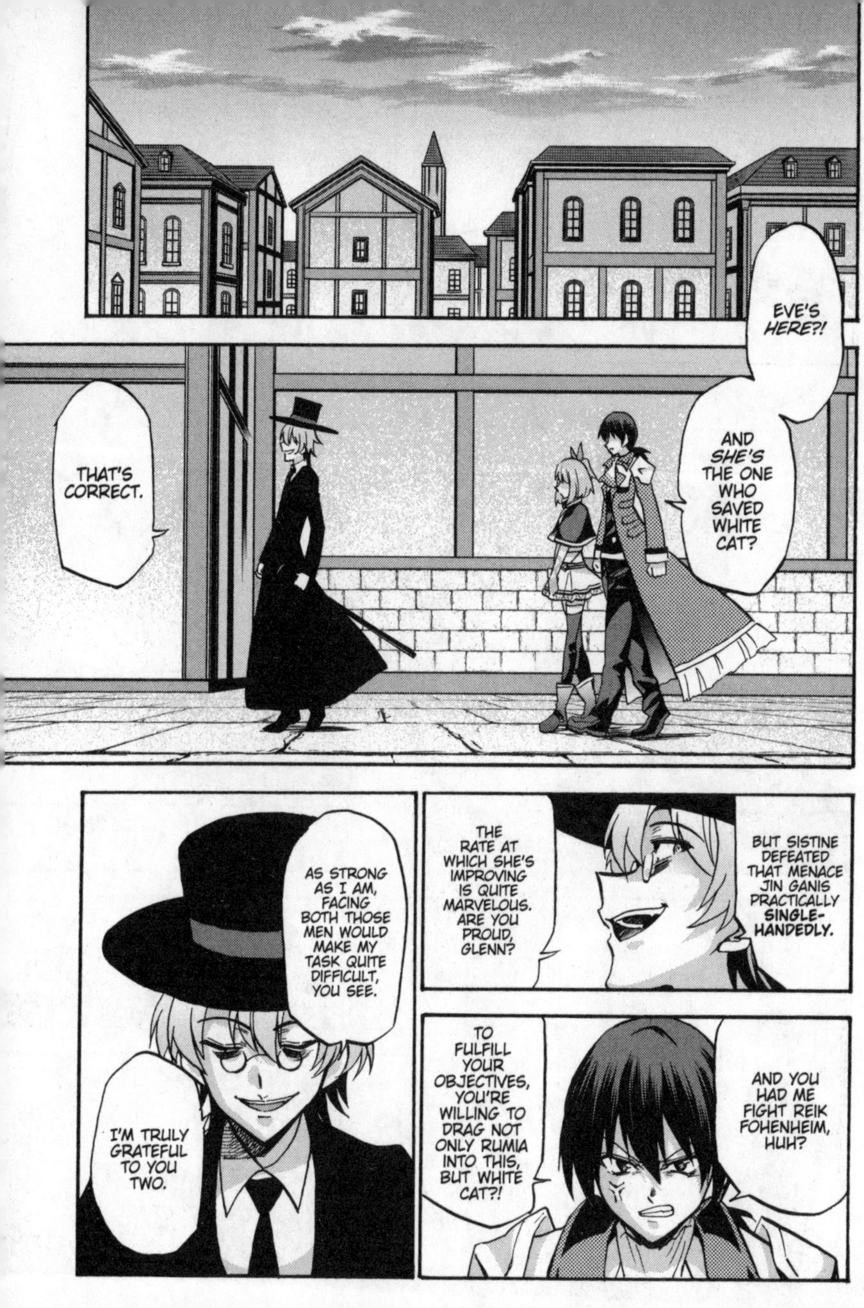
EVE'S HERE?!
AND SHE'S THE ONE WHO SAVED WHITE CAT?
THAT'S CORRECT.
BUT SISTINE DEFEATED THAT MENACE JIN GANIS PRACTICALLY SINGLE-HANDEDLY.
THE RATE AT WHICH SHE'S IMPROVING IS QUITE MARVELOUS. ARE YOU PROUD, GLENN?
AND YOU HAD ME FIGHT REIK FOHENHEIM, HUH?
TO FULFILL YOUR OBJECTIVES, YOU'RE WILLING TO DRAG NOT ONLY RUMIA INTO THIS, BUT WHITE CAT?!
AS STRONG AS I AM, FACING BOTH THOSE MEN WOULD MAKE MY TASK QUITE DIFFICULT, YOU SEE.
I'M TRULY GRATEFUL TO YOU TWO.

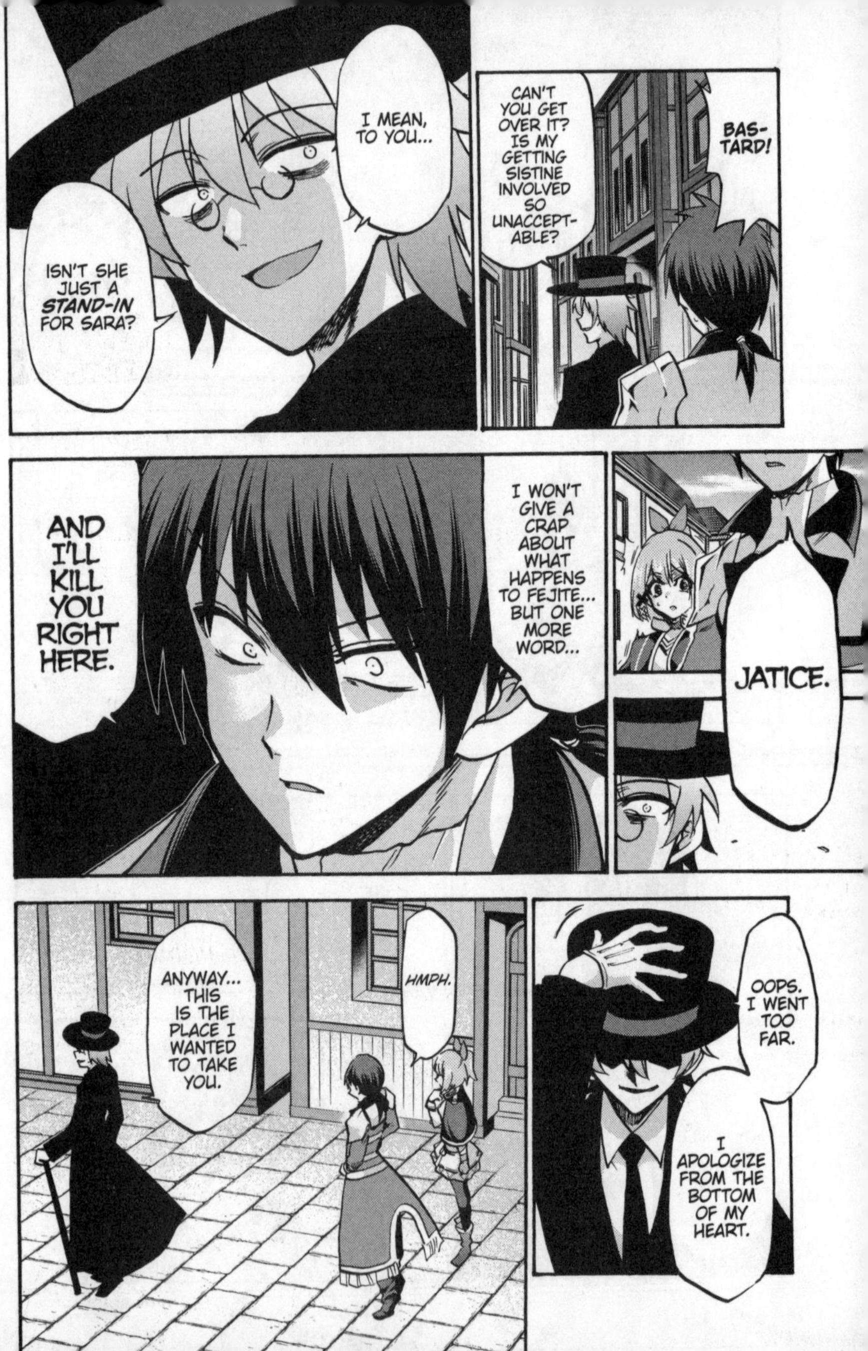
BASTARD!
CAN'T YOU GET OVER IT? IS MY GETTING SISTINE INVOLVED SO UNACCEPTABLE?
I MEAN, TO YOU...
ISN'T SHE JUST A *STAND-IN* FOR SARA?
JATICE.
I WON'T GIVE A CRAP ABOUT WHAT HAPPENS TO FEJITE... BUT ONE MORE WORD...
AND I'LL KILL YOU RIGHT HERE.
OOPS. I WENT TOO FAR.
I APOLOGIZE FROM THE BOTTOM OF MY HEART.
HMPH.
ANYWAY... THIS IS THE PLACE I WANTED TO TAKE YOU.

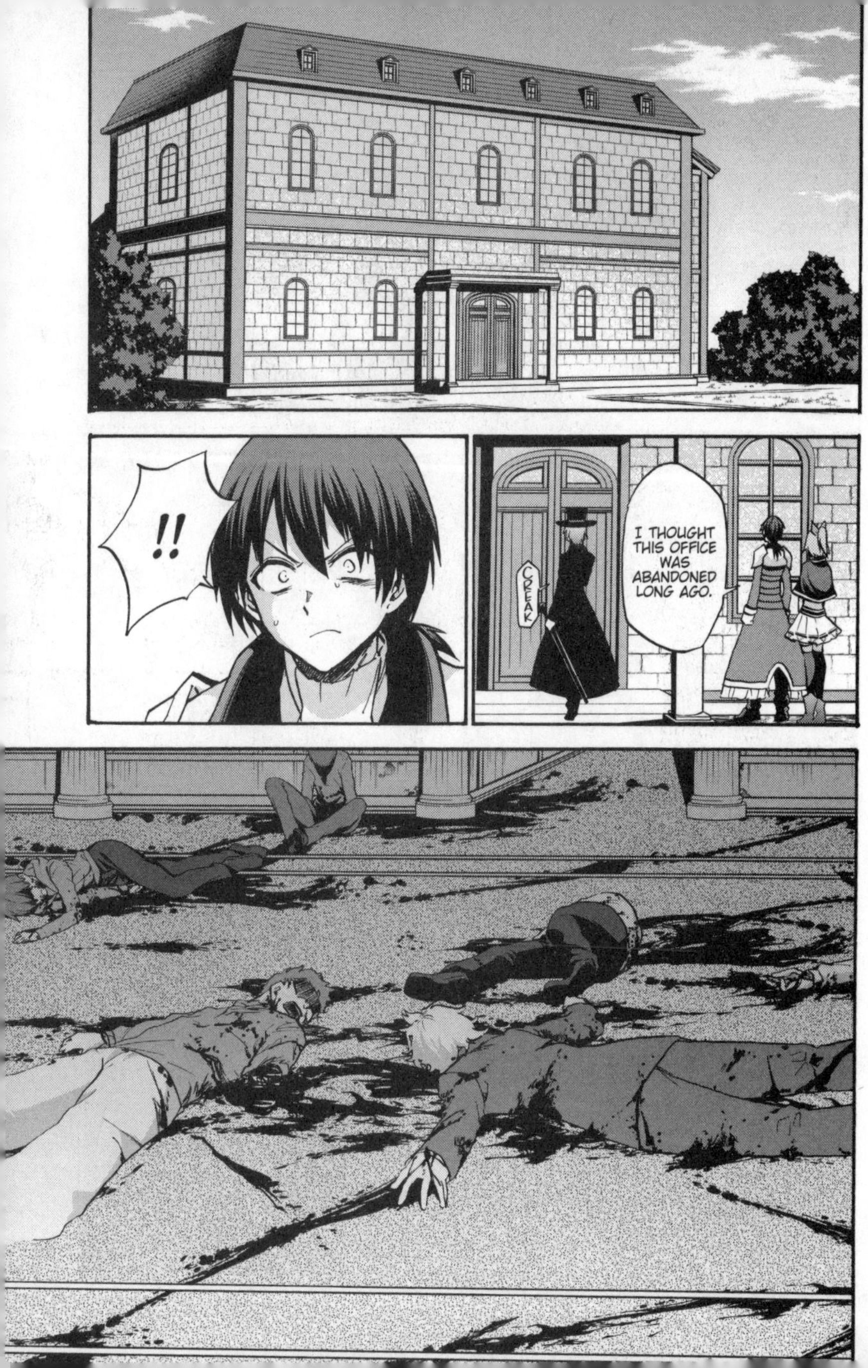
I THOUGHT THIS OFFICE WAS ABANDONED LONG AGO.
CREAK
!!

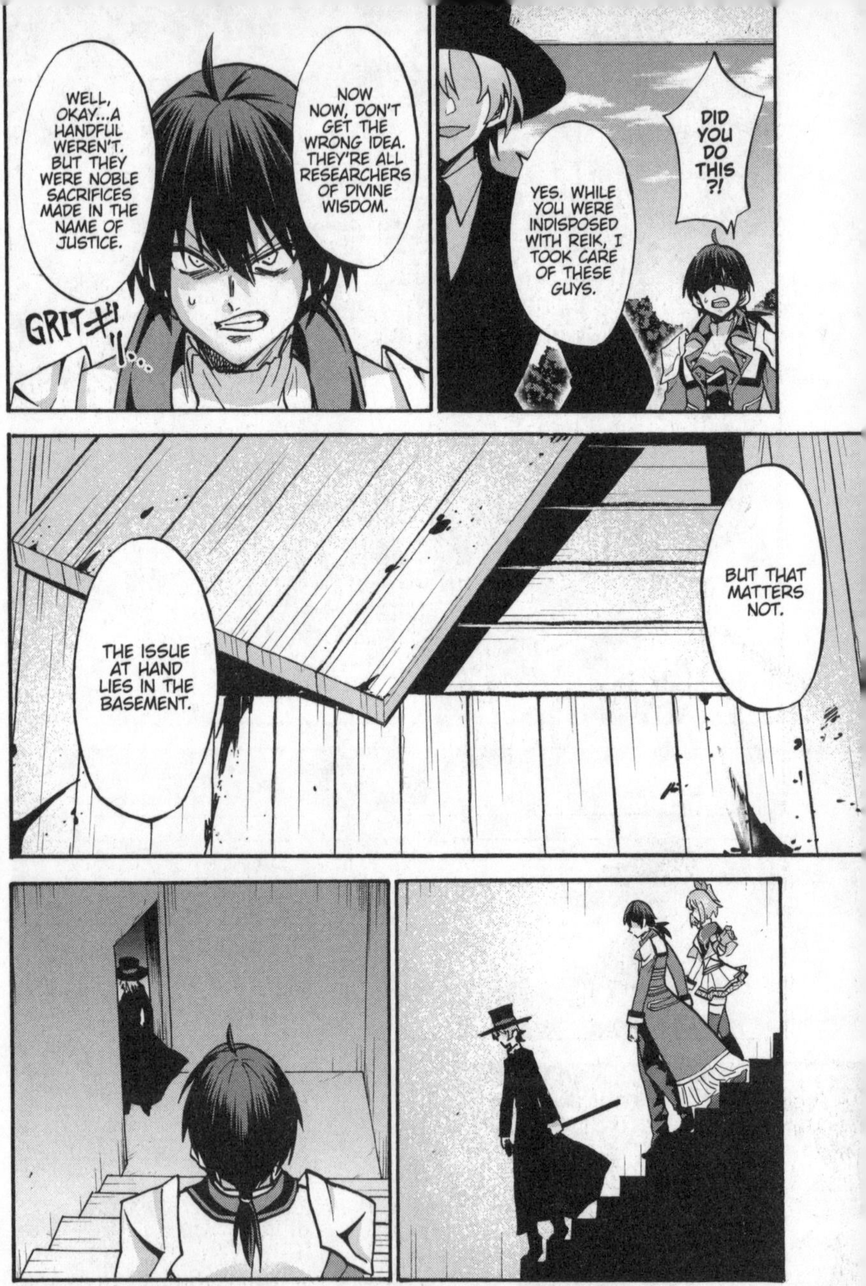
DID YOU DO THIS?!
YES. WHILE YOU WERE INDISPOSED WITH REIK, I TOOK CARE OF THESE GUYS.
NOW NOW, DON'T GET THE WRONG IDEA. THEY'RE ALL RESEARCHERS OF DIVINE WISDOM.
WELL, OKAY...A HANDFUL WEREN'T. BUT THEY WERE NOBLE SACRIFICES MADE IN THE NAME OF JUSTICE.
GRIT
BUT THAT MATTERS NOT.
THE ISSUE AT HAND LIES IN THE BASEMENT.

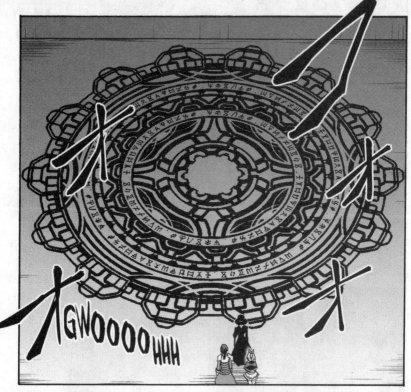

GWOOOOOHHH

SWF...

ALL RIGHT.

STEP ONE IS TO DISPEL THIS MAGIC CIRCLE.

COME, RUMIA.

GWOOOOOO

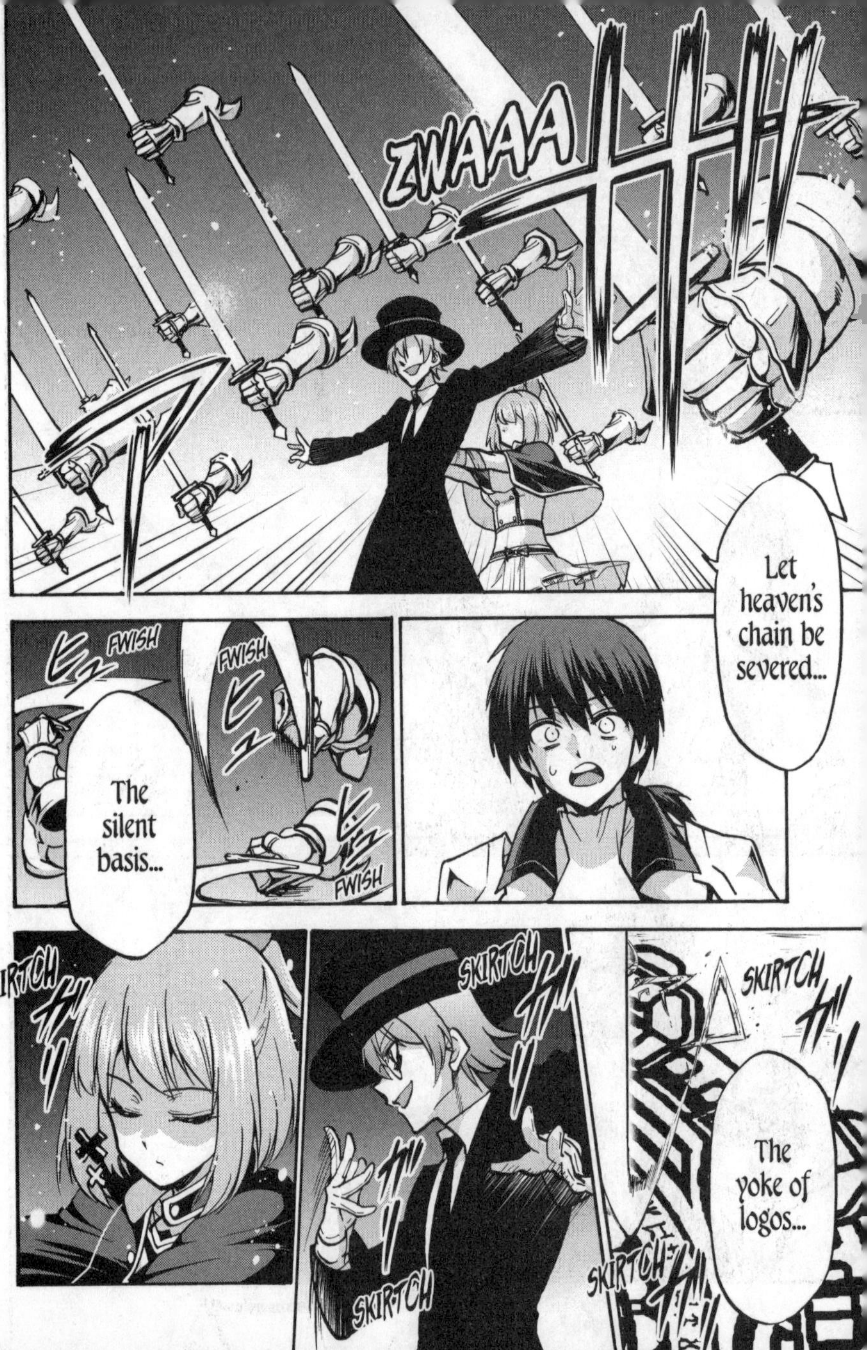
ZWAAA
Let heaven's chain be severed...
FWISH
FWISH
FWISH
The silent basis...
SKIRTCH
The yoke of logos...
SKIRTCH
SKIRTCH
SKIRTCH
SKIRTCH

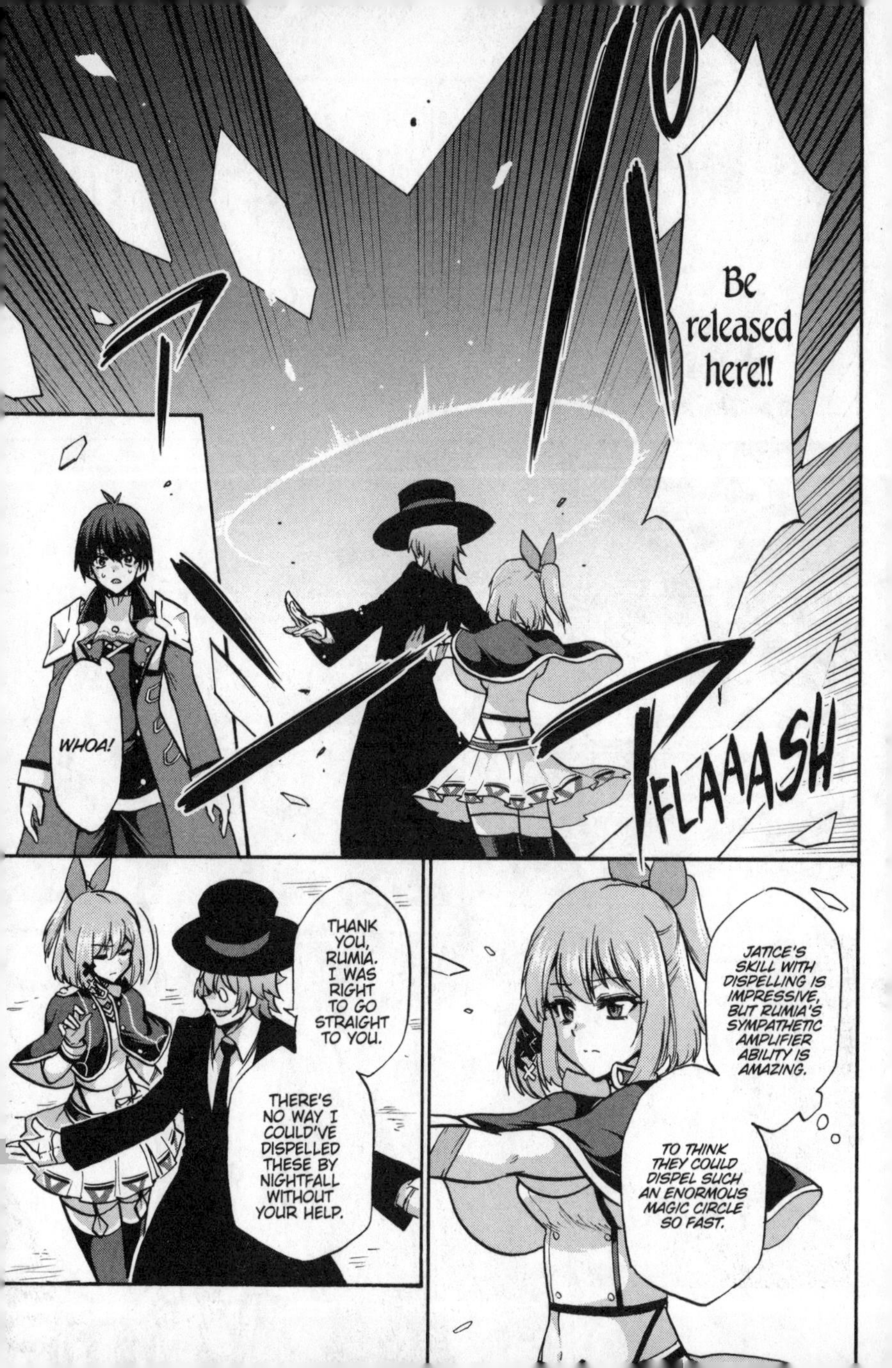
Be released here!!
WHOA!
FLAAASH
JATICE'S SKILL WITH DISPELLING IS IMPRESSIVE, BUT RUMIA'S SYMPATHETIC AMPLIFIER ABILITY IS AMAZING.
TO THINK THEY COULD DISPEL SUCH AN ENORMOUS MAGIC CIRCLE SO FAST.
THANK YOU, RUMIA. I WAS RIGHT TO GO STRAIGHT TO YOU.
THERE'S NO WAY I COULD'VE DISPELLED THESE BY NIGHTFALL WITHOUT YOUR HELP.

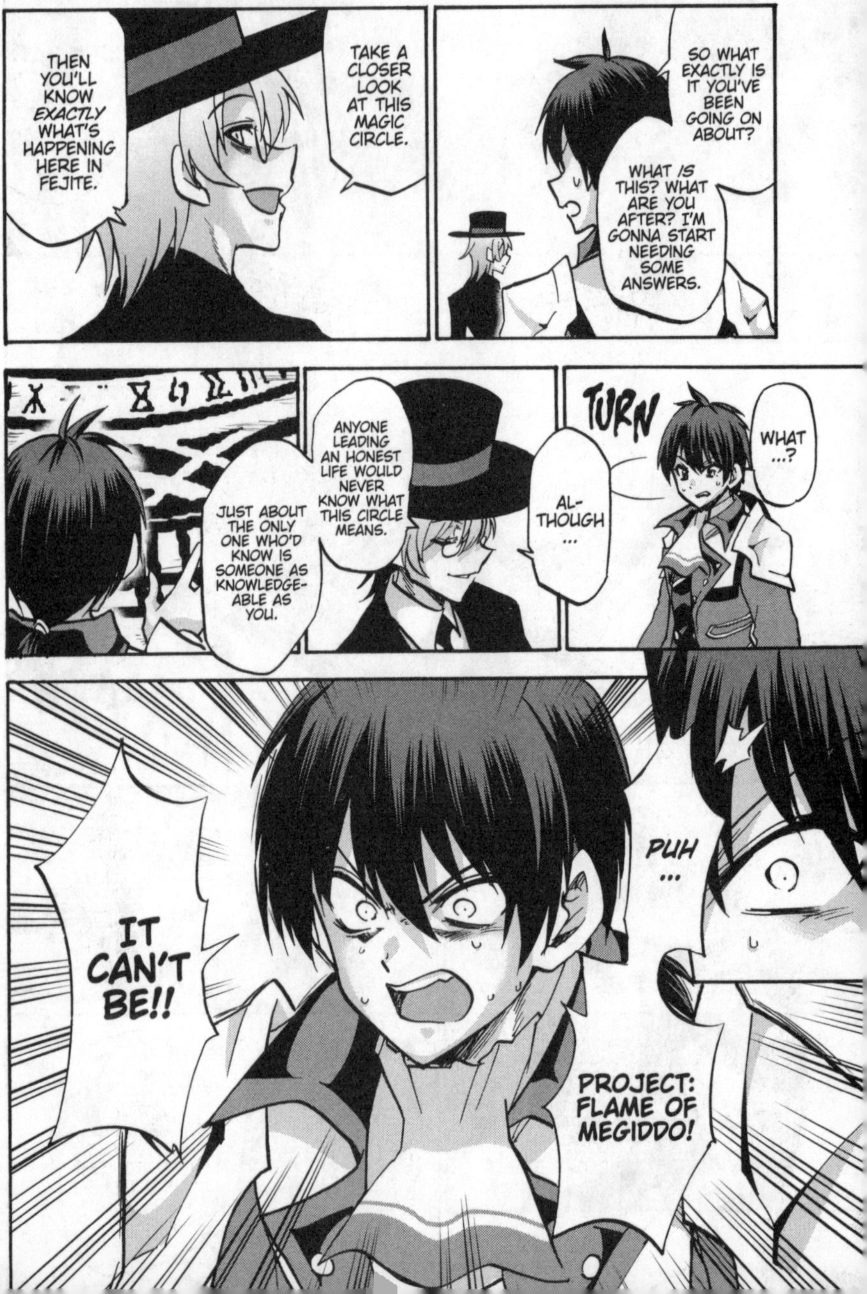
SO WHAT EXACTLY IS IT YOU'VE BEEN GOING ON ABOUT?
WHAT *IS* THIS? WHAT ARE YOU AFTER? I'M GONNA START NEEDING SOME ANSWERS.
TAKE A CLOSER LOOK AT THIS MAGIC CIRCLE.
THEN YOU'LL KNOW *EXACTLY* WHAT'S HAPPENING HERE IN FEJITE.
TURN
WHAT ...?
AL-THOUGH ...
ANYONE LEADING AN HONEST LIFE WOULD NEVER KNOW WHAT THIS CIRCLE MEANS.
JUST ABOUT THE ONLY ONE WHO'D KNOW IS SOMEONE AS KNOWLEDGE-ABLE AS YOU.
PUH ...
PROJECT: FLAME OF MEGIDDO!
IT CAN'T BE!!

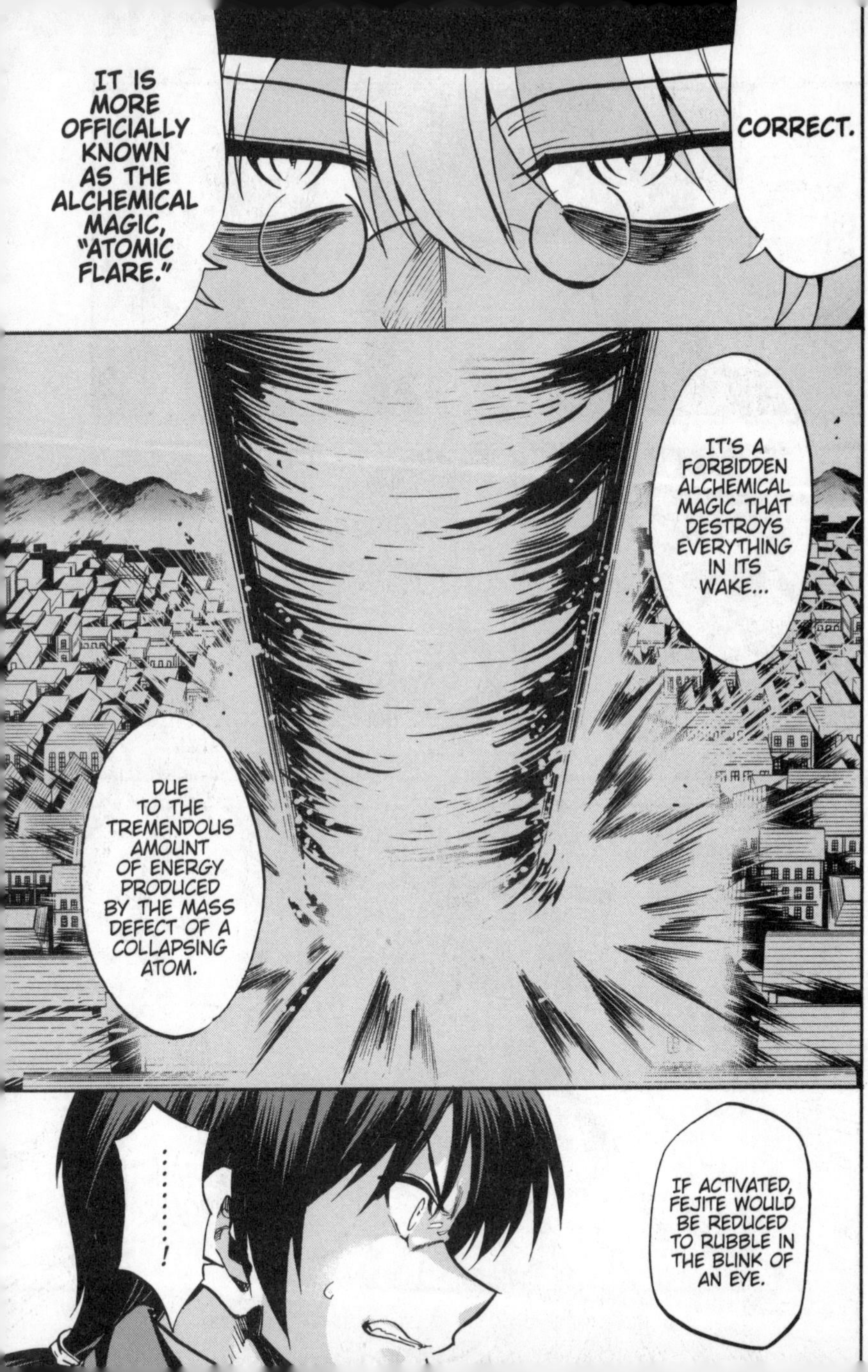
CORRECT.
IT IS MORE OFFICIALLY KNOWN AS THE ALCHEMICAL MAGIC, "ATOMIC FLARE."
IT'S A FORBIDDEN ALCHEMICAL MAGIC THAT DESTROYS EVERYTHING IN ITS WAKE...
DUE TO THE TREMENDOUS AMOUNT OF ENERGY PRODUCED BY THE MASS DEFECT OF A COLLAPSING ATOM.
IF ACTIVATED, FEJITE WOULD BE REDUCED TO RUBBLE IN THE BLINK OF AN EYE.
......!

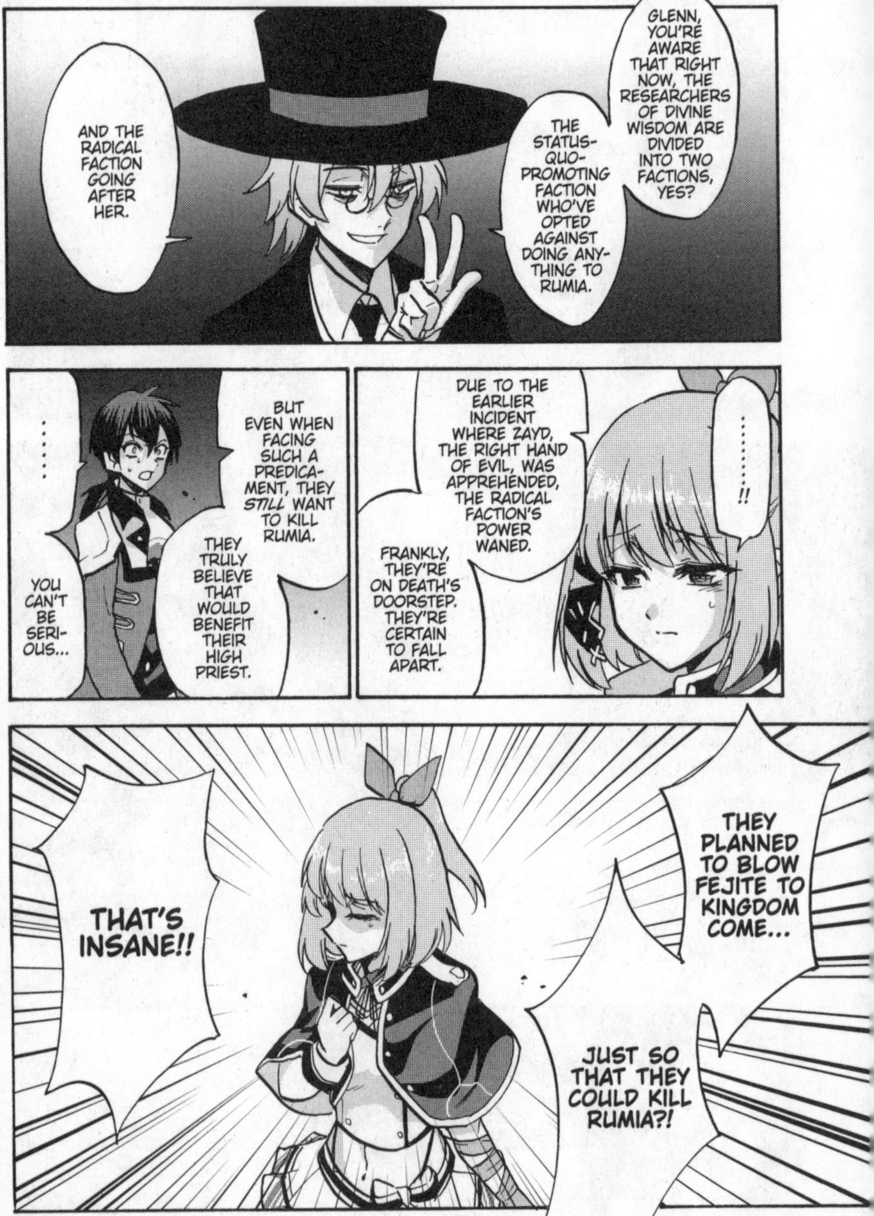
GLENN, YOU'RE AWARE THAT RIGHT NOW, THE RESEARCHERS OF DIVINE WISDOM ARE DIVIDED INTO TWO FACTIONS, YES?
THE STATUS-QUO-PROMOTING FACTION WHO'VE OPTED AGAINST DOING ANY-THING TO RUMIA.
AND THE RADICAL FACTION GOING AFTER HER.
......!!
DUE TO THE EARLIER INCIDENT WHERE ZAYD, THE RIGHT HAND OF EVIL, WAS APPREHENDED, THE RADICAL FACTION'S POWER WANED.
FRANKLY, THEY'RE ON DEATH'S DOORSTEP. THEY'RE CERTAIN TO FALL APART.
BUT EVEN WHEN FACING SUCH A PREDICA-MENT, THEY *STILL* WANT TO KILL RUMIA.
THEY TRULY BELIEVE THAT WOULD BENEFIT THEIR HIGH PRIEST.
......
YOU CAN'T BE SERI-OUS...
THEY PLANNED TO BLOW FEJITE TO KINGDOM COME...
JUST SO THAT THEY COULD KILL RUMIA?!
THAT'S INSANE!!

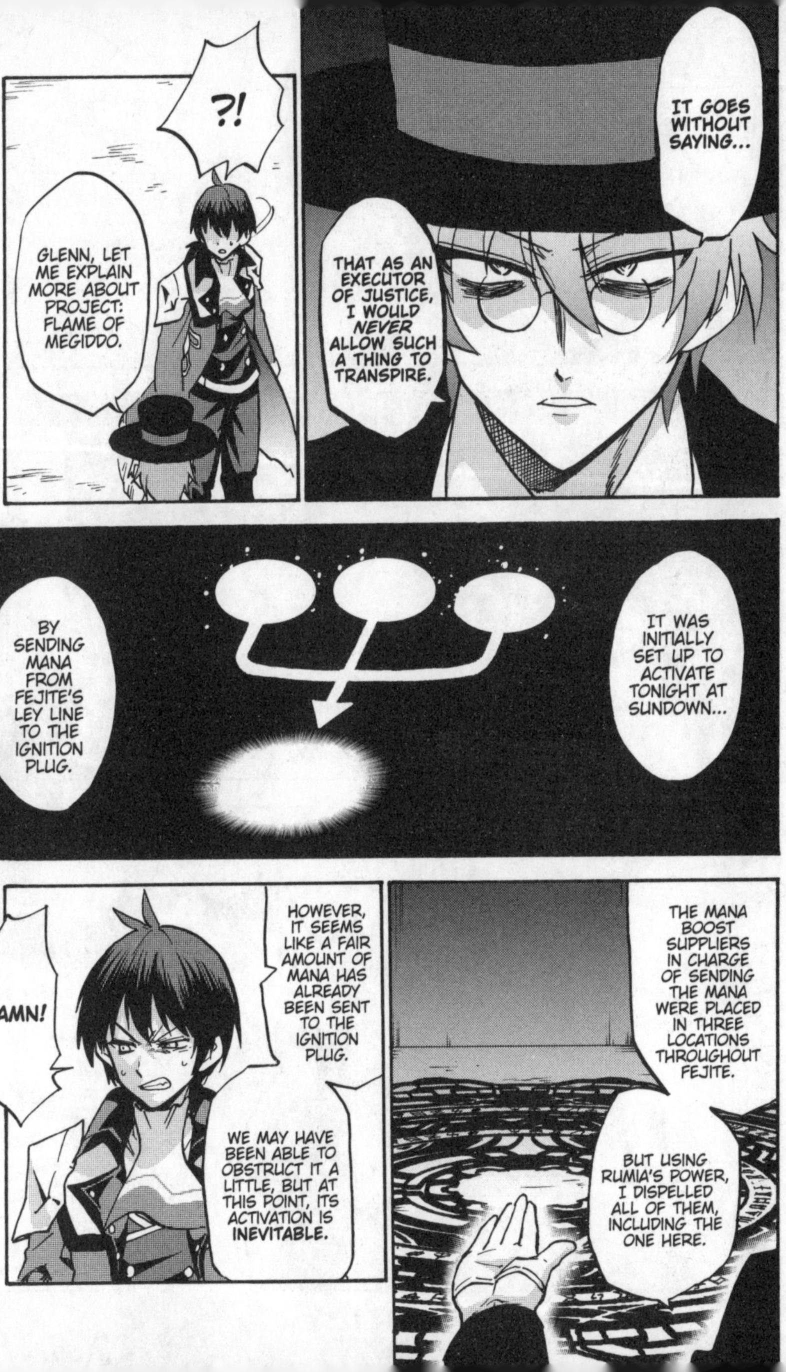
IT GOES WITHOUT SAYING...
THAT AS AN EXECUTOR OF JUSTICE, I WOULD *NEVER* ALLOW SUCH A THING TO TRANSPIRE.
?!
GLENN, LET ME EXPLAIN MORE ABOUT PROJECT: FLAME OF MEGIDDO.
IT WAS INITIALLY SET UP TO ACTIVATE TONIGHT AT SUNDOWN...
BY SENDING MANA FROM FEJITE'S LEY LINE TO THE IGNITION PLUG.
THE MANA BOOST SUPPLIERS IN CHARGE OF SENDING THE MANA WERE PLACED IN THREE LOCATIONS THROUGHOUT FEJITE.
BUT USING RUMIA'S POWER, I DISPELLED ALL OF THEM, INCLUDING THE ONE HERE.
HOWEVER, IT SEEMS LIKE A FAIR AMOUNT OF MANA HAS ALREADY BEEN SENT TO THE IGNITION PLUG.
WE MAY HAVE BEEN ABLE TO OBSTRUCT IT A LITTLE, BUT AT THIS POINT, ITS ACTIVATION IS **INEVITABLE.**
DAMN!

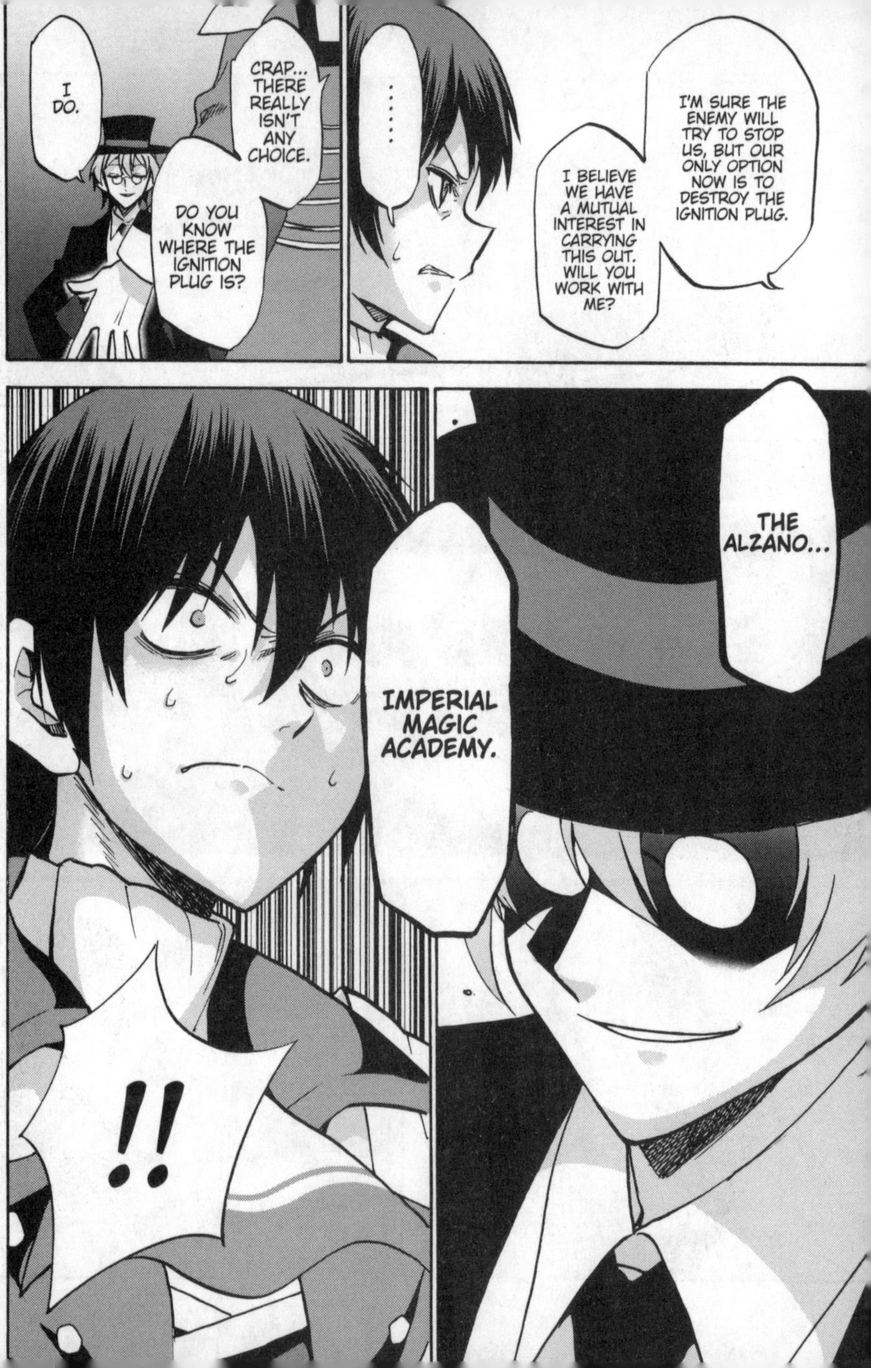
I'M SURE THE ENEMY WILL TRY TO STOP US, BUT OUR ONLY OPTION NOW IS TO DESTROY THE IGNITION PLUG.
I BELIEVE WE HAVE A MUTUAL INTEREST IN CARRYING THIS OUT. WILL YOU WORK WITH ME?
......
CRAP... THERE REALLY ISN'T ANY CHOICE.
DO YOU KNOW WHERE THE IGNITION PLUG IS?
I DO.
THE ALZANO...
IMPERIAL MAGIC ACADEMY.
!!

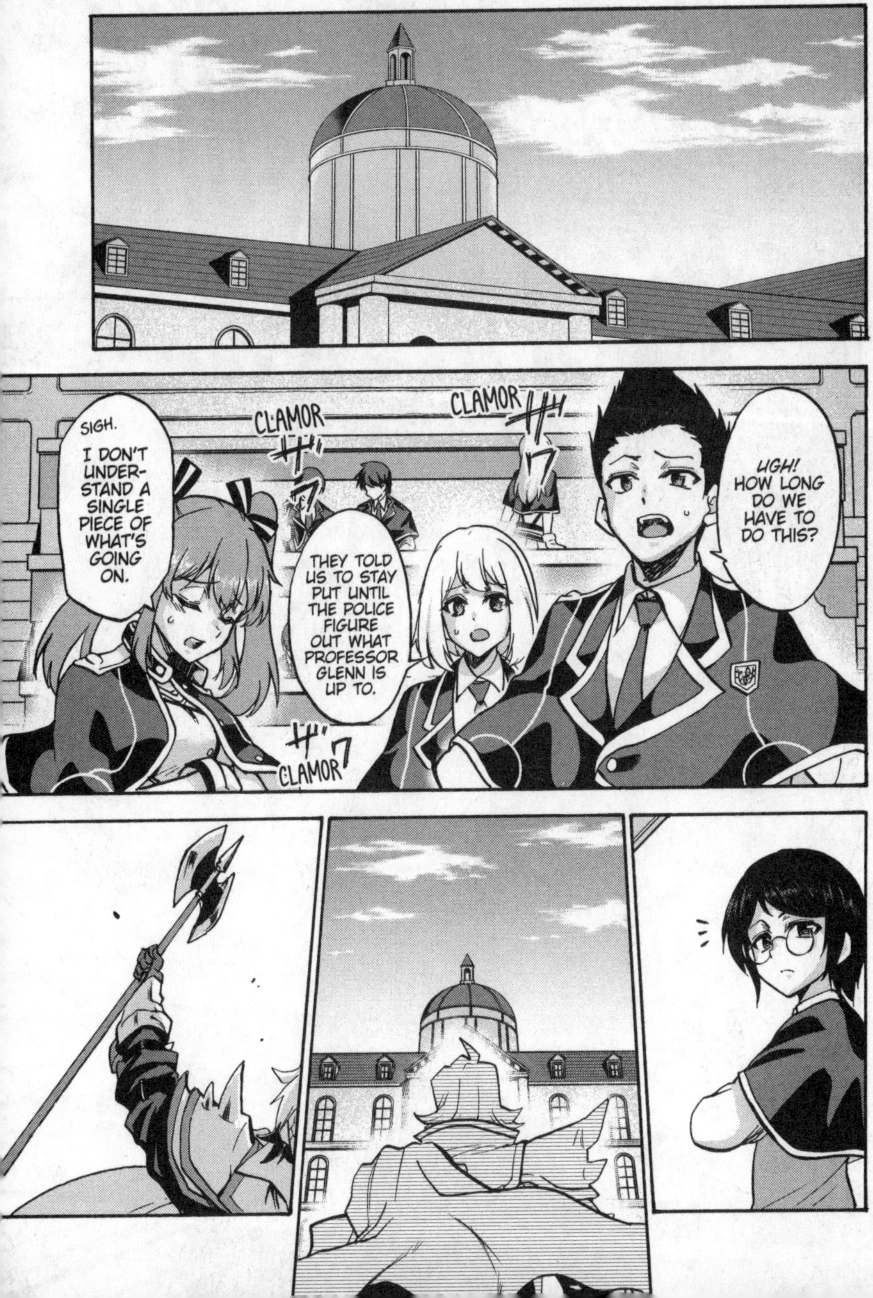
UGH! HOW LONG DO WE HAVE TO DO THIS?
CLAMOR
CLAMOR
THEY TOLD US TO STAY PUT UNTIL THE POLICE FIGURE OUT WHAT PROFESSOR GLENN IS UP TO.
SIGH. I DON'T UNDER-STAND A SINGLE PIECE OF WHAT'S GOING ON.
CLAMOR

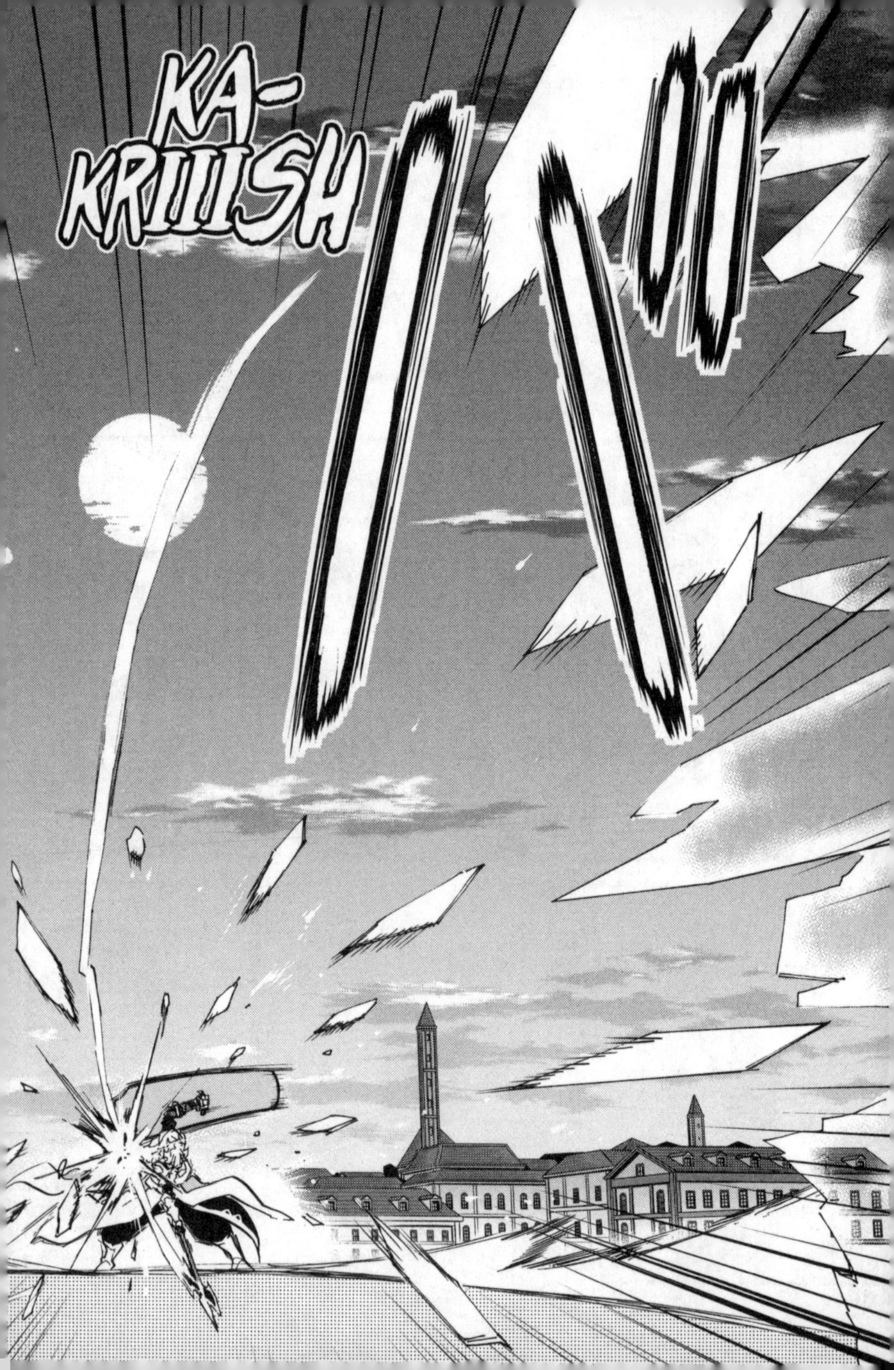
KA-KRIIISH

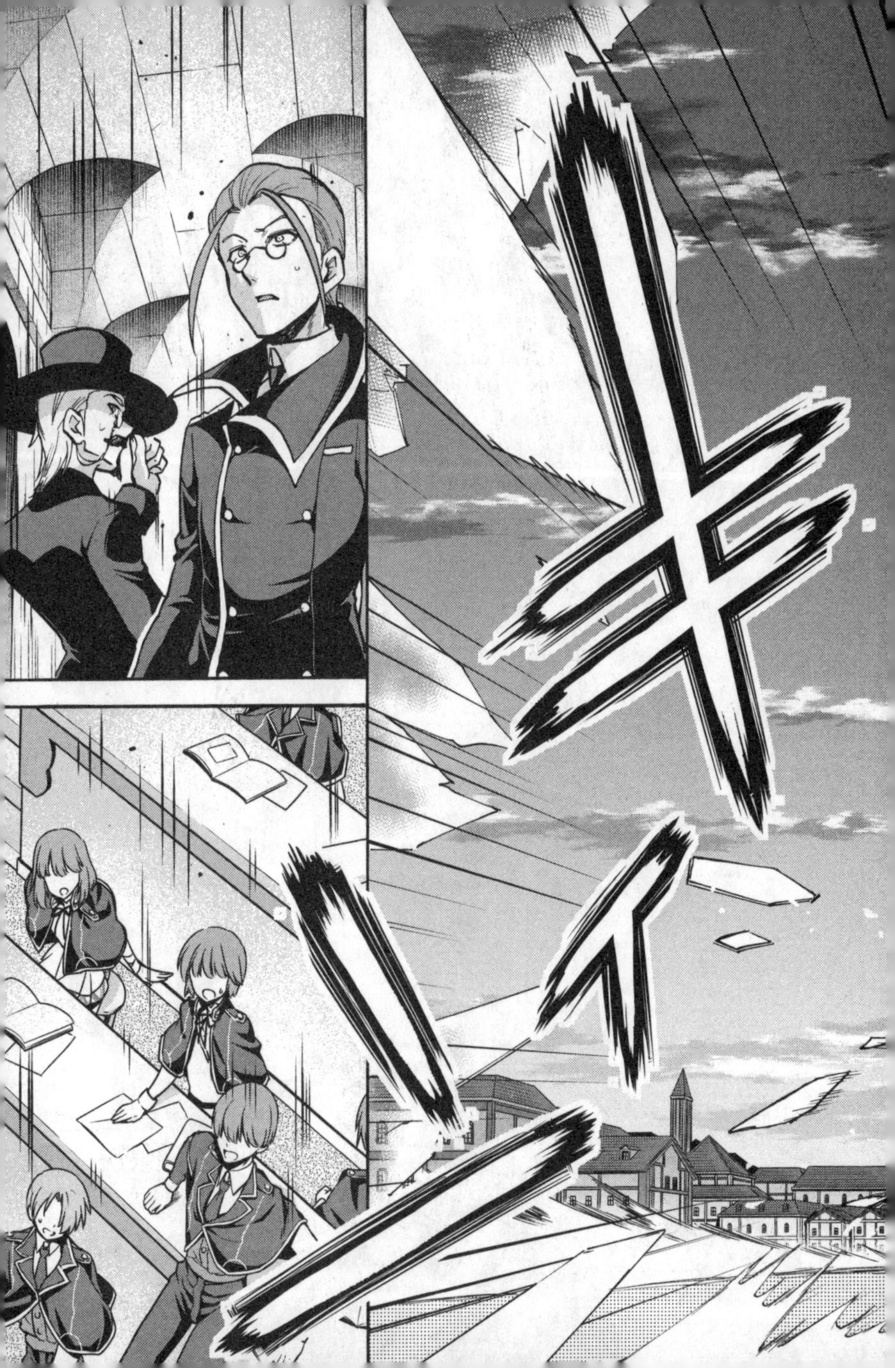

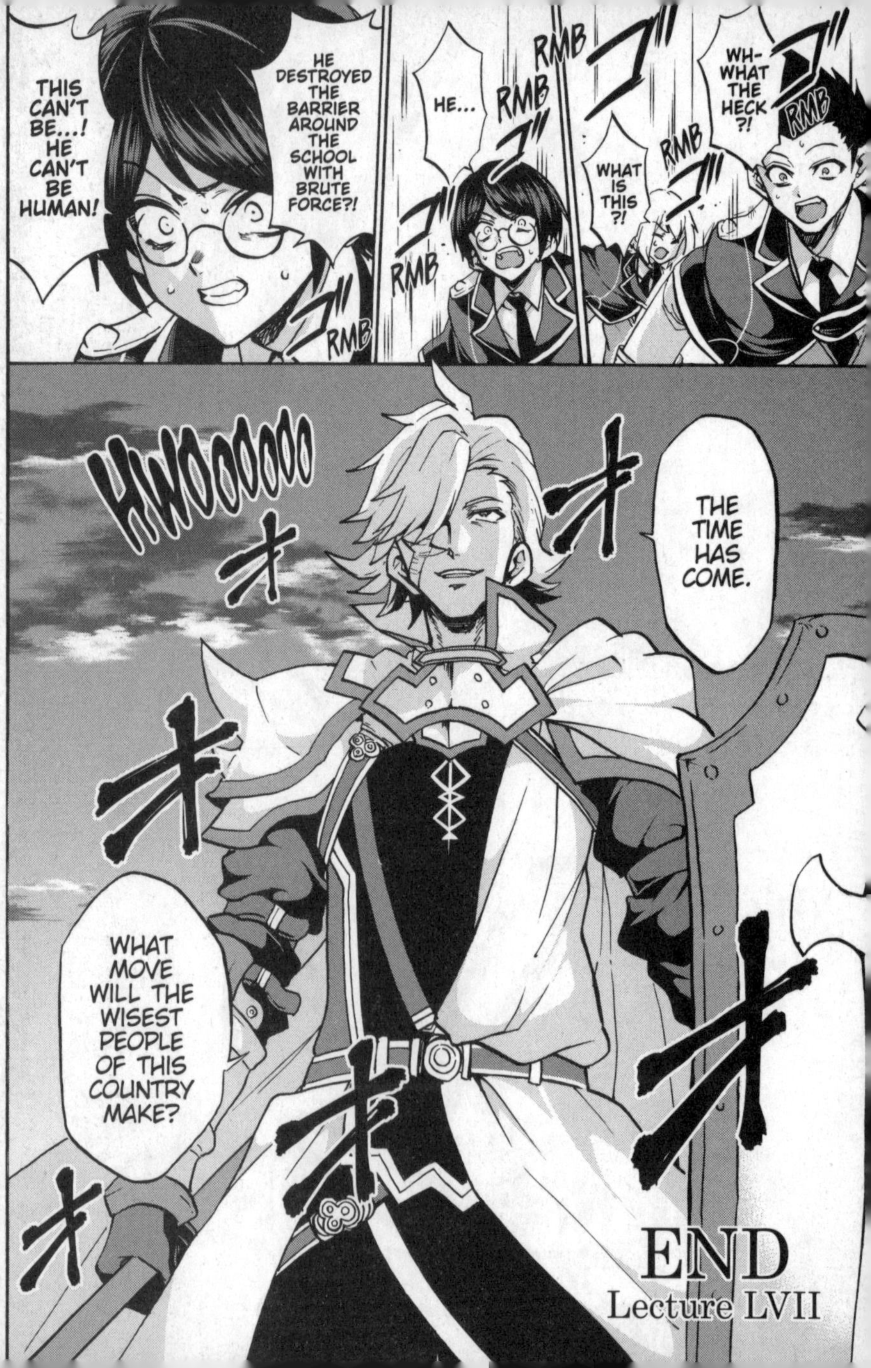
RMB
WH- WHAT THE HECK ?!
RMB
WHAT IS THIS ?!
RMB
HE...
RMB
RMB
HE DESTROYED THE BARRIER AROUND THE SCHOOL WITH BRUTE FORCE?!
THIS CAN'T BE...! HE CAN'T BE HUMAN!
RMB
THE TIME HAS COME.
HWOOOOOO
WHAT MOVE WILL THE WISEST PEOPLE OF THIS COUNTRY MAKE?
END
Lecture LVII

Akashic Records

of ***Bastard*** Magic ***Instructor***

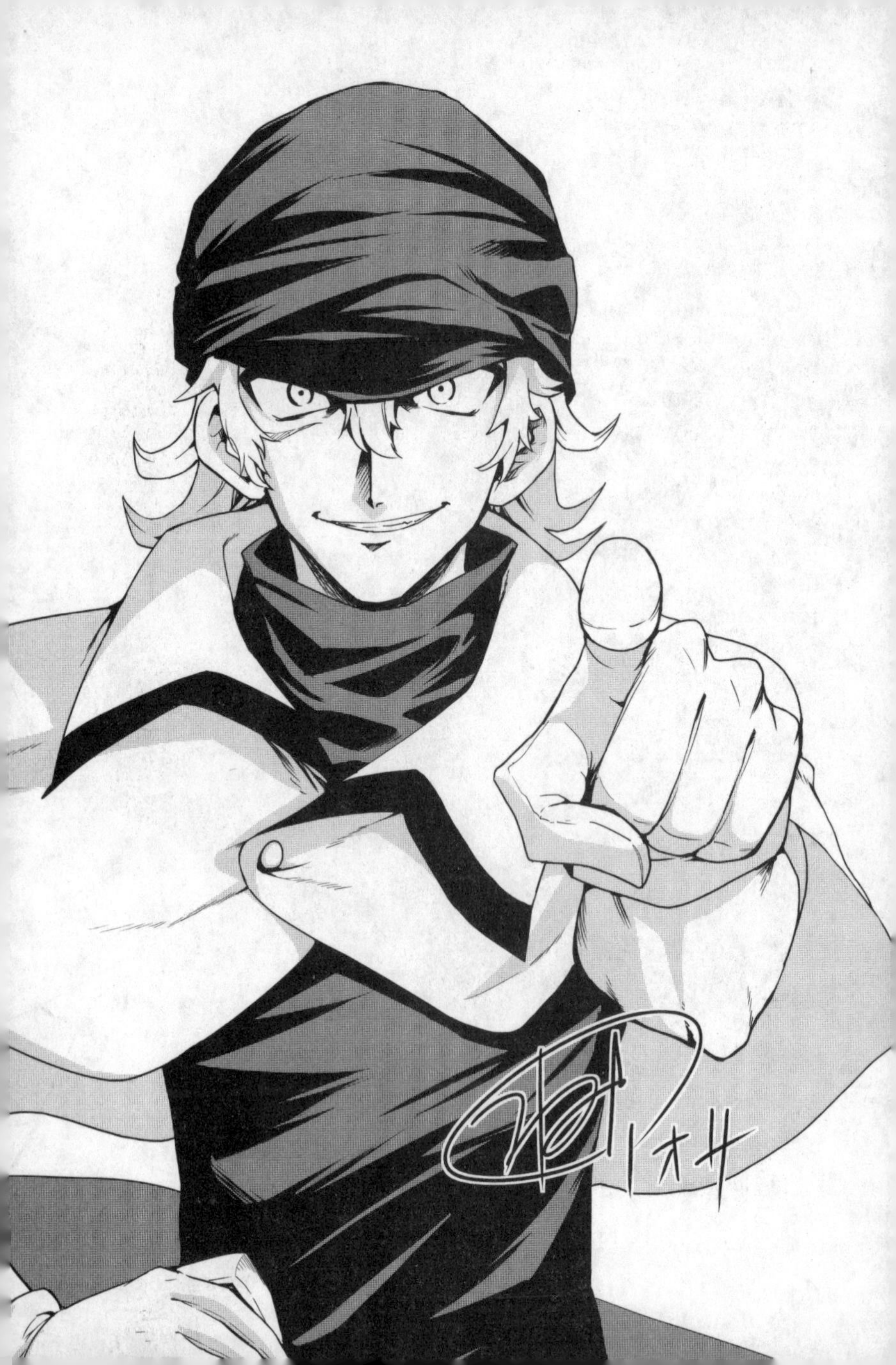

Thank you so much for picking up volume 13 of *Akashic Records of Bastard Magic Instructor.* This is Aosa Tsunemi.

The world's certainly become rough as of late, but thanks first and foremost to my assistants, editor, and all my readers, we were able to release this book.

Now then, it had been a while since these guys showed up. Since they were the first villains, I felt some nostalgia while drawing them, so that was fun. There's a bunch of battle scenes, so I hope you enjoyed reading them.

Well, until next volume!

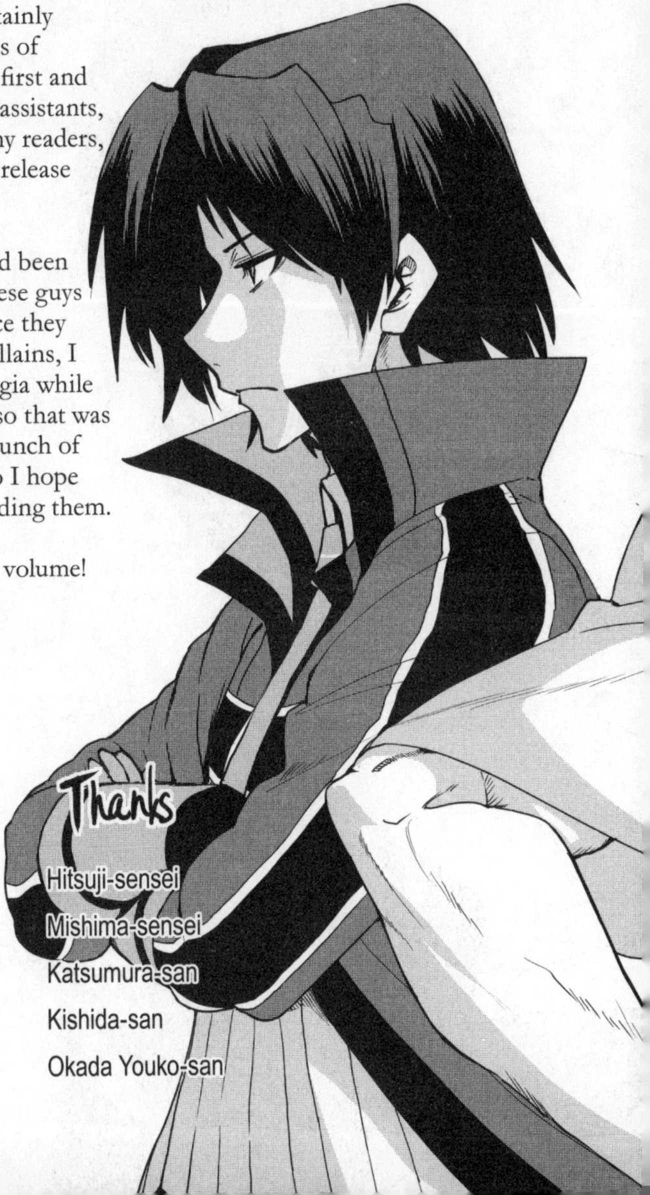

Staff	Thanks
Asahi Ruyoru	Hitsuji-sensei
Piko	Mishima-sensei
Yoshimaru	Katsumura-san
Morita Kanna	Kishida-san
	Okada Youko-san

AKASHIC RECORDS OF BASTARD MAGIC INSTRUCTOR

Story by Taro Hitsuji
Art by Aosa Tsunemi
Character design by Kurone Mishima

●